Futu

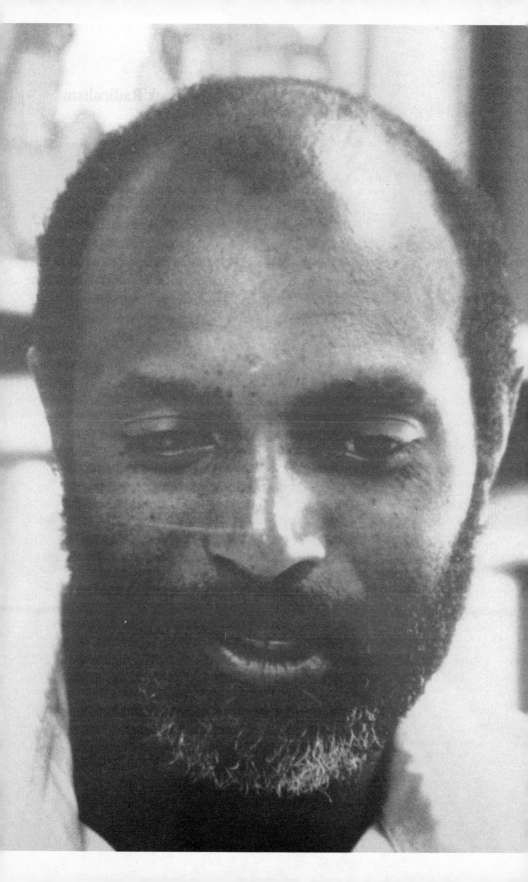

Futures of Black Radicalism

Edited by Gaye Theresa Johnson
and Alex Lubin

VERSO

London • New York

First published by Verso 2017
Contributions © The Contributors 2017
Collection © Verso 2017

3 5 7 9 10 8 6 4

Verso
UK: 6 Meard Street, London W1F 0EG
US: 20 Jay Street, Suite 1010, Brooklyn, NY 11201
versobooks.com

Verso is the imprint of New Left Books

ISBN-13: 978-1-78478-758-5
ISBN-13: 978-1-78478-757-8 (US EBK)
ISBN-13: 978-1-78478-756-1 (UK EBK)

British Library Cataloguing in Publication Data
A catalogue record for this book is available from the British Library

Library of Congress Cataloging-in-Publication Data
Names: Johnson, Gaye Theresa, editor of compilation. | Lubin, Alex, editor of
  compilation.
Title: Futures of Black radicalism / edited by Gaye Theresa Johnson and Alex
  Lubin.
Description: London ; Brooklyn, NY : Verso, 2017. | Includes bibliographical
  references. |
Identifiers: LCCN 2017009449 (print) | LCCN 2017013686 (ebook) | ISBN
  9781784787578 () | ISBN 9781784787561 () | ISBN 9781784787585 (paperback)
  | ISBN 9781784787578 (ebook : US) | ISBN 9781784787561 (ebook : UK)
Subjects: LCSH: African Americans—Politics and government. |
  Blacks—Politics and government. | Radicalism—United States. |
  Radicalism. | Radicals—United States—Biography. | Radicals—Biography. |
  United States—Race relations—Political aspects. | Race
  relations—Political aspects. | Internationalism—Political aspects. |
  Anti-globalization movement. | BISAC: SOCIAL SCIENCE / Ethnic Studies /
  African American Studies. | SOCIAL SCIENCE / Black Studies (Global). |
  POLITICAL SCIENCE / History & Theory.
Classification: LCC E185.615 (ebook) | LCC E185.615 .F88 2017 (print) | DDC
  323.1196/073—dc23
LC record available at https://lccn.loc.gov/2017009449

Typeset in Minion Pro by Hewer Text UK Ltd, Edinburgh
Printed and bound by CPI Group (UK) Ltd, Croydon, CR0 4YY

Contents

Preface

Cedric J. Robinson and Elizabeth P. Robinson

When Cedric committed to preparing this preface, he did so on the condition that we do it together, perhaps already aware that his health was failing, but at a rate neither of us anticipated. Alas, his death has left the task in my hands and though we had talked about some possibilities, we wrote not a word together. I would never presume to speak for him despite our fifty years together. Our styles have always been too different, mine more journalistic, sometimes more polemical. His analytic, elegant, meticulously documented. And always going to places I could never anticipate. So I have sat for months trying to figure out how to procede and have finally been delivered thanks to the transcription of a series lectures he gave at UC Irvine in 2012. Thank you, Tiffany Willoughby Herard for organizing the seminar, Kyung Kim for videoing it, and Mohsin Mirza, Yoel Haile, and Marisela Marquez for providing me with the transcription. Much of what you read is literally in Cedric's voice with only minor corrections from me. His contributions, in italics, were unwritten, so they lack his usual copious footnotes and careful construction. And it is impossible to convey the humor, emphasis, et cetera, of the seminar. But I hope that it gives you a sense of Cedric as teacher.

Elizabeth P. Robinson

Joshua Fit De Battle . . .

This story in some places might exaggerate possible actual events, but if the truth is here, it can be found. The theme is segregation.

Joshua Cole, a negro of sixty or more years, was sitting on the old broken steps of his shack on his side of town, thinking of the sun and how hot it was, when his musing was interrupted by someone calling his name, "Joshua, Josh' Cole," the excited voice cried, "Josh' yo' Freddy is dead!"

Suddenly realizing what was being said, Joshua rose quickly then fell back onto the wall of the building, more weight on his shoulders than even his age could account for.

The facts were made known to him, one by one. One of his neighbors, Zeke, had found the body of ten-year-old Freddy near the old tracks in the bushes. His neck was broken, not from a rope but a mighty blow . . .

. . . Going inside his shack, Joshua confronted Zeke who rapidly told Joshua in his eighty-year-plus-voice what he had seen. Zeke had done more than find the body, he had been sleeping in the nearby brush when Tom Caspine had chased Freddy after the boy had called Tom "white trash." Caspine had turned red with rage and had struck the boy with a vicious sweep of his fist. Caspine had left the boy lying in a peculiar position, not noticing the sightless eyes of the peculiarly positioned head . . .

. . . His last words before his blood flowed like wine, were "Lord, ain't you nevah goin' to give the world to the meek?"

Cedric Robinson
Jan. 8, 1957, English V

The last line in the essay quoted above was penned in the pall of the lynching of Emmett Till, as well as the promise of the mid-twentieth-century Civil Rights movement. The story was about a brutal murder of a Black child and the denial of justice in the aftermath. In looking for the antecedents of Black radicalism, we should consider our individual moments of awakening. Was this one? Or maybe listening to an old man's stories of courage and valor as his grandson helped him mop floors in government buildings. We might consider the little girl in Detroit who found something like the life of Sojourner Truth to read every day over breakfast. Maybe a young Arab woman's discovery that the movie *Exodus* told a particular and peculiar history of Palestine and that race and racism were entirely mutable. Or maybe being scolded for addressing a Black man as "Sir." Surely the affronts that are experienced because we've had the audacity to be somewhere we don't belong, the racial taunts and aggressions experienced repeatedly must be factored in to the formation of our racial identities. But the critical moment comes when we realize the political, historical, and social connectedness of those experiences and move from the personal, however important it might be, to the necessity of engagement, to the Black radical tradition. Also, to remember that this is not only about pain, but also about shared knowledge, joy, and humor that are integral to those experiences.

In compiling this collection of essays, the editors and authors invite or insist that we project a tradition, Black Radicalism, into the future. It is certainly our intention to celebrate that and suggest some ways in which we can find inspiration in our histories for our present moment. In the latter, we are confronted daily with police lethality and other abuse, mass incarceration, and a politics of greed. It is difficult to keep feelings of depression and defeat at bay, but our histories, perceived in all their dynamism, their resistance and resilience, can give us heart and direction. Our pasts are not dead; why else are there repeated attempts to bury them, to erase or forget them? Why does generation after generation have to rediscover W. E. B. Du Bois, Pauline Hopkins, Oliver Cox, and so many others? How is it that the indigenous people at Standing Rock, North Dakota, are telling us about massacres we've never heard of? Why don't we know about Black and white workers who made common cause for mutual benefit? Beyond US borders, why is it not common parlance that peoples' movements from Vietnam, Algeria, Iran, Lebanon, South Africa, Zimbabwe, Chile, Guatemala, to name but a few, were undermined or simply destroyed by Western capitalist greed and militarism? Perhaps it is simply too painful to remember these assaults; but burying them also buries the rich histories of resistance. While slavery and emancipation are part of our official histories, maroons and marronage, Palmares, quilombos, and the Great Dismal Swamp are unknown or little known when they should be the bedrock of contemporary struggles.

I had argued in Black Marxism *that Black Radicalism critically emerges from African culture, languages, and beliefs, and enslavement. What emerged from that conjunction were powerful impulses to escape enslavement.*

At some point when I was writing Black Marxism, *I came across the notion of the "runaway." Most historians talk about runaways, write about runaways. But I became convinced that that language contained and persisted in the notion that slave agency was childlike. Children run away, but what these people were doing was achieving fugitive status. So I began to use the term "fugitive" instead of the term "runaway." But you have to use the term runaway sometimes because, when you're looking at archival material, it is the term that is in fact being employed. The first impulse of these Africans was to remove themselves from the slave system. Rather than going after slavery, they wanted to recreate their African homelands. Rather than confront the system as the system, they removed themselves from it. They created maroon communities which in some instances became so massive and so powerful that, as in Palmares in seventeenth-century Brazil, they became republics themselves. Palmares persisted for ninety years or so. And there were similar kinds of adventures (you might call them) in the West Indies, in Jamaica, and elsewhere. In the North American colonial situation, one area that became famous for marronage was the Great Dismal Swamp. And indeed, in 1857 or so, Harriet Beecher Stowe wrote her second anti-slavery novel,* Dred: A Tale of the

Great Dismal Swamp. *Meaning, in effect, that she understood, as many did, that there in the swamp were to be found fugitives from not only slavery, but Native American fugitives, and poor white fugitives. And Stowe was suggesting in* Dred *that her earlier proposal for a muscular Christianity had to be replaced. And so she invented a son for Nat Turner in her novel. In that sense, she was of course engaging in the Black Radical Tradition as well.*

To return to this question of sovereignty, Palmares, in Brazil, had to be destroyed, and several armies were sent to destroy it in the seventeenth century. In a similar sense, Haiti at the beginning of the nineteenth century had a similar trajectory. Haiti was not only an instance of an extraordinary achievement—slaves having created a republic—but it was a constant threat to the slave-owning planter class in North America. What becomes of the notion of Haiti, what becomes of the notion of Black sovereignty in the nineteenth century? One of the maneuvers to deal with Haiti was to extract from the Black population in North America its freed Black population on the presumption that the free Black population could only contaminate the slave population. Black radicalism led to a particular maneuver which created Liberia. Liberia was supposed to function to siphon off the free Black population, and that maneuver was a fairly successful one in many ways. But the plague of Black sovereignty continued to be a part of American consciousness and that plague resurfaced at the end of the nineteenth century, and the beginning of the twentieth century. At the end of the nineteenth century the plague was in part carried by the Black soldiers who entered the Philippines. We have some sense of how they saw this war from 1899 on because they wrote letters which were published in Black newspapers in the late nineteenth and early twentieth century. Willard Gatewood allowed those letters to resurface in his study called "Smoked Yankees." One of the stories that was revealed there was the defection of Black troops from the American military to the Philippine independent national soldiers. One particular Black trooper, David Fagan, became so well known that the US military put out a reward not for his capture but for his being killed and beheaded. He became a commandante in the Philippine army and was killed in two or three years' time. But again, his was a kind of expression of Black radicalism, as well as a notion of Black sovereignty.

These narratives are found in popular media as well as in the hallowed halls of universities. And those media constructions span far more than 100 years and remain a contemporary practice, not just a historical one. Consider the 2012 film, *Lincoln*: how was it possible to make a film about the post–Civil War United States with barely a presence of Black people as *agents* in the events at hand? Perhaps, given some particularly mean moments in US politics, the film-maker thought we needed an "uplift" film with a great man at the helm. But like most "great men" versions of history, it is at best a partial truth, at worst, a persistent lie. Of course, these predilections are rife and can be found in old as well as new forms. Just as Spielberg told a convenient story, so too did Eugene O'Neill, and each would argue a sensitivity to, even an affinity for, Black people.

Now let me offer you a reading of some of the language that O'Neill thought was useful and necessary in constructing this Black figure [Emperor Jones]. And this is the speech in the original play which eventually becomes the architecture around which Dubose Hayward produces the first two-thirds of the film. He is talking to his Cockney collaborator, a merchant who has been cheating the islanders for years and selling them goods. In Emperor Jones's final moments of rule, he threatens the Cockney in this way.

> *Maybe I goes to jail for getting in an argument with razors over a crap game. Maybe I gets 20 years when that colored man dies, maybe I gets in another argument with the prison guard who oversee us when we are working the road, maybe he hits me with a whip and I splits his head with a shovel and runs away 'n files the chain and gets away safe. Maybe I does all that and maybe I don't. It's a story I tells you so you know I used to be the kind a man that if you ever repeat one word of it, I end your stealing on this earth mighty damn quick.*

I can't read it the way Charles Gilpin or Paul Robeson read it, because it's difficult. It's that invented Black speech that we find both in film and on stage during the 1920s and 1930s.

Now Charles Gilpin has maintained that he created the Emperor Jones, that Eugene O'Neill had merely written it. Part of that claim to authority by Charles Gilpin was that, after performing it several hundred times over the years, Gilpin had begun to change the play. He changed it in this way, one of the ways in which we know that he changed it. In a one-act play, there are fifty or sixty occasions in which the Emperor Jones uses the word "nigger." Gilpin started changing that language, and O'Neill was very upset with him and eventually maintained that he was going to beat Gilpin up if he continued to change his play. Eventually, O'Neill would replace Gilpin with Paul Robeson. Robeson, of course, would perform it not only on stage but also when it became a film. The film went back to the original play, so all those "niggers" reappear in the film the way O'Neill had written them originally in the one-act play. Alright, so of Gilpin's performance as Emperor Jones, we have no historical archive. Of Gilpin's other work, we know he made one silent film in about 1927 or so. But what we are told is that Gilpin's performance as Emperor Jones was awesome because of the nature of his voice, the power of his voice, but we'll have to take his contemporaries' word for it.

To be sure, Gilpin's subversion of O'Neill's written words seems to have represented a refusal to accede to the lie that Black people were brutes, incapable of mastering the English language.

It is easy for us to presume that Blacks have always existed in this country since the occasion of the African Slave Trade. But understand the contest that was taking place in the end of the nineteenth and early part of the twentieth century. That is, the kind of savages—how would you put it? —well, let me put it simply in the terms we addressed earlier. The "Negro" was in place; that is, his docility, igno-rance, bestiality, child-like inferiority, that was in place. But a strata was emerging in conflict with that, to contest it. Some of the strata contested it by in effect compet-ing with the standard for becoming white, Anglo-Saxons. Others turned in the direction of W. E. B. Du Bois, who wrote The Negro *in 1915. Understand when Du Bois writes* The Negro *in 1915, there is no history of Black people published!* [Cedric pounds his fist into his hand as he makes this point.] *This is the first, that is, Du Bois is a part of the invention or reinvention of Blackness, which a small part of his class has undertaken.*

They will write a history of Blackness in the place of a vacuum of such mate-rial, and they're saying that in effect all of these people who have in some sense an immediate origin in Africa are **one** *people. This is an entirely new idea, because what they are adding to it, codifying with it, is in effect a sense of a historical people. Not simply of origins, but a historical people. A people who achieved civili-zation, who have achieved cultures, who have left a mark on the world. Gathering all that material together, Du Bois's excerise in 1915,* The Negro, *is a massive propaganda ploy: we are a people, it doesn't matter whether we're in Brazil, on the African Continent, in Mexico, doesn't matter where we are, we are the same people, and these are the things we can accredit to ourselves. Consequently, we have had a past, we can have a future . . . Black Sovereignty!*

Of course, Du Bois was not alone or the first and hardly the last who would reject the degradation of Black people. Others too would reimagine, resurrect narratives which were/are repeatedly buried. We might not find all of them compelling, some even odious, but they were all rejections of a fundamental, willful error in the imagined Black people that demanded correction. Many of the proponents were a part of the elite, but not all. Many were Black, but not all.

[Pauline] Hopkins was not a member of that strata. Hopkins comes out of the arti-sanal class in Massachusetts. She was apparently a genius: eighteen years old, she writes a musical which is preformed in San Francisco, as well as in other places, about the Underground Railroad. She is eighteen years of age—1879! By 1899, twenty years later, she is such a powerful alternative locus that Booker T. Washington proceeds to try and deliberately destroy her, and he succeeds. How many have heard of Pauline Hopkins? [Cedric scans the room for raised hands. Few appear.]

He vanquished her. She constructed a publishing cooperative in Boston, published her own magazine, The Colored American. *She edited, wrote biogra-phies for it, wrote studies for it, wrote four novels, if not five, and in each of her novels she proceeded to interrogate a way out. Assimilation? Hagar's Daughter proves that that is unacceptable, it is a way towards collective tragedy. She pursues Pan Africanism in another of her novels,* Contending Forces, *and earlier she pursues in effect some resolution to the exploitation of black women. So this is an* *extraordinary individual, pushed to the side, pushed to the margins, pushed into obscurity, never to resurface until almost sixty or seventy years after her death in 1930. But she was part of that legion of people that were moving toward a recovery of a kind of Blackness which had nobility and had a past. One of the weaknesses of Black radicalism in most of its forms is that it lacks the promise of a certain future. Unlike Marxism [where] victory is inevitable eventually, in Black radicalism it is not. Only when that radicalism is costumed or achieves an envelope in Black Christianity is there a certainty to it. Otherwise it is about a kind of resistance that does not promise triumph or victory at the end, only liberation. No nice package at the end, only that you would be free. It comes, as I said at the beginning, out of the insult to African identities that slavery represents. This was unacceptable. **This was unacceptable**.*

And I guess the most poetic representation of that I've ever seen is when Eula tells her story in Daughters of the Dust *of why Ibo Landing has its name. Do you remember the story in* Daughters of the Dust? *The Ibo were brought here in chains, and in chains they were marched from the big boats and conveyed in smaller boats to the shore. They looked at this land and they saw what their future was, and they turned around . . . and walked back into the ocean.*

Only the promise of liberation, only the promise of liberation!

If we are to move the Black Radical Tradition forward, it is imperative that we understand that it is not utopian. Rather it is about questing for freedom. It is about the necessity of recognizing the importance of struggle regardless of outcomes. Nor does it begin and end intellectually. We must look beyond the straightjackets of race to understand common histories in order to make common cause.

Some of you are interested in why I pursued the Irish in Black Marxism *as well as in the latest work,* Forgeries of Memory and Meaning. *In part, I'm trying to give a great deal of our audience a purchase point. There's no possibility of really telling a Black story without telling other peoples' stories. I can tell it in the nationalist trope. And the nationalist trope, in effect, will be guilty of repeating the artificialities that I'm trying to oppose, those kinds of boundaries. The Irish and the Irish Americans are, to a certain degree, opportunistic subjects. Opportunistic in the sense that a lot of their history is coincident with Blackness . . . Coincident with Blackness. But also because I want you to understand that the Irish were negatively racialized, even before the Africans, in the European imagination. We were simply a lob to occupy a category already established. And given the irony that is history, it became the impression that the category had always been ours, always been ours, exclusively. That simply isn't how human affairs have been conducted.*

So the Irish and their history are our teachers as well as our compatriots. Likewise, we must look beyond the writers to our colleagues such as Otis F.

Madison, Mary Agnes Lewis, and Travis Tatum (to name too few) who have steeped thousands of students in the Black Radical Tradition without writing about it and sent them out into the world to carry on. We must look to the activists, actors, and athletes who insist on using their bully pulpits to call attention to realities that corporate media chronically neglect. And we must look to our families, our children, for their particular wisdom. Like the eleven-year-old who tearfully and angrily shouts at her mother, who has insisted to her daughter that she read a text one more time if she didn't understand it, 'But, Mom, it doesn't make sense because it says that after slavery, the slaves couldn't take care of themselves. But they'd been the ones taking care of everything!" Ah hah! We must know that the truth will win out and most likely be buried yet again.

Only the promise of liberation, only the promise of liberation!

Introduction

Gaye Theresa Johnson and Alex Lubin

> For the vast majority of the planet's peoples, the global economy publicizes itself in human misery. Thus, the simple fact is that liberationist movements abound in the real world—a reason for attention far more weighty than the self-serving conceits of capitalist triumphalism and incessant chants of globalism which followed upon the disintegration of the Soviet Union.
>
> —Cedric J. Robinson, *Black Marxism*[1]

Amid a global wave of uprisings, Black protest against police repression and security regimes in the United States has reoriented a conversation about anti-Black racism on an international scale, generating new narratives of struggle and revealing the persistence of racial capitalism and its assault on dispossessed and working people around the world. Developing connections across multiple currents of resistance, a new generation of social actors has met the escalation of anti-Black state violence in the United States with an astonishing matrix of oppositional strategies, enlivening the intersection between domestic antira-cism and global anti-imperialist struggles.

It is the enduring truth of Black rebellion that its traditions, strategies, and representations abide variously in dynamic intersections of radical thought. Today, Hong Kong's pro-democracy marches have been productively linked to Black Lives Matter actions on Staten Island; in Ferguson, violence by the Baltimore Police Department is connected to Palestinian subjugation and containment; and in North Dakota, anticolonial resistance to an oil pipeline is linked to environmental justice actions in the Black communities of Detroit, Atlanta, New York, and Los Angeles.

A persistent distinction of twenty-first-century Black struggles has been the ways in which diverse individuals and communities—from students and cultural workers to activists and intellectuals—have redefined the concept of Black radicalism for Afro-diasporic scholarship. This has inspired new para-digms for interdisciplinary research across the disciplines in which both the manifesto and the monograph become equally, though distinctively, significant projects for reimagining Black radicalism as an enduring weapon against successive racial regimes. The individuals and communities who author and

---

1 Cedric J. Robinson, *Black Marxism* (Chapel Hill: University of North Carolina Press, 2000), xxviii.

enact it find themselves struggling amid multiple contradictions—between neoliberalism and democratic governance, between settler colonialism and the promise of marketplace participation. Therefore, freedom seekers and cultural workers, as they have at every new political conjuncture, have found it necessary to transform this work into more than an intellectual exercise—it is a critical practice.

Some of the most generative scholarship on contemporary capitalism, racism, and rebellion has resulted from studying what Cedric J. Robinson famously described as "the Black Radical Tradition," a tradition of resistance honed by the history of racialized, permanent, hereditary, and chattel slavery that formed the contours of civic and social life in the Americas, Europe, and Africa. Grounded in Black resistance more than five centuries in the making, this practice produced an enduring vision of a shared future whose principal promise is the abolition of all forms of oppression. From *The Terms of Order: Political Science and the Myth of Leadership* to his more recent works, including *Forgeries of Memory and Meaning: Blacks and the Regimes of Race in American Theater and Film Before World War II*, Robinson's work is some of the most significant of its kind on Black political economy, culture, and dialectical thinking.

Taking Robinson's work as a point of entry, the essays in this book consider the history and ongoing struggle against racial capitalism, from the roots of Black radical thought to a shared epistemology of the present political moment. The contributors animate a challenge posed by Robinson in *Black Marxism*: to recuperate and recover the Black Radical Tradition and to enliven it in the academy and the community. Together, they expose the structural dimensions of racialized capital, reveal particular specificities of anti-Blackness and Black liberation, and produce new questions and answers that offer generative critiques and project new visions of justice and democracy. They are an innovation, an advancement of the work on Black radicalism, Black internationalism, and cultural struggle through an engagement with the historical consciousness embedded in the Black Radical Tradition.

Robinson's project was to explore the Black Radical Tradition as it developed in the peripheries of Europe and during the pre-history of capitalism. This tradition demonstrated forms of resistance and rebellion that drew not on European theory, but on cultural resources taught to slaves by their ancestors in Africa. For example, in *An Anthropology of Marxism*, Robinson argues that the foundations of socialist communities lay in pre-capitalist relations among slaves, mystics, and other members of the Black Radical Tradition who contested church and other forms of subjugation. In so doing, Robinson challenged Marx's understanding of the European proletariat as the main revolutionary force in the world, an understanding that did not acknowledge Black liberation movements. Robinson's scholarship thereby "served the purpose of resurrecting events which have systematically been made to vanish from our intellectual consciousness."[2]

Although engaged with Marxist thought, Robinson's project ultimately critiqued its elision of Black radical philosophy. While Marxism can be and has been a useful portal through which to envision a political future, dialecticism precedes Marxism, and the Black Radical Tradition has had to contend not only with the totality of domination under racial capitalism, but also with the limitations of enlightenment philosophy to adequately explain the force of racial regimes. Although Marxism had seemed "for a time" to be a useful theory for Black liberation, Robinson wrote in the preface to the 2000 edition of *Black Marxism*, ultimately:

> Marxism's internationalism was not global; its materialism was exposed as an insufficient explanator of cultural and social forces; and its economic determinism too often politically compromised freedom struggles beyond or outside of the metropole. For Black radicals, historically and immediately linked to social bases predominantly made of peasants and farmers in the West Indies, or sharecroppers and peons in North America, or forced laborers on colonial plantations in Africa, Marxism appeared distracted from the cruelest and most characteristic manifestations of the world economy. This exposed the inadequacies of Marxism as an apprehension of the modern world, but equally troubling was Marxism's neglect and miscomprehension of the nature and genesis of liberation struggles which already had occurred and surely had yet to appear among these people.[3]

Given his criticisms of Marxism, it is ironic that *Black Marxism* has come to represent Robinson's enduring scholarly legacy. And yet, this magisterial study is neither a story of Marxists who were Black, nor an intellectual history of Black (male) radicalism, despite the fact that some readers have wished it so. These errors mistake Robinson's purpose, and worse, suffocate the lifeblood of Robinson's subject—the Black Radical Tradition.

Where Marx believed the potential for revolution lay in the European proletariat, *Black Marxism* grants historical and revolutionary agency to the Black radical subject, placing the start of the project of liberation before capitalism's development. Further, *Black Marxism*'s radical approach revises what Walter Mignolo calls the "geopolitics of knowledge" by locating Black radicalism outside of the Eurocentric core.[4] In this way Robinson accounts for the

---

2   Cedric J. Robinson, quoted in "An Anthropology of Marxism," chapter 17 of Avery F. Gordon's *Keeping Good Time: Reflections on Knowledge, Power, and People* (Boulder, CO: Great Barrington Books, 2004), 134; this chapter originally appeared as the preface to Cedric J. Robinson's *An Anthropology of Marxism* (Oxford: Ashgate, 2001), i–xvi.

3   Robinson, *Black Marxism*, xxx.

4   Walter Mignolo, "The Geopolitics of Knowledge and the Colonial Difference," *South Atlantic Quarterly* 101, no. 1 (Winter 2002): 57–96.

making of racial capitalism in feudal societies external to Europe, while placing revolutionary agency in the hands of Black freedom thinkers often struggling to escape Western civilization, or to reject the racial capitalist order altogether.

Rendering the Black Radical Tradition meant shifting the scholarly gaze beyond Eurocentrism, but it also meant forging new methodologies for writing about communities of struggle that might focus on intellectuals but only insofar as the intellectual was part of a larger collective. While *Black Marxism* focused on radical thinkers and activists like W. E. B. Du Bois, C. L. R. James, and Richard Wright, it did so to offer neither purely intellectual history nor hagiography but rather an enactment of the Black Radical Tradition that viewed individuals as products of historical forces and radical social movements. Hence, Robinson identified the struggles and people surrounding Du Bois, James, and Wright whose collective actions provided them with the theoretical insight required to imagine freedom: "Marxism became a staging area for their immersion into the [Black Radical] tradition," when they began to study the "anticolonial and revolutionary struggles of Africa, the Caribbean, and the Americas."[5]

Robinson's contemporary Grace Lee Boggs was similarly interested in dialectical thought, or the necessity, as she put it, to know "what time is it on the clock of the world."[6] Robinson knew what time it was because he was part of communities of struggle (as Robin Kelley describes in his afterword to this volume), because he saw the contradictions of the moment, and because he theorized from below. Dialectical thinking allowed Robinson to see the ferocity, violence, and seemingly natural "terms of order" of racial capitalism as signs of its weakness and not its dominance. In the Black Radical Tradition he saw a constant struggle for freedom against the forms of oppression that converted humanity and earth into objects of radically different value to be accumulated and owned. In this sense Black liberation included not just Black freedom, but a break with the totality of racial capitalism.

Abolition—the destruction of racial regimes and racial capitalism—entails not only the end of racial slavery, racial segregation, and racism, but also the abolition of a capitalist order that has always been racial, and that not only extracts life from Black bodies, but dehumanizes all workers while colonizing indigenous lands and incarcerating surplus bodies. W. E. B. Du Bois was the first to discuss (though not enact) abolitionism in this sense of the word in *Black Reconstruction* (and Ruth Wilson Gilmore elaborates on the term in chapter 14 of this volume). Du Bois saw abolition democracy during the era of Reconstruction as a political struggle for collective liberation; it brought freedom to Black and white workers in the form of redistributed wealth (jubilee), free public education across poor working communities in the South, and the franchise to many. In this way, and in this book, Black radicalism refers to

5   Robinson, *Black Marxism*, xxxii.
6   Grace Lee Boggs, *Living for Change: An Autobiography* (Minneapolis: University of Minnesota Press, 1998).

demands and articulations of freedom by Black activists, artists, and intellectuals on behalf of everyone's freedom. Black freedom is freedom for all.

An intellectual reckoning with the magnitude and significance of Robinson's contributions is an endeavor whose end, blessedly, can never come. In the wake of his departure, there has been an unprecedented elevation of his work in workshops and panels, tributes and accolades. Teachers, activists, and scholars whose own labors have been long and profoundly influenced by Robinson's pursuits note that his writings went largely unacknowledged for much of his professional career, even in the most recognized scholarship on political economy and Black history. This is merely fact, which reveals the various manifestations of racism and enforcement of pecking order in the structure of academe that stifle radical scholars and radical scholarship, and of which Robinson was witness, target, and foe. We recognize the limitless benefits of evoking the singular contributions of Cedric J. Robinson—to celebrate them but also to recognize what it meant for him to write about Black radicalism during the events that characterized the political economy of the late twentieth and early twenty-first century: Reaganomics, Thatcherism, neoliberalism, the escalation of police violence in aggrieved communities, occupation and genocide in the Middle East, and the expansion of modern security states.

Moreover, and likely most significantly, it was in this context that Robinson refused to merely describe Black radicalism but instead called Black scholars to a recognition of and engagement with the insistence of Black radical actors upon an uncompromising liberation from all forms of oppression, a labor made more difficult by allies whose proposals often reflected the bourgeoisie's construction of class struggle. In this way, his work was much, much more than a celebration of the Black Radical Tradition. And in that spirit, this book is much more than a tribute or hagiography: it is intended to draw us into closer proximity not to the description (nor the illusion, for that matter) of freedom struggles, but closer to the spirit of abolition, the work of revolutionary change, the relentless critique of oppression by *all* of those engaged in that work.

Collectively, these essays emerge from an aspiration for more than the promise of liberation, as Elizabeth Robinson details so eloquently in the preface. The essays in this volume, indeed the volume as a whole, are an incitement, the product of a wish fulfilled by the Robinsons to see Cedric's work engaged by this particular group of scholars. To that end, we wish to assert that this book is not intended to be definitive: the editors are merely archiving a moment in Black radical thought, one which exceeds the pages of this book, and which is always more expansive than the people writing here. Our role is to characterize the moment, not to limit it. And with that intention, we hear the echo of Robinson's words in the preface to the 2000 edition of *Black Marxism*: "In short, as a scholar it was never my purpose to exhaust the subject, only to suggest that it was there."[7]

---

7   Robinson, *Black Marxism*, xxxii.

The Black Radical Tradition has in practice refused the masquerade of natural orderings that racial regimes project.[8] Because this is the central innovation of twenty-first-century Black protest—from the poetry of Danez Smith ("I am sick of writing this poem / but bring the boy. his new name / his same old body") to the social media activism of a new generation of protestors—studying this tradition holds renewed significance for struggle in the twenty-first century. Thus, we must renew our commitments.

It is no irony that two disparate but temporally identical experiences of this historical moment have accumulated into a similar apex. Both Black protest (necessarily) and white supremacy (in its endeavor to maintain its covering conceits) in the United States have doubled down with more international exposure and force than at any other time in the past forty years. As capital flight, neoliberal asset stripping, unprecedented investment in mass incarceration and immigrant detention, and wage theft have escalated, radical protests over the past five years have produced robust platforms demanding reinvestment in public education, local economies and Black communities, food justice, the living wage, and the value of Black life itself.

The pernicious intentions and specific harms of white supremacy, whose designs and delegations began long before Trump's election, have found more stable sanctuary in the reinvocation and embrace of racist expression in the name of national securitization. While the state was enjoined to project official opposition to racism in the post–Civil Rights era, in the days since November 8, 2016 we are assured in both dramatic simile and witness that racism and the privileges of whiteness will enjoy an ascension into the limitlessness of official endorsement. Considering the quotidian struggle for Black life in the face of state counterinsurgency, anti-Black austerity, and domestic neoliberal experimentation, we are obliged to acknowledge the steady organizing of the Right that has culminated in the capture of official power. The logic at play in these maneuvers has been to deny the racial conditions of oppression as not racial, the consequence of which is now a turn to authorized neofascism. The forces of white supremacy—of racial capitalism—have been organizing for this moment for some time, but so too have the forces organized to struggle against it. This book is intended to register those forces, to recognize that while the terrain of struggle has indeed shifted, many who draw on the freedom dreams of liberation movements both past and present are equipped to meet the present challenges, insidious as they are.

Despite the resurgence of Black internationalist politics and new social movements to confront white supremacy and racial capitalism, mainstream media pundits and white liberalism in general have ignored not only the scope and breadth of Black Lives Matter and Black radical protest, but their significant

---

8   See Robinson, *Forgeries of Memory and Meaning: Blacks and the Regimes of Race in American Theater and Film Before World War II* (Chapel Hill: University of North Carolina Press, 2007), xii.

challenge to the hegemony now cumulatively manifest in Donald J. Trump's success. This deliberate exercise effects the same "vanishing" of the historical significance of Black protest that Robinson described. Moreover, liberal commentators turn not to the radical history of social movements with demonstrated evidence of community transformation, but to a contrived and insidious "innocence" that refuses the link between Trump's worldview and the triumph of racial capitalism over both the global economic system and its representations and imaginings by those who maintain it. For these and many more reasons, our commitments to writing, thinking, and acting amid a new generation of scholars and practitioners of radical abolition, and to bringing the practices of Black radicalism into broader cognizance, remain ardent. Therefore, we have much to learn from a movement enacted by Black queer feminists whose central concern is to abolish all forms of oppression. Black Lives Matter (BLM) as well as other organized, antiracist actions by Black communities and abolitionists has enlivened intersectional and international analysis through remarkable acts of solidarity with Palestine and Standing Rock. These sensibilities inspire a steady focus on a new moment when neoliberal economic restructuring converges with global counterinsurgency measures that target Arab and Muslim populations abroad and Black people and Muslims at home.

BLM's avowedly internationalist view of liberation echoes the Black Radical Tradition's insistence on political imaginaries beyond Eurocentrism. The sources of liberation theory in Black radical movements are multiple; the theories arise from social struggles, take into account the needs of the many, and concern intersecting forms of power. Protracted, material, and symbolic struggles against segregation, surveillance regimes, mass incarceration, and environmental racism are also cumulative. We propose that this moment is to be understood as itself more than a culmination of white supremacy: it is also and more significantly a moment characterized by the righteous fury and felt entitlement born of increasingly sophisticated diagnoses of state power, accompanied by powerful and material imaginings of justice, peace, and the promise of abolition democracy.

The driving intellectual task of Black protest in the twenty-first century has been to engage in a renewed and relentless practice of exposing the "covering conceit" of racial regimes: their history. As Robinson instructs us,

> racist regimes do possess history . . . but racial regimes are unrelentingly hostile to their exhibition. This antipathy exists because a discoverable history is incompatible with a racial regime and from the realization that paradoxically, so are its social relations.[9]

This instruction reveals Trump's success as an indication not of the strength of white supremacy and the dominance of the United States in the global market,

---

9   Ibid., xii–xiii.

but of the fragility and fissures in their constructions. Though the most important contrivance of these regimes has been the appearance of fixity and strength, it has historically been a façade that Black struggle has been compelled to disbelieve. It is a necessary and true discernment, and in the protests against the election results, clearly transmissible, even if temporarily. The protests we now see in the wake of the election stand on the shoulders of Black protest in the wake of anti-Black violence; they follow on the heels of a tradition both intended and compelled to endure.

While this book exists in the expansive shadow of Cedric J. Robinson's example, as well as that of the communities of activists and intellectuals from which he drew inspiration and into which his work breathed life, it also looks to the future, imagining the possibilities for abolitionism and freedom given the present conjuncture. Like Robinson himself, the intellectuals writing in this book are committed to thinking dialectically, and often outside the philosophical frameworks authorized within the Western academy. Commissioning an anthology around a profound political and spiritual subject always comes with a risk, primarily that of not including everyone writing on this particular subject in this particular moment. This volume came out of Elizabeth and Cedric's desire to see these particular scholars engage with these questions, to elevate discussion around racial capitalism and the Black Radical Tradition. It is the fulfillment of a wish. To that end, the book is an invocation of a certain conversation at a certain moment, not meant to canonize one view of a set of politics.

Just as the subjects of Robinson's scholarship are the artists, workers, prisoners, slaves, domestics, and anticolonial radicals who theorized their condition and plotted freedom from within particular historical moments, *Futures of Black Radicalism* is inspired by several traditions. While the collection is ostensibly curated by the esteemed and inspirational authors of each chapter, the subjects and sources of this project far exceed the pages of this book and extend back in time to ancestors and internationally to freedom strivers everywhere. This is a book about the worlds that Cedric J. Robinson sought to enliven during his lifetime and the ways that Robinson's legacy is enlivening new imaginaries in changing times. In this way, the book is part of the Black Radical Tradition, which is to say it is a collective endeavor including scholars, activists, artists, the incarcerated, freedom fighters, and more.

Futures of Black Radicalism is organized around three thematic frames that reflect the broad terrain of Robinson's contructions: understanding racial capitalism, the Black Radical Tradition, and imagining the future. We chose these frames in order to enact the kind of dialectical thought process required for these times. No movement forward can rest on a faulty foundational understanding of racial capitalism. This is why, in the first section of the book, scholars engage the intersecting logics of race and capitalism as conditions that confront social movements in the United States today. Steven Osuna and Damien Sojoyner are especially interested in the formation of anti-Blackness in an era of neoliberal racial capitalism. Nikhil Pal Singh, as well as Stefano Harney and Fred Moten examine the micropolitics of racial capitalism, as articulated in the formation of so-called primitive accumulation and in the racialized construction of things to be exchanged for value. Françoise Vergès explores the convergence of racial capitalism and environmental racism.

The second section of the book focuses on the Black Radical Tradition and its capacity to not only negate the conditions of racial capitalism but also to survive and thrive under conditions of racial terror. In this section scholars consider the forms of dialectical thought that have informed various freedom struggles, beginning with an interview featuring Cedric and Elizabeth Robinson and moving to a consideration of various political struggles that, in the words of George Lipsitz, "responded consistently by forging advanced concepts of a deeply politicized love." In addition, this section engages various international struggles for Black liberation in order to stretch the horizons of the Black Radical Tradition beyond the United States and outside the West. For example, Greg Burris looks at the global solidarity uniting Black protest in the United States with Palestinian protest, Paul Ortiz considers the applicability of the Black Radical Tradition to Latin American social movements, and Darryl Thomas recalls the internationalism of Malcolm X in order to locate Black radicalism in North Africa and the Middle East.

In the final section of the book, scholars think about the future by identifying new forms of imagination and struggle through which to achieve liberation. The chapters in this section take up various aspects of abolitionist politics, from prison abolition to Black music and visual culture, that attempt to imagine new futures. H. L. T. Quan explores the concept of ungovernability through the figure of the fugitive and Afrofuturist. Avery Gordon analyzes the aesthetic politics of Black radicalism in three newly commissioned works by African American artist Glen Ligon, a series titled Call and Response. Shana Redmond and Kwame Phillips curate a sonic mixtape of Black liberation music. Ruth Wilson Gilmore outlines the possibility of abolitionism given the present conjuncture of incarceration and policing. Angela Davis discusses the possibilities for new political imaginaries linked to previous ones.

There are two afterwords. Erica Edwards returns us to Cedric Robinson, of what she calls "Cedric People," in order to demonstrate the communities of fate that sustained and enlivened Robinson's study of Black radicalism. Robin Kelley focuses on the ancestors who created Robinson's worlds. Edwards's and Kelley's afterwords enact the Black Radical Tradition by excavating a history of friendships and familial relations that helped Robinson think dialectically. These pieces remind us how love and kinship, often some of the most significant forces available to us, can be transformed into powerful actions in the service of a just future.

In all of his writings on the Black Radical Tradition, Robinson revealed with great care the precision with which Black freedom fighters discerned the fractures in regimes of racism and state power. He archived their commensurate insurrections, seen and unseen, as evidence of an uncompromising struggle to end tyranny and oppression. The endurance of these practices has done more than bolster the courage of Afro-diasporic people: it has commissioned imaginaries and generated epistemologies that have shaped radical intellectual traditions across the world.

It is our hope that this book will inspire a greater consciousness of the specific inheritances of the Black Radical Tradition. The futures of Black radicalism depend on it.

Part One
Racial Capitalism

Chapter 1

Class Suicide

The Black Radical Tradition, Radical Scholarship, and the Neoliberal Turn

Steven Osuna

Each generation must discover its mission, fulfill it or betray it, in relative opacity.
—Frantz Fanon, *The Wretched of the Earth*[1]

The shared past is precious, not for itself, but because it is the basis of consciousness, of knowing, of being.
—Cedric J. Robinson, *Black Marxism*[2]

I write this in a state of urgency—one troubled by the decadence of a capitalist system that is undermining and exhausting the ability of many to live a dignified life. As you read this, Mexican and Central American women, including transwomen and youth are fleeing their countries due to the violence of economic restructuring, only to be detained at the US border and sent to private detention facilities. Drone strikes in the global "war on terror" in countries such as Pakistan have made children fear the beauty of clear, blue skies. Across the United States, state-sanctioned violence in the form of police terror is producing an unrelenting crisis in Black and brown communities, leaving many without their mothers, fathers, sisters, and brothers. All these atrocities emerge in the process of protecting and maintaining a social organism that accumulates wealth and privilege at one pole and misery, degradation, and the torment of labor (or the lack thereof) at the other. As this unfolds, aggrieved communities organize, fight back, and walk tall—a continuous dialectical struggle.

While the movements and voices of these communities are rarely heard or taken seriously, the capitalist state's repressive response to them constantly legitimates itself through political, economic, and ideological apparatuses. As Stuart Hall reminds us, keeping hegemony in place is hard work, and those with an interest in maintaining order will go to great lengths to defend it. One apparatus that does this work is the academic institution. Schools, colleges, and universities reproduce the social relations of oppression and exploitation. The struggle in

---

1 Frantz Fanon, *The Wretched of the Earth*, trans. Richard Philcox (New York: Grove, 2004), 145.

2 Cedric J. Robinson, *Black Marxism: The Making of the Black Radical Tradition*, 2nd ed. (Chapel Hill: University of North Carolina Press, 2000), xxxv.

these terrains to shape interpretations, solutions, and responses to public concerns is, therefore, of the upmost importance. Interventions from radical scholarship that identify the root causes and structural conditions of exploitation and oppression and that prioritize the interests of aggrieved communities are vital, and will occur only if scholars and intellectuals are in conversation with these communities. This is easier said than done, however. Professionalization in academic institutions distances many scholars and intellectuals from people and communities in radical social movements who are struggling against oppression. Instead of engaging and building with social movements that are seeking solutions and strategies to combat the ravages of racial capitalism, scholars and intellectuals remain entangled in bourgeois academia. This has worked in concert with the "neoliberal turn" of the university and social life in general.[3]

At a 2013 academic conference in Chicago, Cedric J. Robinson shared his generation's experience of entering the academy and producing radical scholarship. He argued that many who entered academic institutions in the late 1960s disrupted an academy that had been purged of social justice. They challenged the normalization of brutality that oppressed communities faced in the United States and around the globe. Newly emerging Black Studies, Chicana/o Studies, and Native American Studies functioned as spaces to unsettle the normativity of the white academy. "We came into the academy in the 1960s and we began for a moment, to redeem it," Robinson argued, "but the period of redemption is now under enormous threat by . . . the further incorporation of the academy."[4] The intervention of radical scholarship was crucial for the advancement of social justice and liberatory struggles for aggrieved communities within bourgeois academic institutions. But attacks by reactionary forces from outside and within the academy and the neoliberal subjectivity of many scholars have thwarted their relationship to the public and social movements. Robinson argued that radical and critical scholarship was urgently needed, and that radical scholars and intellectuals needed to be rooted with the people struggling against oppression and exploitation. "We are not possible," he argued, "without the encouragement, the urgency, and the requirement that we be here by those who are in fact being trampled on, being imprisoned."[5]

In his intervention, Robinson provided a suggestion for how radical scholarship engaged with aggrieved communities might endure during the current neoliberal turn. Describing his work on radicalism from the vantage point of American slaves, Robinson reminded the audience of the slaves' revolutionary visions—that they had never experienced or succumbed to what some have

---

3   Lester K. Spence, *Knocking the Hustle: Against the Neoliberal Turn in Black Politics* (New York: Punctum Books, 2015), 3–25.

4   Cedric J. Robinson, "What Is to Be Done? The Future of Critical Ethnic Studies," plenary session, Critical Ethnic Studies Conference, Chicago, September 21, 2013, quoted from the author's notes.

5   Ibid.

called "social death." "That's nonsense," he argued, "because they were some-thing more than what was expected of them—they could invent, manufacture, conspire, and organize way beyond the possibilities."[6] Robinson noted that the slaves' visions of liberation are evident in spirituals, or what Frederick Douglass and W. E. B. Du Bois termed the "sorrow songs,"[7] whose import was commonly overlooked by whites at the time.[8] The spirituals were a cultural formation created by slaves to express their religious faith and provide guidance, instruc-tion, and critiques on how to survive and make sense of their conditions. They were a framework for imagining possibilities beyond the brutality and barba-rism of slavery. White supremacy viewed them simply as noise. Robinson concluded: "What is the noise of 2013? That's what we have to ask today . . . Record the noise."[9]

This mandate provides a radical framework for scholars and intellectuals in our current moment, urging us to listen to the sounds, visions, and cries of the aggrieved, oppressed, and exploited who struggle every day while maintaining their dignity. What are the noises emerging under racial capitalism during the neoliberal turn? How can academics and intellectuals drop the "megaphone," put on the "hearing aid," and join the collective struggle?[10] This undertaking requires a commitment to ending racial capitalism and the numerous oppres-sive conditions it upholds and reproduces. A key site from which to develop this commitment, I argue, is the Black Radical Tradition. As Robinson notes, the Black Radical Tradition is an "accretion, over generations, of collective intelli-gence gathered from struggle,"[11] which compels us to address the contradictions of racial capitalism and the neoliberal turn that has only exacerbated the brutal-ity that so many face. The Black Radical Tradition reveals the shared history of struggle that is a basis not only of consciousness, but of knowledge and being. Awareness of this history is necessary for the future of radical scholarship and struggles for liberation.

In this essay I want to focus, for a moment, on the academic labor of scholars and intellectuals, not to privilege them but rather to suggest and heed a call to action. I ask what scholars and intellectuals—the petit bourgeois intellectual[12], in other words—can learn from the Black Radical Tradition in order to challenge the neoliberal turn of social life, avoid acting as mandarins for white supremacy and

6   Ibid.

7   W. E. B. Du Bois, *The Souls of Black Folks* (Toronto: Dover, 1994), iv.

8   Robinson referenced the scholarship of sociologist Jon Cruz in his discussion of spirituals: Jon Cruz, *Culture on the Margins: The Black Spiritual and the Rise of American Cultural Interpretation* (Princeton, NJ: Princeton University Press, 1999).

9   Robinson, "What Is to Be Done?".

10   George Lipsitz, *American Studies at a Moment of Danger* (Minneapolis: Universty of Minnesota Press, 2001), 282.

11   Robinson, *Black Marxism*, xxx.

12   I use the classical Marxist term "petit bourgeois" to describe the class position of many intellectuals and scholars. The petit bourgeois is the middle strata, or professional middle class, under the capitalist system.

the capitalist classes, and instead join the global struggle against racial capital-ism.[13] To work through these questions, this chapter returns to the radical analysis and process described by many Black radicals, including Walter Rodney, Amilcar Cabral, and Frantz Fanon. For the petit bourgeois intellectuals and scholars to challenge the seductions of neoliberalism and transform their consciousness and being, they must commit "suicide as a class"[14]—a process that speaks to the urgent need to struggle with and for aggrieved, oppressed, and exploited communities. It challenges the petit bourgeois intellectual and scholar to disinvest from their social positions, produce radical scholarship whose research, arguments, and conclusions have a preferential option for the poor, and be informed by the sounds and visions emerging from the trenches of racial capitalism. Class suicide chal-lenges the professionalization process that disconnects the intellectual and scholar from aggrieved communities, the neoliberalization of academic scholarship, and the brutality of racial capitalism. Revisiting the liberatory praxis of Rodney, Cabral, Fanon, and Robinson will be instructive in this endeavor.

THE NEOLIBERAL TURN AND INTELLECTUAL LABOR

The current era has seen rapid acceleration in the unequal distribution of global wealth and resources and in damage to the planet's ability to replenish itself. An ecological, ideological, political, and economic crisis is unfolding, while demands from the global majority are met with repressive, and increasingly normalized, transnational social control. This crisis of global capitalism has unleashed rampant barbarism on the masses of the world even as they continue to fight back.[15] Fueling an increasingly uneven distribution of wealth and resources, the system is, at its core, profoundly unstable. As of October 2015, the wealthiest 1 percent of the global population owned half of all household wealth.[16] Roughly sixty-two individuals around the world have the same wealth as 3.6 billion people. Income for the poorest 10 percent of the world has increased only $3 a year for almost a quarter of a century.[17] This unequal distri-bution of wealth is endemic throughout the United States and has increased racial oppression and exploitation, particularly since the financial crisis of 2008. The Institute for Policy Studies has calculated that the twenty richest Americans

---

13   I use the term "mandarin" in reference to the mandarinate bureaucracy of the Chinese Empire. Members of this bureaucracy served as intellectuals for the elites, as many intellectuals and petite bourgeoisie do today.

14   Amilcar Cabral, *Unity and Struggle: Speeches and Writings of Amilcar* (New York and London: Monthly Review Press, 1979), 136.

15   For a discussion of the crisis of global capitalism, see William I. Robinson, *Global Capitalism and the Crisis of Humanity* (New York: Cambridge University Press, 2014).

16   Richard Kersley and Markus Stierli, *Global Wealth Report 2015* (Credit Suisse Research Institute, October 2015), available at publications.credit-suisse.com.

17   Oxfam, "An Economy for the 1%: How Privilege and Power in the Economy Drive Inequality and How This Can Be Stopped" (Oxfam, January 18, 2016), available at oxfam.org.

own more wealth than the bottom half of the US population combined, a total of 152 million people in 57 million households. The richest tenth of the richest 1 percent in the United States, in the second decade of the twenty-first century, has seen even greater income and wealth gains. For example, the billionaires on the Forbes 400 list now have as much wealth as all Black households and more than one-third of the US Latina/o population combined. Blacks make up 13.2 percent of the US population yet control only 2.5 percent of the nation's wealth, while Latina/os make up 17 percent of the population and control 2.9 percent of the wealth.[18]

In Los Angeles County, where I live, 28 percent of working Angelenos earn poverty pay, while 40 percent live "in what only can be called misery."[19] There is a 10 percent unemployment rate and jobs have been declining since 1990. In 2007 the poverty rate was 13.3 percent; by 2012 it was 17 percent. If Los Angeles County were a country, it would be the nineteenth largest economic power in the world. The Los Angeles region is the trade leader in the United States, with 44 percent of the nation's cargo passing through its ports. Despite these numbers, the poverty rate in Los Angeles County is higher than that of the nation as a whole. Over 1.47 million, or 15 percent, of Angelenos are living in poverty. Nearly 30 percent of full-time workers earn less than $25,000 a year. Four in ten people live in extreme poverty, defined as living on less than $5,400 a year for a single person, or about $11,000 for a family of four. One in five children live in poverty. It is estimated that 11 percent of Asians, 19 percent of Blacks, and 20 percent of Latina/os—and only 8 percent of whites—live in poverty. The percentage of working poor in the county is higher than in the United States as a whole. Adjusted for inflation, in the past twenty years, the average worker actually saw income fall nearly $2 an hour, while the top 1 percent of salaried workers saw significant income growth. In the early 2000s, 14,000 new housing units were built in the city of Los Angeles, but 90 percent of them were affordable only to those earning $135,000 a year or more.[20] The right to housing in Los Angeles is nonexistent, leaving many on the streets to fend for themselves and face the criminalization and surveillance of poverty.

The unequal distribution of the world's wealth produces the misery, starvation, and degradation that we see on our television and computer screens and every day on the streets. These are the savage results of what Robinson called the historical development of a racialized social structure emerging from capitalism.[21] Racism and capitalism must be analyzed as intimately linked concepts. As

18   Chuck Collins and Josh Hoxie, *Billionaire Bonanza: The Forbes 400 and the Rest of Us* (Institute for Policy Studies, December 2015), available at ips-dc.org.

19   Los Angeles 2020 Commission, *A Time for Truth* (Los Angeles, December 2013), available at la2020reports.org.

20   United Way of Southern California, *L. A. County 10 Years Later: A Tale of Two Cities, One Future* (Los Angeles, February 2010), available at wlac.edu.

21   Robinson, *Black Marxism*, 2.

sociologist Kyra R. Greene argues, scholars and activists must study and highlight how the material realities of the political economy exacerbate racialized inequality, thus demonstrating the continued significance of race under capitalism as racism produces a "consistent disadvantage" for racially oppressed communities. The exploitation wrought by capitalism is racialized.[22] "Like the impact of Hurricane Katrina," Greene contends, "it may be raining on all Americans, but people of color are drowning."[23]

Racial capitalism has assumed a distinct shape under the neoliberal turn.[24] The term "neoliberalism" has been used to describe the social formation that emerged once capital broke free from the nation-state in the 1970s. This term, Hall argues, does not satisfactorily describe the complexity and specificities that have materialized in the last four decades. He notes, however, that neoliberalism provides a useful, provisional "conceptual identity" for consistent underlying features of the global political economy.[25] Primarily, neoliberalism signifies an ensemble of economic policies that promote structural adjustment, austerity, free markets, private property, and free trade through deregulation of industry and capital flows and the privatization of public goods—effecting a restoration of class power for global economic elites.[26] Yet, beyond economic policy, neoliberalism is also a culture, philosophy, and worldview that expands neoclassical economics beyond the economic realm. According to Wendy Brown, neoliberalism is also "an order of normative reason" that has taken shape as "a governing rationality extending a specific formulation of economic values, practices, and metrics to every dimension of human life."[27] This strategy has gone global, starting with its implementation in Chile following the 1973 coup d'etat and subsequent execution in the United States and Britain in the 1980s while the International Monetary Fund (IMF) and World Bank (WB) promoted and enforced it throughout the Global South.

The neoliberal turn has exacerbated the inequalities produced by racial capitalism. Instead of providing public housing, unemployment insurance, living wages, and public infrastructure through a social wage, public policy under the neoliberal turn has enforced and encouraged government dismantling of these resources and opened them to market and entrepreneurial forces. As Lester K. Spence highlights, "Under the neoliberal turn progressive policies like welfare, public housing, and unemployment insurance are either slashed or attacked, as these policies are viewed to make people *less* entrepreneurial and

---

22   Kyra R. Greene, "Why We Need More Marxism in the Sociology of Race," *Souls: A Critical Journal of Black Politics, Culture, and Society* 13, no. 2 (2011): 168.

23   Ibid., 166.

24   Spence, *Knocking the Hustle*.

25   Stuart Hall, "The Neoliberal Revolution," *Soundings: A Journal of Politics and Culture* 48 (2011): 10.

26   David Harvey, *A Brief History of Neoliberalism* (Oxford: Oxford University Press, 2010), 16.

27   Wendy Brown, *Undoing the Demos: Neoliberalism's Stealth Revolution* (New York: Zone Books, 2015), 30.

less responsible for their own choices."[28] In this context race and racism have worked in tandem with class exploitation. United for a Fair Economy argues, for example, that the US subprime mortgage crisis that led to the global financial collapse in 2008 caused the "greatest loss of wealth to people of color in modern US history."[29]

The neoliberal turn has created a precarious condition for working-class communities, and should be attacked and critiqued by the intellectual labor of scholars, academics, activists, and organizers. But it is also a "governing rationality" that spreads market values to every sphere of social life, and the academy and activist spaces are no exception. As Brown notes, "*Knowledge, thought,* and *training* are valued and desired almost exclusively for the contribution to capital enhancement."[30] Academic scholarship, for one, has become a form of human capital that offers rewards and status—including foundation grants, money, and prestige—that isolate the intellectual from those struggling to remain alive. As Marx notes in the *Communist Manifesto*, the petit bourgeois intellectual belongs to a conservative middle class that acts as a buffer between capitalists and the working classes and endeavors to keep from extinction. "If by chance they are revolutionary," Marx notes, "they are so only in view of their impending transfer into the proletariat, they thus defend not their present, but their future interests."[31]

With other middle classes, the intellectual often acts as a reactionary in contrast to those striving for liberation from racial capitalism. Ideologically, intellectuals are more inclined to maintain their position in the class-stratified society than destroy it. An agent who emerged from liberal bourgeois academic institutions, the petit bourgeois intellectual's role has been to legitimate the social order. As the Gulbenkian Commission on the Restructuring of the Social Sciences notes, "The intellectual history of the nineteenth century is marked above all by disciplinarization and professionalization of knowledge, that is to say, by the creation of permanent institutional structures designed both to produce new knowledge and to reproduce the producers of knowledge."[32] Through a racialized, gendered, and especially class-specific project, academic institutions have privatized and restricted knowledge production to elites and those from the upper classes. Any knowledge production by the lower orders of society has been interpreted as illegitimate, backward, or nonscientific, thereby allowing the knowledge produced through academic institutions by

---

28   Spence, *Knocking the Hustle*, 38.

29   Amaad Rivera, Brenda Cotto-Escalera, Anisha Desair, and Jeannette Huezo, *Foreclosed: State of the Dream 2008* (Boston: United for a Fair Economy, 2008), available at faireconomy.org/reports.

30   Brown, *Undoing the Demos*, 177.

31   Karl Marx and Friedrich Engels, *The Marx-Engels Reader*, 2nd ed., ed. Robert C. Tucker (New York and London: W.W. Norton, 1978), 482.

32   Immanuel Wallerstein, *Open the Social Sciences: Report of the Gulbenkian Commision on the Restructuring of the Social Science* (Stanford, CA: Stanford University Press, 1996), 7.

intellectuals to mask power relations through claims of objectivity and positivism.

Academic scholarship continues this practice under the neoliberal turn. Although people who were historically excluded from the academy have entered it, many have followed the path of becoming "private intellectuals."[33] In her discussion of academic scholarship by those once marginalized by the academy, Ruth Wilson Gilmore notes several broad, overlapping tendencies that have shaped "oppositional studies" under neoliberalism, including "individualistic careerism," "romantic particularism," and "luxury production." These tendencies, according to Gilmore, produce scholars and intellectuals who are disconnected from larger struggles for social change, who write about oppressive conditions in the abstract, and who produce knowledge accessible only to a specific few.[34] As much as they claim to be "oppositional," such scholars and intellectuals "waste precious intellectual resources and displace needed energy from where it is most needed,"[35] a learned behavior that emerges from the social and cultural pedagogies of neoliberalism. As Barbara Tomlinson and George Lipsitz demonstrate, "neoliberal subjects" are produced in "entrepreneurial" universities that function through market competition and market subjects. Neoliberalism has been "invented, learned, and legitimated"[36] in the academy, where the petit bourgeois intellectual becomes an entrepreneur. Their scholarship is aimed at acquiring social capital and material rewards rather than producing knowledge that advances, informs, or supports the social struggles of those most marginalized.

No research is value-free; therefore all intellectual labor is political. Though guided by the rules and logics of academic research, the intellectual's knowledge is never divorced from the historical context of its production.[37] There is no free-floating, neutral intellectual, and the petit bourgeois intellectual is part of an institution structured by dominance; this requires them to reflect on what their scholarship is doing and not doing. Does it follow the path of individualistic careerism, romantic particularism, or luxury production? Or does it pursue what Gilmore calls "organic praxis"? Does it connect to struggles in and outside of the academy? Does it recognize that the "street has always run into the campus"[38]? The neoliberal turn is seductive; it inhibits radical scholarship that

33   Ruth Wilson Gilmore, "Public Enemies and Private Intellectuals: Apartheid USA," *Race and Class* 35, no. 69 (1993).

34   Ibid., 71–2.

35   Ibid., 73.

36   Barbara Tomlinson and George Lipsitz, "Insubordinate Spaces for Intemperate Times: Countering the Pedagogies of Neoliberalism," *Review of Education, Pedagogy, and Cultural Studies* 35, no. 1 (2013): 17.

37   Although we must also challenge the rules and logics of academic research, which often reproduces white supremacy and class oppression. See Tukufu Zuberi and Eduardo Bonilla-Silva, eds., *White Logic, White Methods: Racism and Methodology* (Maryland: Rowman & Littlefield, 2008).

38   Gilmore, "Public Enemies and Private Intellectuals," 73.

reveals the contradictions in its practice and ideology. To challenge this, the petit bourgeois intellectual and scholar must come to terms with their own positionality. They must, as the Italian socialist strategist Antonio Gramsci argues, develop a "new intellectual" grounded in social struggle:

> The mode of being of the new intellectual can no longer consist in eloquence, which is an exterior and momentary mover of feelings and passions, but in active participation in practical life, as constructor, organizer, "permanent persuader" and not just a simple orator (but superior at the same time to the abstract mathematical spirit); from technique-as-work one proceeds to technique-as-science and to the humanistic conception of history, without which one remains "specialized" and does not become "directive" (specialized and political).[39]

The petit bourgeois intellectual can take the side of aggrieved communities. Alternatively, they can maintain their historical role of legitimating the social order and defending their position within the class structure. The latter is seductive, yet the following discussion should be useful in imagining the former.

THE BLACK RADICAL TRADITION AND CLASS SUICIDE

Have there been petit bourgeois intellectuals and scholars that have gone against their class interests and struggled from the position of the oppressed? What examples can the petit bourgeois intellectuals of today follow to challenge the neoliberal turn? A key site of such inspiration is the Black Radical Tradition. It is here where intellectuals and organizers from a petit bourgeois background but an enslaved and colonized past have emerged to exploit the contradictions of the system in order to speak, write, and organize against it. It is in the Black Radical Tradition that we find the emergence of a radical intelligentsia inspired by the historical struggles of their pasts and present and looking toward a future alongside the masses. As Robinson notes, those inspired by the Black Radical Tradition "began the realization of their history and their theoretical task" and became Black radicals whose work served the people.[40]

Political scientist Michael Hanchard argues that Black political thought and theory have two distinct but interrelated purposes. The first is the practice of theorization and conceptualization in response to racial domination. The second consists of producing political writings and scholarship that center race and racism at the core of the Western modernity project.[41] Black political thought from the Black Radical Tradition pursues these two goals. However, before it

---

39   Antonio Gramsci, *Selections from the Prison Notebooks*, ed. Quintin Hoare and Geoffrey Nowell Smith (New York: International Publisher, 1971), 10.

40   Robinson, *Black Marxism*, 184.

41   Michael Hanchard, "Contours of Black Political Thought: An Introduction and Perspective," *Political Theory* 38 (2010): 512.

embarked on theorization and conceptualization of race and racism, the tradition materialized from the struggles against European slavery, capital accumulation, and its inherent racialism.[42] "Even then," Robinson notes, "the more fundamental impulse of Black resistance was the preservation of a particular social and historical consciousness rather than the revolutionary transformation of feudal or merchant capitalist Europe."[43] Robinson illuminates the emergence of this tradition from surviving the destruction of Western civilization even before it began to provide a ruthless critique of it. It inspired many radical intellectuals through what Robinson refers to as "an ideology of liberation" against racial capitalism, while also challenging Western Marxism and its lack of accounting for the revolutionary forces of the Third World.[44] It showed that Marxist analyses must always be "stretched" to take into account the contradictions within social formations.[45] Moreover, Black radical intellectuals such as W. E. B. Du Bois and C. L. R. James critiqued and reflected on their own positions within the petite bourgeoisie and encouraged others to do the same. They, like Robinson, suggested that a radical tradition existed to inform revolutionary praxis.

Through the act of "accompaniment" with aggrieved communities, this praxis emerges from the scholarship of the petit bourgeois intellectual.[46] This is done by highlighting not individuals but rather communities in struggle. H. L. T. Quan argues that Robinson's scholarship on the Black Radical Tradition provides a method for doing this kind of work—one that avoids the pitfall of centering individuals that is often encouraged by masculinist historiographies. "As in the case of Robinson's work," Quan suggests, "when the focus is on communities rather than individuals, and democratic and communitarian practices rather than elitism, we are able to make that shift from great men's history to people's history."[47] In his scholarship Robinson shows that the brilliance of the radical intellectuals he highlights was derivative. "The truer genius," he argues, "was in the midst of the people of whom they wrote."[48]

The Black Radical Tradition that Robinson shares with us provides many examples of petit bourgeois intellectuals and scholars who have challenged their positions within the political, economic, and ideological system, endeavoring to struggle alongside the masses against the "fatal couplings of difference and power."[49] Anticolonial revolutionary Amilcar Cabral described how they

---

42   Robinson, *Black Marxism*, 310.

43   Ibid.

44   Ibid., 317.

45   Fanon, *The Wretched of the Earth*, 5.

46   For a discussion of "accompaniment," see Barbara Tomlinson and George Lipsitz, "American Studies as Accompaniment," *American Quarterly* 65, no. 1 (2013).

47   H. L. T. Quan, "Geniuses of Resistance: Feminist Consciousness and the Black Radical Tradition," *Race and Class* 47, no. 2 (2005): 49.

48   Robinson, *Black Marxism*, 184.

49   Stuart Hall, "Race, Culture, and Communications: Looking Backward and Forward at Cultural Studies," *Rethinking Marxism: A Journal of Economics, Culture, & Society* 5, no. 1 (1992): 17.

did it. In a 1966 plenary speech delivered at the First Solidarity Conference of the Peoples of Africa, Asia, and Latin America in Havana, Cuba, Cabral discussed socialist strategy, the importance of ideology in national liberation struggles, and his analysis of direct and indirect forms of imperialism. Toward the end of his speech, Cabral addressed the role of the petite bourgeoisie in national liberation struggles. "It is important to stress that the mission with which it is entrusted demands from this sector of the petty bourgeoisie a greater revolutionary consciousness," Cabral notes, "and the capacity for faithfully expressing the aspirations of the masses in each phase of the struggle and for identifying with them more and more."[50] He argues that in the colonial context, the petite bourgeoisie had not acquired as much capital as the colonial bourgeoisie and still had the ability to act as a revolutionary force against imperialism and neocolonialism. Cabral was clearly aware that their class position was seductive and could encourage their "natural tendencies" to become a pseudonational bourgeoisie.[51] Cabral's radical suggestion for avoiding this was class suicide.

> This means that in order to play completely the part that falls to it, in the national liberation struggle, the revolutionary petty bourgeoisie must be capable of committing suicide as a class, to be restored to life in the condition of a revolutionary worker completely identified with the deepest aspirations of the people to which [they belong].[52]

As Robinson notes, Cabral was shaped by the contradictions of domination that emerged from the dialectics of Portuguese imperialism in Guinea-Bissau.[53] This experience made him one of the world's foremost revolutionary theorists and practitioners of liberation. According to Basil Davidson, "there are many stories about [Cabral's] habit of linking the everyday scene, the banal scene you take for granted and barely even see, with the intellectual groundwork of an overall theory of society: of a theory, that is, always riveted to the reality of time and place."[54] Class suicide for Cabral was the ability to tie the everyday struggle of his people to his theoretical analysis, to build an organization like the African Party of Independence of Guinea-Bissau and Cape Verde (PAIGC), and to keep the aspirations and needs of his people at the forefront. Cabral had realized that the Marxism in which he was trained while studying agronomy in Portugal needed further development.[55] His application of Marxism required actual engagement

---

50   Cabral, *Unity and Struggle*, 135.
51   Ibid., 136.
52   Ibid.
53   Cedric J. Robinson, "Amilcar Cabral and the Dialectic of Portuguese Colonialism," *Radical America* 15, no. 3 (1981).
54   Cabral, *Unity and Struggle*, xi.
55   Robinson, "Amilcar Cabral."

with material conditions in Guinea-Bissau. This allowed him to reformulate his theorization and program, evident in his speeches and writings on the peasantry, the culture of resistance, and national liberation.[56]

Cabral had a clear understanding of the class and colonial conditions in Guinea-Bissau and encouraged the petite bourgeoisie to strive for similar awareness. In a message to Guinean and Cape Verdian civil servants and employees in commerce, Cabral reminded them that they were "servitors of Portuguese colonialism,"[57] and therefore received rewards such as homes, bread, health, and education that the majority of their compatriots were denied. Cabral recognized the class anxiety that these segments of the population felt toward national liberation, but urged them to revise their outlook. They had a responsibility to the African continent to join the struggle against colonialism. "Many with awareness of this necessity have bravely put themselves on the side of our people and our companions in struggle," Cabral declared.[58] The destiny of the petite bourgeoisie must mirror the destiny of the people. "Turn each post you hold, in the civil service or in commerce," he argued, "into a fortress of combat for the immediate destruction of Portuguese colonialism."[59] It was time to recognize their historical role and refuse the "selfishness and blind" ambition inflicted on them by Portuguese colonialism. To achieve success in these efforts, Cabral believed that the culture of Guinean society had to be replaced with a revolutionary culture that would counter petit bourgeois class interests. This would include, as Patrick Chabal argues, a "set of beliefs" and "political experiences, which would lead them to accept their responsibilities as revolutionaries."[60] Cabral's involvement in the struggle for national liberation rejected notions of bourgeois individualism: "Nobody is indispensible in this struggle; we are all needed but nobody is indispensable."[61] It was his loyalty to this struggle that led to his assassination.

Frantz Fanon also discussed the notion of class suicide. Born in Martinique, Fanon attained revolutionary consciousness in Algeria and learned to challenge and disinvest in the class position he had obtained through bourgeois academic institutions in France. Although, as Robinson notes, Fanon was struggling with his own personal contradictions, he soon learned about the importance of liberation from the revolutionary struggles of the Algerian people.[62] It was in this period that Fanon wrote his most important work, *The Wretched of the Earth*, which described the struggles he was witnessing. Fanon began his work thus: "National liberation, national reawakening, restoration of the nation to the

---

56   Ibid., 50.
57   Cabral, *Unity and Struggle*, 157.
58   Ibid.
59   Ibid., 158.
60   Patrick Chabal, *Amilcar Cabral: Revolutionary Leadership and People's War* (London: Africa World Press, 2003), 180.
61   Quoted in Robinson, "Amilcar Cabral," 54.
62   Cedric J. Robinson, "The Appropriation of Frantz Fanon," *Race & Class* 35, no. 1 (1993).

people or Commonwealth, whatever the name used, whatever the latest expression, decolonization is always a violent event."[63] He was not speaking from an abstract position but from the trenches of revolutionary struggle. In a letter written days before his untimely death, he declared: "We are nothing on earth if we are not in the first place the slaves of a cause, the cause of the people, the cause of justice and liberty."[64]

In his liberationist theorizing, Fanon provides a critique of the national bourgeoisie and colonized intellectuals that emerge in the anticolonial struggle. Fanon argues that historically, the national bourgeoisie "often turns away from his heroic and positive path, which is both productive and just, and unabashedly opts for the antinational, and therefore abhorrent, path of a conventional bourgeoisie, a bourgeois bourgeoisie that is dismally, inanely, and cynically bourgeois."[65] In the colonial context, Fanon illustrates that colonized intellectuals are trained to think of society in individualist terms, clinging to the "notion of a society of individuals where each is locked in his subjectivity, where wealth lies in thought."[66]

The only way for the intellectual and the national bourgeoisie to avoid these conceits, according to Fanon, is to struggle alongside the people for liberation, educating themselves through the strength of collective knowledge sharing: "Village assemblies, the power of the people's commissions and the extraordinary productiveness of neighborhood and section committee meetings."[67] The real-life struggles of the people, Fanon argues, provide the colonized intellectual with better knowledge of real-world struggles than the "falsity" of the theories, values, perceptions, and cultural preoccupations taught to them by Western civilization.

Just as the intellectual should depart from their "egoism, arrogant recrimination, and the idiotic, childish need to have the last word," the national bourgeoisie should repudiate its class position and serve the people it represents. Fanon notes:

> In an underdeveloped country, the imperative duty of an authentic national bourgeoisie is to betray the vocation to which it is destined, to learn from the people, and make available to them the intellectual and technical capital it culled from its time in the colonial universities.[68]

Fanon, like Cabral, held ambitiously to the (some may argue idealist) vision of the national and petite bourgeoisie coming to terms with their class illusions

---

63   Fanon, *The Wretched of the Earth*, 1.
64   Quoted in Hussein Abdilahi Bulhan, *Frantz Fanon and the Psychology of Oppression* (New York: Plenum Press, 1985), 35.
65   Fanon, *The Wretched of the Earth*, 99.
66   Ibid., 11.
67   Ibid.
68   Ibid., 99.

and enlisting in national liberation. Both men were exemplars of this process. To Fanon, the colonized intellectual must engage in dialogue with those suffering and organizing against oppression and exploitation. At first the interaction would be difficult given the intellectual's training by bourgeois institutions in false notions of objectivity and neutrality, but, through the process of active engagement, their academic labor would change:

> Whereas the colonized intellectual started out by producing work exclusively with the oppressor in mind—either in order to charm him or to denounce him by using ethnic or subjectivist categories—[they] gradually [switch] over to addressing [themselves] to [their] people.[69]

To Fanon, the colonized intellectual and national bourgeoisie have a historic mission. Either they fulfill it by joining the revolutionary struggle, or they betray it and capitulate to the seductions of class aspirations.

Radical writings were important to Fanon as tools for building a liberatory culture with visions of an alternative social structure.

> When the colonized intellectual writing for [their] people uses the past [they] must do so with the intention of opening up the future, of spurring them into action and fostering hope. But in order to secure hope, in order to give it substance, [they] must take part in the action and commit [themselves] body and soul to the national struggle.[70]

The writings of Fanon and Cabral show us their vision of how a petit bourgeois intellectual could contribute to social struggle when informed by the people. As Robinson notes, Fanon's and Cabral's analyses of the national bourgeoisie in the colonial context can and must be linked to the discussion of the petit bourgeois intellectuals and scholars that emerge from academic institutions in the United States and around the globe.[71] Robinson provides an important critique of US intellectuals and their appropriation of Fanon's work for the sake of their own arguments. Rather than using Fanon to prove an academic argument, we should learn from Fanon's organic praxis inspired by the Black Radical Tradition. Fanon demonstrated the power of the people and how their struggle for liberation could provide the fuel for radical scholarship.

Cabral and Fanon were part of the tradition of radical intelligentsia informed by struggle, yet they were not academic intellectuals. Walter Rodney, on the other hand, was a Guyanese historian, professor, organizer, and public intellectual whose organic praxis showed the revolutionary role of the petit bourgeois scholar and intellectual. In his classic work, *How Europe*

---

69   Ibid., 173.
70   Ibid., 167.
71   Robinson, "The Appropriation of Frantz Fanon," 84.

Underdeveloped Africa, Rodney explores the damaging effects of one continent on the other. "Racism, violence, and brutality," he argues, "were the concomitants of the capitalist system when it extended itself abroad in the early centuries of international trade."[72] His work begins with an analysis of the development of Africa and Europe before their encounter, and then of the development and underdevelopment that followed it. He shows how European capitalists ransacked the African continent and placed it in an underdeveloped state. In the first chapter of his study, "Some Questions on Development," Rodney critiques the European scholars who have written about development from a modernization perspective. His critique employs a dialectical analysis that incorporates relations of exploitation. "First, the answer is that the imperialist system bears major responsibility for African economic retardation by draining African wealth and by making it impossible to develop more rapidly the resources of the continent," Rodney contends. "Second, one has to deal with those who manipulate the system and those who are either agents or unwitting accomplices of the said system."[73] His discussion of the power relations between nations and continents and the evasions by bourgeois economists of these relations demonstrates how underdevelopment goes beyond economics. Rodney unmasks how the racist assumptions of European economists naturalized the underdevelopment of the African continent. He argues that these scholars' interpretations adhere to white supremacist discourse maintaining that European countries were more developed because they were innately superior and that the responsibility for the economic underdevelopment of Africa lies with the inherent backwardness of African peoples.[74]

> Mistaken interpretations of the causes of underdevelopment usually stem either from prejudiced thinking or from the error of believing that one can learn the answers by looking inside the underdeveloped economy. The true explanation lies in seeking out the relationship between Africa and certain developed countries and recognizing that it is a relationship of exploitation.[75]

Rodney's scholarship exemplifies a people-centered analysis that places the workers of the world and the oppressed at the center and frames them as historical agents. To understand what Rodney refers to as the "situation from which we move," petit bourgeois intellectuals and scholars must not only read scholarly work on the topic of inequality, but also, and perhaps more importantly, ground themselves with those who struggle every day. In the last chapter of *The Groundings with My Brothers*, Rodney provides intellectuals with three essential

---

72   Walter Rodney, *How Europe Underdeveloped Africa* (Washington, DC: Howard University Press, 1981[1972]), 90.

73   Ibid., 27.

74   Ibid., 21.

75   Ibid., 22.

suggestions for producing scholarship in opposition to exploitation and oppression.

> I suggest first that the intellectual, the academic, within his own discipline, has to attack those distortions which white imperialism, white cultural imperialism have produced in all branches of scholarship . . . My second point is that the black intellectual has to move beyond his own discipline to challenge the social myth, which exists in the society as a whole . . . Thirdly, the black intellectual, the black academic must attach himself to the activity of the black masses.[76]

Rodney's essay was informed by his experiences in Jamaica and his interactions with Rastafarians there. "Grounding" with them wherever he could allowed him and the "brothers" to learn from each other. This was important to Rodney:

> The system says they have nothing, they are illiterates . . . but you learn humility after you get into contact with these brothers. And it is really great . . . I find my colleagues, my so-called peers, white people, black bourgeoisie all frustrate me and I get annoyed.[77]

Rodney's experiences in Jamaica are a clear example of a scholar grounded among the people. He argues in *Groundings* that addressing contradictions among academic disciplines, challenging societal common sense, and staying connected to and informed by struggle produces better scholarship. It is vital for scholars to remain accountable to the people whose lives depend on it. The petit bourgeois intellectual must struggle with common sense, which is both complex and contradictory. Rodney's experience demonstrates the importance of engaging in dialogue outside the confines of the academy. Understanding the rich totality of many determinations and relations demands a complex understanding of social formations that only emerges when scholarship is connected to struggle. In Jamaica, Rodney was grounded with his brothers and was attacked because of it. This was a small price to pay, as his brothers paid it daily.

In a 1978 talk titled "Crisis in the Periphery of the World System, Africa and the Caribbean," Rodney analyzes the historical moment and its relationship to racialized class struggles around the world.[78] During his talk, Rodney highlights the importance of recognizing the role of the petit bourgeois intellectual. He warns the audience of the dangers of "petit bourgeois hegemony" over working-class movements. He argues, like Cabral and Fanon, that the role of the petite

---

76   Walter Rodney, *The Groundings with My Brothers* (London: Bogle-L'Ouverture Publications, 1996[1969]), 62–3.

77   Ibid.

78   Walter Rodney, "Crisis in the Periphery of the World System, Africa and the Caribbean," speech delivered at an unknown university (1978). See the Walter Rodney papers, 1960–1987, Box 31, Robert W. Woodruff Library at the Atlanta University Center.

bourgeoisie is limited—that working people, not the petite bourgeoisie, must lead the struggle for liberation.

> And if the petite bourgeoisie has a role, as one would hope, at least I would hope so for my own sake being located in that class. If we have a role, it has to do with the shift of the initiative into the hands of workers and peasants and then for a change we begin to serve those classes. Because mostly we have been serving other classes anyhow. Mostly we have been serving the capitalist class. So for a change we may begin to service the working people, service the working class.[79]

Serving the working class, according to Rodney, requires a change in the aspirations of the petit bourgeois intellectual: going against their interest in acquiring the material rewards of serving capitalist classes and instead serving working people. The ideology and frameworks developed by scholars must emerge from the needs of working people, not their own.

> When we import our concern it's amazing what the petite bourgeoisie can be concerned about. We have all kinds of preoccupations, which are very little or have nothing to do with what working people say and do out of their own immediate activity in production.[80]

The organizing of aggrieved communities was a priority to Rodney. It formed the foundations for his scholarship. He refused to indulge class seductions. He chose to aspire towards class suicide.

THE BLACK RADICAL TRADITION AND CLASS SUICIDE AS A "WAR OF POSITION"

The organic praxis of Black radical scholars and intellectuals illuminates the importance of the Black Radical Tradition and class suicide during the current moment, when the neoliberal turn is destroying entire communities. It provides useful examples to petit bourgeois intellectuals and scholars for their ideal roles and contributions within racial capitalism. Instead of being seduced by the benchmarks of bourgeois success, Cabral, Fanon, and Rodney chose to struggle with the people and, most importantly, to learn from them. They had acquired a bourgeois education from academic institutions, but realized, as Robinson notes in *Black Marxism*, "that for a people to survive in the struggle it must be on its own terms: the collective wisdom which is a synthesis of culture and the experiences of that struggle."[81] They recognized that their work should be guided by a liberationist perspective, a perspective coming from the aspiration of the

---

79 Ibid.
80 Ibid.
81 Robinson, *Black Marxism*, xxxv.

people struggling against capital, white supremacy, and oppression, and not from the confines of academic institutions.

According to Gramsci, wars of position are used by disparate social forces to generate hegemonic ideas, morals, influence, and power in society, in a slow, protracted process connecting forces that gain momentum through movement building. The Black Radical Tradition and the analysis of class suicide that emerged from it can serve as a war of position for petit bourgeois intellectuals whose academic labor must serve and support the wretched of the earth. Radical research and theorization, including the work of Fanon, Cabral, Rodney, and Robinson, must be useful to and remain in conversation with radical social movements. Class suicide by the petit bourgeois scholar and intellectual is essential. As Maria Poblet from Causa Justa/Just Cause, an organization fighting gentrification in Oakland and San Francisco, notes, "Class suicide is an amazing concept: a vision of profound transformation and alignment with the revolutionary project, on a collective level that breaks open the next stage of development for the movement."[82] The petit bourgeois intellectual must break free from the chains of the neoliberal university and struggle with the people to challenge the ravages of private property and privilege.

As a recently hired academic intellectual and scholar, I hold a position that my mother and others from my communities have never entered or been invited to assume. This is a seductive position that requires self-criticism and organic praxis, and must be used to serve and work with those who are most aggrieved and oppressed. "What would be the consequences of all of us succeeding and in effect the next generation see further developments, further expansions of incarceration?" Cedric Robinson asks us. Although class suicide as a strategy is an opaque process, with many, ever-unfolding contradictions, it is a mission that must be fulfilled or betrayed. I was taught that when we produce our scholarship, we should have liberation on our hearts and minds.[83] We can do better. We can be better. The Black Radical Tradition and its collective wisdom will help us remember that.

---

82 Maria Poblet, "Lessons from Amílcar Cabral: Revolutionary Democracy, Class-Consciousness, and Cross-Class Movement Building," *Left Roots*, available at leftroots.net.

83 I learned this as a graduate student at the University of California, Santa Barbara, while "choppin' it up" with Cedric J. Robinson and Clyde A. Woods. I will be forever grateful for this experience and their guidance.

Chapter 2

On Race, Violence, and "So-Called Primitive Accumulation"[1]

Nikhil Pal Singh

Many of the black carpenters were freemen. Things seemed to be going on very well. All at once, the white carpenters knocked off, and said they would not work with free colored workmen. Their reason for this, as alleged, was, that if free colored carpenters were encouraged, they would soon take the trade into their own hands, and poor white men would be thrown out of employment . . . My fellow apprentices very soon began to feel it degrading to them to work with me. They began to put on airs, and talk about the "niggers taking the country," saying we all ought to be killed.
—Frederick Douglass, *Narrative of the Life of Frederick Douglass*[2]

When we look at social relations which create an undeveloped system of exchange, of exchange values and of money . . . it is clear from the outset that the individuals in such a society, although their relations appear to be more personal, enter into connection with one another only as individuals *imprisoned within a certain definition, as feudal lord and vassal, landlord and serf etc. or as members of a caste etc. or as members of an estate etc.* In the money relation, in the developed system of exchange (and this semblance seduces the democrats), the ties of personal dependence, the distinctions of blood, education, etc. are in fact exploded, ripped up . . . and individuals *seem* independent (this is an independence which is at bottom merely an illusion, and it is more correctly called indifference) . . . The defined-ness of individuals, which in the former case appears as a personal restriction of the individual by another, appears in the latter case as developed into an objective restriction of the individual by relations independent of him and sufficient unto themselves . . . A closer examination of these external relations shows, however . . . [that] these external relations are very far from being an abolition of "relations of dependence"; they are rather the *dissolution of these relations into a general form*; they are merely the elaboration and emergence of the general *foundation* of the relations of personal dependence . . . in such a way that individuals are now ruled by

1   Anupama Rao encouraged me to write the original version of this essay. I thank her and the participants in the Caste and Race Workshop at Columbia University in October 2013 for their engagement with this work. I especially want to thank Harry Harootunian, Tavia Nyong'o, Neferti Tadiar, and Jennifer Morgan for their critical and generative comments on an earlier draft of this essay.

2   Frederick Douglass, *Narrative of the Life of Frederick Douglass, An American Slave, Written by Himself*, eds. John R. McKivigan, Peter P. Hinks, and Heather L. Kaufman (New Haven: Yale University Press, 2001[1845]), 71.

abstractions . . . The abstraction, or idea, however, is nothing more than the theoretical expression of those *material relations which are their lord and master.*

—Karl Marx, *Grundrisse*[3]

The fifth day after my arrival I put on the clothes of a common laborer and went upon the wharves in search of work . . . I saw a large pile of coal . . . and asked the *privilege* of bringing in and putting away this coal . . . I was not long in accomplishing the job, when the dear lady put into my hand two silver half dollars. *To understand the emotion which swelled my heart as I clasped this money,* realizing I had no master who could take it from me, that it was mine—that my hands were my own, and could earn more of the precious coin—*one must have been himself in some sense a slave.*

— Frederick Douglass, *Life and Times of Frederick Douglass*[4]

In this essay, I offer provisional thoughts about the links between human bondage and capitalist abstraction and subsequent racial differentiation under capitalism. My concern is to complicate a tendency in radical thought influenced by Marx, and more specifically by the strand of Marxist theorizing—sometimes defined as political Marxism—that insists upon a definition of capitalism that assumes the structural separation of a productive regime of superior efficiency based on the economic exploitation of wage labor from forms of extra-economic coercion in support of modes of accumulation whose lineages are frequently ascribed to non-capitalist, or pre-capitalist histories. This view, which despite its historicist bent can unfortunately converge with a modernization paradigm, is based upon a strict, single-country origin story of capitalist "takeoff," defined by the establishment of a specific set of class and property relationships in the sixteenth- and seventeenth-century English countryside. These relationships are said to have inaugurated an era of radical market dependency, in turn propelling a shift toward radically self-generating productivity and capital accumulation.[5]

What is gained by the analytical and historical precision of this important body of scholarship is lost in theoretical scope and political capaciousness. These scholars tend to dismiss or diminish the importance of simultaneous

---

3   Karl Marx, *Grundrisse: Foundations of the Critique of Political Economy*, trans. Martin Nicolaus (New York: Penguin, 1993[1857]), 163–4. Emphasis added.

4   Frederick Douglass, *Life and Times of Frederick Douglass*, vol. 3, *The Frederick Douglass Papers*, ed. John R. McKivigan (New Haven: Yale University Press, 2012[1881]), 163. Emphasis added.

5   For an original and exemplary statement of this viewpoint, see: Robert Brenner, "Agrarian Structure and Economic Development in Pre-Industrial Europe," *Past and Present* 70 (February 1976): 30–75. Brenner sharpens the polemical stakes of this argument, taking on various modes of "dependency" and "world-systems theory" which he faults for "displac[ing] class relations from the center of economic development," and for failing to recognize "the productivity of labor as the essence and key of [capitalist] economic development." See also Brenner's "The Origins of Capitalist Development: A Critique of Neo-Smithian Marxism," *New Left Review* 104 (July–August 1977).

modes of economic expansion, particularly slavery and the slave trade, whose links to the rise of industrial capitalism may be acknowledged but whose contribution to the *form* of capitalism remains radically underspecified.[6] More problematic, this scholarly approach supports a tendency in Marxist thought to think of slavery as capitalism's antecedent—a historical *stage*—which glosses over a startling fact affirmed in much recent historiography: that the chattel slave was a new kind of laboring being and new species of property born with capitalism.[7] Slavery, as Sven Beckert writes, especially on North America's "cotton frontier," was not only a labor regime but also a means to allocate capital "tightly linked to the intensity and profits of industrial capitalism" that was gradually able to dispense with direct coercion of producers.[8] Marx's oeuvre, which frequently compares labor by workers and slaves during this time, exemplifies the problem we face, both offering support for what W. E. B. Du Bois once

---

6   Ellen Meiksins Wood, *The Origin of Capitalism: A Longer View* (London: Verso, 2002). Following Brenner, Wood writes, "The wealth amassed from [slavery and] colonial exploitation may have contributed substantially to further development, even if it was not the necessary precondition for the *origin* of capitalism . . . If wealth from the colonies and the slave trade contributed to Britain's industrial revolution, it was because the British economy had already for a long time been structured by capitalist property relations" (149).

7   Stephanie Smallwood, *Saltwater Slavery: A Middle Passage from African to American Diaspora* (Cambridge: Harvard University Press, 2007). As much as any other contemporary thinker, Smallwood strives to link the logics of slavery as social death and as a novel form of commodification: "The Atlantic market for slaves changed what it meant to be a socially, politically or economically marginalized person . . . Captivity . . . was not a temporary status . . . not [a situation] of extreme alienation within the community, but rather of absolute exclusion from any community," the fashioning of "bodies animated only by others' calculated investment in their physical capacity" (30, 35).

8   Sven Beckert, *The Empire of Cotton* (New York: Vintage, 2014), 92, 114. Also see Eric Williams, *Capitalism and Slavery* (New York: Putnam, 1966[1944]). Important contributors to the contemporary resurgence of this argument include Walter Johnson, Edward Baptist, Stephanie Smallwood, and Julia Ott, but its key originator was Eric Williams, who argued that slavery profits were central to industrial capitalist takeoff. This controversial thesis (which bears the traces of stagist thinking) died by a thousand historiographical cuts in the decades following the publication of Williams's book. What was arguably most disturbing about Williams's argument was his more fundamental challenge to those who emphasized slavery's relative historical insignificance in order to moralize and legitimate subsequent capitalist development—in effect, freeing capitalism from a debt to slavery. Writing in a period in which international capitalism spearheaded by the United States sought to detach itself from the racism and imperialism from which it had developed, Williams provided an unsettling dose of skepticism: "This does not invalidate the arguments for democracy, for freedom now or for freedom after the war . . . But mutatis mutandis the arguments have a familiar ring," he wrote. "We have to be on our guard, not only against the old prejudices, but against the new which are being constantly created" (210–12). Historian Frank Tannenbaum exemplified the kind of orthodoxy that Williams unsettled in his writing. "The Negro race has been given an additional large share of the face of the globe for its own. It received this territory as a kind of unplanned gift," Tannenbaum wrote. "It is in its own nature, no different than the process which has occurred as a result of the allurement which led millions of Americans to labor in American mines, fields, and factories . . . The result has been moral. It has proved a good thing for the Negroes in the long run. They have achieved a status both spiritually and materially, in the new home to which they were brought as chattels." Frank Tannenbaum, "A Note on the Economic Interpretation of History," *Political Science Quarterly* 61 (1946): 248–9.

called the "slavery character" of capitalism, particularly in its Anglo-American ascendancy, and contributing to a problematic conceptual relegation of African slavery within capitalism's history that has haunted radical politics ever since.

The outstanding trace of that haunting is a political imagination that separates race, sex, and gender domination from capitalist exploitation both conceptually and in terms of strategic priorities for working-class unification and struggle. Ironically, this understanding of anti-capitalist struggle presents an impediment to the kind of solidarity required in a world characterized by "intimate and plural relationships to capital"[9] It also forfeits a powerful analysis by Marx himself of capitalism as a machine whose productive expansion rests on enlarging the fields of both appropriation and dispossession.[10] Marx not only describes capitalism as "veiled slavery," he also takes "slave management in slave-trade countries" as a reference point for thinking about capitalism's seizure of vital life processes, including what he describes as the wageworker's "premature exhaustion and death."[11] As subsequent anti-Marxist critics have pointed out, however, this aspect of slavery is in one instance indispensible as a lens through which to examine capitalism: sometimes slavery seems "closer to capitalism's primal desire . . . than wage [labor]," while at other times, it represents what has been replaced by a form of oppression whose covert power rests upon its supposed ability to dispense with violent dominion.[12]

Strictly distinguishing between the worker's exploitation and the slave's "social death"—a common move within an important strand of contemporary Black critical theorizing often called "Afro-pessimism"—offers no better answers to this conundrum, merely a kind of inversion, in which slavery and the anti-Blackness that proceeds from it are excluded from politics. This approach further precludes an understanding of slavery tied to the development of

9   Dipesh Chakrabarty, "Universalism and Belonging in the Logic of Capitalism," *Public Culture* 12, no. 3 (2000): 653.

10   For a powerful contemporary theory that develops this view, see: Jason Moore, *Capitalism in the Web of Life: Ecology and the Accumulation of Capital* (New York: Verso, 2015).

11   Karl Marx, *Capital*, vol. 1 (New York: Vintage, 1967[1867]), 925, 374–81, 225. Here are the respective quotations in full: "Whilst the cotton industry introduced child-slavery into England, in the United States it gave the impulse for the transformation of the earlier, more or less patriarchal slavery into a system of commercial exploitation. In fact the veiled slavery of the wage-laborers in Europe needed the unqualified slavery of the New world as its pedestal" (925). "Capital therefore takes no account of the health and the length of the life of the worker, unless society forces it to do so. Its answer to the outcry about the physical and mental degradation, the premature death, the torture of over-work, is this: Should that pain trouble us, since it increases our profit (pleasure)?" (381). "If labor-power can be supplied from foreign preserves . . . the duration of [the worker's] life becomes a matter of less moment than its productiveness while it lasts . . . It is accordingly a maxim of slave management in slave importing countries, that the most effective economy is that which takes out of the human chattel in the shortest space of time the utmost of exertion that it is capable of putting forth" (225).

12   Frank Wilderson, "Gramsci's Black Marx: Whither the Slave in Civil Society," *Social Identities* 9, no. 3 (2003): 230. For a related argument more in keeping with the spirit of my approach in this essay, see Walter Johnson, "The Pedestal and the Veil: Rethinking the Capitalism/Slavery Question," *Journal of the Early Republic* (Summer 2004): 299–308.

capitalism, and with it any impulse to overcome the problematic severing of racial domination and class subordination. In order to bridge this analytical and political divide, we might instead begin by recognizing how the production of racial stigma that arises in support of chattel slavery contributes to developing the material, ideological, and emotional mechanisms for appropriation and dispossession that are indispensible to capitalism.

The uneven valuation of human subjects in slavery along ethical and political lines derives from how slave status was explicitly raced, gendered, and sexed via privatized household violence formally backed by state power, even as wage labor (and even indentured servitude) was increasingly becoming nationalized and linked to social standing and state protection. As historian Jennifer Morgan observed, the main legal innovation of chattel slavery as it grew in seventeenth-century North America was assigning it a hereditary force through the reproductive capacity of captive African women, who could thereby only ever give birth to future slaves.[13] Underlying the unpaid labor of slaves was another layer of unpaid work: social and biological reproduction, conducted by women. The process of conception and reproduction under slavery, however, was violently coerced and attached to the creation of a new species of human capital, "sustained," in the words of Frederick Douglass, "by the auctioneer's block."[14] This bio-capitalist innovation was in turn married to a necro-capitalist prerogative, expanding the scope and forms of corporeal violence that could be visited upon the bodies of slaves with or without legal sanction, up to and including homicide.[15]

The rise of the commodity form, as Marx famously tells us, helped to advance ideas of universal exchangeability, formal equality, general abstraction, and the idea of a human subject without particular properties. The legal/governmental procedures and material processes that produced these effects, however, operated in a context of human beings who were themselves commodities (as well as instruments of credit and capital investment), and on the grounds of socially constructed differences and divisions that ultimately found their way into separate bodies of abstract thinking, most notably racial science, whose

---

13   Jennifer Morgan, "Archives and Histories of Racial Capitalism: An Afterword," *Social Text* 33, no. 4 (2015). Also see Morgan, "Partus Sequitur Ventrum: Slave Law and the History of Women in Slavery" (forthcoming).

14   Frederick Douglass, "Reception Speech at Finsbury Chapel, Moorfield, England, May 12, 1846," in *My Bondage and My Freedom* (New York and Auburn: Miller, Orton and Mulligan, 1855). "We have in the US slave-breeding states . . . where men, women and children are reared for the market, just as horses, sheep and swine are raised for the market. Slave-rearing is there looked upon as a legitimate trade; the law sanctions it, public opinion upholds it, the church does not condemn it. It goes on in all its bloody horrors, sustained by the auctioneer's block" (412).

15   What Wilderson has termed "gratuitous violence" retained an instrumental value as exemplary violence in the face of much feared resistance and revolt. More recently Edward Baptist has also made a compelling case for the relationship between bodily torture and surplus extraction under slavery: *The Half That Has Never Been Told: Slavery and the Making of American Capitalism* (New York: Basic Books, 2015).

lineage contaminated the development of the human sciences more generally. In this view, racial subordination materialized along with class differentiation and inequality as a building block of the capitalist social formation through an association of whiteness with property, citizenship, wages, and credit, along with the reproduction of surplus and super-exploited populations through openly coercive capitalist accumulation by dispossession.[16]

This is not a definitive assertion about the capitalist "origins" of race and racism, but rather a claim that racial differentiation is intrinsic to capitalist value-creation and financial speculation, changing an idealized game of merit and chance into a stacked deck, with racially disparate fates manifest in devalued land, degraded labor, permanent indebtedness, and disposability. In short, there has been no period in which racial domination has not been woven into the management of capitalist society, and yet, with important exceptions, there has been a lack of sustained, sympathetic attention to this issue from within the Marxist tradition. Exploitation and the constitution of an objective order of market dependency, not direct racial violence and domination, are thought to continuously reproduce capitalist relations of production. But if land, labor, and money are "fictitious commodities" that form the foundations of capitalism,[17] they also constitute what Patrick Wolfe has called the "elementary structures" of race.[18] This insight complicates common tendencies within both liberal and Marxist intellectual traditions to consider racial differentiation in terms of static

---

16   The notion of accumulation by dispossession is a contemporary reframing of Marx's "so-called primitive accumulation." See Gillian Hart, "Denaturalizing Dispossession: Critical Ethnography in an Age of Resurgent Imperialism," *Research Report 27*, UC Berkeley (2004). Also see Michael Perelman, *The Invention of Capitalism and the Secret History of Primitive Accumulation* (Durham: Duke University Press, 2000).

17   Karl Polanyi, *The Great Transformation: The Political and Economic Origins of Our Time* (Boston: Beacon Press, 2001[1944]). By describing land, labor, and money as "fictitious commodities," Polanyi emphasizes the imposition of the logic of the self-regulating market and universal commodification as the defining features of capitalism. Further, he emphasizes how processes of commodification broadly encompass not only the domain of labor and its social and biological reproduction, but also the ecological matrix of life itself, as well as the mediums and modes of exchange that constitute social horizons. The subjection of all three domains to the "market mechanism" threatens the very conditions of social existence, stripping human beings of "the protective covering of cultural institutions," "defiling neighborhoods and landscapes," and subjecting purchasing power to disastrous "shortages and surfeits of money" (76). This formulation challenges both liberal and Marxist tendencies to construct the economy as an analytically autonomous domain. At its best, the notion of fictitious commodification draws our attention to the ongoing, state-enforced, noncontractual, and dominating bases of capital accumulation, as well as to dynamics of "social protection" or resistance that often draw upon non-market norms of land, labor, and money (including, potentially, reactionary ones). "Laissez-faire was planned, planning was not," Polanyi famously writes, and "the stark utopia" of the free market was the fascist response to its deepening crisis. See also Fred Block, "Karl Polanyi and the Writing of 'The Great Transformation,'" *Theory and Society* 32, no. 3 (2003): 275–306, and Nancy Fraser, "Can Society Be Commodities All the Way Down? Polanyian Reflections on Capitalist Crisis," *Fondation Maison des Sciences de L'Homme*, Working Papers Series, no. 18 (August 2012).

18   Patrick Wolfe, "Land, Labor and Difference: Elementary Structures of Race," *American Historical Review* 106, no. 3 (2001): 866–905.

visions of pre-capitalist history.[19] It further highlights the modern, fabricated quality of racial distinctions that continue to support institutionalized coercion and surplus extraction and deeply influence value formation within certain capitalist societies.[20]

Specialization in violence was integral to capitalism's origins. Beckert names this "war capitalism": a form of capitalist privateering backed but unimpeded by sovereign power, and most fully realized in slavery, settler colonialism, and imperialism. Following Cedric Robinson, we might rename it "racial capitalism," recognizing with Beckert that while it preceded industrialization, it is also an integral part of capitalism's ongoing expansion. Returning to Marx, we can observe how racial differentiation as a directly violent yet also flexible mode of arbitrary social categorization at first appears similar to the conscription, criminalization, and disposability of poor, idle, and surplus labor: the historical process of forcibly divorcing "the producers from the means of production" that Marx posits as the precondition for the emergence of capitalism. The creation of a pool of free wage-laborers through the "bloody legislation against the expropriated," turning feudal peasants into beggars and vagabonds "whipped, branded, [and] tortured by laws grotesquely terrible, into the discipline necessary for the wage system" appears to closely parallel slavery in its overt violence and direct coercion of producers of value. "The starting point of the development that gave rise both to the wage-laborer and the capitalist," Marx writes, "was the enslavement of the worker. The advance made consisted in a change in the *form* of . . . servitude."[21]

Yet as capitalism becomes what Marx called "a never-ending circle," the dynamic changes. Capital now requires that labor both appear and disappear. What Marx described as the "tendency of capital to simultaneously increase the laboring population as well as to reduce constantly its *necessary* part (constantly to posit a part of it as reserve)" comes to possess a more or less automatic, even natural character.[22] "The disposable industrial reserve army," he writes in another veiled reference to chattel slavery, "belongs to capital just as absolutely as if the latter had bred it at its own costs." While the initial "barrier [to forming a pool of wage labor] could only be swept away by violent means," the mechanism for creating a labor surplus develops into what Marx terms an "economic law," one that divides labor into "overwork" and "enforced idleness" as "a means of enriching individual capitalists." This process internalizes competition and precarity among workers themselves, and in doing so "completes the despotism

---

19   David Kazanjian, *The Colonizing Trick: National Culture and Imperial Citizenship in Early America* (Minneapolis: University of Minnesota Press, 2003).

20   The literature on varieties of capitalism argues that there is no capitalist mode of production compatible with actually existing capitalism, only "configurations" or "forms of capitalism" "compatible with a variety of forms of labor-exploitation." See Jairus Banaji, *Theory as History: Essays on Modes of Production and Exploitation* (London: Historical Materialism, 2010), 11.

21   Marx, *Capital*, vol. 1, 875. Italics added

22   Marx, *Grundrisse*, 400. Italics added.

of capital." Marx goes on to detail various forms taken by the "relative surplus population . . . the floating, the latent and the stagnant," or lowest strata comprised of "vagabonds, criminals and prostitutes . . . the actual lumpenproletariat . . . who succumb to their incapacity for adaptation."[23] In these passages, Marx recognizes capitalism's active production of a dependent and motley working class. He also reserves some of his most scornful writing for these degraded, unwaged laborers—who are even more categorically marked for premature death, but who nevertheless remain to haunt socialist militants who dream of class simplification or a unitary proletarian consciousness.[24]

As Marx famously wrote, mature capitalism exists when "the silent compulsion of economic relations sets the seal on the domination of the capitalist over the worker." At this point, "direct force, extra-economic force is still of course used, but only in *exceptional* cases."[25] In this moment, the proximity of wage labor to the violent conditions that produced its dependency gives way to a divided working class: one group whose productive capacities have been harnessed by the industrial machine, and the other whom Marx describes as "sharply differentiated from the industrial proletariat . . . a recruiting ground for thieves and criminals of all kinds."[26] This intra–working-class differentiation cuts against the grain of Marx's radical recuperation of the term "proletarian"— formerly a reference to those left without reserves—as a figure of collective struggle. Yet, it also coincides with his periodic recourse to a progressive view of history that assumes capitalism's civilizing potential, sacrificing a proper understanding of the myriad forms of labor that he simultaneously uncovers. The direct application of state-sanctioned force and violence once required to create wage labor, moreover, did not disappear. It remains in hierarchy and competition between workers, in the policing of unwaged labor that has migrated to poverty and the informal economy, and in imperial and nationalist conscription of the metropolitan working class.

The inattention to these political effects that frame but appear to no longer define relations of production has led to confusion between forms of domination and stages of development, in which the unevenness of unpaid, disposable, and surplus labor is opposed to the orderly fluctuations of waged and reserved labor on what Marx tellingly calls "the normal European level." The exceptional cases in which direct force is used include colonial spaces where slavery and other forms of coerced labor took root and where, Marx writes, "artificial means," including "police methods," are required "to set on the right road that

---

23   Marx, *Capital*, vol. 1, 784, 789, 793, 797.

24   The slave and lumpenproletariat may resemble each other when outside a relationship of capitalist exploitation. This insight, for which I am indebted to Tavia Nyong'o, is not pursued here but, of course, has been a spur to thinkers like Fanon and George Jackson. See Peter Stallybrass, "Marx and Heterogeneity: Thinking the Lumpenproletariat," *Representations* 31 (1990): 81.

25   Marx, *Capital*, vol. 1, 940, 899. Emphasis added.

26   Quoted in Stallybrass, "Marx and Heterogeneity," 84.

law of supply and demand which works automatically everywhere else."[27] Marx's description of colonialism and slavery as matrices of "so-called primitive accumulation" highlights the value and limitation of his work for thinking about the ongoing development of racial categories, and particularly the social reproduction of race through ongoing violence, dominion, and dependency. Marx skewers the bourgeois fairy tale of a virtuous phase of so-called "original" accumulation achieved via the thrift and ingenuity of a "frugal elite" that condemned the unfortunate majority to a situation in which they would be forced (in Marx's words) "to sell . . . their own skins." In oft-quoted lines from volume one of *Capital*, Marx emphasizes the murderous origins of capitalism in Europe's armed commercial expansion, colonialism, racial slavery, and genocide:

> The discovery of gold and silver in America, the extirpation, enslavement and entombment in mines of the indigenous population of that continent, the beginnings of the conquest and plunder of India, and the conversion of Africa into a preserve for the commercial hunting of black-skins, are all things which characterize the dawn of the era of capitalist production. These idyllic proceedings are the chief moments of primitive accumulation.[28]

An enduring historical and theoretical challenge posed by this sketch is how to interpret Marx's view of "the dawn of the era of capitalist production" as a separate historical moment and concept, reliant upon force and violence, from the era of capitalist accumulation proper, when the "silent compulsion" of market discipline supplanted the need for coercion through noneconomic means. "Primitive accumulation" is not yet capitalism for Marx; it is plunder. Its relationship to the more fundamental process of divorcing the producer from the means of production remains unclear. Marx's analysis in some ways blurs the distinction, for example, in his parallel references to "commerce in skins." Yet, new world primitive accumulation is an indictment of capitalism, not an explanation of its dynamics. Much like the nineteenth-century workers who spoke of "wage slavery" to distinguish themselves from rather than align themselves with racial slaves, moreover, Marx (who knew better than to do this) further suggests that a focus upon the direct coercion of the producers not only misreads the source of capital accumulation, but deflects from the central challenge of anti-capitalist politics by reinforcing the "illusion" of independence and freedom

---

27   Marx, *Capital*, vol. 1, 937. Marx writes: "In the old civilized countries the worker, although free, is by a law of nature dependent on the capitalist; in the colonies this dependence must be created by artificial means." (Note: he is not referring to slavery here, but his comments are applicable to it.) The problem of the colonies is that there is too much freedom for workers to opt out and become "independent landowners, if not competitors with their former masters in the labour market." Marx also hastens to add: "We are not concerned here with the condition of the colonies. The only thing that interests us is the secret discovered in the New World by the political economy of the Old World" (936, 940).

28   Marx, *Capital*, vol. 1, 873, 915.

proffered by capitalism's more "developed system of exchange"—that semblance of freedom—that "seduces the democrats."[29]

This passage affirms Marx's tendency to characterize political inclusion as an illusion. Ironically, however, Marx's effort to undermine what he calls the "rule of abstractions" depends upon the opposition between ascribed or coerced status and abstract labor. In the second epigraph to this essay from the *Grundrisse*, Marx presents ascribed status as a kind of immobility or "imprisonment," in contrast to wage labor in which "individuals seem independent." Liberal social-contract theory sees this arbitrary assignment and enforcement of status—feudal, caste, estate, blood, we might add *slave*— as opposed to an ostensibly modern, mobile, and dynamic social order based on contracts and free exchange. Where the majority of liberal thinkers view education as an engine of meritocratic distinction and class mobility, Marx's analysis moves in the opposite direction, emphasizing capitalism's leveling *indifference* to any prior social condition or status. He does so, however, in an effort to unmask this "seeming" or "apparent" freedom from direct coercion and hierarchy as the grounds for increasingly universal domination under capitalist *abstraction*: the "general form" and "theoretical expression of those material relations which are lord and master."[30]

Yet, Marx's analysis, insofar as it adopts the standpoint of "developed" capitalism in England, can lead to an inattention and even indifference to how capital differentiates between free labor and less-than-free labor according to racial, ethnic, and gender hierarchies as a means of both labor discipline and surplus appropriation. Suggesting a tendency to render these hierarchies anachronistic over the long run will even begin to function as a measure of capitalism's progressivism. It is significant in this regard that Marx not only contrasts the free worker and the slave, but also the different relationships that the English yeomanry and former slaves have to capitalism. For the emancipated slave, Marx writes, "the capitalist relationship appears to be an improvement in one's position on the social scale . . . It is otherwise when the independent peasant or artisan becomes a wage-laborer. What a gulf there is between the proud yeomanry of England . . . and the English agricultural laborer!" Ironically, although the yeomanry may have fallen further, they can recuperate pride in a different form. "The consciousness (or better: the idea) of free self-determination, of liberty, makes a much better worker of the [free worker] than the [slave], as does, the related feeling (sense) of responsibility . . . *He learns to control himself, in contrast to the slave*, who needs a master."[31] This explains, as Marx notes elsewhere, why emancipated slaves reverted to producing only what they needed to live or self-provisioning, regarding "loafing (indulgence and idleness) as the real luxury good . . . Wealth confronts direct forced labor not as capital,

---

29   Marx, *Grundrisse*, 164.
30   Ibid., 164.
31   Marx, *Capital*, vol. 1, 1031, 1033. Emphasis in original.

but rather as a relation of domination ... which can never create *general industriousness.*"[32]

The differentiation between slavery and capitalism here effectively widens the gulf between slaves and workers. As Marx writes, in a key definitional statement: "Capital ceases to be capital without free-wage labor ... as its general creative basis."[33] In this view, slavery's inefficiencies, including the impossibility of increasing labor productivity by reducing socially necessary labor time, actively *impeded* the development of capitalism.[34] What is curious is that Marx, who persistently compares capitalism with slavery in order to undermine what he calls "a liberalism, so full of consideration for 'capital,'"[35] seems to yield to his opponents' intellectual tendency to frame capitalist social relations through "a seductive dichotomy of 'free' and 'unfree' labor, as if these categories were really opposites."[36] His remarks on the affect, cognition, and habit formation of free workers and freed slaves reinforces distinctions between them, even problematically linking them to prior conditions of servitude: while the English workers' loss of customary rights and subsequent proximity to the engines of value-creation place them in the vanguard of class struggle, both slave and ex-slave remain passive figures (indelibly linked together) and unable to connect to history's forward movement.[37]

Marx, of course, notes: "In the United States of America, every independent workers' movement was paralyzed as long as slavery disfigured a part of the republic. Labor in a white skin cannot emancipate itself, where in the black it is branded."[38] Yet, slave emancipation for Marx is but a prelude to a unified working-class struggle for the eight-hour day. It is difficult to imagine Marx having any insight into ongoing social dynamics and movements that proceed directly from slavery. C. L. R. James observed of the Haitian slaves that "they were closer to a modern proletariat than any other group of workers in existence at that time," and capable of enacting a "thoroughly prepared and organized mass movement."[39] At the same time, Eric Williams, in an argument indebted to James, warned that the "outworn interests [of slavery] whose bankruptcy smells

---

32 Marx, *Grundrisse*, 326.

33 David Roediger, *The Wages of Whiteness: Race and the Making of the American Working-Class* (New York: Verso, 2007).

34 Charles Post, *The American Road to Capitalism: Studies in Class Structure, Economic Development and Political Conflict, 1620–1877* (New York: Haymarket Books, 2012).

35 Marx, *Capital*, vol. 1, 391.

36 Banaji, *Theory as History*, 13.

37 Marx, *Capital*, vol. 1, 382. Just as the worker's feeling of freedom has important material effects, so too does the transformation of freedom into a kind of status distinction. "Capital ... takes no account of the health and length of the life of the worker," Marx writes, "unless society forces it to do so." This is of course a reference to the English class struggle, mostly one-sided in Marx's view, in which the worker may achieve a normal working day, but is "compelled by social conditions to sell the whole of his active life, his very capacity for labor in return for the price of his customary means of subsistence, to sell his birthright for a mess of pottage."

38 Ibid., 414.

39 C. L. R. James, *The Black Jacobins* (New York: Vintage, 1989[1938]), 86.

to heaven in historical perspective, exercise an obstructionist and disruptive effect" into the future, based upon the "powerful services it had previously rendered and the entrenchment previously gained."[40]

In part the limitation derives from Marx's indebtedness—even in his critical stance towards it—to a conception of freedom defined as political opposition to arbitrary power, which fails to fully interrogate what the grounding of freedom in chattel slavery and its violent household manifestations means for the development of capitalist freedom going forward. Marx holds on to an ultimately problematic distinction between ancient forms of slavery that have what he terms a "patriarchal character" and historical slavery "drawn into the world market dominated by the capitalist mode of production."[41] However, when he formulates an opposition between (an illusory) political freedom and (a metaphorical) economic slavery, Marx is thinking of the former, not the latter. In this way, the Marx-inspired critique of capitalism, like popular nineteenth-century critiques of wage slavery, can unwittingly become what Mary Nyquist terms "an important conductor of racialization . . . that severs or weakens the 'free' citizen's affective ties with enslaved Africans" and others imagined to be lodged within dependent, coerced identities.[42] Put differently, although Marx wants to overturn the idea that capitalism does away with servitude, when he adopts a Eurocentric historical focus he participates in a larger conversation in which slavery is discussed less in terms of its material relationship to capitalism and more as a kind of insult and humiliation, a lack of political standing and social honor. Capitalist indifference and Marxist indifference ideologically intersect here to divide capitalist power, which publicly deepens the worker's dependency, from despotic power, which privately strips the enslaved worker of rights and public standing.

Marx describes both "direct private violence" and organized state violence as the "midwife" of a capitalist mode of production, whose development, maturity, and superior productivity is predicated on an ability to dispense with cruder forms of coercion. Capitalism is still a violent system, but its violence is immanent within a developmentally superior labor relation that no longer requires direct applications of coercive force. Indeed, direct coercion is not only a fetter on productivity gains—the representation of the absence of direct coercion—in both legal and ideological terms, is also one of the main ideological bulwarks of capitalist domination.[43] Given the sexual and gendered nature of slavery and colonization, the metaphor of the "midwife" whose reproductive labor is essential but historically dispensable retains a certain resonance for framing the

---

40   Williams, *Capitalism and Slavery*, 211.
41   Marx, *Capital*, vol. 1, 345.
42   Mary Nyquist, *Arbitrary Rule: Slavery Tyranny and the Power of Life Over Death* (Chicago: University of Chicago Press, 2013), 366.
43   Heide Gerstenberger, "The Political Economy of Capitalist Labor," *Viewpoint Magazine* (September 2014), available at viewpointmag.com.

relationship of slavery and capitalism. The Marxist view of capitalism as a progressive historical force and superior mode of production and social reproduction tends to either remove or freeze our vision of the gendered racial violence indispensible to its "birth." This violence appears static, non-historical, and non-reproductive—a historical event that ended in time, and whose remains or traces in the present are marginal or anachronistic. Capitalism may "come into the world dripping from head to toe in blood," as Marx writes, but it manages to clean itself up, at least in certain spaces and places. The true novelty of its forward march, particularly when conceived on the narrow terrain of the free-labor contract, depends upon its abstract reproductive capacity.

It would be a mistake to end the analysis here, however. Marx, as already observed, is decidedly hesitant, even ambivalent on this issue. The English economist Malachy Postlethwayt, whom Marx read, was perhaps the first to describe the "African trade" as a "prop and support" of British free trade. Marx takes up this figure in various forms, writing, for example, that "the veiled slavery of the wageworkers in Europe needed, for its pedestal, slavery pure and simple in the new world."[44] Elsewhere Marx recognizes without illusions that the "business of slavery is conducted by capitalists," that slavery only "appears as an anomaly opposite the bourgeois system itself" and that, under the spur of the cotton trade, "the civilized horrors of overwork [have been] grafted onto the barbaric horrors of slavery and serfdom."[45] Indeed, one of his clearest statements on the issue was penned two decades before *Capital* and evinces what might be considered a more clear-sighted abolitionism, interpreting capitalism and slavery as conjoined within a single, global space:

> Direct slavery is just as much the pivot of bourgeois industry as machinery, credits, etc. Without slavery you have no cotton; without cotton you have no modern industry. It is slavery that has given the colonies their value; it is the colonies that have created world trade, and it is world trade that is the precondition of large-scale industry. Thus slavery is an economic category of the greatest importance.[46]

By these lights we might begin by rewriting Marx's axiomatic statement, "Capital ceases to be capital without wage labor" in the following way: *Capital ceases to be capital without the ongoing differentiation of free labor and slavery, waged labor and unpaid labor.* This differentiation provides the indispensible material

---

44   Marx, *Capital*, vol. 1, 925. Postlethwayt is quoted in David Waldstreicher, *Slavery' Constitution: From Revolution to Ratification* (New York: Hill and Wang, 2010), 27.

45   Kazanjian, *The Colonizing Trick*, 21; Marx, *Grundrisse*, 464.

46   Karl Marx, *The Poverty of Philosophy* (Moscow: Foreign Language Publishers, 1958[1847]), 125. Gopal Balakrishnan describes the early Marx of this period as an "abolitionist" in a set of brilliant essays, writing, "Only later would Marx come to see a contradiction between free wage labor and slavery. Now he assumed that American slavery was an integral part of the world system of bourgeois society . . . The Marx of this period was a ruthless abolitionist." Gopal Balakrishnan, "The Abolitionist—II," *New Left Review* 91 (January–February 2015).

and ideological support for capitalism's continued development. The absolute separation of freedom and slavery operates in the interests of capital. It is only by retaining an understanding of their overlapping dimensions that we attain a critical perspective adequate to oppose it.

These moments—and they are only moments—since Marx never delivers on an analysis of slavery as an "economic category of the greatest importance," are well worth holding onto. Here Marx evinces a refusal to separate capitalism and slavery that sharpens the argument that capitalist development represents a broader form of domination. Exploring this connection pulls our thinking toward rather than away from the legacy of slave capitalism and capitalist slavery and enduring interactions of race and capital, what Robinson has termed "racial capitalism."[47] Temporal cleavage gives way to simultaneity, and a rejection of "logical formula" that would separate co-existing, mutually supportive elements into sequential time.[48] Only later does Marx characterize this in terms that open themselves up to teleological interpretation, describing "the incompleteness" of the "development of capitalist production," that joins to "modern evils," "inherited evils, arising from the passive survival of archaic and outmoded modes of production with their accompanying train of anachronistic social and political relations."[49] But the marking of certain relations as passive or anachronistic remains problematic. What if this incompleteness is a permanent feature of capitalism? What happens when those supposedly passive or archaic capitalist methods most closely linked to direct coercion are not only retained within the labor process, but also profoundly shape the form of the state?

North American slavery was a mode of social reproduction that was capable of birthing itself. The vitality of this system required it to outgrow the effects of the Atlantic slave trade, building on violent control over the wombs of slave women, along with expanding settlement on and murderous depopulation of the land. Nor did slavery simply wither away; it required a war of cataclysmic proportions and mass death on an unimaginable scale to bring it formally to an end. What followed for the majority of freed blacks was an era equally marked by direct violence and coercion of labor under various types of penal enforcement. Freeing slaves enlarged both the instrumental and popular political ambit of racism as a tool of labor discipline (divide and rule), as a means of introducing new forms of labor coercion (so-called "coolie labor"), as a weapon of class struggle (the wages of whiteness), and, of course, as a tool for empire. It also inaugurated an era of state and private violence that directly seized upon Black household formation, sexuality, and bodies as a means to preserve and reproduce a racial-capitalist political economy with far-reaching, global implications. As Du Bois memorably wrote in his magisterial *Black Reconstruction*, which

---

47   Cedric J. Robinson, *Black Marxism: The Making of the Black Radical Tradition* (Chapel Hill: University of North Carolina Press, 1983).

48   Marx, *The Poverty of Philosophy*, 124.

49   Marx, *Capital*, vol. 1, 91.

adopted a Marxist idiom, the "echo of that philanthropy which had abolished the slave trade, was beginning a new industrial slavery of black and brown and yellow workers in Africa and Asia."[50]

Indeed, if the system built upon racialized chattel slavery is understood as a "variant of capitalism," might we not make the stronger claim that racism is a dimension of the form of capitalism that develops from that system? Insofar as this variety of capitalism reproduces divisions between (re)productive humanity and disposable humanity, might we not further recognize how this very division is mediated by the shifting productions of race as a logic of depreciation linked to: 1) proletarianization as a condition of "wageless life"—the norm of capitalism insofar as it produces radical market dependency and surplus labor— and 2) the regular application of force and violence within those parts of the social that subsequently have no part?[51] Finally, to the extent to which direct compulsion and organized violence is retained within capitalist social formations might the importance of these methods lie not so much in how they relate to the exploitation of labor and the extraction of surplus-value (let alone whether or not they are "anachronistic"), but rather in their indispensable contributions to maintaining capitalist social relations? This includes not only the defense of private property, but also the active management of spaces and times of insecurity and existential threat that threaten or challenge the idea that capitalist social relations successfully encompass an entire way of life.

Within the Marxist tradition, Rosa Luxemburg comes closest to this view when she notes that "the accumulation of capital, seen as a historical process, employs force as a permanent weapon, not only at its genesis, but further down to the present day." It is precisely the limitations placed upon capitalism's global expansion, its ongoing dependence upon "non-capitalist strata and social organization . . . existing *side by side*," she writes, that produces "peculiar combinations between the modern wage system and primitive authority" and enable "far more ruthless measures than could be tolerated under purely capitalist social conditions" citing "the first genuinely capitalist branch of production, the English cotton industry."[52] Unfortunately the lingering references to a "pure capitalism" and "primitive authority" reinforce the very oppositions that she otherwise challenges. Echoing Marx's comment that "war developed earlier than peace . . . in the interior of bourgeois society," and anticipating Foucault—"A battlefront runs through the whole of society, continuously and permanently"— Luxemburg points to militarization, the institutionalization of coercion within

---

50   W. E. B. Du Bois, *Black Reconstruction in America, 1860–1880* (New York: Free Press, 1998), 632–4.

51   It is important to note that the term "proletariat" in Marx literally means "those without reserves." As Michael Denning writes, it is not a synonym for wage labor "but for dispossession, expropriation and radical dependence on the market." Michael Denning, "Wageless Life," *New Left Review* 66 (November–December 2010): 81.

52   Rosa Luxemburg, *The Accumulation of Capital* (New York: Monthly Review Press, 1968 [1951]), 372.

capitalism, as a method not only of "primitive accumulation" but of enforcing capitalist discipline and disposability at the shifting borders of its circulatory movement.[53]

Civil society, as both Foucault and Marx argue in different ways, is the perfect site for capitalism, as a realm of economic freedom that fundamentally modifies the terms of political authority. While Marx attempted to demystify this process by describing the actual subordination of sovereign political status to forceful economic tyranny, Foucault at times emphasizes the real limitations placed by market freedom on the political life of the state. "The condition of governing well," he writes, "is that freedom, or certain forms of freedom are really respected."[54] The idea of a totalizing police power gives way to a police force focused upon the prevention and management of the probability of "disorders" and "disasters." At the same time, both Marx and even Foucault exceptionalize the phenomenon that at different points preoccupies both of them: the bloody, annihilating violence that haunts modern social existence. In an echo of Marx's account of the decreasing frequency in use of overt force, Foucault, for example, calls Nazi genocide an "eruption of racism," an expression of the outdated right of a sovereign to kill that is retained alongside normative governmental imperatives of population management and biopolitical growth. But like Marx, he ultimately begs the question of how to account for the enduring nature of this always waning, quasi-hallucinatory genocidal force.[55]

It is not, moreover, only spectacular violence, but the slow, repetitive, incremental, often concealed violence of appropriation that needs to be considered here. If socially necessary labor time constitutes value for capital, as Jason Moore writes, such value is embedded in a "web of life" that capital uses to exploit formally free wage labor. Marxist theory that considers the most distinct undertakings of capitalism to be economic exploitation and the production of surplus value separating economic compulsion from direct domination fails to recognize what may be an even greater capitalist novelty: the dynamic by which capital is able to "identify, secure and channel unpaid work outside the commodity

53   Marx, Grundrisse, 109; Michel Foucault, Society Must Be Defended: Lectures at the College de France, 1975-1976 (New York: Picador, 2003), 51.

54   Michel Foucault, Security, Territory, Population: Lectures at the College de France 1977-1978 (New York: Picador, 2009), 353.

55   Foucault, Society Must Be Defended, 260. While Foucault develops an idea of "race war" as integral to modern statecraft, his account is idiosyncratic and noncommittal. He appears to view Nazi violence through the lens of exceptionalism: "A society which generalized biopower in an absolute sense . . . has also generalized the sovereign right to kill. The two mechanisms—the classic, archaic mechanism that gave the State the right of life and death over its citizens, and the new mechanism organized around discipline and regulation . . . of biopower—coincide exactly . . . We can therefore say this: The Nazi state makes the field of life it manages, protects, guarantees and cultivates in biological terms absolutely coextensive with the sovereign right to kill anyone, meaning not only other people, but also its own people." Discussing the "final solution," he writes, "Nazism alone took the play between the sovereign right to kill and the mechanisms of biopower to this paroxysmal point. But this play is in fact inscribed in the workings of all states. In all modern states, in all capitalist States? Perhaps not."

system into the circuit of capital." As Marxist-feminists have long noted, "The appropriation of accumulated unpaid work in human form," including the labors of biological and social reproduction undertaken the world over by women, provides the real historical conditions for "socially necessary labor time." A "narrow sphere" of productive relations, in this view, depends upon a "more expansive sphere of appropriation" in which cheap human and extra-human nature "are taken up by commodity production."[56]

Embodied in the figures of the slave, the migrant worker, the household worker, the chronically unemployed, and others like them, appropriation encompasses both privatized and publically sanctioned coercion and ethico-political devaluation inseparable from capitalist processes of assigning value. Thus, rather than opposing notions of absolute sovereignty and its power of life over death with a biopolitically, productive materialist history, we might instead recognize how the two are inextricably linked through the conquest/commodi-fication of Black bodies (as well as in the conquest/commodification of indige-nous lands) that for Marx comprises the moment of "so-called primitive accu-mulation." This connection extends to the ongoing unpaid work of women the world over, accumulated unpaid work represented by labor migration, and war capitalism's differentiation between internally ordered, rule-bound spaces of production and market exchange and exceptional zones of armed appropria-tion. The latter are not only domains for enacting "plunder"—that is, primitive accumulation (or accumulation by dispossession)—but also for developing cutting-edge procedures, calculations, and fungible systems of commercial and military infrastructure—the slaver's management of human cargo, railways of extraction and settlement, coerced urbanisms, strategic hamlets and forward military bases—that are able to proceed insofar as they are unfettered by legally protected human beings, thus advancing new prejudices that build upon the old.[57]

With respect to slavery, we might recognize how the supposedly lessening frequency of noneconomic coercion, which defines the emergence of the economic and the political as analytically distinct domains, is accompanied by continued racialization, defined first via war-slavery doctrine (by Grotius, Hobbes, Locke, and others) and later in terms of race war, amid capitalism's recurrent crises and attempts at universalization. The concept of actual slavery, which Locke describes as the development of a pre-civil state of war into a rela-tionship between lawful conqueror and captive, allows theorists of modern poli-tics to imagine the conquest of freedom as the end of *political slavery* and arbi-trary rule within Euro-American colonial contexts. Here, the actual slaveholder's power over life and death is retained by the sovereign political subject. Meanwhile, the logic of racialization "generates heritable liberties along with

---

56   Jason Moore, "Endless Accumulation, Endless (Unpaid) Work?," *The Occupied Times* (2015), available at theoccupiedtimes.org.

57   Moore, *Capitalism in the Web of Life*, 70, 224. Also see Smallwood, *Saltwater Slavery*, 35.

heritable slavery"; servility and incapacity (conceived as either inherent to or derived from the condition of enslavement) are used to explain subjects whose very existence counts as an aggression not only against freedom, but also against life itself, and who therefore can be permanently sequestered, governed without rights, or killed with impunity.[58]

As a final illustration (and by way of conclusion), I turn briefly to the archives of Black radicalism to consider the passages from Frederick Douglass quoted at the outset of this chapter. In the first passage, published three years before the *Communist Manifesto*, Douglass marks what I would suggest is a new production of race at the moment of transition from one labor regime to another: slavery to wage labor. At this moment, Black entry into the wage relation was understood by whites as a threat to their own wage-earning capacity, and, indeed, a loss of country—or sovereign capacity—which in turn called forth the fantasy of a war of extermination against the offending party. This moment in Douglass's text is interesting for the ways in which it illuminates race-making as a social, political, and emotional process—that constitutes a warlike relationship. Yes, Black and white, slave and free already existed as distinctions. But at first, Douglass tells us, the presence of the "free colored" posed no special problem. What initiated the shift "all at once"?

At first glance the passage appears to confirm the conventional wisdom of contemporary theorists writing about racially segmented labor markets. However, emphasizing that "things seemed to be going very well" and noting that white fears of potential Black monopolization of the trade were mere "allegation," Douglass is in fact doing more than making a claim about anti-Black racism as a historically given condition. What was it about the mere presence of a "Black carpenter" that meant total loss of livelihood? Why was the sense of threat so readily amplified and defined in terms of political identity and national subjectivity ("niggers taking the country")? Finally, how did the affect (fear, anger) get translated into a genocidal impulse ("we all ought to be killed")? Put simply, how did the race-labor juxtaposition become a race-war situation? My suspicion is that the figure of race war, far from being an afterthought, in fact controlled and mediated the entire sequence that Douglass describes. Indeed, one of the most striking aspects of Douglass's *Narrative* is the ways in which he consistently describes slavery as something other than the theft of Black labor, emphasizing instead its violent, totalizing claims on Black life as a thoroughly militarized and policed social relation.

In explaining this sequence of events, Douglass intentionally highlights the double threat of wagelessness and political degradation that the considered presence of the "Black carpenter" evoked. In turn, he depicts the production of race (in this case, whiteness) as a process of binding legal status and despotic

---

58   This discussion is heavily indebted to Nyquist, *Arbitrary Rule*, especially chapter 10 and the epilogue.

power—maintaining control of the "country," "putting on airs," and laying claim to the expansive, extra-judicial right to kill. He defines all of this, moreover, in relation to the transition from slavery to capitalism. The development of race as a form of generic whiteness in this view is revealed as a specific relationship to Blackness in its relationship to capital—one that is based upon a deferral of the haunting specter of wageless life evoked by the prior association of Blacks with slavery, as well as by actual, ongoing conditions of market dependency. Indeed, it is worth recalling in this context Du Bois's famous description of whiteness in *Black Reconstruction* as "a *public* and psychological wage." The association of whiteness with wages through the monopolization of fields of employment has been widely discussed. Less fully examined is how the transfer of whiteness to nationality actively links freedom with the management of public authority, specific mechanisms of violence, and the notion of a racial nemesis.

The second passage from Douglass's *Notebooks* in the third epigraph above offers final amplification of my (admittedly provisional) efforts here to revisit the relationship between race and capital. It is tempting on initial reading to interpret Douglass's lines *against* the claims developed here. After all, assuming the garb of the common laborer, Douglass seems precisely to affirm as directly *emancipatory* the movement from household slavery to wage labor. On closer inspection, however, Douglass is actually making a more specific claim about what the capitalist wage relation looks and feels like from the standpoint of slavery. The feeling of joy ("the emotion which swelled my heart") produced by recognition of self-possession ("my hands were my own") and the possibility of accumulating "more of the precious coin" are in this view entirely contingent upon the condition of enslavement ("one must have been in some sense a slave"). Here, we might wonder about the ways in which Douglass and Marx converge. For in both, a critical sense of the deep violence of being reduced to a proletarian condition and radical market dependency (within the *ongoing* transitions to capitalism) appears most directly in reference to slavery (and for Douglass, within Black life that emerges from it). Indeed, the fact that it was Anna Murray, a free Black woman, whose savings from domestic labor paid for the disguise that Douglass used when he escaped slavery deepens further the webs of dependency upon which any so-called freedom depends. As Du Bois would go on to argue, the "real modern labor problem" lies closer to the condition of racial dispossession than to the prospects of normative, wage-earning stability. Capitalist freedoms and their enjoyment (life, liberty, and the pursuit of happiness) require us continuously to "put on airs" and to cultivate a generous rage against the prospects of a bare life.

Atlantic slavery emerged as the foundational expression of exploitation, appropriation, and dispossession under capitalism over the course of the long sixteenth and seventeenth centuries. But it also bequeathed something that lasted—an enduring cheapness of black life. The production of race as a method for aggregating and devaluing an entire group has depended on assessing the value of Black social and biological reproduction in terms of capital accumulation and its social reproduction. From medical experimentation to crime statistics, debt peonage, labor market manipulation, rent harvesting, infrastructural exclusion, and financial speculation, the racial differentiation that many have considered only tenuously related to the itinerary of capitalism during slavery and its afterlife, has directly produced capitalist value and contributed in an ongoing way to the technical development of capitalism on its alleged frontiers, where new specializations in violence can be tested free of ethical judgment, and new harvests of people separated from land and resources consumed within the web of capital.

Marx recognized that capital formed in contradiction not only to exploited labor, but to life itself. Capital accumulation spurs population increase while voraciously depleting living labor. The societal crisis that capitalism constantly faces is the ongoing violent dislocation of these two processes. Racial marking through directly coercive interventions by the police and military is a response to those whose very existence affronts or resists capitalist assignment of value. It spurs the fabrication of moral, temporal, and spatial sequestration that becomes part of the ideological and institutional framework of crisis management through which the production of growth and death can be viewed less as a contradiction in the present than as a necessary dimension of historical progress itself.[59] Racism's toxicity, in this view, is a product of capitalist theft of resources and a material event. It is as much our inheritance as the environmental degradation from capitalism's appropriation of cheap nature that now widens the bandwidth of morbidity for everyone and everything in its path. The relationship of capitalism and slavery is in this way far-reaching. By exposing the proximity of violence and economy and the heterogeneity of historical time, it also exposes "the broken time of politics and strategy."[60] Rather than being a cause for disorientation, it is the starting point for any reconstruction.

---

59   Melinda Cooper, *Life as Surplus: Biotechnology and Capitalism in a Neoliberal Era* (Seattle: University of Washington Press, 2008), 60.

60   Daniel Bensaid, *Marx for Our Times: Adventures and Misadventures of a Critique* (New York: Verso, 2002), 23.

Chapter 3

Dissonance in Time

(Un)Making and (Re)Mapping of Blackness

Damien M. Sojoyner

In preparation to write this essay, I culled through my notes taken during weekly meetings with Cedric Robinson while I was a postdoctoral fellow in the Department of Black Studies at the University of California, Santa Barbara. The notes left me in awe: it was quite obvious from our weekly sessions that Cedric had figured out all of my weaknesses and very meticulously brought me along without condescension or judgment. While experience had taught me that his kindness and generosity knew no bounds and that he was, without a doubt, the smartest person that I had ever met, there was something about rereading the notes that intensified my appreciation for Cedric as a scholar and mentor. It took me a while to figure out what it was, but after a few sleepless nights, it finally hit me. Cedric, who was working on several projects at once, had spent time and energy adopting my project as his own. He brought countless resources to every meeting that shaped and informed my research and spent countless hours taking me through the flaws and strengths of my argumentation. Our meetings focused not so much on the particulars of crafting an argument (although we certainly discussed them), but the nuances of how to think about pursuits of study. The very fundamental exercise of thought itself was vital to each and every one of our discussions and it is in that spirit that I write this piece.

Under the guidance of Cedric, I have spent considerable time thinking about the relationship between schools and prisons. Throughout the following pages, my aim is to intently focus on one of the root connections between these vast structures: time. My framing of time is understood in its intimate proximity to Western constructions of difference. Time is the lifeblood of Western civilization. It is both the conduit that transfers vital information and bolsters key tenants of western modalities of being. Time, through manipulation, can be limitless; it can also be punitive. Thus, it is the rare vehicle that is both a matter of ideology and an instrument that imposes the weight of ideological adherence. Within Western norms, time represents the ideological manifestation of freedom; the ability to wield time for one's material benefit is a central part of the Western educative process. However, time is also an instrument utilized to levy punitive force upon those who Ruth Wilson Gilmore calls the "unfree"—those confined to the precarious politics of carcerality.[1] Time has been central to the imposition of disciplinary mechanisms aimed at ideological positions that counter Western notions of law and order. The punitive nature of time is thus linked to perhaps its most critical inflection use: as of time—an ideological and instrumental force in efforts to establish difference-making projects that attempt to legitimize race. Time is critical in making race appear logical and commonsense where it is in fact fictive and quite fragile. Having no historical other than mythical deployments of crafted reality, time is utilized to shore up the gaps left by inconsistencies within the Western imagination.

At the intersection of time and Western fantasies of racial making, a tension is exposed—a tension that can be understood as a key site of ideological struggle between Western manifestation of time on one hand, and time as interpolated within the Black Radical Tradition. As a means to explore this tension, I provide a brief ethnographic snapshot into organizing efforts against police brutality and education in Los Angeles that configure time in vastly different ways than western normative standards. Black radical time is not something that is employed to be inflicted upon people; rather, it is central to organizing against structures of domination (such as prisons and education). It is a shared resource that fosters collectivity in the midst of struggle and does not adhere to Western conventions of day/night and free/unfree. Such a paradigm provides a means to analyze and break away from western-time-induced trappings of the material and to synthesize, creating a politics based upon love of community and shared human experience. The power to tear asunder commonsensical understandings of time is a generative force for the Black Radical Tradition and a serious threat to obliterate the difference-making projects of Western society.

TIME IN THE WEST

Time is an elusory term. We often think of it as an objective unit of measurement associated with the mundane—the time of day or the amount of time it will take to get from point A to point B. Yet, just beneath the layer of banal superficiality, time is exposed as the not-quite-tangible but ubiquitous linchpin of Western civilization: the marker of difference. Difference of course is the vital source of energy by which racially charged exploitative practices are made logical. In his opus *Black Marxism*, Cedric Robinson beautifully explains that difference has been at the center of Western epistemological explanations of culture, economies, and general configurations of life dating back to the foundations of nation-state development:

---

1   Ruth Wilson Gilmore, "Forgotten Places and the Seeds of Grassroots Planning," in Charles R. Hale and Craig Calhoun, eds., *Engaging Contradictions: Theory, Politics, and Methods of Activist Scholarship* (Berkeley: University of California Press, 2008), 31–61.

The tendency of European civilization through capitalism was thus not to homogenize but to differentiate—to exaggerate regional, subcultural, and dialectical differences into "racial" ones. As the Slavs became the natural slaves, the racially inferior stock for domination and exploitation during the early Middle Ages, as the Tartars came to occupy a similar position in the Italian cities of the late Middle Ages, so at the systemic interlocking of capitalism in the sixteenth century, the peoples of the Third World began to fill this expanding category of a civilization reproduced by capitalism.[2]

The trick and abject horror of time is its covert use in the reinforcement of difference (i.e., race, gender, sexuality). On a very basic level the manifestation of such difference is understood within the context of *how* time is applied and to *whom*.

The annals of late twentieth- and early twenty-first-century US federal and state judicial and incarceration records provide evidence of the imposition of time. Ranging from months to hundreds of years, time is utilized as the preemptive disciplinary force to regulate the quality and quantity of life. The common sense connections between time and incarceration are evident in how time is invoked as a possessive action. "Just put your head down and do your time." "How much time did you get?" "Will I get credit for time served?" "Where do I have to do my time?" These inquiries resonate loudly within Black working-class and impoverished neighborhoods across the United States, for the application of time as a disciplinary mechanism of power has been key to the corralling of Black freedom.

Yet, just as harshly as time is applied to Black people, its application to constructions of whiteness stands in contradistinction. Rather than signifying an action served, time in the context of whiteness is fueled by notions of "inventible" and "unbounded" development and progress. The grand narrative of expansion in the United States is governed by omniscient renderings of time. The ideological underpinning of manifest destiny, the violent nation-driving process that provides contemporary boundaries (or lack thereof) to the United States, is governed by this limitless sense of time. Time in this sense is something that can be controlled and manipulated in order to provide meaning to that which defies both history and logical explanation. As in the case of manifest destiny, the possession of time provides the binary (and necessary) opposite of time's punitive nature in relation to Blackness.

Yet, in order for time to be made whole, the structural formations that drive whiteness have to be made real on the level of the individual subject. The immense amount of social, political, and racial indoctrination to reify the individual also erases the structure of whiteness from the collective discourse. In its

---

2   Cedric J. Robinson, *Black Marxism: The Making of the Black Radical Tradition* (Chapel Hill: University of North Carolina Press, 2000), 26.

place are rhetorical strategies that depend upon time to govern collective thought toward the individual. Ironically, the nation-state utilizes structural apparatuses such as public education and the film industry to develop a cognitive dissonance against structural argumentation through a hypervigilant focus on the individual. Elementary-, middle-, and high-school textbooks are littered with white masculine leaders who, acting alone, changed the hands of time.[3] Mythical constructions in these narratives include George Washington waiting for the perfect time to lead a band of wayward and tawdry soldiers in the Battle of Valley Forge, and Bill Clinton deftly pushing the limits of time to safely guide the United States out of a recession and usher in an economic revitalization fueled by technological innovations. Such constructions are central to the focus on the individual.

Similarly, the film industry works tirelessly to reinforce the trope of the individual and to avoid examination of the racialized other. Writing about the centrality of film at the dawn of the twentieth century, Cedric Robinson argues that the film industry became the central means by which race was reinforced:

> In the United States, the technical development of moving pictures in the late nineteenth century was so enveloped in the formation of an industry, which, in turn, became an agency of power and wealth. Prior to these events, the disintegration of a centuries-long slave system had deposited a racial regime in American culture. Without a hint of irony, that racial regime had achieved its maturity at precisely the moment when its internal contradictions were most marked (the great slave rebellions of the nineteenth century) and domestic and international opposition was amassing. With the collapse of the slave system, a different racial regime was required, one which adopted elements from its predecessor but was now buttressing the domination of free labor.[4]

Popular and financially successful films of the late twentieth and early twenty-first century such as *Glory, Dangerous Minds, Amistad,* and *Freedom Writers* operate as difference-making projects within the contemporary racial regime. A central component of these films is the manipulation of time—specifically, control of time by white agents of the state (e.g., teachers, politicians, soldiers) over Black subjects. More insidious, the erasure of Blackness from film in the case of the *Tarzan* films of the early twentieth century and in animated depictions of Africa such as *The Lion King* and *Madagascar* during the late twentieth and early twenty-first centuries, occurs through a manipulation and re-historicizing of time. Such tropes also solidify the ways through which time works on Black people;

---

3   Ellen Swartz, "Emancipatory Narratives: Rewriting the Master Script in the School Curriculum," *Journal of Negro Education* 61, no. 3 (1992): 341–55.

4   Cedric J. Robinson, *Forgeries of Memory and Meaning: Blacks and the Regimes of Race in American Theater and Film before World War II* (Chapel Hill: University of North Carolina Press, 2007), xv.

importantly the lack of agency and intentional omission is directly tied to the manner in which time works on and against Black people.

Time serves as a dual processer—an instrument and ideology—on one hand it functions on the meta-level of structural imposition to buttress grand narratives of the state; however it simultaneously works to reinforce the mythical power of the individual. This latter function, in turn, effectively overwrites the social memory of the former. Thus, in our collective thinking, the history and contemporary narratives of politics, economies, and culture shrink down to encompass only the ability (or inability) of the racialized individual to reorder time and place, omitting any structural analysis of power. Time's structural effect on Black people dissolves and is reconfigured as Black people's lack of desire, will, or internal fortitude to change their circumstances in the present moment. Additionally, the concealed nature of the societal structure enables time to appear as a racial blank slate. Historically manipulated and ideologically driven, the individual within such a construct is free to dictate the parameters of time without constraint, limited only by the bounds of their free will. The strong association of time with the individual, absent any structural forces, provides the perfect milieu for *choice* to become the governor of lived experience.

CHOICE AND TIME

Choice is the operative that masks racial realities and seamlessly blends the myth of the individual to bend time with unseen violent affront of structural forces that impose time. Within the paradigm of choice, the individual chooses how to use time. Choice as an operative of western constructions of time works to move the individual beyond the perils of structural circumstance. As a tool of ideological subterfuge, choice has had a profound impact upon two racialized groups: working- and middle-class white people and a burgeoning Black middle class. To the former, choice is critical as it allows for material life decisions to be achieved through mythical notions of hard work. The purchase of a home, attainment of a high salary, and access to the college of one's desire are all filtered through the narrative of choice. Time becomes the mitigating factor that reinforces the framing of choice through the politics of the individual. Rhetorical inflections such as "I spent all of those hours studying in school" or "All of the time that I spent working well into the night got me that promotion" become the dominant understanding of how one makes a choice to advance within modern society. It is the relationship with time that enables choice to carry with it underlining advantages. Within the context of the racial blank slate, if everyone were to manipulate time then they would be able to reap the benefits of "good" choices. Thus, the "failure" of Black youth in school or the inability of Black people to gain access to the housing market are all systematic of not being able to use time in the manner that would ensure "good" choices.

However, it is not merely that Black people do not understand how to control time. Within the western popular social canon there is a clear understanding of the effect of time upon Black people. To this end, it is not just that Black people cannot make good decisions, it also that time works differently upon Black people. There is something akin to a biological determinism that works on Black people to prevent the manipulation of time and further, time becomes an albatross around their collective necks. Following such logic the political, economic, and racial intergration with Black people defies the laws of common sense and rational economics. Mass segregation in US housing, schools, financial systems, and health care found in the United States is not a matter of systematic injustice, but instead a most profoundly logical development to ensure the ability of non-Black people to manipulate time.

For the burgeoning Black managerial middle class, choice is critical as it serves two functions. Similar to the white working and middle classes, choice provides the language to validate personal achievements in the face of daunting odds. Vast institutions such as colleges and universities, the formal political sector and the modern film industry invent and prey upon stories of Black youth from structurally devastated communities who have been able to jump over, through, and around obstacles to achieve greatness. The choice to follow the correct path in the face of a myriad of "bad" choices is hailed as a characteristic of the highest form of moral integrity. The trappings of such an ideological construct are seductive, offering material rewards that are accompanied with blinders that prevent any discussion beyond the purview of the individual.

The most devastating function that is associated with choice in relation to the burgeoning Black managerial class is the disciplinary work that goes into the management of the Black working and poor classes. The logical conclusions drawn from "following the wrong path" or "hanging out with the wrong group" is that a particular individual made the choice and they undoubtedly knew the consequences that would be associated with such choices. The infamous phrase, "You did the crime, now you have to do the time," can only be understood within a context of choice as the dominant narrative of racialized time, mediated by the burgeoning Black middle class who look with disdain upon the wayward Black masses while offering grossly ironic solutions based upon the manipulation of time. This was most famously evident during the early part of the twenty-first century when iconic Black celebrities and "leaders" such as Bill Cosby, Oprah Winfrey, and Barack Obama implored the Black working and poor classes to take individual responsibility for their woeful stations in life. Prior to the public revelations of his sexually violent acts toward women, Bill Cosby had cornered the market on shaming the Black poor. With several books under his belt and increasing success on the college lecture circuit, Cosby's invocation of personal responsibility was lauded by his middle-class brethren and white contemporaries alike. Winfrey, widely praised for her philanthropic work in South Africa, asserted that she would not donate money to inner-city schools in the United States because "the sense that you need to learn just isn't there."[5] Using South Africa as the imagined counterweight whose success was yet untapped, she stated, "In South Africa, they don't ask for money or toys. They ask for uniforms so they can go to school."[6] (The irony of Winfrey, who has made millions of dollars from the shilling of consumptive goods, chastising Black youth for wanting material possessions is laughable at best.) President Barack Obama, who publicly declared his intention to save the middle class, had no problems continuing the misguided critique of Black male responsibility, attributing its alleged absence to a broken Black family structure. Speaking to an overflowing congregation at the Apostolic Church of God in Chicago, Illinois, then presidential candidate Obama said, "Too many fathers are MIA, too many fathers are AWOL, missing from too many lives and too many homes. They have abandoned their responsibilities, acting like boys instead of men. And the foundations of our families are weaker because of it."[7] Through a narrative of personal responsibility and accountability, Cosby, Winfrey, and Obama demand that the Black poor change the dynamics of Western imposition of time—an impossible task that to attain at the invocation by the Black middle class only serves to reinforce the material rewards gotten at the expense of critiques and analysis developed from within poor and working-class Black communities.

Cloaked in the ill-fitting suit of racial uplift politics, the narrative of choice silences discussion of the structural conditions that develop and maintain whiteness. Models that emanate from poor and working-class communities, on the other hand, are not stymied by a politics of choice and by extension a manipulation of time; rather, they operate with a profound understanding of how time functions. The option of choice is just as logical as the practicality of turning into a winged creature and flying into space. The reality is that the material conditions do not exist for choice to be a viable option. When the closest large-scale medical facility is a thirty-minute car ride away, the best job that one can hope for with a high-school degree pays under the poverty wage, and the prospects of attaining housing are slim to nil, and the option of choice is beyond irrational.

TIME IN THE BLACK RADICAL TRADITION

It is here, within the logic of Black communal spaces, that modes of analysis dramatically shift from the individual and choice to models based upon a collective understanding of the severe limitations of Western philosophical traditions. Rather than an intense focus upon the individual or choice, the

---

5   Allison Samuels, "Oprah Goes to School," *Newsweek* (January 7, 2007), available at newsweek.com.

6   Ibid.

7   Julie Bosman, "Obama Calls for More Responsibility From Black Fathers," *New York Times* (June 16, 2008), available at nytimes.com.

analysis that develops is based upon the structural apparatuses and conditions that fuel the state projects governed by the logics of racial capitalism. Thus, the lived experience of being Black dictates that choice is a fleeting proposition that has very little bearing on the outcome of one's family and neighborhood. For example, counter to the rhetoric of "school of choice" that supposedly grants individuals the opportunities to attend any school that they want to, the reality is that for the vast majority of Black people, the options of schools are predetermined and have nothing to do with choice. The fantasy of choice in this narrative is cloaked by imposed racial structures: Schools are determined by neighborhoods; neighborhoods in turn are determined by planned patterns of racial and economic segregation; Black neighorhoods are marked by the constant presence of police surveillance, which leads to incarceration. The litmus test for gaining admission to a school of choice (with, for instance, high test scores, music and art programs, and extracurricular activities) is based upon a testing mechanism (which proves nothing other that a student can pass a test) that is predicated on the financial resources available to prepare for the test. Given that Black communities are economically stymied by housing options dictated by racial segregation and lack of employment opportunities, as well as by the financial imposition of incarceration, financial resources are not available for test preparation. Thus, schools in Black communities have the lowest test scores and are deemed the least desirable, which feeds into the racialized construction of Black educational failure. The result is that Black youth do not have the option to attend a school of their choice, as that choice has already been structured for them.

Rather than feed into the limitations of choice, promising solutions involve radical transformations of education, housing, and health care in Black neighborhoods, of Black people. Beyond financial considerations, there is an understanding that the type of education that is being received is not commensurate with the lived experience of being Black. It is not a question of how much money is allocated by federal and state governments for housing, rather it is a question of who controls how the money is dispersed. It depends not merely on access to healthcare facilities, but much more substantive questions that pertain to both the quality of health care provided and the financial burdens incurred by a system funneled through a government-subsidized private administrative market infrastructure, as well.

It is within this framework that time transforms from something that is to be manipulated and controlled to a paradigm where time is a shared construct that enables creative dialogue around rigorous analysis and solutions. It is here that we see the development of an alternative understanding of the reckoning with time and how time operates to facilitate interpersonal and metaphysical growth. The following sections are ethnographic moments that illustrate the development of alternative social visions of time. The first is taken from an experience with the archival records of the Coalition Against Police Abuse

(CAPA). Housed at the Southern California Library, CAPA's archive is an excruciating mix of joy and pain. A collection of monumental victories and just as many stories of painful defeat, the archive is an amalgamation of the transformation of time. At the hands of the community, the enforcement of Western impositions of time via the strong arm of the law—the police—is not only challenged, but also supplanted by a radical organizing strategy that bends the normative boundaries of time. Necessitated by the need to serve neighborhoods throughout South Central Los Angeles, the CAPA archive is a look into Black visions of the future: a future that places human concerns over the material demands of a Western racial capitalist infrastructure.

The second snapshot is taken from a conversation with a young Black man by the name of Marley. An insightful, caring, charismatic individual with the organizing tenacity and self-awareness to quickly humble police and professors alike, Marley had made the decision to withdraw from the formal education process. This was not a rash decision but a well-conceived plan that embodied a radical understanding of social arrangements and the politics of education in Los Angeles. Marley's testimony must be read as an indictment of the structural implementation of time via public education to suppress Black organizing and Black movement. Read side by side, the CAPA archive and Marley's testimony represent the power of the transformation of time in a manner that is both threatening and empowering to communities.

A BEAUTIFUL STRUGGLE—ARCHIVES OF THE COALITION AGAINST POLICE ABUSE

I sat down at the elongated beige table, daunted by the task of going through the archival records of an organization that had such deep ties and such a profound impact on the Black residents of South Central Los Angeles. Stacked in boxes, the enclosed documents held tales of the past and key insights for the future. I opened the lid and deep inside were bundles and bundles of five-by-eight-inch index cards. Slightly faded from the accumulation of dust in the CAPA office, the cards archived the process of struggle against the Los Angeles Police Department from the 1980s through the 1990s. Some of the cards contained meticulously handwritten notes, while others had been carefully placed into the capable metal arms of a typewriter. Each card told a different story but all were framed by a common theme: police violence.

Michael Zinzun knew the horrors of police violence all too well. A former member of the Black Panther Party, Zinzun was savagely attacked by officers of the Pasadena Police Department. Having lost an eye in the brutal encounter, Zinzun successfully won a million-dollar lawsuit against the department and immediately went to work. With the money collected from the suit, he started CAPA. The aim of the organization was multifaceted, but these cards were the embodiment of the overarching aims of the organization. Zinzun quickly spread the word about CAPA and soon just about everybody in South Central Los Angeles knew its phone number. Promising to take calls any time day or night, CAPA became a clearinghouse for Black grievances against police violence. Members of CAPA and quite often Zinzun himself would take down over the phone details of individuals who had been harassed or brutalized by the police. Zinzun would transfer the intimate details from notepads onto the index cards, in effect archiving the long history of brutal police repression in Los Angeles. From his days of organizing with the Panthers, Zinzun had developed an extensive database of attorneys and paralegals. He paired individuals who had called in with representation, in an effort to take on the Los Angeles Police Department and the Los Angeles County Sherriff's Department.

I sat on the chair in amazement culling through the cards reading story after story of harrowing encounters with the police. Even more astonishing was the amount of time that was put in collecting these stories. Not just the time to make sure that the details of the story was correct and accounted for, but also the complete disregard for conventions of time to be a caretaker to the stories. Whether it was one o'clock in the afternoon or one o'clock in the morning, the only time that matter was that moment. Zinzun knew all too well that the physical and psychological trauma that was accompanied by police violence needed immediate response. There was something cathartic about being able to tell one's story to an individual who not only would listen to your story without judgment but would also advocate and fight on your behalf. The level of selflessness that such caretaking involved and the level of commitment without the need for self-aggrandizement, took me aback. With his charismatic leadership style and highly attuned wit, Zinzun could have easily taken his experience and personally monetized his story through various media platforms. Like many who had been seduced by the lure of fame at the expense of dignity, Zinzun held a moral conviction for the community.

CAPA's work was instrumental in building new forms of communal alliance without the politics associated with state-based reform. The index cards held stories of lived experience and detailed a model to collectively address the violence of police brutality. Zinzun understood that a voice standing alone stood no chance against the tentacles of city power and the police was the strong arm. Rather, there was an understanding that it took a disparate coalition of people across class lines whom could provide redress and effectively counter decades of systematic brutality.

PLANNING FOR A DEMISE—MARLEY'S ANALYSIS

We sat in the car at a red light a momentary pause in our drive down San Pedro Street in the heart of South Central Los Angeles. The light turned green and we continued on, passing a massive construction site that was to be the home of a new high school—the third to border the street. Marley's face held a mix of frustration and anger. Marley and I had become very close over the past few years, and I knew that he didn't wait to be told when to speak his mind. True to his disposition, he wasted very little time getting his words out:

This is what I don't get. They are building all these new schools all over the place, right. They are building this school over there in between Vermont and the 110 Freeway. That is a recipe for disaster. That school is going to be right in between two rival hoods. As soon as that school opens, there are going to be problems. Then they are building that other school right off of San Pedro, which is going to be the same thing. I mean, it is like you have to sit back and think and wonder if they are doing this on purpose. Why in the world would you intentionally build a school right in between two groups that you know don't like each other?

The only thing that I can think of, and you know I am not big on conspiracies, but they are building these schools because they don't want us here much longer, like they want us to kill each other or have more reason to bring in more police and lock us up for stupid stuff. They have to know that . . . this hood that is right over here . . . [has] been having problems with this other hood that is right next to them and now you are forcing them to have contact with each other without any type of mediation from people who they respect or . . . some sort of peace agreement, it is going to be just chaos. I mean, that just does not make sense at all.

Or they want to put all this money into education and say, "See, we tried to give you something. We poured all this money into getting you educated and you did not want to do anything with it. So, now we are going to take it over. We are going to do our way, when the truth of the matter is that we had nothing to do with it in the first place." I mean, there was no plan that I saw or heard about where they sought me or anybody that I knew out to ask them about the building of these schools. I would have told them right away that this is a bad idea! I bet that they had some meeting downtown or somewhere far off in [the] middle of the day when no one could go [to] the meeting. Then they could say that they had a meeting and that we gave the people a chance to speak. The reality of the situation is that building up all of these schools like they are is pouring water on a grease fire. Everybody around here knows that all that it is going to do is make the fire even stronger. What they need is to give complete control to the community. Let us determine how we want the schools to operate. Let us determine what type of education that we want and what type of place that we want to live in. Until that happens, there is no reason to even believe what they say or even think that what they say is going to happen. This is not education that we are getting. This is a setup and pretty much everybody around here is smart enough to see that coming from a mile away. So, let me ask you, what is the point of even going to these new schools? I know that if I go, I am going to run into trouble of some sort. Either I am going to see someone that I have some problems with and it is going to be an issue, or because of all these police that you know are going to be at these schools . . . I am more than likely [to] have some sort of problem. So, you tell me why should I go. On top of that, I know that I am not going to learn anything that I need to live and no [one] around here is getting out of any of these schools and going to anybody's college. So, you tell me what is the point in going. It is not that I am against education, you know I love education. But I am against being told that something is good for me, when I know and everybody around me knows that if you follow that plan, you might as well be planning your own funeral.

The Black Radical Tradition's reckoning with Western philosophical renderings of time is illustrative of both the destructive capacity of time as a difference-making project and also the beauty of the transformative capacities of radical social visions. In the case of CAPA, time is constituted as a marker of the immediate concerns of Black residents in the vast sprawl of urban space and the binding agent that connected people across lines of imposed difference. With respect to Marley, the boundaries of Western constructions of time imposed upon Black communities both incapacitated Black thought and laid waste to Black lives in the creation of neighborhood chaos. Marley's social vision was based not on the consent of state governing structures (e.g., public education) and instead was based upon the ceding of power to his community to control time and, by extension, their lived experience. Read together both the formation of CAPA to counter police repression and the withdrawal from violent state structures represent uses of time by the Black Radical Tradition that are critical to social visions. Resistant to individualized, difference-making projects, time is altered to support communal organized strategies that affirm Black life.

In an era marked by brutal forms of racial confinement and captivity, the rabid fangs of Western civilization have been exposed. Western constructions of difference have been laid bare and in their naked state, the response has been a violent, vicious attack to protect the ideological undercurrents that buttress mythical fallacies central to race and race-making. In this manner, the vulnerability of western civilization has been over the creation, maintenance, and reproduction of ideology. Throughout this piece, my goal has been to demonstrate how time, as both a manifestation of ideology, and an instrument of ideological implementation is a terrain of struggle. While Western civilization has tried to impose particular renderings of time as a means of racial maintenance, organizing efforts molded by the Black Radical Tradition have demonstrated the fallacy of Western difference-making projects and fostered new methods to construct reality. The effect of such organizing efforts has made it quite obvious that the social mapping of Western chronologies are no longer commensurable in a society that registers time in different scales. Simply thinking about time and the registers of time has forced us to reconsider the intent of prisons, policing, and education. The development of thought, such as thinking about the construction of a world without prisons, is Western civilization's greatest fear and a core tenet of the Black Radical Tradition—the restructuring of the mind. Taken from Robinson's account of the Black Radical Tradition, "But always, its focus was on the structures of the mind. Its epistemology granted supremacy to metaphysics not the material."[8] The reconceptualization of time based upon Black radical practices provides a means to destabilize the consruction and maintence of difference and develop a society indebted to a social vision immersed in communal bonds and shared human experiences.

---

8 Robinson, *Black Marxism*, 169.

Chapter 4

Racial Capitalocene

Françoise Vergès

In the debates on the "Anthropocene," global warming, and climate change, voices of the South and of minorities—the prime victims of these phenomena's consequences—have developed an analysis that brings together race, capitalism, imperialism, and gender. This analysis rests on past struggles, such as the organization of farmworkers led by Cesar Chavez in California in the early 1960s for workplace rights, including protection from toxic pesticides, and of African American students in 1967 to oppose a city dump and in 1979 to oppose a landfill in Houston. Environmental racism became a site of struggle. The publication in 1987 of *Toxic Waste and Race in the United States*, a report by the Commission for Racial Justice of the United Church of Christ, was a turning point.[1] It showed that race was the single most important factor in determining where toxic waste facilities were sited in the United States and that the siting of these facilities in communities of color was the intentional result of local, state, and federal land-use policies. In the 1980s, the Reagan administration's practice of cutting the budgets of federal environmental agencies had aggravated racist decisions. The report demonstrated that "three out of every five Black and Hispanic Americans lived in communities with uncontrolled toxic waste sites."[2] Twenty years later, the United Church of Christ published another report confirming that "people of color make up the majority of those living in host neighborhoods within 3 km of the nation's hazardous waste facilities. Racial and ethnic disparities are prevalent throughout the country."[3]

Between the two reports a global movement for environmental justice had emerged. In October 1991, the Delegates to the First National People of Color Environmental Leadership Summit drafted and adopted the "Principles of Environmental Justice," which became a defining document for the growing grassroots movement for environmental justice. The preamble read:

---

1   United Church of Christ Commission for Racial Justice, *Toxic Wastes and Race in the United States: A National Report on the Racial and Socio-Economic Characteristics of Communities with Hazardous Waste Sites* (New York: 1987).

2   Ibid, xiv.

3   United Church of Christ Justice and Witness Ministries, *Toxic Waste and Race at Twenty, 1987–2007: Grassroots Struggles to Dismantle Environmental Racism in the United States* (March 2007), 11.

WE, THE PEOPLE OF COLOR, gathered together at this multinational People of Color Environmental Leadership Summit, to begin to build a national and international movement of all peoples of color to fight the destruction and taking of our lands and communities, do hereby re-establish our spiritual interdependence to the sacredness of our Mother Earth; to respect and celebrate each of our cultures, languages and beliefs about the natural world and our roles in healing ourselves; to ensure environmental justice; to promote economic alternatives which would contribute to the development of environmentally safe livelihoods; and, to secure our political, economic and cultural liberation that has been denied for over 500 years of colonization and oppression, resulting in the poisoning of our communities and land and the genocide of our peoples.[4]

The authors of the 2007 report warned that "for many industries, it is a 'race to the bottom,' where land, labor and lives are cheap."[5] Similar studies in India, South Asia, South America, Africa, and Europe demonstrated a global pattern of environmental racism and the ways in which states and multinationals have been avoiding environmental justice.

In this chapter, I try to answer the following question: Though minorities and peoples of the South have shown that they are the victims of racialized environmental politics—toxic waste, polluted water and rivers, pesticides, polluted food—have studies on the emergence of the "Anthropocene" addressed the role of race in its making? In other words, is the Anthropocene racial? Scholars have studied race as a central element of destructive environmental policies, but what connection can be made between the Western conception of nature as "cheap" and the global organization of a "cheap," racialized, disposable workforce, given the conception of nature as constant capital and the fact that "the organizers of the capitalist world system appropriated Black labor power as *constant* capital"[6]? What methodology is needed to write a history of the environment that includes slavery, colonialism, imperialism and racial capitalism, from the standpoint of those who were made into "cheap" objects of commerce, their bodies as objects renewable through wars, capture, and enslavement, fabricated as disposable people, whose lives do not matter?

What does this have to do with Cedric Robinson? In *Black Marxism*, Robinson writes that "for the realization of theory we require new history." He adds, "Black radical theory was not made by choice but dictated by historical inheritance."[7] In the spirit of Robinson's advice, I will try in this chapter to

---

4   First People of Color Environmental Leadership Summit, "Principles of Economic Justice" (1991), available at ejnet.org.

5   United Church of Christ, *Toxic Waste and Race at Twenty*, 14.

6   Cedric J. Robinson, *Black Marxism:The Making of the Black Radical Tradition* (Chapel Hill: University of Carolina Press, 1983), 309. Emphasis in original.

7   Robinson, *Black Marxism*, 307.

suggest ways of writing a history of environment that takes into account the history of racial capitalism. My interest in the history of racialized environmental politics is partly biographical: I come from Réunion Island in the Indian Ocean, which became a French colony in the seventeenth century and is today a French department. Growing up in a communist, anticolonial, and feminist family, I learned early that the environment had been shaped by slavery and colonialism—a reading of space that gave meaning to where cities were built, where poor people lived, and how the large sugarcane fields, rivers, mountains, volcano, and beaches had been inscribed in the colonial and postcolonial economy. I studied the combined work of scientists (first botanists, then biologists, oceanographers, and volcanologists), engineers, soldiers, and business executives (whether slave traders, slave owners, bankers, or multinational CEOs), which fabricated "nature" as excess that needed to be tamed and disciplined and, through the tourism industry, enjoyed. I observed how the Cold War and studied the nature of the "green revolution" continued to transform nature in the Indian Ocean and the alliance between the military, the engineering company, the multinational, and the scientist. More recently, understanding what is at stake in the negotiations about "climate change" means considering the place of these stakeholders in the context of a global counterrevolution—the erosion of rights, the politics of nonraciality beneath which, as David Theo Goldberg has argued, lurk more sinister shadows of the racial everyday and persistent institutional and structural racisms—and racial capitalism. Global warming and its consequences for the peoples of the South is a political question and must be understood outside of the limits of "climate change" and in the context of the inequalities produced by racial capital.

ANTHROPOCENE OR RACIAL CAPITALOCENE?

The term "Anthropocene" to describe the "human dominance of biological, chemical and geological processes on Earth" was first introduced in 2000 in an article jointly written by Paul Crutzen and Eugene Stoermer. They dated its emergence to the latter part of the eighteenth century, admitting that

> alternative proposals can be made (some may even want to include the entire Holocene). However, we choose this date because, during the past two centuries, the global effects of human activities have become clearly noticeable. This is the period when data retrieved from glacial ice cores show the beginning of a growth in the atmospheric concentrations of several "greenhouse gases," in particular CO_2 and CH_4. Such a starting date also coincides with James Watt's invention of the steam engine in 1784.[8]

---

8   Paul J. Crutzen and Eugene F. Stoermer, "The 'Anthropocene,'" *International Geosphere-Biosphere Programme* 41 (2000): 17–18.

When and why the Anthropocene had occurred, its dangers, and what could stop them were widely debated in scientific journals and conferences. The narrative centered on the threat to human beings as an undifferentiated whole and was summarized thus: humanity would not survive if it did not slow down the emission of CO_2. Films and advertisements began to highlight the dangers of climate change, accentuating the loss of animal species and the idea of Earth as a common good. These media did not, however, take into account the asymmetry of power and instead marginalized what had been demonstrated in the 1980s: the role of racialized policies of public health and toxic waste disposal, weapons and pollution, land grabs and deforestation, the importance of the Cold War with its alliance between the chemical industry and the military, laws of commerce and monopolies. It was remarkable that these studies did not seek to locate points of intersection with emerging studies on imperialism and environment.[9] When Dipesh Chakrabarty wrote "The Climate of History: Four Theses" in 2009, the hope was that a dialogue was finally starting between scientists and postcolonial thinkers.[10] By focusing on the immediacy of climate change as a crisis, Chakrabarty framed the Anthropocene as a current transformation. This presentism ignored a deeper history and created the illusion of an organic and undifferentiated universal humanity. In his 2012 essay "Postcolonial Studies and the Challenge of Climate Change," Chakrabarty referred again to the abstract figure of "the human in the age of the Anthropocene," but, moving away from his 2009 conclusion somewhat, stated: "There is no corresponding 'humanity' that in its oneness can act as a political agent. A place thus remains for struggles around questions on intrahuman justice regarding the uneven impacts of climate change."[11] In answering his critics especially about "the rich always having lifeboats and therefore being able to buy their way out of all calamities including a Great Extinction," he asked, "Would not their survival also constitute a survival of the species (even if the survivors quickly differentiated themselves into, as seems to be the human wont, dominant and subordinate groups)?"[12] Chakrabarty defends a notion of the Anthropocene that, according to Aaron Vansintjan, infers a "blanket humanity, a blanket history, a

9   See William Beinart and Lotte Hughes, eds., *Environment and Empire* (Oxford: Oxford University Press, 2007); Alfred W. Crosby, *Ecological Imperialism: The Biological Expansion of Europe, 900–1900* (New York: Cambridge University Press, 2004); Daniel R. Headrick, *Power over Peoples: Technology, Environments, and Western Imperialism, 1400 to the Present* (Princeton: Princeton University Press, 2012).

10   Dipesh Chakrabarty, "The Climate of History: Four Theses," *Critical Inquiry* 35, no. 2 (2009): 197–222.

11   Dipesh Chakrabarty, "Postcolonial Studies and the Challenge of Climate Change," in Pramod K. Nayar, ed., *Postcolonial Studies: An Anthology* (Wiley-Blackwell, 2015), 144–57, 145, and 154.

12   Dipesh Chakrabarty, "Whose Anthropocene? A Response," *RCC Perpsectives: Transformations in Environment and Society*, no. 2 (2016), 112.

blanket geological record"[13] which relies on "apolitical and colonialist assumptions" and "highlights the danger of using one framework (geology and climatology) to make universal claims about the world—it helps make only one world possible."[14]

But the Anthropocene is a catchy term that

> makes for an easy story. Easy, because it does not challenge the naturalized inequalities, alienation, and violence inscribed in modernity's strategic relations of power and production. It is an easy story to tell because it does not ask us to think about these relations *at all.*[15]

The notion "sweeps up within it the diverse, dynamic, and even contradictory discourse of peoples throughout the globe contending with catastrophic environmental change"[16] and maintains the nature/society division dear to Western thought, masking the fact that relations between humans are themselves produced by nature. The notion of the Anthropocene is "de-historicizing, universalizing, eternalizing, naturalizing a mode of production specific to a certain time and place," a strategy of ideological legitimation that blocks off any prospect of change.[17] Student of anthropology Elizabeth Reddy has coined the expression "charismatic mega-category"[18] to describe the temporality and spatiality produced by the notion of the Anthropocene. Sociologist Jason Moore has suggested the notion of a Capitalocene[19] which brings back capitalism "as a world-ecology, joining the accumulation of capital, the pursuit of power, and the co-production of nature in dialectical unity."[20] As Moore puts it, scholarship that posits

> the exploitation of nature as an external relation to the exploitation of labor power does two things. First, it confuses matters, because nature and labor are not comparable entities. Nature is the field within which human activity unfolds, and is also the object, and precondition of, human activity. Second, it confuses matters yet further by establishing an arbitrary discontinuity between human

---

13   Aaron Vansintjan, "Going Beyond the 'Ecological Turn' in the Humanities," ENTITLE blog: A Collaborative Writing Project on Political Ecology (March 1, 2016), available at entitleblog. org.

14   Ibid.

15   Jason Moore, "The Capitalocene Part I: On the Nature & Origins of Our Ecological Crisis" (January 2014), available at jasonwmoore.com. Emphasis in original.

16   Zoe Todd, "Relationships," *Cultural Anthropology* (January 21, 2016), available at culanth. org.

17   Andreas Malm, *Fossil Capital: The Rise of Steam Power and the Roots of Global Warming* (London: Verso, 2016), 271.

18   Elizabeth Reddy, "What Does It Mean to Do Anthropology in the Anthropocene?" Platypus: The CASTAC Blog (April 8, 2014), available at blog.castac.org.

19   Moore, "The Capitalocene, Part I."

20   Ibid.

environment-making—the exploitation of nature—and environment-making by other forms of life.[21]

Moore dates the beginning of the Capitalocene to the sixteenth century, which also witnessed the "discovery of the New World" into which people were brought through the force of "blood and fire,"[22] the slave trade, the division of colonies among European powers, and the organization on a global scale of a mobile, racialized, gendered, and bonded workforce. Slavery and colonialism had a deep impact on the world-ecology.

To the historian Joachim Radkau, "the chief problem of colonialism seems to have been not so much its immediate ecological consequences as its long-term impact, the full extent of which became apparent only centuries later, in the era of modern technology, and many times only after the colonial states had acquired their independence."[23] We must, in our narrative of the racial Capitalocene, integrate this long memory of colonialism's impact and the fact that destruction in the colonial era becomes visible in the postcolonial era. In other words, we must add to the United Church of Christ's 1987 study of racialized policies of the environment in the twentieth century a history of racial Capitalocene, with an analysis of capital, imperialism, gender, class, and race and a conception of nature and of being human that opposes the Western approach. In the 1991 "Principles of Environmental Justice," the first principle stated that "Environmental Justice affirms the sacredness of Mother Earth, ecological unity and the interdependence of all species, and the right to be free from ecological destruction." The principle posits a new understanding of what it is to be human and challenges the international dialogue on climate change that focused on a strategy of adaptation. Adaptation through technology or the development of green capitalism has indeed been presented as a good strategy. Yet it does not thoroughly address the long history and memory of environmental destruction about which Radkau has written, nor the asymmetry of power.

In the reconfiguration of the world that followed the colonization of the Americas and the Caribbean, nature was transformed into a cheap resource, as endlessly renewable as the bonded workforce. It is human praxis as labor and the global use of a color line in the division of labor that must be studied, and not a "human" death drive. When Andreas Malm argues that "there is also a different kind of violence, not rapid but slow motion, not instantaneous but incremental, not body-to-body but playing out over vast stretches of time through the medium of ecosystems," he raises the question of the narratives that

---

21 Jason Moore, "Beyond the 'Exploitation of Nature'? A World-Ecological Alternative" (April 25, 2014), available at jasonwmoore.wordpress.com.

22 Karl Marx, *Capital: A Critique of Political Economy* (New York: Random House, 1906), 786.

23 Joachim Radkau, *Power and Nature: A Global History of the Environment* (New York: Cambridge University Press, 2008), 153.

would bring to light this kind of violence. Indeed, if we find and read "stories and essays on the slow violence of the Bhopal disaster, oil exploitation in the Arabian Gulf and the Niger Delta, mega-dams in Indian, depleted uranium in Iraq"—to which we can add Katrina in New Orleans, the moving tide of toxic iron-ore residue in Brazil, polluting the water supply of hundreds of thousands of residents as it makes its way to the ocean, the consequences of nuclear tests in French Polynesia, the polluted water in Flint, Michigan, and the negative impact of agro-business—there are none "on climate change as such," as if "the capacity to imagine violence seems to have reached its limits."[24] We have to renew the ways that violence is narrated.

APOCALYPTIC/OPTIMISTIC VIEWS OF CLIMATE CHANGE AND ENVIRONMENTAL HISTORY

Two views about climate change and the environment have been dominating the media and politics shaping the public debate: apocalyptic (humans are responsible for ecological destruction) and optimistic (scientists and engineers will find solutions). In 1991, Clive Ponting's book *A Green History of the World* offered a wide view of human and ecological history that covered the globe and centuries. Though Ponting discussed slavery, colonialism, and the creation of the Third World, "Man" was his main culprit. But it was his narrative of the ecological suicide of Easter Islanders that became the exemplary apocalyptic narrative. In his opening paragraph, Ponting wrote:

> Easter Island is one of the most remote, inhabited places on earth. Only some 150 square miles in area, it lies in the Pacific Ocean, 2,000 miles off the west coast of South America . . . At its peak the population was only about 7,000. Yet, despite its superficial insignificance, the history of Easter Island is a grim warning to the world.[25]

Ponting's analysis blamed the disappearance of Eastern Islanders on a human predisposition for destruction. His book was an instant success, offering a paradigm for the whole environmental history of the world that both frightened and pacified: if there was nothing to do, there was nothing to do. The book inspired, and continues to inspire, movies and novels. A whole genre of popular cinema has blossomed that offers a narrative of human hubris in which a white American male saves first "his" family and then "his" community. Individual mad scientists or cynical politicians are the villains; nothing is said of an economic system that privileges profit and fabricates racialized, disposable beings. The success of Ponting's book shows why the apocalyptic

---

24   Malm, *Fossil Capital*, 9.
25   Clive Ponting, *A Green History of the World* (London: Sinclair-Stevenson, 1991).

narrative is an ideological strategy that blames out-of-control forces rather than structures of power. But Easter Islanders did not commit suicide; they were the victims of systematic murder committed by Peruvian slave traders in the nineteenth century. The apocalyptic view rests on a pessimistic view of human nature. The optimistic view, on the other hand, is deeply steeped in the tradition of belief in progress. Ferdinand Braudel, whose work has been vital to historians of the environment, embodies that tradition. To him, climate is a longterm, mostly stable element which changes more slowly than historical time (though Braudel sometimes portrays nature—the sea, the mountains, rice, maize—as the main actor of history). Yet, as Eyal Weizman has written,

> the climate can no longer be considered a constant . . . The current acceleration of climate change is not only an unintentional consequence of industrialization. The climate has always been a project for colonial powers, which have continually acted to engineer it.[26]

Apocalyptic and optimistic approaches have inspired the current rhetoric of a "crisis" produced by human nature or by an error in progress, evident in three recent moments in politics of the environment. The first moment is the emergence of a Western-led transnational network of conservation work which appeared in the years before World War I. The second is the Western-led boom of environmentalism that appeared around 1970 and developed rapidly in response to decolonization, the first oil crisis, the alliance between the chemical industry and the army (pesticides for war and the green revolution), the culmination of international programs on birth control in the Third World,[27] the War in Vietnam, the proxy wars in Africa, revolutionary social movements, the dictatorships in South America, the interventions in the Middle East. Indeed, Starting in the early 1970s, European States as well as the United States started to issue regulations about clean air, clean water, and the protection of nature. In 1972, *The Limits to Growth* by the Club of Rome became an international best seller; that year in Stockholm, representatives from more than 100 countries met for the first United Nations Conference on the Human Environment and the United Nations Environment Programme (UNEP) was created. The third moment is the upswing of environmental issues all over the globe at the end of the Cold War, culminating in the Earth Summit in Rio de Janeiro in 1992. In December 2015, not long after the Paris attacks, the Cop21

---

26   Cited in McKenzie Wark, "Climate and Colonialism" (November 5, 2015), available at publicseminar.org.

27   In the late 1950s, at a series of World Congresses on world population, representatives of the US government started an ideological campaign in which they argued that global security and peace were tied to a low birth rate in the Third World. It became a truth: Third World countries were said to be condemned to poverty and underdevelopment if their birth rate was not controlled.

opened. The rhetoric on the relationship between political opposition to climate change and world security, and the "war on terror," has opened a new chapter in the development of the racial Capitalocene.

To unpack the different levels of racialized environment we need to go back the long sixteenth century, the era of Western "discoveries," of the first colonial empires, of genocides, of the slave trade and slavery, the modern world mobilized the work of commodified human beings and uncommodified extra-human nature in order to advance labor productivity within commodity production. Racialized chattel were the capital that made capitalism. Africa was forced to share its social product—human beings—with the Atlantic slave system. But the slave trade consisted of not only the organized deportation of millions of Africans to continents and islands, but also a massive transfer of plants, animals, diseases, soil, techniques, and manufactured goods from Europe. Capitalism relied for growth on an endless access to nature as excess, as a "bounty of extra-human biological systems and geological distribution: plants, silver, gold, iron, coal."[28]

RADICAL AGENDA

A history of the racialized Capitalocene à la Cedric Robinson will help us understand that climate change is not about human hubris, but the result of the long history of colonialism and racial capitalism and its Promethean thinking—the idea that "Man" can invent a mechanical, technical solution to any problem. To develop a theory from a renewed history of the racial Capitalocene is to study the matrix constructed by the army/science/engineers/business/state alliance. On January 8, 2016, a court in Oregon fined the Biotech firm ArborGen $53.5 million in compensation and punitive damages for using "trickery and deceit" to defraud workers. ArborGen is a US-based company, a leader in research and development for genetically engineered trees. It presents itself as a "leading global provider of conventional and next generation plantation trees."[29] The company develops mostly eucalyptus, which is the second-most-popular tree for the paper industry (pine is the first). On its website appear the following questions and their answers: "What Makes a Profitable Forest? Advanced Technology, Incomparable Value"; "What Makes a Valuable Tree? Superior Growth, Maximum Value"; "What Makes a Superior Seed? Exceptional Breeding, Outstanding Results." It is the vocabulary of profit for profit. ArborGen has a rival: the Israeli biotech company Futuragene, which has developed a

---

28   Jason Moore, "The End of Cheap Nature. Or How I Learned to Stop Worrying about 'the' Environment and Love the Crisis of Capitalism," in C. Suter and C. Chase-Dunn, eds., *Structures of the World Political Economy and the Future of Global Conflict and Cooperation* (Berlin: LIT, 2014), 285–314.

29   See arborgen.com.

unique technology that accelerates tree growth, again mostly eucalyptus. It is now a branch of the Brazilian plantation group Suzano, which grows 500,000 hectares of eucalyptus trees a year and has partners in China, Thailand, and South Africa. ArborGen and Suzano compete in an industry (forestry and paper) which generates $400 billion annually. The eucalyptus is known for being invasive and contributing to the depletion of water, desertification of soils, and loss of biodiversity. Once they are engineered, these effects are multiplied. Further, the paper industry always hides the waste it produces. Yet, waste embodies, more than ever before, the new era of the Capitalocene. Capitalist production is waste production. According to a 2000 study carried out by five major European and US research centers, one-half to three-quarters of annual resource inputs to industrial economies are returned to the environment within a year as waste. It must be said, however, that there is a huge gap between the amount of waste produced by multinationals and countries of the North and the amount of waste produced by populations of the South.[30]

Green capitalism and the biotech industry hold the optimistic discourse, offering seductive solutions: a green and sustainable future created by engineers and scientists, with the help of drones, satellites, and the new international laws of property and trade. Philosopher Isabelle Stengers has argued that we are witnessing an authoritarian management of societies based on Margaret Thatcher's "There Is No Alternative." Stengers argues for a "skepticism of the probable" in order to take a stand with the "possible" and commit to the multiple and always precarious attempts which bet on the possibility of a world which does not answer the probabilities offered by green capitalism. Building counterpowers means exposing the dangers of bioengineering to human health, biodiversity, and the lives and well-being of minorities, indigenous communities, and poor peasants, the majority of whom are women. It also means developing a radical curriculum based on a decolonization of knowledge production and institutions and a de-nationalization of knowledge. Knowledge production must take place with an awareness of diverse living realities and multiple publics without imposing the distance, disregard, or disdain of privilege. World citizenship and humanism must be brought in as decolonializing alternatives. A curriculum of radical pedagogy for the politics of the possible will challenges all forms of dehumanized work in favor of shared, life-affirmative labor practices, resisting the economy of speed for efficiency and acknowledging that time is needed to nourish knowledge. The politics of the possible also rest on the imagination—on the freedom to dream other pasts and imagine other futures than those suggested by the racial Capitalocene. Afrofuturism, for example, offers a way of looking at possible

---

30   Emily Matthews et al., *The Weight of Nations: Material Outflows from Industrial Economies* (Washington, DC: World Resources Institute, 2000).

futures or alternate realities through a Black cultural lens, blending the future, the past, and the present. "Each generation must out of relative obscurity discover its mission, fulfill it, or betray it," Frantz Fanon wrote in 1961. We are at a critical juncture, a historical moment that sends us into our inheritances to find sources and references for the struggle ahead.

Chapter 5

Improvement and Preservation

Or, Usufruct and Use

Stefano Harney and Fred Moten

0.

"The idea that modernity is, properly speaking, the globalization of Europe" is what the African philosopher Tsenay Serequeberhan calls the pre-text of the European Enlightenment, that "metaphysical belief that European existence is qualitatively superior to other forms of human life." This metaphysical belief is grounded in the very idea of Europe as geographical and geopolitical embodiment and exception. The European exception has certainly been well diagnosed. Critics of colonialism such as Sylvia Wynter have noted that one cannot produce the self-owning, earth-owning individual without producing the figure of man, whose essential inhumanity is evident in the restless theorizing and practicing of race. Indeed, how could a self-owning, earth-owning man *not* belong to a self-owning group instantiated in and on a self-owning world that is, at once, an absolute and expansive locale? The self-owning, earth-owning group sets itself apart from other groups—particularly, fundamentally, in violent speciation, from groups that do not own (either self or earth). The cost of this speciation, which is carried out in invasion and enclosure, accrues to those with whom the ones who would be one say they don't belong, as a matter of blood and soil—those whose failure to (want to) be exceptional constitutes a sub- or pre-European (souther or eastern or negro or immigrant or terrorist) problem/question. What is implied in imagining that one has become (exceptional)? There will have been the gift to Europe of its own place, at once insular and unlimited, and its own singular and sub-divisible time. This transcendental honorarium, wherein gift is conceptualized as the given and the given is conceptualized as gift, will have granted Europe (the) world as the place and time of exception. But someone will have had to except Europe, to allow the constantly emergent state of its exception, to sacralize its politico-theological ground and atmosphere. Someone will have had to give the Europe(ans) the capacity to be one. (Some) one will have given man the power of being one, a completeness that will have been as if it were given. It is by way, and not in spite, of all this that we speak, in echo of Frantz Fanon, of "that same Europe where they are never done talking of Man" as "an avalanche of murders," a bloody history of slavery and colonialism that suggests the exception is always insufficiently granted and involuntarily

accepted, that it is the illusory object of an empty will's incapacity for self-impo-
sition. If the assertion of the European exception is its condition of im/possibil-
ity, then the avalanche of murders is that assertion's expressive operation.

Exception is a categorization one grants oneself only at the price of imagining
that it has been granted by an Other. To declare one's exceptionalism is not a
matter of exempting, or excluding, or excusing oneself, all of which are transitive.
Exceptionalism imagines the intransitive and attributes action to Others and,
more importantly, an originary kind of power to someone else. And it is here that
we see how the pre-text Serequeberhan identifies is in fact pre-given in a double
sense—it must be given but in order to be given it must also have been granted.
There is no dialectic here. Rather, we might say it is only the European who has
ever been both master and slave. This is his drama, held in the body, and enacted
in the world, he has to have. The exception will have been a power given by an
Other to selves who, in taking it and its accompanying knowledge on, are supposed
to have been provided, in this give and take, their own confirmation. But the pre-
text is never truly grounded, never truly granted, never truly given. Europe is
constantly disestablished by what it seeks to envelop, which, in and out of turn,
envelops it. What surrounds the European even in his midst is the native inform-
ant Gayatri Spivak identifies as a creation text for a world of exception, against, but
nonetheless within, the general antagonism of earthly anarrhythmia and displacement. The paradox of the pre-text is thus that being exceptional can no more be
taken than it can be given and can no more be claimed than it can be granted. This
simultaneity of being-master and being-slave is sovereignty's static, omnicidal
decline. This is what it is to be chained to the struggle for freedom, a "rational"
instrument run amok in place, as man's perpetually stilled motion.

1.

What does it mean to stand for improvement? Or worse, to stand for what business calls a "commitment to continuous improvement"? It means to stand for the
brutal speciation of all. To take a stand for speciation is the beginning of a diaboli-
cal usufruct. Improvement comes to us by way of an innovation in land tenure,
where individuated ownership, derived from increasing the land's productivity, is
given in the perpetual, and thus arrested, becoming of exception's miniature. This
is to say that from the outset, the ability to own—and that ability's first derivative,
self-possession—is entwined with the ability to make more productive. In order
to be improved, to be rendered more productive, land must be violently reduced
to its productivity, which is the regulatory diminishment and management of
earthly generativity. Speciation is this general reduction of the earth to productivity and submission of the earth to techniques of domination that isolate and
enforce particular increases in and accelerations of productivity. In this regard,
(necessarily European) man, in and as the exception, imposes speciation upon
himself, in an operation that extracts and excepts himself from the earth in order

to confirm his supposed dominion over it. And just as the earth must be forcefully speciated to be possessed, man must forcefully speciate himself in order to enact this kind of possession. This is to say that racialization is present in the very idea of dominion over the earth; in the very idea and enactment of the exception; in the very nuts and bolts of possession-by-improvement. Forms of racialization that both Michel Foucault and, especially and most vividly, Cedric Robinson identify in medieval Europe become *usufructed* with modern possession through improvement. Speciated humans are endlessly improved through the endless work they do on their endless way to becoming Man. This is the usufruct of man. In early modern England, establishing title to land by making it more productive meant eliminating biodiversity and isolating and breeding a species—barley or rye or pigs. Localized ecosystems were aggressively transformed so that monocultural productivity smothers anacultural generativity. The emergent relation between speciation and racialization is the very conception and conceptualization of the settler. Maintenance of that relation is his vigil and his eve. For the encloser, possession is established through improvement—this is true for the possession of land and for the possession of self. The Enlightenment is the universalization/ globalization of the imperative to possess and its corollary, the imperative to improve. However, this productivity must always confront its contradictory impoverishment: the destruction of its biosphere and its estrangement in, if not from, entanglement, both of which combine to ensure the liquidation of the human differential that is already present in the very idea of man, the exception. To stand for such improvement is to invoke policy, which attributes depletion to the difference, which is to say the wealth, whose simultaneous destruction and accumulation policy is meant to operationalize. This attribution of a supposedly essential lack, an inevitable and supposedly natural diminution, is achieved alongside the imposition of possession-by-improvement. To make policy is to impose speciation upon everybody and everything, to inflict impoverishment in the name of improvement, to invoke the universal law of the usufruct of man. In this context, continuous improvement, as it emerged with decolonization and particularly with the defeat of national capitalism in the 1970s, is the continuous crisis of speciation in the surround of the general antagonism. This is the contradiction Robinson constantly invoked and analyzed with the kind of profound and solemn optimism that comes from being with, and being of service to, your friends.

2.

At the end of the movie *Devil in a Blue Dress*, which is based on the Walter Mosley novel of the same name, and which Robinson delighted in teaching us how to read and see, what comes sharply into relief is the persistent life—which survives under the rule of speciation; which surrounds the speciation that would envelop it; which violates the speciation by which it is infused; which anticipates the speciation that would be its end—of a neighborhood of neat lawns, small family houses, and the

Black people who live in them. The movie's last line simultaneously belies and acknowledges speciation's permanent crisis. Is it wrong to be friends with someone you know has done bad things? asks the movie's protagonist, Easy Rawlins. All you got is your friends, replies Deacon Odell. That's right. That's all. Tomorrow the cops could come back, or the bank, bringing the violence of speciation, against which there is just this constant and general economy of friendship—not the improvement that will have been given in one-to-one relation but the militant preservation of what you (understood as we) got, in common dispossession, which is the only possible form of possession, of having in excess of anyone who has. Neither the globalization of possession-by-improvement nor the achievement of being exceptional is possible. We live (in) the brutality of their failure, which is a failure in and as derivation. Moreover, the sovereign declension (given, in a variation of Denise Ferreira da Silva's grammar as God: Patriarch—Possessive Individual—Citizen) is a derivative—a rigid, reified, securitized understanding of difference. Meanwhile, in the scene it constantly sets on Easy's porch, in Joppy's bar, at John's Place (the illegal speakeasy above a grocery store), *Devil in a Blue Dress* keeps reminding us that the task at hand is, as Manolo Callahan would say, to renew our habits of assembly, which implies a turn, a step away from the derivative. We ain't studying the failure, just like Easy ain't studying no job. We ain't trying to enter the declension that instigates what it implies: the (necessarily failed) separation, speciation, and racialization—the enclosure and settlement—of the earth. The play, as Callahan and Nahum Chandler teach us, is to desediment, to exfoliate, to renew the earthly and inseparable assembly, the habitual jam, by way of and in the differentiation of what will be neither regulated nor understood. All we got is us in this continual giving away of all. And, as Robinson also took great care to teach us in his critical admiration of Easy's friend Mouse, who is always about to blow somebody's nose off, all depends upon our readiness to defend it.

3.

Here is the famous passage on slavery in *Elements of the Philosophy of Right* where the "not yet"—its phase as mere "natural human existence"—of the universal appears as a tainted and unnecessary remedy:

> If we hold firmly to the view that the human being in and for himself is free, we thereby condemn slavery. But if someone is a slave, his own will is responsible, just as the responsibility lies with the will of a people if that people is subjugated . . . Slavery occurs in the transitional phase between natural human existence and the truly ethical condition; it occurs in a world where a wrong is still right. Here, the wrong *is valid*, so that the position it occupies is a necessary one.[1]

---

1   G. W. F. Hegel, *Elements of the Philosophy of Right*, ed. Allen W. Wood, trans. H. B. Nisbet (Cambridge: Cambridge University Press, 1991), 88. Emphasis in original.

This "not yet" of the universal, of global history, is subsequently reinforced when Hegel says, "The same determination [absolute right] entitles civilized nations to regard and treat as barbarians other nations which are less advanced than they are in the substantial moments of the state."[2] But before then, Hegel immediately turns from the first passage and towards the subject of "taking possession" and the "use of the thing." This "natural entity"—the thing—exists only for its owner "since this realized externality is the use or employment to which I subject it, it follows that *the whole use* or employment of it is *the thing in its entirety*."[3] But then Hegel reaches a problem, just after paradoxically asserting the necessary rectitude of the necessary wrong of slavery in progressive history.

> If the whole extent of the use of a thing were mine, but the abstract ownership were supposed to be someone else's, the thing as mine would be wholly penetrated by my will . . . while it would at the same time contain something impenetrable by me, i.e. the will, in fact the empty will, of someone else.[4]

He calls this a relationship of "absolute contradiction" and then introduces the Roman idea of "*usufructus*."[5] In theory, Hegel is addressing feudal property rights, with their shared ownership. But it is he in "natural human existence," who has failed, as Hegel says in his previous consideration of slavery, to take "possession of himself and become his own property." Usufruct demands this natural entity be "subordinated to its useful aspect." Hegel speaks of Roman and feudal property but his concern is world history, this (necessarily European) world where a wrong is still right. His concern is with how to become one's own property and with the usufruct that intitiates and confounds this project. Improvement is granted and haunted by an illusory and impenetrably empty will.

4.

The moment you say it is mine because I worked it and improved it, or you say that I am me because I worked on myself and improved myself, you start a war. And by misattributing the initiation of this war to nature, you then codify this war as the (anti)social contract.

It is said that the (anti)social contract and the public sphere it creates is a reaction to feudalism and absolutism. But this is only half the story, and an inaccurate half at that. Perhaps it's better to think of the (anti)social contract as emerging, as Angela Mitropoulous says, not in opposition to absolutism but as

---

2 Ibid., 376.
3 Ibid., 90. Emphasis in original.
4 Ibid.
5 Ibid., 91.

the democratization of sovereignty. Even that might have had an inadvertently anarchic quality, as every man considered himself a king. But the (anti)social contract not only reacts to, while also reflecting, absolutism, making every home/castle/hovel a hall of mirrors, it also emerges as a way to explain and justify the violence of European man. Everyone from Adam Ferguson to Kant tries to explain why the Africans, Asians, and indigenous people being extermi- nated and enslaved are so much less warlike than Europeans. The Crusades misled Europeans into believing their brutality was part of humanity rather than an exception, even as religious war gave them a taste for blood that they could not ignore. So the (anti)social contract emerges less to confront absolut- ism than to contain the obvious historical exceptionalism of European savagery. Clearly the world could not be ordered around good and evil without some dire consequences for Europe. Those who conceive of the (anti)social contract mistake the wars it instigates: wars of sovereigns against contractors, and of contractors against each other, and of contractors against those whom Bryan Wagner describes as "being subject to exchange without being a party to exchange," the ones not quite accurately called third parties in a formulation that is misleading not only because they are not parties to what passes for exchange but also because they are innumberable and un(ac)countable even in having been accumulated, even in having been financialized. Perhaps, in this regard, it would be even better to think of the (anti)social contract as emerging against a history of revolt: the peasant revolts that buried European feudalism, and which Robinson understands as "the socialist exchange" comprising Marxism's anthropological (under)ground is the revolt of nature, prosecuted by those who are made to stand in for nature, having been philosophically rele- gated to some essentially paradoxical state of nature, by the ones who seek to engineer nature's subordination to and within the socioecological disaster of improvement.

This is to say, again, that the political half of the story, in which the social contract is understood as improvement rather than its ge(n)ocidal imposition, is wrong and incomplete. The (anti)social contract is not only a political theory but also an economic practice: the practice of the juridical regulation and anti- socialization of exchange in the imposition of improvement. In particular, the social contract specified the individuation of its parties. Individuals now must be formed in order to enter into contract. And the economic contract emerges not in exchange but from the idea that ownership derives from improvement. As a result it is not simply the individual, but rather the individual capable of self-improvement who must and can enter into the contract. The self-improving individual can also be thought of as the self-accumulating individual: not possessive (this is stasis without movement), not acquiring (this still bears the trace of anarchic exchange), but self-accumulating—that is, property-gathering in order to put property to work, including and most especially the properties of the self that can be deployed and improved while being posited as eternal and absolute. "Properties of the self" is not a pun here. Properties that can be accumulated and put to work include race, religion, and gender but also class, standing, trust, thrift, reliability, and punctuality. These can all be used to improve where to improve is to own, and own more, and thus set in motion further accumulation of self, others, and nature that all might be put to work.

Maybe it can be stated this way: ownership emerges in Europe as usufruct, in the improvement of land that grants and justifies it. It is extended and diffused throughout the regime the social contract defines in the self-ownership that will have taken its completed form in the individual—that brutal, brittle crystallization of an always and necessarily incomplete melding of subject and object. Ceaselessly at work in the task of making everything, including himself, subject to being put to work, the European is the usufruct of man. Man's endless improvement, in which necessity is enforced as an absolute contingency, is fixed in European thought as the vicious grasping of its objects, including itself. The historical unfolding of this fixation on fixing, the murderous interplay of capture and improvement, is given in and as *self*-improvement-in-*self*-accumulation's violence towards whatever shows up at the rendezvous of differentiation, incompletion, and affection. The constantly changing activity of what appears to what appears as the self as the continual undoing of the very idea of the self and its eternally prospective completion-in-improvement can only be met, from the self's myopic and impossible perspective, with a nasty combination of regulation and accumulation. The one who accumulates does so at the expense of what it takes to be its others—women, slaves, peasants, beasts, the earth itself. Thus the social contract, as a contract between the improving and accumulating ones, is inscribed upon the flesh of those who cannot be, and in any case refuse to be, a party to antisocial exchange under the terms of the (anti)social contract. Meanwhile, as much as the contractors are united in a strategy to subject to usufruction whatever cannot or will not be a (numerable, individuated) party to antisocial exchange, they are also dedicated to killing each other, to war in and as their beloved public carried out in the name of the improvement of that public and its problems—that is, its denizens. The self-accumulating individual's war, his total mobilization against the innumerable and against his fellows under the sign of ownership as improvement, carried out in order to prevent the recrudescence of the natural, renders irredeemable the very premise of the (anti)social contract.

And every subcontract within the (anti)social contract must result in improvement. It's not a matter of both parties being satisfied with what they have exchanged. Such a contract was not just badly made but at odds with the desired identity of the contractors. And here we can put it the other way around: the social contract is conceived by the political theorist also as a contract amongst those capable of self-improvement, or what they called progress, and this is why it was essentially destructive of the notions of exchange encountered amongst feudal rebels (Robinson's *Anthropology of Marxism* is instructive here) or of exchange encountered amongst Africans who would rather move elsewhere than enter into conflict to gain improvement (Robinson's *Black Marxism* is instructive here). Ferguson and Kant both say war is about improvement of the European race. And Robinson teaches us that this is carried out as a violent intra-European racialization of difference, a continually barbaric festival in which incursion and the instantiation of improvement as militarily enforced externalities produce Europe, and then the globe, as dead and deadly bodies politic, monsters whose mechanized, drone-like simulations of spirit regulate the social with the kind of latex affability and latent menace commonly associated with police commissioners and university provosts. Antisocial sociability is the basis of the social contract. In the end, improvement is war, which is why the public sphere is war, and why the private—in its anti- and ante-individual impurity, as refuge even under constant pressure—is a porch.

The (anti)social contract is haunted by the economic contract, which is not a contract of exchange like one might find in friendship, but a contract based on the claim to ownership of oneself, others, and nature that is always tied to what more one can make of, which is to say accumulate in and through, oneself, others, and nature. In other words, the expanding universe of ownership took a contractual form that was not limited, as is sometimes supposed, to free individuals—that is, to the European subject imagined by the European theorist; it is a contractual form, rather, that requires broad-spectrum contact as the material ground of its exclusive and exclusionary network. What makes it truly dangerous is that it could never get free of that from which it wished to distinguish itself; what is truly dangerous to it is that what is forced to grant its exception can refuse the contract to which it is a third (or an innumerable or a non) party. Exchange, on the other hand, is a practice that prevents accumulation at, and as the elimination of, its source—the self-improving individual. Instead, exchange, given in and as the differential and differentiating entanglement of social life, even under the most powerful forms of constraint and regulation, is about a social optimum.

5.

George Clinton teaches us this:

> I'm always waiting to see what dance they're gonna do, because dance is always changing. But I trust the fact that funk affects the booty. So when I see somebody doing some type of dance, I always try to figure out what groove does it take to make the booty move like that? I'm really a bootyologist. I don't just look at it cause it looks good, but how can I make sure with my music, the booty is at its optimum?[6]

6 Conversation with Jeff Mao at the Red Bull Music Academy, quoted in Matthew Trammell, "How to Stay Cool as Fuck Forever, According to George Clinton," *The Fader* (May 14, 2015), available at thefader.com.

And Jacques Derrida teaches us to ask:.

> When will we be ready for an experience of freedom and equality that is capable of respectfully experiencing that friendship, which would at last be just, just beyond the law, and measured up against its measurelessness?[7]

It's just that we could only learn these lessons from them in having learned first from Cedric Robinson that the social optimum derives from social wealth, stepping out only to step back in all good, optimally, even under absolute duress, as the preservation in friendship of the socio-ontological totality. Like him, we look forward to getting back to the optimum we never left.

---

7   Jacques Derrida, *The Politics of Friendship*, trans. George Collins (London and New York: Verso, 2005), 306.

The Black Radical Tradition

Part Two

The Black Radical Tradition

Chapter 6

The World We Want

An Interview with Cedric and Elizabeth Robinson

Jordan T. Camp and Christina Heatherton

Cedric and Elizabeth Robinson have influenced generations of scholars, activists, and community journalists. Their work is a product of conversations through the global struggles against racial capitalism, militarism, and imperialism. Accordingly, their conclusions arrive through dialogue both with the world and with each other. Together, they co-hosted the *Third World News Review*, a weekly television and radio show in Santa Barbara. Elizabeth Robinson was the advisor and associate director for media for KCSB 91.9 FM in Santa Barbara. She produces the weekly radio show *No Alibis* and is a longtime grassroots activist and community radio advocate. This two-part interview took place in Robinson's home in Santa Barbara, California, in December 2013 and 2015.

Heatherton: This interview is taking place partially in celebration of the thirtieth anniversary of *Black Marxism: The Making of the Black Radical Tradition*, first published in 1983 by Zed Press and republished in 2000 by the University of North Carolina Press with a foreword by Robin D. G. Kelley.[1] Reflecting on the past thirty years, how do you both feel about the book's reception?

Cedric Robinson: I have been deeply appreciative of the reception. The book was written in an extraordinary frenzy of work. In a sense, it was an attempt to respond to several remarkable moments in American scholarship, most directly of course Harold Cruse and, in terms of the style, Immanuel Wallerstein. Cruse's *Crisis* opened an extraordinary space of recalling that there had been a radical Black intellectual past.[2] As a participant, he had every right to recall it in the terms that he did. But in doing so he, in a sense, succumbed to the conceit that I was addressing—that radicalism is dependent upon an intelligentsia. One of the things that I've been most impressed by is *Black Marxism*'s extraordinary following. I expected the book to be a site from which people did

---

1 Cedric J. Robinson, *Black Marxism: The Making of the Black Radical Tradition* (1983; Chapel Hill: University of North Carolina Press, 2000).

2 Harold Cruse, *The Crisis of the Negro Intellectual: A Historical Analysis of the Failure of Black Leadership* (New York: New York Review of Books, 1967); Immanuel Wallerstein, *The Modern World System* (New York: The Academic Press, 1974), and Wallerstein, *The Modern World System II* (New York: Academic Press, 1980).

work. Those whose work has come after *Black Marxism* have deepened the original work.

Elizabeth Robinson: In the same way that Cedric was jousting with Cruse, he was certainly doing the same with C. L. R. James. At the time he was writing, there was new attention being paid to people like Amilcar Cabral and others in Africa and the West within leftist progressive thought. This happened while we were living in England for the first time. There was an anniversary of the Paris Commune and a lot of focus on Marx and Marxism there, much more than in the United States, where universities were focused on Freud, psychology, and so forth. These things all informed the work that you started doing.

CR: In a certain sense, my own training in the Cold War incited me to do something of this nature. We had gotten a grant from the Ford Foundation for *Black Marxism*. When we went to the foundation's annual gathering of past and present recipients, I was astounded by the depth of fear that established the ceiling of work that could be done with respect to the Left at the time. A British editor for Zed Press [which eventually published *Black Marxism*] later commented that he never encountered as much fear about the Left in his own country as he had in the United States. There was a compelling impulse to try and get something better on page for both Americans and those beyond.

Heatherton: I'm guessing the Ford Foundation didn't support a lot of projects like *Black Marxism* during that period.

CR: Actually I was the first recipient who was supported to go outside the United States. My fellow recipients of that year were confounded by the book's subject and astounded by the choice to do work outside the United States.

Camp: As you've described, *Black Marxism* was intended as an intervention in multiple conversations. It contributed to debates about the origins and development of the world capitalist system among your colleagues at SUNY-Binghamton, including Immanuel Wallerstein. It was also the product of dialogues with your colleagues at the Institute of Race Relations in London, such as A. Sivanandan, Jenny Bourne, Colin Prescod, Paul Gilroy, Hazel Waters, Lou Kushnick, and others. Can you talk about the transatlantic conversations that you were participating in at the time—specifically as you developed the concept of racial capitalism? How was it shaped by those dialogues?

CR: There is a kind of liberal historiography about race which sees it as thin and superficial and presumably antithetical to capitalism. My research revealed racializations which anticipated capitalism. This is the context, the field, the very cultural tapestry in which capitalism develops. I was trying to make the argument that race became a way of controlling labor. I was unsatisfied with the notion that in the modern new world experience, there had only been one labor force. There were many academic propositions that insisted that that was the case. I was trying to burrow through these imaginary histories, particularly imaginary American histories.

My own experience as a young man was with a multiplicity of ethnicities: Mexican, Chinese, Asian, particularly Japanese, and so forth. I saw how many communities had accepted a certain kind of amnesia about their past. I was stunned by my Nisei [second-generation Japanese American] peers in high school and university who knew less about their experience than I did. I grew close to several of them and inquired about their parents and their grandparents. I wondered why they knew so little about their past. Why, for example, did my friend Sandra not realize that she had been born in a relocation camp? I was trying to make sense of an accumulation of experiences, of multiple forms of abuse, expropriation, oppression. I wanted *Black Marxism* and subsequent works to constantly challenge duality as an appropriate racial configuration. Concealed behind the privileging of one particular oppression was a failure to recognize those moments when there was a convergence, an overlap, as well as resistance to those oppressions.

Heatherton: You've mentioned some of the events that were happening in the production of *Black Marxism*. I want to invite you to talk a little bit more about other events in the late 1970s and early 1980s that shaped the research and writing of the book.

ER: The first time we lived in England and moved from one social context to another, we saw how race played out differently. We had encounters where, for example, we were each identified as Pakistanis—whereas most people in the United States would rarely put us in the same racial category. In that context, I discovered that Arabs were not considered white. With the conflict between the British and the Irish in the 1970s, we also encountered very negative reactions to Irish people, the telling of "Paddy" jokes and the like, even among progressive British people. These were all significant realizations that were very important to the research Cedric did, especially his work on the role of the Irish. During our second period in England in the early 1980s, we encountered a different notion of Blackness altogether. The uprisings in Brixton had occurred. We explored those things at the Institute of Race Relations in London where people very warmly embraced Cedric's work.

CR: The first time we were in Britain we also encountered Veronica Sankey, who had just arrived in Britain from Nigeria. She was Irish and a raconteur. I have never heard anyone tell stories like she did. She had gone to Nigeria in about 1948. On the ship with her was a man named Francis Nkrumah, who became her son's godfather. She had lived in a British colony and subsequently in the Nigerian Republic. She was an Irish woman who married a Black man, so she was doubly cursed in the eyes of the English. Because she came from an Irish Republican past, she deeply appreciated her expulsion from the colonial society. To a certain extent, the beginnings of our appreciation for the Irish experience came through her.

One day she showed up at our house with a woman who had been out of a convent for about a week, an Irish woman.

ER: May I just add that she had come from a cloister in which the women were not allowed to speak. This woman had been there for years.

CR: There was a huge silk screen of Angela Davis on the wall. This woman walked in, looked at Angela Davis's image, and the first words out of her mouth were, "You know they framed her." [*Laughter.*] We had many encounters with remarkable Irish women, not only in England but in Central America, places like Nicaragua, and so forth.

Camp: Let me ask you about another famous political prisoner and Black revolutionary of this period, Nelson Mandela. We witnessed various commemorations and co-optations following Mandela's death. The struggle against apartheid spurred intense debates about the relationship between race and class and the apartheid state, debates which influenced liberation movements as well as the social sciences. To what extent did these debates inform your theoretical work around racial capitalism?

CR: I think I became much more aware of that later on. In the period of writing *Black Marxism*, the anti-apartheid movement was a ghost in the world.

ER: One of the people who had been involved with *Third World News Review*, almost from its inception in 1980, was a young man named Peter Shapiro who was entirely focused on the apartheid horror and the freeing of Nelson Mandela. I think the anti-apartheid movement may have had more impact on some later things.

Camp: Your book *Forgeries of Memory and Meaning* demonstrates how apartheid became an instrument of American capital. You interrogate how appeals to a mythical racial unity have helped justify class formations in the United States. In doing so, you offer a rather complicated analysis of whiteness as a system of class discipline. Can you elaborate on this insight?[3]

---

3   Cedric J. Robinson, *Forgeries of Memory and Meaning: Blacks and the Regimes of Race in American Theater and Film before World War II* (Chapel Hill: University of North Carolina Press, 2007).

CR: The American context is still to be fully realized, in my thinking. Recently I've been reading historical research into "poor white trash." I am fascinated by this formation. One of my current students is researching white women in Appalachia. She's lived there for many years. I'm trying to get her to think about their political consciousness. The rebellions and resistances that were emerging from the poor whites before and during and after the Civil War is of real significance in terms of the constant reinvention of whiteness.

Another area that I'm currently fascinated with is the intersection of gender and Black studies. I think I would've written some things differently in *Black Marxism* if I had been more aware. Jennifer Morgan's *Laboring Women* is just a brilliant intervention.[4] It is so central to encounter plantations in Barbados that are all female and to begin to transfer our sense of the fundamental economy of slave production and how African and Black women were involved in it. Talk about the kind of resistance that some African women put up in the nineteenth century in West Africa and elsewhere! I allude to them in my description of the nanny towns in Jamaica, but there's so much more to discuss.

ER: I think of the conversation you had with H. L. T. Quan about *Black Marxism* and feminism in *Race & Class*.[5] *An Anthropology of Marxism* also explores the role of women, not just in resistance but also in the practice of Christianity.[6]

Camp: One thing that was really vivid for me in *Black Movements in America* was its focus on the centrality of Black women's activism in the freedom movement—particularly as carried out by figures like Ella Baker and Fannie Lou Hamer.[7]

CR: I was just bowled over when I read Erica Edwards's *Charisma and the Fictions of Black Leadership*. I thought, "Oh my goodness, this is a bold thesis which reflects what Baker was saying so many years earlier." Erica's thesis describes, in effect, how a gendered political construction is exchanged for political currency.[8]

Heatherton: In addition to this being the thirtieth anniversary of the publication of *Black Marxism*, 2013 also marks the 150th anniversary of the Emancipation Proclamation, a historical event depicted in films such as *Lincoln*, *Django Unchained*, and *Twelve Years a Slave*. *Forgeries* revisits this moment. You

---

4   Jennifer L. Morgan, *Laboring Women: Reproduction and Gender in New World Slavery* (Philadelphia: University of Pennsylvania Press, 2004).

5   H. L. T. Quan, "Geniuses of Resistance: Feminist Consciousness and the Black Radical Tradition," *Race & Class* 47, no. 2 (2005): 39–53.

6   Cedric J. Robinson, *An Anthropology of Marxism* (Oxford: Ashgate, 2001).

7   Cedric J. Robinson, *Black Movements in America* (New York and London: Routledge, 1997).

8   Erica Edwards, *Charisma and the Fictions of Black Leadership* (Minneapolis: University of Minnesotta Press, 2012).

describe how film emerged at the very moment in which the slave system had disintegrated and, as you say, a new racial regime was being stitched together. You argue that motion pictures critically mobilized racial imaginaries that were tied to the needs of finance capital. Can you explain the concept of racial regimes and its importance in analyzing the relationships between race and class, culture, and capitalism?

CR: What I wanted to stress in *Forgeries* is that racial regimes are inventions. As inventions—and this is something that I wanted the movement to hear—resistances are always leaving residues. As E. P. Thompson said with respect to the English worker and the British working class, there is going to be documentation of rebellion, resistance, outcry, and so forth.[9] In *An Anthropology of Marxism*, for example, I draw on Franciscans in the twelfth and thirteenth centuries who attended the trials of people who claimed they were not heretics. I wanted to show what inventions were used to constrain and contain the memory of the issues they were raising.

As I said in the introduction to *Forgeries*, racial regimes are not actualities but inventions; they constantly fray and fall apart, so they have to be repaired. We were talking about the advent of moving pictures at the end of the nineteenth and early twentieth centuries, how so many suppressions had to occur and what phenomenal possibilities were available through technology. Lester Walton, a Black theater owner and film critic, among other things, was so impressed by the impact of these moving pictures that in 1909 he wrote a column about an on-screen fabricated lynching. Whiteness was being contested in so many ways, and it responded through brutality, brutal violence, and what we would call pseudoscience: eugenics, sterilization, and so forth. Some of the earliest thinking about moving pictures recognized their function in repairing a racial regime.

The regime had to be reformulated so that it could capture all these fugitives. Earlier, we were talking about the film series *The Godfather*. How could you imagine transforming Italian immigrants into white people, Polish immigrants into white people, Irish immigrants into white people, Eastern Europeans, Central Europeans, Southern Europeans into white people? One way is that you had to invent an imaginary Blackness.

Camp: There's a continuity between *Forgeries* and *Black Marxism*: specifically your chapter on W. E. B. Du Bois and his *Black Reconstruction in America* (1935), which claims that the Reconstruction period was "one of the most extraordinary experiments of Marxism that the world, before the Russian Revolution, had seen."[10] In *Forgeries* you show how mythical constructions of

---

9   E. P. Thompson, *The Making of the English Working Class* (New York: Vintage Books, 1966).
10   W. E. B. Du Bois, *Black Reconstruction in America: An Essay Toward a History of the Part Which Black Folk Played in the Attempt to Reconstruct Democracy in America, 1860–1880* (1935;

the Reconstruction period obscured how Black workers and poor whites coop-
erated at that time. You argue that it was this concealment, this obfuscation of a
radical past, that was critical in finance capital's project to make European
immigrant workers identify with an ideology of whiteness. So there's a persistence in this focus, isn't there?

CR: And you know how remarkable it is because of its obfuscation. It took me
until the research on *Forgeries* to find it necessary to look at the etymological
origins of the term "slave." I have looked at slaves other than Africans and Blacks
and West Indians, but I don't think it had yet occurred to me that when you
talked about Black slaves, you were talking about transforming Blacks into
slaves. I'd done the research about the implications of that, but I hadn't put it as
simply or as directly as the linguistic evidence would allow. That's the answer to
the notion of racial regimes.

Heatherton: You highlight three figures in *Black Marxism*: W. E. B. Du Bois,
C. L. R. James, and Richard Wright, all of whom were critically shaped by
the 1930s. This was an era that witnessed war, depression, and the most
profound crisis in the history of world capitalism. These were conditions
that propelled many Black radicals to the Left. The Black freedom and labor
struggles of the period determined the liberation agenda for decades to
come. Could you talk about the importance of the 1930s to the Black Radical
Tradition?

CR: Part of the narrative that I was looking at was the degrading of Black labor
in the post–Civil War period, and particularly that of skilled and semi-skilled
laborers. This new racial regime that I'm looking at in *Forgeries* has to expel the
possibility of skilled and semi-skilled Black labor. In the same way that poor
whites remain excluded, it's rather remarkable that poverty is still portrayed as
an aberrational phenomenon. Now in public discourse, poverty is only refered
to obliquely. No public official will run on a platform of addressing the American
poor. There's a racialization of the American, not in Black/white terms, but in
terms of genetic inferiority. They are deemed biologically incapable, disqualified
from being Americans.

ER: One thing that I always want to do when you're talking about these imaginaries is to stand up and shout, "They're purposeful imaginaries!" It's not just
that they're fanciful; they're pernicious because they're so intended.

Camp: One thing *Black Marxism* shows is that Black radicalism and the turn
towards Marxist theory during the radical 1930s were fashioned in a crucible of

New York: The Free Press, 1992), 358.

imperialism and fascism. Indeed, *Black Marxism* critiques European Marxist history for not coming to terms with the impacts of racism and nationalism on the organization of labor under capitalism, and argues that radical intellectuals such as Du Bois, James, and Wright made that theoretical advance. It concludes that "Marxism was (and remains) a superior grammar" for the critique of racial capitalism. Can you reflect on the connection between Black radical historiography and Marxist theory?

CR: Over and over again we're led to misrepresentations of the responses and reactions to exploitation and oppression. I think I was reiterating Du Bois when I said Marxism is a superior grammar, as opposed to James in *Black Jacobins* trying to reconfigure the Haitian events in terms of class.

Camp: James argued that enslaved Africans working on the sugar plantations in Haiti were the most well-organized proletariat that the modern world had seen.[11]

CR: It's rhetorically powerful.

Camp: I was captivated by it, as you know.

CR: So were we all. So were we all. It's an intervention by James, making the case that Black people have a radical history. In a sense, I was making a rhetorical gesture. I knew it was easier for a radical intelligentsia to be drawn to James and Du Bois, but what about Wright? He came from the peoples to whom all the earlier parts of *Black Marxism* is addressing itself. He came from sharecroppers. We have to pay as close attention to him and to the dilemmas that he was addressing as we do to James and Du Bois. Wright was trying to say that capitalism doesn't always or ordinarily produce rational opposition: racial capitalism also produces a kind of insanity.

Heatherton: In the conclusion of *Black Marxism*, you note that Black radicalism remained a currency of resistance and revolt for revolutionaries like Angela Y. Davis. In the present moment, how do visions of liberation articulated by the Black Radical Tradition help us in developing a philosophy of praxis?

CR: Part of it is, in effect, developing a method of understanding the world around you. Our communities are marvelous phenomena. In a sense, the totalities that we have experienced historically have each, in the moment, seemed unassailable. At each crisis we shouldn't have survived, but we have. The current

---

11 C. L. R. James, *The Black Jacobins: Toussaint L'Ouverture and the San Domingo Revolution* (New York: Vintage Books, 1989), 86.

ordering of the world is so fragile. That is the lesson: in each historical moment, justice, social justice, and moral authority are questioned. They seem to be on their last legs, but that has never proven to be the case. That's one of the lasting lessons of *Black Marxism*.

ER: I always have thought that *Black Marxism* was badly received or not received at all. Without Robin D. G. Kelley's intervention, it wouldn't have been reprinted. The work that all of Cedric's students have done has, in some sense, saved it from what was meant to happen. Robin said something in his foreword [to the 2000 edition] about how the work is dangerous; it's not meant to be seen and read.[12]

One of the things I learned from Cedric is that there are these repetitions of the Black Radical Tradition. Sometimes it's scholarship and sometimes it's the audaciousness of individuals. Whether it's Oliver Cromwell Cox, Du Bois, or any number of people, their work has disappeared. My presumption is that this is the course that Cedric's work should have followed and often has. His book *Anthropology of Marxism*, and until recently *Terms of Order* were essentially unavailable. But the way younger scholars have taken up his work and pushed it, as Cedric has said, beyond where he intended it or was able to go, is critical.[13]

That, for me, is the lesson. This work will be buried unless there are people like all of you who are refusing to let it happen. It's not just Cedric's work, of course. The academy is not amenable to scholarship like this. It's not amenable to things that are meant to be transforming. So everybody's tasks are cut out for them. As Cedric says, we have not been defeated, but the attempts are there. It will probably take thirty years for the work to be really appreciated. In some ways, it's still invisible—as is *Forgeries,* unfortunately.

Part II

Heatherton: There's been a renewed interest in the Black Radical Tradition, particularly in wake of protests against police killings in Ferguson, Baltimore, Chicago, New York City, and beyond during 2014 and 2015. You both coauthored a piece titled "Ferguson, Gaza, and Iraq: An Outline of the Official Narrative in 'Post-Racial' America," which points out the difficulty of fighting racism in a world that considers itself post-racial. You make a compelling argument about how Ferguson was depicted in a "familiar, manageable, and seductive narrative" along the lines of the civil rights era of the 1960s and 1970s. You say that the freedom movement has been covertly reversed through race projects such as mass incarceration.[14] How do we think about freedom struggles when

---

12   Robin D. G. Kelley, "Foreword," *Black Marxism*, xi-xxiii.

13   Cedric J. Robinson, *Terms of Order: Political Science and the Myth of Leadership* (1980; Chapel Hill: University of North Carolina Press, 2016).

14   Cedric J. Robinson and Elizabeth Robinson, "Ferguson, Gaza, and Iraq: An Outline of the

those histories are presented as if they're resolved? How can we struggle against racism in a world that considers itself post-racial?

CR: Those of us who are active in the liberation movement are sensitive to when we can speak directly and candidly and when our listeners might be so alienated by hearing a bold truth that we might lose credibility with them. Obama's campaign in 2008 presented him as capable of turning America as a culture away from blatant, vicious racism. We were saying that that was merely an obfuscation, that the naked opposition to racial justice can only be encouraged by Obama's presidency. Obama's presidential success was supposed to have eviscerated racism, when in fact it reanimated it. In other words, beneath the surface, something very different was happening: not post-racialism but, in effect, the anticipation of the deployment of racism.

Jordan may remember that I used this exercise in my undergraduate courses: I had people look at the labels on their phones, their shoes, their shirts, and so forth, and imagine the conditions in which those people were working and the conditions in which they were living. It's really remarkable how seldom we think about the people who are feeding us and clothing us and the conditions in which they labor. Obama's presidency made American society more accepting by obscuring the fundamental nature [of labor].

Camp: In that same article, you note that Black and Brown people are targeted for surveillance, harassment, police violence, and state terror. You write that "Ferguson is about poverty and the lengths to which the state and its local tributaries have gone to control the poor." You conclude that "race and racism are merely covers for class."[15] We wondered if you could say more about this conception of the relationship between race and class?

ER: Well, that's a position that Cedric has certainly long held and that gets obscured very often. I see race mentioned a lot more than I see class. Racism is a moving concept—it appears when class interests become threatened. That's a really hard thing to grasp for a lot of people—that racism is not about color.

Camp: It turns out phenotypes have been poor indicators.

ER: I think it's about how narrowly we define race and how exclusive it becomes.

CR: A more narrow appropriation of it. That is one of the reasons why the Irish sections are in *Black Marxism*.

Official Narrative in 'Post-Racial' America," *Commonware*, September 4, 2013, commonware.com.
    15   Robinson and Robinson, "Ferguson, Gaza, and Iraq."

Heatherton: *Forgeries* offers a provocative quotation from Otis Madison: "The purpose of racism is to control the behavior of white people, not black people. For blacks, guns and tanks are sufficient."[16] Can you talk about why this is an important insight?

CR: We can describe this moment in many of the cultures with which we are most familiar as a modern phenomenon in historical terms. The blatant, vicious characterization of the Irish by English spokespersons, writers, and so forth has largely dissipated since the early part of the twentieth century. Irish communities carry these wounds much longer than the rest of us. Irish historians reminded me of these earlier moments when they were defined as objects of vilification. As E. P. Thompson suggests, much of the vilification of Blacks was transferred from the Irish in the nineteenth century. Racism has the advantage of being able to move and transfer its disaffections from one group to another without being held accountable.

ER: Otis's quotation is a very clear way of addressing the issue: Who is racism serving?

Heatherton: How do you understand his claim that the purpose of racism is to control the behavior of white people?

CR: Well, as I understood it, "white people" is a voluntary identification. If you put enough pressure on European communities, they will re-imagine their identity in terms of race—in terms of whiteness. It embraces extraordinarily distinctive people. One of the things we found when we went to England the first time in the 1970s was how many South Asians had been considered white in England. But it was not a clear, all-or-nothing sort of division. Many of the South Asians we met were moving away from white working-class identities, white middle-class identities, English identities, and so forth, and toward a kind of militancy which whiteness would've denied them. After the militancy, they were often reenergized by their ethnic and historical identities.

Heatherton: In "Ferguson, Gaza, and Iraq," you're careful to describe the ways in which the media sanctioned the death of Michael Brown during the very same summer that they were sanctioning the deaths of Palestinians in Gaza. Can you say a bit more about understanding both processes at the same time?

CR: The basic division of humanity between the rational and the irrational has for centuries been coded by color. The current debate over who has the right to

---

16 Quoted in Robinson, *Forgeries*, 82.

atomic weapons and who is going to hold managerial authority over weapons of mass destruction continues that.

ER: One thing we wanted to say in the Ferguson piece is that this is not new; this has been going on and on and on. In the mid to late 1990s, there was a group in Los Angeles who published a book documenting police killings. I had a bunch of students record a PSA with me in which they read from the book, reciting the names of each person and a description of the circumstances of their death. Young people, old people, and people of all races had died at the hands of the police. The issue was not just about policing; it was and continues to be about determining legitimate and illegitimate authority.

Camp: You both recently produced the last episode of the *Third World News Review* in 2015, a show which had been airing in Santa Barbara for three decades. You were also awarded the 2015 Media Access Award by TVSB in Santa Barbara for building community and increasing diversity in local media. Can you talk about the importance of community-based media in providing an alternative to the corporate media?

ER: Well, where else are you going to hear it? That is my short answer. Corporate media is critical in the way it constructs our reality. Creating a little alternative space is always really important; it's always about being able to think about things differently. You might not be able to do anything this very moment, but at least you can hold up some alternate possibilities. That's part of what alternative media does.

I think social media is doing a little bit of this sometimes, but it's not the same as coming together in person and talking about something. There's something about the dialogic nature of community media that makes it different than social media. Or maybe I'm just an old dog. I don't know. I'll allow for both things.

CR: Well, I won't. (*Laughter.*) We had this conversation thirty years ago when you were thinking about *No Alibis* and I was thinking about *Third World News Review*. We continue to have this debate about format, presentation, and so forth. Eventually each of us reconciled the corporate media with the theater of distraction. Every now and then the Third World perspective leaks into the very severely restricted space of that theater. Have you seen the Obama imitation that Keegan-Michael Key and Jordan Peele do?

Heatherton: The anger translator?

CR: Yeah. And they couldn't keep that up because it started bouncing against the wall of actual Black and Latino anger.

Heatherton: That's a great point. I would love to figure out exactly when they stopped doing it, when parody maybe started cutting too close to the bone. One last question: What do you both consider the most important thing for activists today to grapple with? What are your resources for hope?

CR: Simply walking down the streets of Goleta and in many locations in Santa Barbara, you get a sense of the vivid and vivacious alternatives that exist. That's politically crucial, but even more encouraging are the lyrics of much of what they play on the popular music stations. When Elizabeth and I came back from England in 1971, we were listening to the radio while we were driving across the Bay Bridge and marveling at how acute Marvin Gaye's representation of Black ideas were and how stunning and direct his critiques were. But of course, he was writing about a whole culture, a whole community's critiques.

ER: Cedric answered this in probably the boldest way when he was at University of California, Irvine, a couple of years ago. He'd done a two-day seminar there. At the end of it, people wanted to know, When does it all get better? Cedric said something to them about the struggle being important, regardless of whether or not you are going to win. If it's some kind of salvation you're looking for, I don't think it's going to happen. It's not like a football game that's going to end with your team either winning or losing. We have to understand that there is value in trying, not in winning. It's important to recognize small victories and celebrate them and one another. There is not just victory at the end of the struggle. There's value in recognizing that. Trying to change things has a value in and of itself.

I've told students in the past that they can make choices about what their lives are going to be like when they leave the university. I've told them that most of them are going to go into all-white environments or racially and ethnically segregated environments, unless they choose to do something different. And you can choose to do something different. You can choose to participate in racist and classist structures, or you can choose not to. That is really important.

I want people to be free to enjoy the fullness of their experiences, whatever they are, wherever they are. Cedric was talking earlier about being able to say boldly what it is we think about something. There's so many instances where we can't do that. To try to create more spaces where we can at least approximate it, where we can talk openly and freely with each other, that is important.

Chapter 7

What Is This Black in the Black Radical Tradition?

George Lipsitz

Three miracles seem to characterize the history of Black people in the United States. The very survival of Black people in the face of murderous brutality and genocidal intent qualifies as a miracle. The enduring reality of Black humanity in a society that has used every means at its disposal to destroy Black dignity and deny Black people the opportunity to exercise their full humanity appears miraculous. The historical record of democratic aspiration and achievement by Black people, of creating democratic opportunities for themselves and extending them to others, seems to defy normal rational explanations. Despite the social death at the center of the slave system and the organized abandonments of today's neoliberal capitalism, despite beatings, lynchings, shootings, mass incarceration and systematic impoverishment, Black people have survived and thrived. In slavery, African people in the Americas owned virtually nothing, not even the skin on their backs. They had every reason to give in to despair. Yet they somehow managed to survive, to extend recognition and respect to each other while in bondage, and to maintain a commitment to the linked fate of all humans. Time and time again, Black people have countered vicious dehumanization with determined and successful re-humanization. Insisting on their own humanity and the humanity of all people, even that of their oppressors, they have been at the forefront of what Dr. King called "the bitter but beautiful struggle" for a more just and better world. From the egalitarian politics of abolition democracy in the wake of the Civil War and the participatory democracy of the civil rights movement to the contemporary insurgencies waged under the banners of #BlackLivesMatter and #SayHerName, struggles for Black survival and Black humanity have repeatedly linked the termination of existing racist policies to the creation of new democratic practices and institutions. Forced to cope with the nadir of political evil over centuries, Black people have responded consistently by forging advanced concepts of a deeply politicized love. Perhaps precisely because brutality and oppression can make people decidedly unlovable, African people in America have been adept at finding ways to perceive something left to love inside themselves and in others. That ability has enabled their survival, the preservation of their humanity, and their emergence as the nation's foremost champions of democracy and social justice. The people who were systematically denied access to the fruits and benefits of democratic citizenship and social membership turned out to be the people who valued democracy the most and who did the most to extend it to others.

Cedric Robinson has demonstrated that the three miracles were not really miracles at all, but rather products of a collective intelligence developed over generations of struggle. In *Black Marxism*, Robinson defines the Black Radical Tradition as "the continuing development of a collective consciousness informed by the historical struggles for liberation and motivated by the shared sense of obligation to preserve the collective being, the ontological totality."[1] Thus in many ways, the greatest achievement of the Black community was itself, its emergence as an aggrieved and insurgent polity committed to social justice. The "Black" in the Black Radical Tradition is a politics rather than a pigment, a culture rather than a color. Yet this Blackness does not presume a unified homogenous community with only one set of interests, needs, and desires. On the contrary, Robinson's research reveals that the key building blocks for Black survival, Black humanity, and Black democracy came from the lower rungs of Black society, from the plantations and slave quarters, out of the contradictions of the rural regimes of slavery and debt peonage and the living conditions in ghettos of northern and western cities. Experience taught the Black poor and the Black working class that racial capitalism entailed "an unacceptable standard of human conduct"[2] that they needed to counter with a politics that was "inventive rather than imitative, communitarian rather than individualistic, democratic rather than republican, Afro-Christian rather than secular and materialist."[3]

Robinson's emphasis on political struggle as the main explanation for Black survival, humanity, and democracy reminds us not to confuse the grandiose aspirations and illusions of the powerful with the actual lived experiences of those they control. Slavery did mandate legally and militarily supported social death, but slaves worked assiduously and effectively each day, every day, each year, and every year to create a rich social life.[4] As Robinson argues, "Slavery gave the lie to its own conceit: one could not create a perfect system of oppression and exploitation."[5] Domination produces resistance, and resistance plants the seeds of a new society within the shell of the old. As Robinson explains in *Black Movements in America*, "The resistances to slavery were the

---

1 Cedric J. Robinson, *Black Marxism: The Making of the Black Radical Tradition* (Chapel Hill: University of North Carolina Press, 2000), 171.

2 Cedric J. Robinson, *Forgeries of Memory and Meaning: Blacks and the Regimes of Race in American Theater and Film Before World War II* (Chapel Hill: University of North Carolina Press, 2007), 308.

3 Cedric J. Robinson, *Black Movements in America* (New York and London: Routledge, 1997), 97.

4 Orlando Patterson, *Slavery and Social Death: A Comparative Study* (Cambridge: Harvard University Press, 1985); George P. Rawick, *From Sundown to Sunup: The Making of the Black Community* (Westport: Greenwood Press, 1973); Steven H. Marshall, *The City on the Hill from Below: The Crisis of Prophetic Black Politics* (Philadelphia: Temple University Press, 2011); Stephanie M. H. Camp, *Closer to Freedom: Enslaved Women and Everyday Resistance in the Plantation South* (Chapel Hill: University of North Carolina Press, 2004).

5 Robinson, *Black Movements in America*, 11.

principal grounds for the radically alternative political culture that coalesced in the Black communities of the eighteenth and nineteenth centuries, the era of revolutionary, liberal and nationalist impulses among Europeans in North America."[6]

Declaring Blacks to be less than human could not make them so, even in the eyes of their oppressors. Research by John Blassingame, George Rawick, Sterling Stuckey, Herbert Gutman, and Stephanie Camp (among others) reveals how slaves fused African retention and New World invention to forge a culture that affirmed their humanity and the humanity of others.[7] They recognized this common humanity through multicultural, multiracial alliances with poor whites and others in maroon communities.[8] In colonial Louisiana, Blacks reached out to Native Americans for help in resisting slavery.[9] Slave owners, however, were less successful in preserving their own humanity. In order to maintain the illusion of complete control, they tortured, whipped, hanged, burned, and dismembered their "property" when it displayed signs of having human will.[10] Black people witnessed white people's inhumanity and pitied them. As early as the 1820s, David Walker argued that while whites lost the moral capacity to perceive the evil they enacted, they nonetheless knew "in their hearts" that Blacks were human. He argued that it was precisely this recognition that propelled their cruelty and brutality: they presumed that Blacks resented them and, if given the opportunity, would do to whites what whites had done to Blacks.[11] In his history of the New Orleans slave market, Walter Johnson notes a similar loss of humanity among slave owners. Whites invested more than money in the slave system; they looked to it to elevate them beyond the status of ordinary mortals and became outraged when their chattel refused to conform to the roles they had been assigned. Johnson notes:

> The greater the transformative hopes slaveholders took with them to the slave market, the more violent their reactions to the inevitable disappointment of their efforts to get real slaves to act like imagined ones . . . If they had to, they would use brutality to close the distance between the roles they imagined for themselves and the failings of the slaves they bought as props for their performance.[12]

---

6   Ibid., 19–20.

7   John Blassingame, *The Slave Community: Plantation Life in the Antebellum South* (New York: Oxford University Press, 1972); George P. Rawick, *From Sundown to Sunup*; Sterling Stuckey, *Slave Culture: Nationalist Theory and the Foundations of Black America* (New York: Oxford, 1987); Herbert Gutman, *The Black Family in Slavery and Freedom* (New York: Pantheon, 1976); Camp, *Closer to Freedom*.

8   Robinson, *Black Movements in America*, 13.

9   Ibid., 18.

10   Ibid., 20.

11   Marshall, *The City on the Hill*, 53.

12   Walter Johnson, *Soul by Soul: Life Inside the Antebellum Slave Market* (Cambridge: Harvard University Press, 1999), 206.

Although Black survival, humanity, and democracy required recognition of a linked fate and the production of practices capable of turning radical divisiveness into radical solidarity, the divide-and-conquer tactics of power did not produce a fully unified and uniform Black community. Robinson argues that the Black Radical Tradition in fact emerged from a split in the community: on one side, "a liberal, bourgeois consciousness" that was "packed with capitalist ambitions and individualist intuitions," a stance that sought access to the roles and rewards monopolized by whites,[13] and on the other a radical proletarian consciousness that sought to realize a higher moral standard than the one embraced by whites and their Black imitators.[14] It was this radical consciousness that W. E. B. Du Bois championed when he condemned the "dream of material prosperity" as the nation's emerging ethical and political goal. Du Bois believed that a people whose ancestors had been treated as objects of commerce had especially valuable knowledge about the shortcomings of capitalism, and he worried that commercial values would shatter the social reciprocity needed for the survival, humanity, and democratic hopes of the vast majority of the Black population.[15]

Robinson's location of the Black Radical Tradition in the practices and passions of the Black working class raises questions about how a resource-poor population without access to (much less control over) schools, conservatories, museums, publishing houses, or businesses could create and sustain a politics of survival, humanity, and democracy. In *Black Marxism* and *Black Movements in America*, Robinson describes the important roles played by unions, clubs, organizations, and political parties. In *Forgeries of Memory and Meaning*, he reveals how theater, film, and commercial products and venues served as contradictory sites where new social imaginaries could be envisioned and enacted. Scholarly studies of Black expressive culture reveal another important realm of endeavor where the weapons of the weak could be forged, honed, refined, and deployed without attracting excessive surveillance and suppression: the realm of expressive culture.

Robert Farris Thompson highlights the ways in which artistic creation has helped the Black working class to decorate the way to other worlds. He recounts the trajectory of stonemason Henry Dorsey of Brownsboro, Kentucky, who suffered an industrial accident at the age of twenty-five in 1922 that diminished his ability to hear. The impairment of his hearing made Dorsey eager to see more things, to take in visually what he could no longer register aurally. He left home and wandered across the nation, working on docks and railroads. Much of what he saw appalled him. His travels exposed him to repeated scenes of racial cruelty. Yet he also encountered diverse forms of Afro-diasporic creativity.

13   Robinson, *Black Movements in America*, 96.
14   Ibid., 96.
15   Marshall, *The City on the Hill*, 93–9.

As Dorsey walked through villages and small towns, along deserted road-ways and through farm fields, he witnessed the creativity of a people who, while often broke, were never broken. He noticed trees adorned with bottles, sculptures made up of automobile tires and hubcaps, and installations composed of scrap iron and discarded pieces of plastic. Dorsey felt that these eccentric creations had important work to do in the world. Bottles placed on trees could capture evil spirits and render them incapable of inflicting harm. The circular shape and previous functions of tires and hubcaps and the fluttering in the wind of pinwheels and streamers affirmed the power of movement and the people's right to it. Art made up of discarded trash instructed viewers to find value in devalued things and to discern multiple uses for every object.

After ten years on the road, Dorsey returned home to Kentucky and committed himself to decorating the house he had inherited from his father. He started by carving the names and birth dates of his children on a concrete tablet recessed in the wall of a chimney. He placed commemorative shells next to the initials of their first names. He assembled sculptures that evoked and expressed motion out of metal pipes, pulleys, and tractor tires, adorning them with plastic dolls, ice cube trays, and assorted parts from a washing machine. He marked the death of his sister by inscribing the details of her life on a headstone that he positioned in his yard on top of an iron strongbox and flanked by a one-wheeled locomotive rooted in the ground.

Thompson identifies these eccentric creations as important sites of moral instruction. He argues that they send a message about the importance of mastering things rather than complaining about them, about responding to injury and provocation with laughter and generosity. Thompson interprets Dorsey's redeployments of discarded objects as a lesson in parallel construction, a call for viewers to find more than a single function in any object and social situation. Dorsey's penchant for evoking motion through the use of seemingly static objects like hubcaps, automobile tires, and train wheels, coupled with his skill at bringing broken machines back to life by connecting them to pulleys, levers, and electrical motors, enacts the dramatic inversions, the unities of opposites characteristic of Afro-diasporic epistemologies all around the world.

These kinds of artistic proclivities and practices that Thompson highlights in the art of Henry Dorsey emerged organically and logically from a people whose survival depended upon improvisation. Quilt makers took patches of worn-out garments and cloth bags and stitched them into patterned bed covers that served as both sources of warmth and a material inventory of how patterns of the past persisted in the present.[16] Slaves who were forced to cut sugarcane on Louisiana plantations discovered possibilities in the stems of the cane plants. They drilled holes in the stems and turned them into reed instruments to make

---

16   Patricia A. Turner, *Crafted Lives: Stories and Studies of African American Quilters* (Jackson: University Press of Mississippi, 2009).

music to accompany dancing at secret late-night revels.[17] Dancing constituted another act of inversion. It turned the exploited work body valued only for its labor into an expression of personal value and virtuosity on the dance floor.

Henry Dorsey followed this honorable tradition of using material objects to create new temporal and spatial realities as a means of changing social relationships. He functioned as what Theophus Smith has described as the "conjure doctor." In expressive culture, medicine, and politics, the conjure doctor turns hegemony on its head by transforming the toxic into the tonic, disadvantage into advantage, humiliation into honor. Conjuring "transforms reality by means of prescribed operations involving a repertory of efficacious materials."[18] For Thompson, Dorsey's eccentric creations tell us, "If you know where you are going and where you are coming from, you can decorate the way to other worlds—the road to the ancestors and to God; and your name will merge forever with their glory."[19]

Thompson's formulation enables us to see the larger significance in Dorsey's seemingly small and eccentric artistic practices. They reflect a specific philosophy of life and art that contradicts many of the core premises of Enlightenment and post-Enlightenment art. As Donald Lowe has argued, it took the emergence of typographic culture to produce a new ideal of objective knowledge grounded in the separation of the content of knowledge from the actions of a knowing subject. Lowe explains that the elevation of visual knowledge in Western culture entailed privileging distance and judgment over close intersubjectivity.[20] In the Enlightenment and post-Enlightenment intellectual traditions of Euro-Americans, the road to the ancestors and to God is thus an abstract and interior journey. In the Afro-diasporic tradition, however, it is a practical and physical path. Thompson notes the pervasive presence of interruption, inversion, surprise, and disguise in Afro-diasporic art as ways of using material objects to transform social relations, to envision and enact new possibilities, and to make a way where there seems to be none.

"Inversion signifies perdurance," Thompson explains.[21] Being upside down in this world brings one closer to the realm of the ancestors, who possess the strength, experience, and wisdom that their descendants need. Connections to ancestors recruit new allies and expand the spheres of the present. Broken glasses and plates placed on the graves of the deceased symbolize the ruptures that death enacts across generations. Flowerpots decorated with green tinfoil and turned upside down at grave sites reflect light in a way that is understood as

17 Camp, *Closer to Freedom*, 73–4.
18 Theophus Smith, *Conjuring Culture: Biblical Formations of Black America* (New York: Oxford, 1994), 31.
19 Robert Farris Thompson, *Flash of the Spirit: African and Afro-American Philosophy* (New York: Vintage, 1984), 158.
20 Donald Lowe, *History of Bourgeois Perception* (Chicago: University of Chicago Press, 1983).
21 Thompson, *Flash of the Spirit*, 142.

the flash of the spirits of the dead as they travel to the other world. The roots of trees planted on grave sites seek out the world of the dead.[22] Henry Dorsey's seemingly modest and local artistic practices had world-making implications. They built on advanced abilities to embrace contradictions and adapt them, to produce art outside of official institutions without written sources, to participate in a collective process of re-creation that required no credential for entry.[23]

The artistic imaginary of Henry Dorsey manifested the enduring influence and impact of the Black Radical Tradition. During slavery, men and women slipped away to brush arbors in the woods for midnight ceremonies where they could pray in the African way. As a symbol of inversion, they gathered around overturned pots that symbolized their links to the world of their ancestors and their own pasts.[24] Their covert resistance exasperated the slave owners. The slaves' nighttime prayer meetings and social gatherings manifested a refusal to conform to their designated roles as property rather than people. One outraged slave owner complained that the "night is their day."[25] Thus time itself was turned on its head inside the slave community. The forced labor of slaves during the day, from sunup to sundown, created a world of comfort and ease for slave owners. It produced the products that a rapidly industrializing world required. At night, however, from sundown to sunup, slaves found the way to other worlds in the form of the community they created. At night, descendants of ancestors from diverse places who spoke diverse languages and practiced diverse religions used their linked fate as slaves to commit themselves to life and to one another.

They made music that had meaningful work to do in the world. It did not just express emotions, moods, and thoughts; it produced them. As musicologist Christopher Small explains, the supreme value in the music made by slaves and their descendants has been the preservation of the community. "Without a community for support," Small observes, "the individual is helpless, while with it he or she is invincible."[26] Long after legal slavery ended, the descendants of bondspeople preserved this epistemology and ontology. They expressed their love for one other by citing Proverbs 27:17: "As iron sharpens iron so one person sharpens another." People need people, not only for affection and security, but to become sharper, smarter, braver, and better. Individual actions can fill personal needs, but they also work to enable the entire community to survive.

Thompson's evidence about the role of expressive culture in Black survival, humanity, and democracy, coupled with Robinson's recognition of the existence of two distinct and opposing political cultures in the Black community, helps explain the dynamics and dimensions of the #BlackLivesMatter and

---

22   Ibid., 138, 142.

23   Christopher Small, *Music of the Common Tongue: Survival and Celebration in African American Music* (Middletown, CT: Wesleyan University Press, 1998), 86, 81.

24   Rawick, *From Sundown to Sunup*, 42–3.

25   Camp, *Closer to Freedom*, 69.

26   Small, *Music of the Common Tongue*, 86.

#SayHerName mobilizations that emerged in the wake of the unpunished kill-ings of Trayvon Martin, Michael Brown, Rekia Boyd, Tanisha Anderson, and so many others. When police officers and supervisors left Michael Brown's dead body to fester in the street for four hours in the hot summer sun, the politicians, preachers, professors, and pundits were not the first to respond; it was the people. Brown's stepfather, Louis Head, stood in the street with a sign he had made from a cardboard box that read, "Ferguson Police Just Executed My Unarmed Son!!!" A Twitter post featuring a photo of Michael Brown's dead body facedown on the asphalt declared, "I just saw someone die."[27] Within a week some 3.6 million posts on Twitter revolved around Brown's killing and responses to it.[28] Social media communications punctuated a feeling of shared temporality. Without the lag time inherent in print and electronic journalism or even Facebook, tweets gave participants and followers a sense of simultaneity, of acting together in real time. In addition, the hashtag "#Ferguson" gathered an enormous range of individual statements into a shared historical moment. Social media communication enabled demonstrators in St. Louis to plan and revise strategy in real time, to communicate with each other constantly, and to attract sympathizers from across the nation and around the world to their cause. The medium also offered an opportunity to challenge mainstream manipula-tions of the facts. When an article in the New York Times published one week after the killing on the day of Michael Brown's funeral declared that the teenager was "no angel" because he had "dabbled in drugs and alcohol," scuffled once with a neighbor, recorded a hip-hop song with profane lyrics, and lived in a neighborhood with "rough patches," Twitter lit up with the hashtag #NoAngel to challenge this effort to turn the victim into the perpetrator. "I am #NoAngel, so I guess I deserve to be murdered too. Yep, perfectly acceptable to gun down a person if they aren't a Saint."[29]

As police officers and prosecutors conspired to cover up the facts of the kill-ing and orchestrate a shameful exoneration of the officer who killed Michael Brown, they responded to the protests with massive and violent force. Police officers riding in mine-resistant armored vehicles pointed semiautomatic weap-ons at demonstrators and threatened to kill them. They fired concussion grenades, tear gas, plastic and rubber bullets, and chemical irritants at defense-less demonstrators. Yet young people from the St. Louis area and around the nation continued to flock to Ferguson to insist on their right to grieve the killing of Michael Brown and that his killer be held accountable. When they were attacked, the people fought back and were not ashamed of their actions. Tef Poe—activist, rapper, and participant in the Ferguson movement—explains:

---

27 Yarimar Bonilla and Jonathan Rosa, "#Ferguson: Digital Protest, Hashtag Ethnography, and the Racial Politics of Social Media in the United States," American Ethnologist 42, no. 1 (February 2015): 4.

28 Ibid.

29 Ibid., 9.

When we were at the scene, it was very combustible. Like in St. Louis when the police kill someone of color, it's very aggressive at the scene. A lot of us don't shy from the fact that it's aggressive. I wanted to be aggressive at the scene. I want you to know that if you're going to come to one of these communities where there's black folks and that you're going to pull your gun out and you're going to shoot, you will be met with resistance. This is what that resistance looks like. This is what it feels like. This is what it sounds like. We're going to curse at you. We're going to throw some stuff at you. We might even tip over a police car or two, depending on how we feel that day. But you will not just come into our communities and gun people down and be met with nothing. And when I said that, that's what I meant.[30]

Shocked by this affirmation of the right to resist unjust repression, reporters asked Tef Poe if he wasn't betraying the nonviolent legacy of Dr. King and the civil rights movement. They were referring, of course, to a rhetorical construction of the civil rights movement far removed from the movement that actually existed. This framework remembers the quiet dignity of Rosa Parks and the disciplined collective action of the Montgomery Bus Boycott while ignoring the dozens of prior confrontations between bus drivers and militant, profane, and combative Black women who repeatedly tested the boundaries of bus segregation.[31] It recalls the passive resistance to fire hoses and police dogs in Birmingham in 1963 but not the active hurling of rocks and bottles at police officers by angry Black youths that same year that finally forced the Department of Justice to intervene in that city. It embraces the willingness of Black college students to be beaten and humiliated for ordering hamburgers at lunch counters but erases the efforts at armed self-defense by the Deacons for Defense and the Black Panther Party. Aware of this complex history, Tef Poe rejected the effort to suppress effective means of struggle today by counterposing them against the reverence that white supremacy purports to have for the tactics (but not, of course, the goals) of Dr. King. Poe declared, "This ain't your mama's civil rights movement."

Missouri governor Jay Nixon hopped on Poe's statement in an effort to justify the brutal repression of the movement, presenting himself (and presumably the violence of the police and the National Guard) as the heirs to the legitimate and respectable civil rights movement while dismissing the people in the streets of Ferguson as criminals and hoodlums. He pointed to the prominence of a Black officer placed in charge of the National Guard troops, but said nothing about his own history as one of the state's most determined and resolute foes of school desegregation. Many white liberals and some members of the Black bourgeoisie took up Nixon's line of criticism. They charged that the

---

30   Percy Green, Robin D. G. Kelley, George Lipsitz, Tef Poe, Jamala Rogers, Elizabeth Hinton, and Walter Johnson, "Generations of Struggle: Panel Discussion on Protest Before, During, and After the Ferguson Rebellion," *Kalfou* 3, no. 1 (2016).

31   Robinson, *Black Movements in America*, 141.

demonstrators should register voters and change the system peacefully, not resist its violence with violence of their own.

When he referred to "your mama's civil rights movement," Poe did not mean the heroic legacy of struggle by ordinary people resisting an unlivable destiny and creating new democratic institutions. For years, he and his fellow activists have worked with and learned from grassroots Black activists in their city. But he was rejecting the political culture of placing a few dark faces in high places, the culture that Robinson describes as liberal and bourgeois, as laden with material ambition and individualist consciousness. He was embracing the Black Radical Tradition, the culture of opposition born, nurtured, and sustained within everyday life, honed and refined through expressive culture and underground activism. He walked in the footsteps of Henry Dorsey and many others as an artist whose creation spoke truth to power, exposed the existence of evil, and anticipated and prefigured struggles for justice.

When Michael Brown was killed on Canfield Drive in Ferguson on August 9, 2014, Tef Poe and other activists knew what to do because they had prepared well for that moment. As Poe explains,

> We already had an underground system of activism in St. Louis. A lot of people didn't know about it but it was there. That's why in certain instances things were able to move so quickly because a lot of us were already doing the work and already anticipating a moment like this happening. Maybe two or three years ago, [on] one of the covers of my album I have a kid with a hoodie on walking, and behind him is just pure chaos. You see a tank. You see money on the ground. You see blood on the ground. You see military soldiers. I don't even know what made me say that that should be the album cover, but part of it was that I knew the eeriness of being black in St. Louis and I remember being 13 years old standing on the corner of W. Florissant Avenue and Chambers Road and thinking to myself this isn't normal. I can't even walk to the barber shop to get a haircut without being harassed by a cop. I remember standing there one day on that corner and I just looked up at the sky and I was like I don't know what's going to happen here, but something is going to happen here. I don't know what. I don't know when. I don't know how. But this is so unsustainable that it has to explode one day. And it exploded.[32]

The suggestion that the Ferguson protestors use voting rather than violence to advance their aims has an especially cynical intent and effect. Instead of seeing the routine abuse of Blacks in a city that is two-thirds Black as the fault of its virtually all-white city council, police force, and court system officials, this charge blames Blacks for their own powerlessness. It ignores how housing instability compels working people to move so often that they are rarely eligible to vote, how voter suppression strategies use these changes of address to purge

---

32   Green et al., "Generations of Struggle."

them from the voter rolls, how the war on drugs has saddled 13 percent of the Black electorate with felony convictions that prevent them from voting, and how politicians become more responsive to those who fund them than to those who favor them at the polls. Tef Poe has been part of voter registration drives and campaigns in electoral politics. The killing of Michael Brown and the official responses to it did not increase his respect for the electoral system, but rather made him feel he should apologize to the people he had asked to participate in it. He relates:

> People have to figure out what they believe in. Even for myself, my politics have drastically shifted. There was one night that we were on the McDonald's parking lot surrounded by the National Guard, and I looked at two young women that I had an outstanding relationship with prior to that moment, and I told them I was sorry. I said I'm sorry because I was a part of the regime that told you that a ballot could remove this, and voila! I do believe that voting is a weapon. I do believe that voting is a tool. But I do not believe that oppressed people have to consistently go back to the system to correct those wrongs. I do believe that we as the young people of our race have the artistic foresight, we have the talent, we have the intellect, we have the ability, we have the endurance, we have the hunger to reimagine what being black and what being politicized looks like ... So unfortunately a few folks have been coming to black people's doors for 300 years about why you all ain't voting. Maybe it's more responsible to analyze why people aren't voting and bring mechanisms to them that will spark some type of political interest in them, and then when the time comes that we should vote, then we vote. But we don't just go vote for some Tom, Dick, and Harry just because it's time to vote. White people don't do that. But we as black people are told that's how we get free. I can ask the Palestinians what voting gets you.[33]

The Ferguson uprising reveals the enduring relevance of the Black Radical Tradition. It speaks for and from the experiences of people who cannot make a separate peace with racialized capitalism. For them, the presence of one Black person in the White House does not cancel out the incarceration of millions of Black people imprisoned in the Big House. The civil rights movement they remember was not merely an effort to desegregate the ranks of the pain inflictors of this world, to enable invasions, bombings, drone strikes, and torture to be overseen by Condoleezza Rice, Colin Powell, and Barack Obama, as well as Dick Cheney, George Schultz, and George W. Bush. The individualistic institutions of the Black bourgeoisie have often been of tactical utility, but their collective consciousness has been honed through mass mobilizations and confrontations to be sure, but also struggle inside the alternative academies of prophetic works of expressive culture that manipulate material objects in order to conjure into existence the possibility of justice.

---

33   Ibid.

The Black Radical Tradition is needed now more than ever before. It is not the only source of struggles for social justice and against racialized capitalism. It contains many contradictions and is always in danger of building unity at the expense of its most despised and disempowered constituents. Robinson concludes at the end of *Black Marxism* that it is too much to ask of one social group to be the solution to all the problems perpetuated by racial capitalism, imperialism, and hetero-patriarchy. "But," he writes, "a civilization maddened by its own perverse assumptions and contradictions is loose in the world. A black radical tradition formed in opposition to that civilization and conscious of itself is one part of the solution."[34]

---

34   Robinson, *Black Marxism*, 318.

Chapter 8

Birth of a (Zionist) Nation

Black Radicalism and the Future of Palestine

Greg Burris

It is always possible that the next Black social movement will obtain that distant land, perhaps even transporting America with it.
—Cedric J. Robinson, *Black Movements in America*[1]

If the Palestinian revolution is armed with a philosophy at all, it is armed with the anti-determinist vision of the open-endedness of the future.
—Fawaz Turki, "Meaning in Palestinian History"[2]

One can only wonder what possessed executives at the History Channel to borrow the title of the first Hollywood blockbuster—D. W. Griffith's notoriously racist 1915 epic *The Birth of a Nation*—for a documentary they produced in 1996 celebrating the establishment of the State of Israel: *Israel: Birth of a Nation* (dir. Herbert Krosney). Griffith's silent film was a reactionary reimagining of the American Civil War and the Reconstruction Era which romanticized the Ku Klux Klan as a heroic band of champions guarding white civilization against the threat of Black disorder run amok. Based on Thomas Dixon's 1905 novel *The Clansman: An Historical Romance of the Ku Klux Klan*, the film was even given a special White House screening by the US president Woodrow Wilson, Dixon's former university classmate. "It is like writing history with lightning," Wilson allegedly commented after viewing the Hollywood production, "and my only regret is that it is all so terribly true."[3]

Significantly, *The Birth of a Nation* appeared at a very particular time in US history: the year 1915. As Cedric Robinson argues in his book *Forgeries of Memory and Meaning*, 1915 marked a moment in which the racial constellations that would later come to characterize the twentieth-century American landscape were still in flux. This instability manifested itself in a number of phenomena. That same year, for instance, the second Ku Klux Klan was inaugurated on Stone Mountain, Jewish factory superintendent Leo Frank was lynched

1   Cedric J. Robinson, *Black Movements in America* (New York: Routledge, 1997), 153.
2   Fawaz Turki, "Meaning in Palestinian History: Text and Context," *Arab Studies Quarterly* 3, no. 4 (1981): 381.
3   Quoted in Michael Rogin, "'The Sword Became a Flashing Vision': D.W. Griffith's *The Birth of a Nation*," *Representations* 9 (1985): 151.

by a mob of anti-Semites in Georgia, and Black boxing champion Jack Johnson was defeated by Jess Willard, the latest incarnation of "the Great White Hope." Also of relevance here is the racialized discourse that accompanied the US invasion and occupation of Haiti which commenced that July.[4] Moreover, with the intra-European battles of the First World War entering their second year, large immigrant communities in the United States remained deeply divided, and they still lacked a cohesive collective identity capable of bringing them together.[5]

In the midst of this racial maelstrom, *The Birth of a Nation*, Robinson argues, functioned as an important cinematic counterpart to a broader ideological project—*the whitening of America*. In his words, "What Griffith consciously served as a midwife for was the birth of a new, virile American whiteness."[6] For Robinson, this whiteness—the unifying "myth of white solidarity" as he elsewhere puts it[7]—was not something that had existed from time immemorial; rather, it was a defensive reaction on the part of governing elites and their sympathizers to an underlying disorder: a restless discontent which included, among other things, *Black insurgency*.

While the decision to borrow the title of Griffith's film for a documentary about the founding of the State of Israel might have been accidental, a comparison of these two texts can nevertheless be quite revealing. Indeed, rewatching *Israel: Birth of a Nation* today, one is struck by how much its basic ideological coordinates resemble those of its namesake. If Griffith's infamous film simultaneously whitewashed European immigrant groups in the United States and demonized Blacks, the History Channel's TV documentary homogenized Jews and scapegoated Palestinians; if the former film erased the history of slavery, the latter erased the ethnic cleansing of Palestine; and if the former glorified the KKK, the latter romanticized violent Zionist militia groups like the Irgun.

Comparisons, of course, can easily be refuted, and a list of similarities between any two states, societies, or even cinematic texts can immediately be cancelled by an even longer list of differences—facts negated by counter-facts, evidence by counter-evidence. Thus, if the births of these two nations are to be examined together, it behooves us to go beyond curious coincidences and happenstance analogies. Even more, we must discover how these distinct racial regimes interact with and influence each other. As David Theo Goldberg insists,

---

4   Cedric J. Robinson, *Forgeries of Memory and Meaning: Blacks and the Regimes of Race in American Theater and Film Before World War II* (Chapel Hill: University of North Carolina, 2007), 82–126. An earlier version of this chapter appeared as Cedric J. Robinson, "In the Year 1915: D. W. Griffith and the Whitening of America," *Social Identities* 3, no. 2 (1997): 161–92.

5   As Robinson writes, "From the 1890s to World War I the country had no national political consciousness, no hegemonic cultural core, no dominant historical identity, no definite social solidarity." Robinson, *Forgeries of Memory and Meaning*, 181.

6   Ibid., 108.

7   Cedric J. Robinson, *Black Marxism: The Making of the Black Radical Tradition* (Chapel Hill: University of North Carolina, 2000[1983]), 80.

our analysis must not only be comparative; it must also be *relational*.[8] In this regard, we should follow in the footsteps of scholars like Nur Masalha, Gabriel Piterberg, Shira Robinson, Steven Salaita, and Patrick Wolfe who understand the partnership between the US and Israeli nation-states to be the result of an ideological bind—a common rootedness in *white settler-colonialism*.[9]

But even if we do posit a relational link connecting the US and Israeli settler-colonialist projects—that is, a link between the births of a white American nation and an Ashkenazi Zionist nation—what about the other side of the coin? What about those populations that have suffered under the iron heel of the US and Israel's oppressive governing practices, people including (but not limited to) the Black and Palestinian communities? Can a relational link likewise be drawn between them?

To be sure, such a possibility is not at all guaranteed, and while many prominent members of the African American community have historically gravitated towards Zionism, certain parts of Arab society (including Palestinian society) have harbored anti-Black African sentiments. Nevertheless, activists on both sides of the Atlantic have been articulating connections of solidarity and support for the last several decades—from meetings held in Algiers between representatives of the Black Panther Party and Fatah in 1969 to the contemporary collaboration of Black and Palestinian hip-hop artists like Chuck D, Lupe Fiasco, Jasiri X, DAM, and Shadia Mansour;[10] from the fiery rhetoric of Malcolm X and Stokely Carmichael to the use of civil rights iconography by Palestinians protesting segregated streets and bus lines in the occupied West Bank;[11] from the poetry of June Jordan to the spoken word of Remi Kanazi and

---

8   David Theo Goldberg, "Racial Comparisons, Relational Racisms: Some Thoughts on Method," *Ethnic and Racial Studies* 32, no. 7 (2009): 1271–82.

9   See, for instance, Nur Masalha, *Expulsion of the Palestinians: The Concept of "Transfer" in Zionist Political Thought, 1882–1948* (Washington DC: Institute for Palestine Studies, 1992); Nur Masalha, *The Palestine Nakba: Decolonising History, Narrating the Subaltern, Reclaiming Memory* (New York: Zed Books, 2012); Gabriel Piterberg, *The Returns of Zionism: Myths, Politics and Scholarship in Israel* (New York: Verso, 2008); Shira Robinson, *Citizen Strangers: Palestinians and the Birth of Israel's Liberal Settler State* (Stanford: Stanford University, 2013); Steven Salaita, *The Holy Land in Transit: Colonialism and the Quest for Canaan* (Syracuse, NY: Syracuse University Press, 2006); Patrick Wolfe, "Settler Colonialism and the Elimination of the Native," *Journal of Genocide Research* 8, no. 4 (2006): 387–409; and Patrick Wolfe, *Settler Colonialism and the Transformation of Anthropology: The Politics and Poetics of an Ethnographic Event* (New York: Cassell, 1999). See also Maxime Rodinson's pathbreaking *Israel: A Colonial-Settler State?*, trans. David Thorstad (New York: Pathfinder, 1973).

10   On the Black Panther Party meetings with Fatah, see Keith P. Feldman, *A Shadow Over Palestine: The Imperial Life of Race in America* (Minneapolis: University of Minnesota Press, 2015), 81–6. On Palestinian hip-hop, see Sunaina Maira, "'We Ain't Missing': Palestinian Hip Hop—A Transnational Youth Movement," *CR: The New Centennial Review* 8, no. 2 (2008): 161–92; and Sunaina Maira and Magid Shihade, "Hip Hop from '48 Palestine: Youth, Music, and the Present/Absent," *Social Text* 30, no. 3 (2012): 1–26.

11   On the Palestinian "Freedom Riders," see Maryam S. Griffin, "Freedom Rides in Palestine: Racial Segregation and Grassroots Politics on the Bus," *Race and Class* 56, no. 4 (2015): 73–84.

Suheir Hammad;[12] and from a documentary film about Martin Luther King Jr.'s relevance for Palestine (*Al Helm: Martin Luther King in Palestine* [dir. Connie Field, 2014]) to a recent museum exhibit in East Jerusalem about the slain Black political prisoner George Jackson.[13] In the summer of 2014, the prospect of Black–Palestinian solidarity attained even greater visibility due to the synchronous timing of two events that August: the police murder of Michael Brown in Ferguson, Missouri, and Israel's latest bloodbath in the Gaza Strip. While pro-Palestinian signs and banners began appearing at "Hands Up, Don't Shoot" and #BlackLivesMatter protests in the United States, some Palestinians in the West Bank began tweeting instructions to their would-be comrades in Missouri about how best to deal with the pepper spray and tear gas.[14]

   In recent years, Black–Palestinian racial imaginaries have received growing scholarly attention, resulting in the proliferation of journal essays, conference panels, and even book-length treatments by activists and academics such as Angela Davis, Keith Feldman, Robin D. G. Kelley, and Alex Lubin.[15] Such accounts of Black–Palestinian solidarity are usually intended to contest hegemonic master narratives at the factual level by subversively shedding light on a counter-history of transnational activism and resistance that has otherwise been forgotten or erased. But as essential as such endeavors are, they nevertheless have their blind spots. Indeed, as long as this body of literature limits itself to empirical documentation, it will be unable to respond to the claims of certain skeptics who dismiss Black–Palestinian activism as nothing more than an excuse for anti-Black appropriation.[16] Thus, as important as it may be to document new instances

12   June Jordan, *Moving Toward Home: Political Essays* (London: Virago, 1989); Remi Kanazi, *Poetic Injustice: Writings on Resistance and Palestine* (New York: RoR, 2011); and Suheir Hammad, *Born Palestinian, Born Black* (Brooklyn: UpSet, 2010[1996]).

13   The George Jackson exhibit was curated by Tufts University professor Greg Thomas based on his ongoing research. See Rebecca Pierce, "How the Sun of Palestine Reached a Black Panther in Jail," *Electronic Intifada* (December 15, 2015), available at electronicintifada.net.

14   See my essay, "Palestine in Black and White: White Settler-Colonialism and the Specter of Transnational Black Power," in Sunaina Maira and Paola Bacchetta, eds., *Global Raciality: Empire, Postcoloniality, and Decoloniality* (London: Routledge, forthcoming).

15   Angela Y. Davis, *Freedom Is a Constant Struggle: Ferguson, Palestine, and the Foundations of a Movement* (Chicago: Haymarket, 2016); Alex Kane, "'A Level of Racist Violence I Have Never Seen': UCLA Professor Robin D. G. Kelley on Palestine and the BDS Movement," *Mondoweiss* (February 16, 2012), available on mondoweiss.net; Robin D. G. Kelley, "Another Freedom Summer," *Journal of Palestine Studies* 44, no. 1 (2014): 29–41; Feldman, *A Shadow Over Palestine*; and Alex Lubin, *Geographies of Liberation: The Making of an Afro-Arab Political Imaginary* (Chapel Hill: University of North Carolina, 2014). See also "Roundtable on Anti-Blackness and Black-Palestinian Solidarity," *Jadaliyya* (June 3, 2015), available at jadaliyya.com. For an earlier discussion of Black–Palestinian ties, see Lewis Young, "American Blacks and the Arab-Israeli Conflict," *Journal of Palestine Studies* 2, no. 1 (1972): 70–85.

16   For instance, after the American Studies Association (ASA) passed a resolution in 2013 endorsing the Palestinian call to boycott, divest from, and sanction the Israeli regime (BDS), California-based academic Nicholas Brady authored an online editorial which denounced the ASA's position as one "aris[ing] from an anti-black calculus." Moreover, in a 2014 interview, Frank Wilderson similarly derided Black–Palestinian solidarity as "bullshit." In his words, "The Arabs and the Jews are as much a part of the Black slave trade . . . as anyone else . . . Anti-Blackness is as

of solidarity—another rap song, another YouTube video, another protest spectacle—we must also seek to take our analysis underground and to ask how the
traditions of Black radicalism and Palestinian liberation can speak to each other
at the level of theory, philosophy, and epistemology.

In this essay, I would like to gesture towards one possible way of beginning
this important task by turning our attention to the work of Cedric Robinson,
theorist of the Black Radical Tradition. Although Robinson's oeuvre is chiefly
concerned with Black resistance to racial capitalism from slavery to the silver
screen, we would be doing his work a great disservice if we limited its relevance
to these historical confines.[17] Indeed, Robinson's explication of Black radicalism, in my view, also provides us with a valuable intellectual resource for grasping the meaning and importance of both the Palestinian Liberation Struggle in
general and coalitions of Black–Palestinian solidarity in particular. Furthermore,
while Robinson's work appears to be concerned with the past, I argue that it is
animated by a passion for the future, and this utopian element even suggests a
way for us to conceive of *the future of Palestine*.

Let us return, then, to the focal point of the History Channel's ill-named
documentary, the 1948 establishment of the State of Israel. In Zionist discourse,
the birth of the modern Jewish nation-state is tied to yet another birth: that of
Palestinian liberation. To be sure, Zionists have routinely questioned the existence of Palestine and the Palestinians—from Golda Meir's infamous 1969 assertion that the Palestinians do not exist to the baffling argument recently made on
the floor of the Knesset by an elected politician who claimed that an entity called
"Palestine" logically could not have existed because Arabic does not contain the
letter "P."[18] Most often, the point of such dismissals is not to dispute the empirical presence of non-Jewish, Arabic-speaking bodies in the land of Palestine;
rather, the point is to dispute their status as a *nation*. From a Zionist perspective,
Palestinians existed before 1948—but only as benign peasants, helpful workers,
or hostile militants. As such, they did not constitute a legitimate collective body.

---

important and necessary to the formation of Arab psychic life as it is to the formation of Jewish
psychic life." Going even further, Wilderson warned the Black community against "bonding with
people who are really, primarily, using Black energy to catalyze and energize their [own] struggle."
See Nicholas Brady, "The Void Speaks Back: Black Suffering as the Unthought of the American
Studies Association's Academic Boycott of Israel," *Out of Nowhere* (December 23, 2013), available
at outofnowhereblog.wordpress.com. For Wilderson's original interview, see I Mix What I Like!,
"Irreconcilable Anti-Blackness and Police Violence" (October 1, 2014), available at imixwhatilike.
org. For the transcript, see "'We're Trying to Destroy the World': Anti-Blackness and Police
Violence After Ferguson: An Interview with Frank B. Wilderson, III," Ill Will Editions, available at
ill-will-editions.tumblr.com.

17   The most glaring exception to this overall focus is Robinson's short book *An Anthropology of
Marxism*, which includes a discussion of medieval poverty movements in Europe as an example of
pre-Marxist socialism. See Cedric J. Robinson, *An Anthropology of Marxism* (Oxford: Ashgate, 2001).

18   "Golda Meir Scorns Soviets: Israeli Premier Explains Stand on Big-4 Talks, Security,"
Washington Post (June 16, 1969); and Matt Payton, "Israeli MP Claims the Palestine Nation Cannot
Exist 'Because They Can't Pronounce the Letter P,'" *The Independent* (February 11, 2016), available
at independent.co.uk.

They were Arabs but not Palestinians, people but not *a* people. To recall the words of Chaim Weizmann, Israel's first president, the natives were "the rocks of Judea"—that is, "obstacles that had to be cleared on a difficult path."[19] Accordingly, Palestine is just an accidental by-product of Zionism, and the Palestinian Liberation Struggle is nothing more than a belated, jealous response to Israel's victories.

Significantly, the Zionist linking of Palestinian resistance to the year 1948 is often replicated by the Palestinians themselves, and in Palestinian discourse, the ethnic cleansing of Palestine—the catastrophe or the Nakba—is regularly treated as *the* foundational event of contemporary Palestinian identity.[20] As the editors of an important anthology on Nakba memory write, "There is little doubt that the catastrophe, in all its dimensions, has . . . become the key site of Palestinian collective memory and national identity."[21] In many accounts, the 1948 Nakba is even seen as the glue that holds Palestinians together, the connective tissue that bridges the many religious, socioeconomic, and geographic gaps separating Palestinians from each other. Here, one might be tempted to borrow Robin D. G. Kelley's argument about the role of "ghettocentricity" in Black American identity and claim that the Palestinians are similarly gripped by a certain *Nakba-centricity*. In both cases, the community in question is united by the existence of a perceived underlying tragedy.[22]

The Nakba thus seems to permeate all aspects of Palestinian culture, from the proverbial keys that Palestinians keep as a reminder of the past and a promise for the future to the cinematic texts produced and directed by innovative Palestinian filmmakers, sometimes working in quite adverse conditions. Indeed, the film which arguably inaugurated Palestinian fictional filmmaking, *Return to Haifa* (dir. Kassem Hawal, 1982), opens with reenacted scenes from the Nakba. Based on one of Ghassan Kanafani's most famous novellas and financed by the Popular Front for the Liberation of Palestine, *Return to Haifa* was made with the participation of some 3,000 Palestinian refugees who served as extras. These refugees came to the set dressed in the same clothes that they had been wearing when they were forced into exile three decades earlier, and with their help, the film's production crew temporarily transformed Lebanon's northern port city of Tripoli in 1981 into the port city of Haifa in 1948.[23] Scenes from the Nakba have

---

19   Quoted in Masalha, *Expulsion of the Palestinians*, 17.

20   See Ilan Pappé, *The Ethnic Cleansing of Palestine* (Oxford: Oneworld, 2006).

21   Lila Abu-Lughod and Ahmad H. Sa'di, "Introduction: The Claims of Memory," in Ahmad H. Sa'di and Lila Abu-Lughod, eds., *Nakba: Palestine, 1948, and the Claims of Memory* (New York: Columbia University Press, 2007), 4.

22   Robin D. G. Kelley, *Race Rebels: Culture, Politics, and the Black Working Class* (New York: Free Press, 1996), 209.

23   Annemarie Jacir, "Coming Home: Palestinian Cinema," *Electronic Intifada* (February 27, 2007), available at electronicintifada.net. See also Ghassan Kanafani, "Returning to Haifa," in *Palestine's Children: Returning to Haifa and Other Stories*, trans. Barbara Harlow and Karen E. Riley (Boulder: Lynne Rienner, 2000), 149–96.

also appeared in other Palestinian films—for instance, the traumatic flashbacks in *The Milky Way* (dir. Ali Nasser, 1997), the eerie black-and-white opening montage from *Salt of This Sea* (dir. Annemarie Jacir, 2008), and the early scenes of *The Time that Remains* (dir. Elia Suleiman, 2009).[24]

While I do not contest the tremendous role that the Nakba has played and will continue to play in the formation of Palestinian collective memory and identity, we nevertheless run a great risk when we assign the events of 1948 such a strong degree of determinative agency. That is, by treating the establishment of the State of Israel as the instigator of the Palestinian Liberation Struggle, we are in danger of viewing history through the same interpretive prism employed by the Zionists. In either case, Israel takes historical and logical priority, and Palestinian resistance is treated as an aftereffect or delayed reaction. Israel comes first; Palestinian resistance comes second. In this manner, Israel is inadvertently reified even by its opponents. *Zionism wins.*

A similar roadblock confronts those delving into the history of Black resistance to racial capitalism, and far too often, even the most sympathetic of historians can inadvertently complete a process in theory that the white supremacist overseers were unable to accomplish in reality. The North American slave system separated the African not only from his or her native continent, but also from his or her history, language, and culture. This violent cleavage was intentionally perpetrated as part of a broad, systemic attempt to transform the African into a slave, a project that ultimately failed. Despite the overseers' best efforts, the Africans resisted—from small, daily acts of insubordination to the activities of insurgent leaders like Gabriel, Denmark Vesey, and Nat Turner. As C. L. R. James once remarked, "The only place where Negroes did not revolt is in the pages of capitalist historians."[25] Thus, the question that confronts us is not whether or not the Africans rebelled. Rather, the question that confronts us has to do with the source of the rebellion. That is, the question is not *whether* the Africans rebelled but *why* they rebelled.

One possible answer lies in Western civilization itself. Indeed, many have attempted to locate the source of the Africans' resistance within the conditions of slavery. Simply put, they rebelled because they were oppressed. This is the same logic that was employed by Marx and Engels when they famously contended in *The Communist Manifesto* that capitalism would create its own gravediggers.[26] But by locating the seeds of rebellion within the institution of

24 On the significance of the Nakba to Palestinian cinema, see Haim Bresheeth, "The Continuity of Trauma and Struggle: Recent Cinematic Representations of the Nakba," in Sa'di and Abu-Lughod, eds., *Nakba*, 161–87; and Nadia G. Yaqub, "Narrating the Nakba: Palestinian Filmmakers Revisit 1948," in Dina Matar and Zahera Harb, eds., *Narrating Conflict in the Middle East: Discourse, Image and Communications* (New York: I. B. Tauris, 2013), 225–47.

25 C. L. R. James, "Revolution and the Negro," in Scott McLemee and Paul le Blanc, eds., *C. L. R. James and Revolutionary Marxism: Selected Writings of C. L. R. James, 1939–1949* (Atlantic Highlands, NJ: Humanities, 1994), 77.

26 Karl Marx and Friedrich Engels, *The Communist Manifesto* (New York: Signet, 1998[1948]).

slavery in this manner, one inadvertently replicates the conceit of the slave masters, effectively abolishing the Africans' most important resource: their collective past. This is precisely where Robinson locates the Black Radical Tradition, and for him, Black resistance emanated not from oppression alone but from a consciousness that the North American overseers were simply unable to obliterate. For Robinson, the slave ships not only transported bodies; they also transported "cultures, critical mixes and admixtures of language and thought, of cosmology and metaphysics, of habits, beliefs, and morality." "African labor," he argues, "brought the past with it . . . This was the embryo of the demon that would be visited on the whole enterprise of primitive accumulation."[27]

As counterintuitive as it might initially appear, then, the wellspring of inspiration fueling Black radicalism actually predates the institution against which the Africans rebelled. The slave masters' attempts to brainwash the Africans did not generate a rebellious African consciousness. Rather, Robinson argues that the opposite was the case, and a rebellious African consciousness generated the slave masters' need to brainwash the Africans. However totalizing the slave system might have seemed, it was not a completely dominant enterprise, and it was perpetually plagued by the threat of a consciousness that preceded it and that it could not eradicate.

To be sure, Black thought is hardly a monolithic field, and Robinson's conception of Black radicalism is quite distinct from many other formulations. The film theorist Frank Wilderson, for instance, views Blackness in an almost completely antithetical way. According to Wilderson, Blackness was born in the Middle Passage, and it has no connection whatsoever to the African past. "Blackness," as he puts it, "recalls nothing prior to the devastation that defines it," and "there is no way to Africa through the Black."[28] The gulf separating Wilderson's brand of Afro-pessimism from Robinson's Black Radical Tradition could not be any wider. For Wilderson, Blacks have not stopped being slaves. For Robinson, they were never really slaves to begin with.[29]

Importantly, Robinson's subversive gesture operates on at least two distinct levels. It is both historical and theoretical, concrete and abstract. If Robinson is explicitly addressing a very specific case—Black resistance to slavery—his argument nevertheless has a much broader theoretical purchase. Robinson is arguing that no system of thought—no social science, no economic model, no governing ideology—is ever as hegemonic or dominant as we pretend it is, and

---

27   Robinson, *Black Marxism*, 121–2.

28   Frank B. Wilderson, *Red, White, and Black: Cinema and the Structure of US Antagonisms* (Durham, NC: Duke University, 2010), 280, 47.

29   Wilderson perversely makes a similar point in his effort to distinguish the Africans' experience of slavery from the Jews who were exterminated in the Nazi genocide. As he writes, "Jews went into Auschwitz and came out as Jews. Africans went into ships and came out as Blacks. The former is a Human holocaust; the latter is a Human *and* a metaphysical holocaust." Ibid., 38.

there are always cracks in the ruling regime, holes and gaps from which other forms of thinking, being, and imagining can emerge. Robinson's intellectual project is thus a radically open-ended one, and he refuses to give existing structures and institutions the final say.

Here, it is worth noting a certain overlap between Robinson's work and the writings of another radical intellectual, Edward Said. Indeed, it is significant that Robinson's book on early film history, *Forgeries of Memory and Meaning*, begins with a quotation by that late Palestinian intellectual: "In human history there is always something beyond the reach of dominating systems, no matter how deeply they saturate society."[30] While Robinson does not elaborate on this potential overlap in the subsequent text, I believe that the presence of this epigraph at the beginning of Robinson's book indicates a fascinating possibility that merits further exploration—the prospect of the Black Radical Tradition intersecting with the Palestinian Liberation Struggle.

What would it mean to conceive of Palestine through the work of Cedric Robinson? First of all, it would mean seriously calling into question any historical narrative—be it Zionist or anti-Zionist in political orientation—that gives too much determinative authority to the actions of Israel in the shaping of contemporary Palestinian identity. Indeed, local ways of thinking, being, and imagining already existed before any Zionist feet had even touched Middle Eastern soil, and this indigenous culture and consciousness has shaped the way that Palestinians respond to the litany of tragedies that have befallen them.[31] Just as slavery could not fully brainwash the Africans, Zionism, too, has been unable to fully dominate the Palestinians. While pro-Israeli activists like to claim that Palestine is a modern-day invention, Robinson's theoretical example would suggest that by rejecting the occupation, the Palestinians are not only playing out the internal contradictions of the oppressive power structures they contest, but are also drawing upon local cultures, cosmologies, metaphysics, beliefs, and values—phenomena which the Israelis have been unable to obliterate. Whatever devastation the Nakba wrecked, Israel's oppressive actions do not have determinative power, and Palestinian resistance is not merely an automatic, instinctual reaction against it. Like the Black Radical Tradition, the Palestinian Liberation Struggle has roots older than the occupation itself. However oppressive Zionism is, it can never fully determine the shape that Palestinian resistance takes.

Second, thinking Palestine through the Black Radical Tradition can also help us demystify Zionism by recognizing Israel's expressions and performances

---

30   Edward W. Said, *The World, the Text, and the Critic* (Cambridge, MA: Harvard University Press, 1983), 246–7.

31   As Rashid Khalidi writes, "Although the Zionist challenge definitely helped to shape the specific form Palestinian national identification took, it is a serious mistake to suggest that Palestinian identity emerged mainly as a response to Zionism." Rashid Khalidi, *Palestinian Identity: The Construction of Modern National Consciousness* (New York: Columbia University Press, 2010[1997]), 20. See also Baruch Kimmerling and Joel S. Migdal, *The Palestinian People: A History* (Cambridge, MA: Harvard University Press, 2003[1994]).

of power as indications of its ultimate impotence. Just as the aforementioned project of whitening the United States was a response to an underlying disorder that included Black insurgency, Israel's actions likewise represent a defensive reaction against the Palestinians' continued intransigence. Palestinian liberation should therefore not be seen simply as a reaction to the brutality of the occupation. On the contrary, *the brutality of the occupation is a reaction to Palestinian liberation.* The imposition of hierarchy and apartheid in Palestine—what the Israelis call separation or *hafrada*—is not a principle but a consequence, and it is precisely because Palestinian liberation is constantly threatening to erupt that the Israeli authorities, along with their Palestinian partners, must continually act to contain it, ceaselessly working to paper over power's cracks. Ironically, then, each time a Zionist like Golda Meir denies the Palestinians' existence, he or she is unwittingly indicating the opposite and inadvertently admitting the fragility of Israel itself.

How does this intersection of Black radicalism and Palestinian liberation help us conceive of Black–Palestinian solidarity? To be sure, those who champion such activist networks have sometimes come under fire from other members of the Left who correctly point out a myriad of empirical differences separating the Black and Palestinian struggles. As these skeptics are quick to note, the Black experience with US racial capitalism is quite different from the Palestinians' fate under Zionist settler-colonialism. Simply put, Ferguson is not Gaza, Baltimore is not Jerusalem, and Watts is not the West Bank. By so easily interchanging the two struggles, as these naysayers argue, one may actually be divesting them of their political specificity.

Here, we can again turn to Robinson's work, where a particular historical subject appears again and again—the person who escapes his or her oppressive surroundings by fleeing them. This is the runaway, the fugitive, or the maroon. Marronage, as Robinson points out, was a relatively common practice in pre-colonial US history, even preceding the establishment of Jamestown by some eighty-two years.[32] Significantly, these maroon communities were populated by a diverse mix of peoples—not only self-liberated Africans but also Native Americans and Europeans who were former indentured servants. As if anticipating Fred Hampton's original Rainbow Coalition, these communities exhibited a diverse, multiethnic solidarity that was far more radical than the liberal multiculturalism that would later characterize hegemonic narratives about US civil society.[33] Robinson's interest in marronage should come as little surprise.

---

32 Robinson, *Black Movements in America*, 13.

33 As Robinson contends, "American maroon communities frequently acquired the multicultural and multiracial character that liberal historians of the early twentieth century had expected of the whole nation." Ibid., 13. On the original Rainbow Coalition, see Amy Sonnie and James Tracy, *Hillbilly Nationalists, Urban Race Rebels, and Black Power: Community Organizing in Radical Times* (Brooklyn: Melville House, 2011); and Jakobi Williams, *From the Bullet to the Ballot: The Illinois Chapter of the Black Panther Party and Racial Coalition Politics in Chicago* (Chapel Hill: University of North Carolina, 2013).

By liberating themselves with their own feet, these fugitives enacted literally what Robinson is trying to accomplish theoretically: an escape from dominant ways of thinking, being, and imagining. Ultimately, the Black Radical Tradition is itself a theory of fugitivity.

While the leftist critics of Black–Palestinian solidarity are technically correct that the Black situation vis-à-vis US white supremacy is not the same as the Palestinian situation vis-à-vis Zionist settler-colonialism, they are nevertheless making a great mistake. Declarations of solidarity and political belonging between the two struggles are rarely meant to be scientific comparisons, and Black–Palestinian solidarity does not hinge on absolute sameness any more than did the ties forged in North American maroon communities between self-liberated Africans, Native Americans, and European servants. Those who participate in the imagining of Black–Palestinian ties are not simply describing the world as it already exists; they are creating something new, giving flesh to a potential that had previously been hidden. Their activities are not blind reactions to US and Israeli forms of oppression and injustice but a testament to the radical ways of thinking, being, and imagining which preceded them and continue to inspire social struggle and resistance.

Thus, when Palestinian protesters in Hebron staged a Freedom March in 2013 and desegregated their downtown streets while wearing masks of Martin Luther King Jr. and carrying pictures of Rosa Parks, they were not simply appropriating the Black struggle; they were giving it new life and showing that the emancipatory message of the Black freedom movement cannot be ghettoized into one particular historical and political context.[34] Similarly, when #BlackLivesMatter protesters interrupted traffic on Martin Luther King Day in January 2015 and unfurled a giant Palestinian flag on California's San Mateo–Hayward Bridge, they were not simply turning a protest against white supremacy into anti-Black spectacle.[35] Rather, in both instances, the protesters were letting the submerged and buried traditions of Black radicalism and Palestinian liberation emerge from the shadows of the present. Indeed, we might even go so far as to say that they were acting as twenty-first-century fugitives, metaphysical maroons fleeing oppressive discourses and identitarian boundaries. Just like the runaways that Robinson privileges in his work, they were creating new, imaginative coalitions and racial constructions that defy existing forms of categorization. To recall Robinson's concluding words from *Black Marxism*, "It is not the province of one people to be the solution or the problem . . . But for now we must be as one."[36]

---

34   Alistair Dawber, "'Come Here, Obama, and Visit the Museum of Apartheid': Pro-Palestinian Protesters Clash with Army in West Bank as US President Arrives in Tel Aviv," *The Independent* (March 20, 2013), available at independent.co.uk; and David Shulman, "Hope in Hebron," *New York Review of Books* blog (March 22, 2013), available at nybooks.com.

35   Caleb Smith and Catherine Zaw, "Students Shut Down San Mateo–Hayward Bridge; 68 People Arrested, 11 Jailed," *Stanford Daily* (January 19, 2015), available at stanforddaily.com.

36   Robinson, *Black Marxism*, 318.

The final point I would like to make has to do with our conception of time. Elias Sanbar has suggested that with the Nakba, it was as if the clock stopped for the Palestinians. Since 1948, they have been unable to progress in time, stuck in a seemingly infinite loop of tragedy and trauma.[37] This temporal deadlock is memorably depicted in Annemarie Jacir's 2012 feature *When I Saw You*. The film begins in a fictional Palestinian refugee camp in Jordan which acts as a place of death, a kind of Palestinian purgatory where refugees wait indefinitely for a solution that will never come. Here, old refugees from the 1948 Nakba intermingle with new refugees from the 1967 Naksa, and in their misery, they become virtually indistinguishable from one another. The camp's inhabitants seem to have accepted a helpless, passive existence for themselves, forever in limbo, waiting for the conflict to be settled by other people. Later in the film, the connection between the camp and the Nakba is solidified when we learn that it has been leveled by Israeli jets. Massacre thus follows massacre, and tragedy comes on the heels of tragedy. Within the physical and ideological boundaries of this camp, the cycle of violence and trauma appears inescapable. Time has stopped, and the Nakba appears present and permanent.[38]

But what if the future of Palestine was right before our eyes? What if Zionism has been unable to stamp out the Palestinian future just as it has been unable to erase the Palestinian past? Indeed, what if these two things were actually one and the same, and what if, by seeking out those moments in history when the Palestinian Liberation Struggle emerged from Zionism's cracks, we were simultaneously uncovering fragments of the Palestinian future? While Robinson's writings seem preoccupied with history, I would argue that his vision is actually animated by a passion for the future, and by shedding light on the fugitive moments of the past, Robinson is endeavoring to outline traces of tomorrow.[39] This quasi-mystical dimension of Robinson's work is most apparent in those moments when he dips into theology, identifying the men and women who fight for freedom against oppression as "divine agents" and arguing that Black churches might eventually give birth to a "social movement [that] will obtain that distant land, perhaps even transporting America with it."[40]

Here, we can draw a comparison between Robinson and other utopian thinkers—for instance, the mystical Marxist sage Ernst Bloch or, even better, the

---

37 Elias Sanbar, "Out of Place, Out of Time," *Mediterranean Historical Review* 16, no. 1 (2001): 87–94.

38 Wilderson sees a similar temporal dynamic at work with respect to Black Americans. As he argues, "The Black lost the coherence of space and time in the hold of the Middle Passage." Wilderson, *Red, White, and Black*, 315.

39 This is precisely how Fred Moten describes the role of the prophet who, he writes, "is the one who tells the brutal truth, who has the capacity to see the absolute brutality of the already-existing and to point it out and to tell that truth, but also *to see the other way, to see what it could be.*" Stefano Harney and Fred Moten, *The Undercommons: Fugitive Planning & Black Study* (New York: Autonomedia, 2013), 131. Emphasis added.

40 Robinson, *An Anthropology of Marxism*, 138–9; and Robinson, *Black Movements in America*, 153.

great C. L. R. James, one of Robinson's most influential intellectual forebears. If, for Bloch, "the tomorrow in today is alive," James declared that *the future is already in the present* and needs only to be seized.[41] According to these theorists, the seeds of the future already exist in the here and now, scattered all around us but usually unrecognized and unacknowledged. As a result, revolutionary action does not involve creating something out of thin air. Rather, revolutionary action entails a process of uncovering something that already inhabits the shadows of the present.

In order to discover Palestine's future, then, one does not have to look to the mythical heavens or peer into a crystal ball. Instead, one has only to uncover the ways in which the Palestinian future is already lying dormant all around us. Each moment that Zionism fails—that is, each instance in which the specter of Palestinian liberation manages to seep through the governing order's cracks— we do not only see glimpses of the Palestinian past; we also see traces of the Palestinian future. This also applies to Black–Palestinian solidarity activists. Viewed through this utopian lens, such protesters are not only serving as present avatars of the Black radical and Palestinian liberation struggles of the past; they are also acting as messengers from the future, a Black–Palestinian future that is already with us, hidden within the recesses of the settler-colonialist present.

It is with this particular conception of the future in mind that we can at last return to the place from which we started, D. W. Griffith's *The Birth of a Nation* and its more recent History Channel namesake. As we have already seen, these two films and other cultural products like them represent broad efforts to forge collective unity in the face of sustained insubordination from below. But these narratives should not only be understood as attempts to stamp out a resistant consciousness stemming from the Black and Palestinian pasts. They also represent attempts to suppress the Black and Palestinian futures. Whether or not these efforts will be successful depends on us.

---

41   Ernst Bloch, *The Principle of Hope*, vol. 3, trans. Neville Plaice, Stephen Plaice, and Paul Knight (Cambridge, MA: MIT Press, 1986[1959]), 1374; and C. L. R. James, *Spheres of Existence: Selected Writings* (Westport, CT: Lawrence Hill, 1980), 79.

Chapter 9

Anti-Imperialism as a Way of Life

Emancipatory Internationalism and the Black Radical Tradition in the Americas[1]

Paul Ortiz

But where the true friend of freedom can discover hope for our country, or the oppressed of our land, from anything by him yet done or said, I can't divine . . . To fill the coffers of the wholesale and retail dealers in immorality, and arouse the latent war spirit, and prepare us to crush Cuba, Mexico, South America and accomplish the "destiny" of this "Mighty Republic," and finally to break down the walls of the "City of Refuge," (Canada) and secure the undisputed reign of "Republican" despotism in the Western World, laying broad and firm the foundation of that "Free Government," the "corner stone" of which, is interminable bondage to one sixth of its native born citizens, dooming them and their posterity, during all coming time, to a state, an hour of which is worse to be endured than ages of the oppression our fathers resisted.[2]

I had to leave the United States to understand it. As a sergeant in the US Special Forces in Central America in the mid-1980s, I encountered Augusto Sandino everywhere I went. Representations of the Nicaraguan revolutionary's visage, murals of his guerrilla comrades, and walls etched with Sandino's sayings were ubiquitous in the region. Governments that had aligned themselves with US interests viewed Sandino's words as seditious. No sooner had the *policía* scrubbed Sandino's injunction "Come, you pack of morphine addicts; come to kill us in our own land" from the side of one building, dissenting artists would write, "We will go to the sun of freedom or to death" on a wall on the other side of town. I am not ashamed to admit that I thought for quite some time that Augusto César Sandino (1895–1934) was still alive and that he was our gravest enemy.

Years later, I faced Sandino again. This time, I found him as a historian searching African American newspapers for stories of Sandino's struggles against the American occupation of Nicaragua in the 1920s. While the *New York Times* depicted Sandino as a scoundrel, the *Amsterdam News* argued:

1 I owe a debt of gratitude to Genesis Lara, Richard Lainez, Brittney Meija, and Yareliz Mendez-Zamora, staff members of the Samuel Proctor Oral History Program's Latina/o Diaspora in the Americas Research Project, for their editing and translation expertise.
2 "Letter from B. F. Remington," *Frederick Douglass' Paper* (February 19, 1852).

Sandino has been called a bandit, but his words are not those of a bandit; they would have fitted the mouth of George Washington when he was fighting the British. The worst feature of the business is the curtailing of Latin American freedom of speech by American military power.[3]

African Americans celebrated Sandino's resistance to the US invasion. The *Pittsburgh Courier* noted that "it is assumed that the Nicaraguan patriots who are following Sandino are illiterate. Illiterate they may be, but certainly they are as surely patriots as the ragged hosts that cast their fortune with George Washington in 1776."[4] When the Marines finally prevailed over Sandino, the *Norfolk Journal and Guide* mourned that "the victory of our fighting forces over the Nicaraguan rebels may have been a fine achievement for the military, but it is nothing to reflect credit upon our country's Latin-American policy. In fact, it is rather a discredit, indeed a disgrace."[5]

These meetings with Augusto Sandino taught me that American exceptionalism—the idea that the United States is a uniquely democratic nation with an anticolonial ethos that escaped the tyrannies of Old Europe—is patently false. From the perspectives of African Americans and the residents of Central America, the United States has been as oppressive as Europe ever was. The men and women I was sent to combat in Latin America deployed the image and words of Augusto Sandino against me and my comrades as a reminder that their fight against US imperialism was resilient and longstanding. What I learned first as a soldier and later as a historian was that American foreign policy in the Global South is driven by the pursuit of profits and reinforced exponentially by assumptions of racial superiority. Cedric Robinson's idea of *racial capitalism* gave me a theoretical framework to understand the development of Jim Crow at home and imperialism abroad.[6] At the same time, Robinson's conception of

---

3   See: "Says Sandino Served," *New York Times* (January 6, 1928) and "Republic or Empire?" *New York Amsterdam News* (February 22, 1928). See also: "Nicaraguan War as a Forum Topic," *Amsterdam News* (January 25, 1928).

4   "Uncle Sam's Hot Potato," *Pittsburg Courier* (January 14, 1928); "Nicaraguan War as Forum Topic"; Neill MacAulay, *The Sandino Affair* (Chicago: Quadrangle Books, 1967); Thomas W. Walker, *Nicaragua: Living in the Shadow of the Eagle* (Cambridge: Westview Press, 2003); Max Boot, *The Savage Wars of Peace: Small Wars and the Rise of American Power* (New York: Basic Books, 2003), 231–52.

5   "Our Nicaraguan War," *Norfolk Journal and Guide* (July 23, 1927).

6   Cedric J. Robinson, *Black Marxism: The Making of the Black Radical Tradition* (Chapel Hill: University of North Carolina Press, 2000[1983]). Robinson's work is a reminder that Black radical intellectuals have long studied the relationship between slavery, racial capitalism, and imperialism. See: T. Thomas Fortune, *Black and White: Land, Labor, and Politics in the South* (New York: Fords, Howard, & Hulbert, 1884); W. E. B. Du Bois, *Black Reconstruction: A History of the Part Which Black Folk Played in the Attempt to Reconstruct Democracy in America, 1860–1880* (New York: Free Press, 1998[1935]), C. L. R. James, *The Black Jacobins: Toussaint L'Ouverture and the San Domingo Revolution* (London: Vintage Books, 1989[1938]); Eric Williams, *Capitalism and Slavery* (Chapel Hill: University of North Carolina Press, 1944); Oliver Cromwell Cox, *Caste, Class and Race: A Study in Social Dynamics* (New York: Doubleday, 1948); Paul Ortiz and Derrick White,

the Black Radical Tradition helped me understand how opposition to racial capitalism was internationalist from the beginning, and that African American critiques of US imperialism offer a way to imagine an anti-imperialist politics.[7]

I attempt here to follow Chicana scholar and organizer Elizabeth Martínez's call for a "New Origin Narrative" of American history. Martínez writes:

> We can go on living in a state of massive denial, affirming this nation's superiority and virtue simply because we need to believe in it. We can choose to believe the destiny of the United States is still manifest: global domination. Or we can see a transformative vision that carries us forward, not backward. We can seek an origin narrative that lays the groundwork for a multicultural identity centered on the goals of social equity and democracy.[8]

American history looks quite different when we explore the connections between liberation struggles in Latin America, the Caribbean, and the United States rather than viewing these movements as categorically separate. This essay connects the Mexican War of Independence, the US invasion of Mexico, and the Civil War to argue for an Americas-wide approach to understanding US history. What can an exploration of the Black Radical Tradition, particularly its anti-imperial dimensions in the Americas, teach us about challenging capital and neoliberalism in the age of the global war on terror?

José Maria Morelos, leader of the Mexican War of Independence, wrote to President James Madison in the summer of 1815 requesting the support of the United States in Mexico's struggle against Spanish colonialism. A former mule driver and Catholic priest of African, indigenous, and European descent turned revolutionary general, Morelos had two years earlier presented a new political and social program in a speech titled "Los Sentimientos de la Nación" (The Feelings of the Nation) at the historic National Constituent Congress in Chilpancingo. The program abolished slavery, called for an end to legalized caste oppression of indigenous people, demanded independence from Spain, banned torture, forbade the waging of war on other countries, and promised the "education of the poor."[9]

"C. L. R. James on Oliver Cox's *Caste, Class, and Race*: An Introduction," *New Politics* XV, no. 4 (Winter 2006): 43–7; and C. L. R. James, "The Class Basis of the Race Question in the United States," *New Politics* XV, no. 4 (Winter 2016): 48–60.

7 I expand on these themes in *An African American and Latinx History of the United States* (Boston: Beacon Press, forthcoming). See also: Paul Ortiz, "Making History Matter: Teaching Comparative African American and Latina/o Histories in an Age of Neoliberal Crisis," *Kalfou* 3, no. 1 (Spring 2016): 125–46.

8 Elizabeth Martinez, *De Colores Means All of Us: Latina Views For a Multi-Colored Century* (Cambridge, MA: South End Press, 1998), 48.

9 *Sentimientos De La Nación de José María Morelos: Antología Documental* (Mexico City: Instituto Nacional de Estudios Históricos de las Revoluciones de México, 2013), 116–24. For broader treatments of the Mexican War of Independence, see: Theodore G. Vincent,

"Los Sentimientos de la Nación" was the revolutionary movement's greatest weapon against the Spanish Empire, and represented a rejection of three centuries of European colonialism in the Americas. A few years earlier, Alexander von Humboldt had described the racial caste system of New Spain that Morelos and his soldiers were now risking their lives to overthrow:

> In a country governed by whites, the families reputed to have the least mixture of Negro or mulatto blood are also naturally the most honored. In Spain it is almost a title of nobility to descend neither from Jews nor Moors. In America the greater or less degree of whiteness of skin decides the rank which man occupies in society. A white who rides barefooted on horseback thinks he belongs to the nobility of the country.[10]

Morelos seized every opportunity to publicly denounce slavery as well as caste repression.[11] As Eqbal Ahmad notes, "Revolutionary style and institutions are most successful when they are qualitatively different from the existing ones and, at the same time, appeal to the deepest and most natural yearnings of the masses."[12]

Morelos, Miguel Hidalgo, Vicente Guerrero and their comrades recruited soldiers to their revolutionary columns by invoking the ideals of "civil rights and racial equality."[13] A month after the War of Independence began on September 16, 1810, "the first addition which [Morelos] received to this force, on arriving on the coast, was a numerous band of slaves from Petatlán, and

---

The Legacy of Vicente Guerrero, Mexico's First Black Indian President (Gainesville: University Press of Florida, 2001); Virginia Guedea, "The Process of Mexican Independence," *American Historical Review* 105, no. 1 (February 2000): 116–30; Josefina Zoraida Vázquez, "The Mexican Declaration of Independence," *Journal of American History* 85, no. 4 (March 1999): 1362–9. George Reid Andrews, *Afro-Latin America* (New York: Oxford University Press, 2004), 53–115.

10   Alexander von Humboldt, *Political Essay on the Kingdom of New Spain With Physical Sections and Maps*, vol. 1, trans. John Black (London: Longman, Hurst, Rees, et al., 1811), 246. For discussions of slavery, the imperial Spanish *casta* system and racial formation in colonial New Spain, see: Martha Menchaca, *Recovering History, Reconstructing Race: The Indian, Black, and White Roots of Mexican Americans* (Austin: University of Texas Press, 2001); Ilona Katzew, *Casta Painting: Images of Race in Eighteenth-Century Mexico* (New Haven: Yale University Press, 2004); Herman L. Bennett, *Colonial Blackness: A History of Afro-Mexico* (Bloomington: Indiana University Press, 2009); Dennis N. Valdés, "The Decline of Slavery in Mexico," *The Americas* 44, no. 2 (October 1987): 167–94.

11   On Morelos and his role in the Mexican War of Independence, see: Rubén Hermensdorf, *Morelos: Hombre Fundamental de México* (Mexico: Aeromexico-Grijalbo, 1985); John Charles Chasteen, *Americanos: Latin America's Struggle for Independence* (New York: Oxford University Press, 2008), 89–121; Wilbert H. Timmons, *Morelos: Priest, Soldier, Statesman of Mexico* (El Paso: Texas Western College Press, 1963); Peter F. Guardino, "The War of Independence in Guerrero, New Spain, 1808–1821," in Christon I. Archer, ed., *The Wars of Independence in Spanish America* (New York: Rowman & Littlefield, 2000).

12   Eqbal Ahmad, "The Nature of Counterinsurgency," in Carollee Bengelsdoorf, Margaret Cerullo, and Yogesh Chandrani, eds., *The Selected Writings of Eqbal Ahmad* (New York: Columbia University Press, 2006), 55.

13   Vincent, *The Legacy of Vicente Guerrero*, 84; Andrews, *Afro-Latin America*, 87.

other towns, eager to purchase their liberty on the field of battle."[14] This insurgency was condemned by royalist religious leaders in New Spain as "an uprising against the rich people."[15] Elite independence leaders wanted to maintain as much of their authority as possible in the transition to autonomy; as one historian notes, however, "the peasants and workers who formed the bulk of the insurgent ranks had very different goals, such as access to land and improved working conditions."[16] Royalist General Félix María Calleja wrote to King Ferdinand VII of Spain that Morelos's soldiers wished for "the Independence of the country, and the proscription of all the Europeans, whom they detest."[17] Morelos's troops revered him for his physical courage and his commitment to radical equality. His priestly education could have set him apart from his army, yet, according to one chronicler, "he had not forgotten the twenty-odd years spent as an unlettered mule driver . . . He never became so well educated that the poor and uneducated peasants could not understand him and he them."[18] Astonished at the determined stand of his adversary's heavily outgunned troops at the Siege of Cuautla in 1812, General Calleja called Morelos "a second Mahomet."[19] "In revolutions," Eqbal Ahmad observes, "life begins to manifest itself in forms which are incomprehensible to bureaucrats and social engineers."[20]

Would this new life be explicable to President James Madison? Morelos attempted to garner Madison's support for the cause of Mexican independence by arguing that Mexicans were following in the footsteps of the thirteen colonies in their quest for independence:

> Dear Sir: The Mexican people, tired of suffering under the enormous weight of the Spanish domination, and forever losing their hope of being happy under the government of their conquerors, broke the dikes of moderation, and braving difficulties and dangers that seemed insurmountable for those of an enslaved colony, raised the cry of liberty and courageously undertook the work of their regeneration.[21]

Morelos attempted to sway Madison by pointing out that the two nations could become formidable allies:

---

14 H. G. Ward, *Mexico in 1827* (London: Henry Colburn, 1828), 185.

15 From: "Pastoral Letter of November 28, 1812, Addressed to Parish Priests and Other Clergy of the Diocese of Durango by the Dean and Chapter of the Cathedral," in *Caste and Politics in the Struggle for Mexican Independence*, The Newberry Library, n.d., available at dcc.newberry.org.

16 Guedea, "The Process of Mexican Independence," 119. For a comparative assessment, see: Marixa Lasso, "Race War and Nation in Caribbean Gran Colombia, Cartagena, 1810–1832," *American Historical Review* 111, no. 2 (April 2006): 338.

17 Ward, *Mexico in 1827*, 512.

18 Ibid., 203; Peter B. Hammond, "Mexico's Negro President," *Negro Digest* (May 1951), 11.

19 Ward, *Mexico in 1827*, 197.

20 Bengelsdoorf et al., eds., *Selected Writings*.

21 "To James Madison from José Maria Morelos" *Founders Online*, National Archives (July 14, 1815), available at founders.archives.gov. Translation by author.

I could not forsake the obvious Justice of our cause, nor abandon the righteousness and purity of our intentions aimed exclusively for the good of humanity: we trust in the spirit and enthusiasm of our patriots who are determined to die first rather than return to the offensive yoke of slavery; and finally we trusted in the powerful support of the United States, who has guided us wisely with example . . . There is no power capable of subduing a people determined to save themselves from the horrors of tyranny.[22]

While it is not known if Madison responded to Morelos directly, the man who answered, in a sense, Morelos's overtures on behalf of the United States was John Quincy Adams, the premier American diplomat of his time. In letters to his family, as well as in his diplomatic correspondence with Spain during the negotiations which led to the Adams–Onis Treaty of 1819, James Monroe's secretary of state reflected the thinking of much of the American elite toward the burgeoning independence struggles in Mexico and Latin America.[23] Adams revealed his own attitude toward the Mexican War of Independence and his viewpoints on race and citizenship in a letter he wrote to his brother Thomas in 1818. Secretary Adams contrasted the American Revolution, which he characterized as a "war of freemen," with what he depicted as a "servile war" of slaves bent on destroying society:

The struggle in South-America, is savage and ferocious almost beyond example. It is not the tug of war between Greek and Greek, but the tyger-conflict between Spaniard and Spaniard—The Cause has never been the same in any two of the revolting Colonies—Independence has not even been the pretext during [a] great part of the time—Sometimes they have fought for Ferdinand; sometimes for the Cortes—Sometimes for Congresses and Constitutions, and sometimes for particular leaders, like Morales [sic], Hidalgo, Artigas, or Bolivar—The resemblance between this Revolution and ours is barely superficial. In all their leading characters the two Events, present a contrast, instead of a parallel—Ours was a War of freemen, for political Independence—This is a War of Slaves against their masters—It has all the horrors and all the atrocities of a servile War.[24]

Expansion of the nation's borders and the preservation of slavery were Secretary John Quincy Adams's foremost goals. Adams defended General Andrew

---

22   Ibid.

23   For the Latin American wars of independence, see: Andrews: *Afro-Latin America*; Chasteen, *Americanos*; Peter Winn, *Americas: The Changing Face of Latin America and the Caribbean* (Berkeley: University of California Press, 2006), 39–90.

24   "From John Quincy Adams to Thomas Boylston Adams, 14 April 1818," *Founders Online*, National Archives, available at founders.archives.gov. For elaboration on John Quincy Adams's views on slavery and racial capitalism, see also: "John Quincy Adams to John Adams" (December 21, 1817), in Worthington Chauncy Ford, ed., *The Writings of John Quincy Adams*, vol. 6 (New York: Macmillan, 1916), 276.

Jackson's controversial conduct in the First Seminole War in Florida (1816–19), including his summary executions of two British subjects, because, as Adams told George William Erving, the US minister to Spain, they had

> invited by public proclamations, all the runaway negroes, all the savage Indians, all the pirates and all the traitors to their country, whom they knew or imagined to exist within reach of their summons, to join their standard, and wage an exterminating war against the portion of the United States immediately bordering upon this neutral and thus violated territory of Spain.[25]

Adams instructed Erving to explain to the Spanish government that Jackson's destruction of the Negro Fort on the Apalachicola River was necessary because it had become a "receptacle for fugitive slaves and malefactors, to the great annoyance of the United States and of Spanish Florida."[26]

José Morelos's vision of a "beautiful bond" between Mexico and the United States was sabotaged by the imperatives of racial capitalism. Slave-owning settler-colonialists on slavery's expanding frontier in the South waged war against the Mexican people for decades, culminating in the US invasion of 1846–7 that cost Mexico half of its territory. Early Black newspapers such as *The Colored American* asserted that the goal of this invasion was not to secure boundaries or national honor, but to achieve the expansion of slavery.[27] On a speaking tour in Ohio in 1847, Frederick Douglass railed against the war and what it revealed about the United States. In a letter published in *The National Anti-Slavery Standard*, Douglass wrote:

> The real character of our Government is being exposed . . . The present administration is justly regarded as a combination of land-pirates and free-booters. Our gallant army in Mexico is looked upon as a band of legalized murderers and plunderers. Our psalm-singing, praying, pro-slavery priesthood are stamped with hypocrisy;

---

25 "John Quincy Adams to George William Erving" (November 28, 1818), in Ford, ed., *The Writings of John Quincy Adams*, vol. 6, 486–7. For information on Erving, see: J. L. M. Curry, *Diplomatic Services of George William Erving* (Cambridge, MA: John Wilson and Son, 1890).

26 "John Quincy Adams to George William Erving." See also: Lynn Hudson Parsons, "In Which the Political Becomes the Personal, and Vice Versa: The Last Ten Years of John Quincy Adams and Andrew Jackson," *Journal of the Early Republic* 23, no. 3 (Autumn 2003): 438. For the Negro Fort, see: Matthew J. Clavin, *Aiming for Pensacola: Fugitive Slaves on the Atlantic and Southern Frontiers* (Cambridge, MA: Harvard University Press, 2015).

27 "Our Country," *The Colored American* (September 22, 1838). Black newspapers and the journals of abolitionists featured numerous anti-imperial critiques of US foreign policy. For examples, see: "Manifesto of the Mexican Congress Concerning the Rebellion in Texas," *National Enquirer* (December 10, 1836); "Southern Patriotism & Florida War," *National Enquirer* (January 28, 1837); "Mr. Editor," *The Colored American* (February 17, 1838); "Cuba," *Frederick Douglass' Paper* (October 29, 1852); "Cuba and the United States," *Frederick Douglass' Paper* (September 4, 1851); "Cuba—The Reason," *Provincial Freeman* (June 3, 1854).

and all their pretensions to a love for God, while they hate and neglect their fellow-man, is branded as impudent blasphemy.[28]

The abolition of slavery in Mexico threatened US commercial interests, and numerous articles in the African American newspapers as well as the abolitionist press pressed this point throughout the antebellum period.[29] Equally important, the anti-slavery spirit stoked by Morelos, Vicente Guerrero, and other African indigenous leaders of the Mexican War of Independence persisted, making Mexico a place of sanctuary in the minds of rebellious US slaves in the Deep South.[30] African Americans developed a deep respect for the Mexican War of Independence in the first half of the nineteenth century, as well as towards the Latin American wars of liberation; they understood, however, that the United States would likely respond to Mexico's abolition of slavery with military action. Frederick Douglass articulated this conception of US racial imperialism in Belfast, Ireland, in 1846, noting:

> We do not hear of much confusion in Texas, until 1828 or 1829, when Mexico after having erected herself into a separate government and declared herself free, with a consistency which puts to the blush the boasted "land of freedom," proclaimed the deliverance of every captive on her soil.[31]

Back in the United States the following year, Douglass extended his critique, noting:

28   "Letter from Frederick Douglass," *The National Anti-Slavery Standard* (September 9, 1847). Speaking to members of the Sixth Congregational Church in Cincinnati, Martin Delany excoriated the United States for its imperialism and "affirmed that the war was instigated for the acquisition of slave territory, at the behest of Southern slaveholders." "M. R. Delany," *Frederick Douglass' Paper* (May 19, 1848). US newspapers accused Douglass and other abolitionists who spoke against the war on these terms as traitors. See: "The Negro Douglass," *National Anti-Slavery Standard* (September 9, 1847).

29   See: "Southern Patriotism & Florida War"; "Mr. Editor," *The Colored American* (February 17, 1838); "Our Country"; "The Present Position of Mexico," *The Colored American* (February 2, 1839); "Cuba and the United States"; "Cuba," *The Colored American* (October 29, 1852).

30   A correspondent from Mexico reported in an article titled "A New Plot of the Slave-Drivers" in the *National Anti-Slavery Standard* that slave owners were "trying to acquire Mexican territory, to own slaves there, but to also keep those regions from being available to fugitive slaves to hide" (August 4, 1855). On this topic, see Jeffrey R. Kerr-Ritchie's important work: *Freedom's Seekers: Essays on Comparative Emancipation* (Baton Rouge: Louisiana State University Press, 2013), 21–40. Proof of enduring anti-slavery beliefs among Mexicans can be found in: "Speech of Mr. Clay, of Kentucky, in Support of His Propositions to Compromise on the Slavery Question in the Senate of the United States, February 5, 1850" (Washington: J. T. Towers, 1850), 6–7; "Speech of John Quincy Adams in the House of Representatives, on the State of the Nation: Delivered May 25, 1836" (Whitefish, MT: Kessinger Publishing, 2010); Paul Bryan Gray, *A Clamor for Equality: Emergence and Exile of Californio Activist Francisco P. Ramirez* (Lubbock: Texas Tech University Press, 2012).

31   "Texas, Slavery, and American Prosperity: An Address Delivered in Belfast, Ireland," *Belfast News Letter* (January 2, 1846), in John Blassingame et al., eds., *The Frederick Douglass Papers: Series One–Speeches, Debates, and Interviews*, Gilder Lehrman Center for the Study of Slavery, Resistance, and Abolition, available at glc.yale.edu.

The war with Mexico, undertaken and carried on for the infamously wicked purpose of extending and perpetuating the enslavement of my race, is becoming more and more popular every day, and such is the feeling here, that to denounce this war in the terms which its atrocious character merits, is at once to be branded as a traitor; but justice must be done, the truth must be told, the wicked must be exposed, freedom and righteousness must be vindicated, and with the help of the God of peace and the oppressed, I will not be silent.[32]

Douglass connected the US invasion of Mexico with the oppression of labor, the extension of slavery, and the evils of militarism:

You know as well as I do, that Faneuil Hall has resounded with echoing applause of a denunciation of the Mexican war, as a murderous war—as a war against the free states—as a war against freedom, against the Negro, and against the interests of workingmen of this country—and as a means of extending that great evil and damning curse, negro slavery. Why may not the oppressed say, when an oppressor is dead, either by disease or by the hand of the foeman on the battlefield, that there is one the less of his oppressors left on earth? For my part, I would not care if, to-morrow, I should hear of the death of every man who engaged in that bloody war in Mexico, and that every man had met the fate he went there to perpetrate upon unoffending Mexicans.[33]

José Maria Morelos's overture to the United States and Frederick Douglass's analysis of US imperialism vis-à-vis Mexico deserve to be seen as part of the Black Radical Tradition, a set of ideas and practices built upon grassroots insurgencies and social movements.[34] Morelos's conceptions of liberty were based on his direct observations of the willingness of the people defined by Spanish officials as pariahs to strike decisively for their freedom. Frederick Douglass's attacks on US imperialism were grounded in the anti-slavery movement. Morelos's and Douglass's efforts to imagine international solidarity as well as a struggle against slavery that transcended national borders is an ideological practice that I have called *emancipatory internationalism*.[35]

For African Americans, the struggle against slavery did not begin and end in the United States; it was a conflict that encompassed Latin America, the

---

32   "The Word to America," *National Anti-Slavery Standard* (July 8, 1847).

33   "On Mexico," *The Liberator* (June 8, 1849). See also: Editorial in *The North Star* (January 21, 1848).

34   Robinson, *Black Marxism*.

35   I expand on these themes in *An African American and Latinx History of the United States*. See also: Paul Ortiz, "'Washington, Toussaint, and Bolívar, The Glorious Advocates of Liberty': Black Internationalism and Reimagining Emancipation," in William Link and James Broomall, eds., *Rethinking American Emancipation: Legacies of Slavery and the Quest For Black Freedom* (New York: Cambridge University Press, 2015), 187–215; Paul Ortiz, "Black History Month and the Cuban Solidarity Movement of the 1870s," *Beacon Broadside* (February 25, 2015), available at beaconbroadside.com.

Caribbean, Africa, and beyond.[36] Emancipatory internationalism grew as an idea as it became clearer that the United States had set itself on a path of hemispheric domination premised on spreading slavery through military action, filibustering, or, as in Cuba, direct investment in the island's sugar plantations.[37] As slave-owning colonial settlers swarmed into Northern Mexico in 1827, *Freedom's Journal* published an excoriating critique of white Texans as "advocates for the liberty of enslaving others," and noted:

> The truth is, the new Republics of North and South America have set us an example on the subject of slavery, which we should do well to imitate, under such modifications as our peculiar circumstances render necessary. If we remember right, the last slave in Colombia is to be emancipated within the present year. Peru has essentially lightened the burden which for centuries had oppressed the poor Indians, and Mexico evinced by her decision in enforcing the law in behalf of enslaved Africans, that she is determined not to be behind her sister Republics in this cause of justice, humanity and religion.[38]

Freedom's Journal also emphasized that the liberation forces of the Global South were composed of soldiers who were considered to be the dregs of society: Africans, indigenous people, and *mestizos*. This was vital because it demonstrated an understanding that the individuals who Herman Melville called "the meanest mariners, renegades, and castaways" of the Americas were the linchpins of its future.[39] The centrality of Haiti as the true beacon of freedom in the Americas was stressed:

> What is the complexion of the common soldiery of these states? Has not the independence of their country from the vassalage and bondage of Old Spain, been accomplished by troops composed of negroes, mulattoes and indians? From what

36   I see emancipatory internationalism as a specific form of Black internationalism, the literature on which includes: Julius Scott, "The Common Wind: Currents of Afro-American Communication in the Era of the Haitian Revolution," PhD diss., Duke University (1986); Robin D. G. Kelley, "'But a Local Phase of a World Problem': Black History's Global Vision, 1883–1950," *Journal of American History* 86, no. 3 (1999): 1045–77; St. Clair Drake, "Diaspora Studies and Pan-Africanism," in Joseph E. Harris, ed., *Global Dimensions of the African Diaspora*, 2nd ed. (Washington DC: Howard University, 1993), 11–40; Michael O. West, William G. Martin, and Fanon Che Wilkins, eds., *From Toussaint to Tupac: The Black International since the Age of Revolution* (Chapel Hill: University of North Carolina Press, 2009).

37   Stephen Chambers, *No God but Gain: The Untold Story of Cuban Slavery, the Monroe Doctrine, and the Making of the United States* (London: Verso, 2015).

38   "The Revolt in Texas," *Freedom's Journal* (April 20, 1827). *Freedom's Journal*'s analysis of the outcome of the Latin American independence wars was a bit exaggerated; the final abolition of slavery in Colombia did not occur until 1851. The newspaper's main argument however was that it was necessary to look to Mexico and to Latin America if one hoped to gain greater knowledge about the process of emancipation and freedom writ large.

39   C. L. R. James, *Mariners, Renegades and Castaways: The Story of Herman Melville and the World We Live in* (London: University Press of New England, 2001[1953]).

source did Bolivar derive that aid, when fortune seemed to desert his standard, did not Hayti, furnish him with MEN and MONEY, and enable him when the contest was seemingly hopeless, by a daring effort, with a handful of *sable followers*, to achieve the final emancipation of his native country.[40]

William Appleman Williams established that "empire as a way of life" has been a central theme of US history.[41] However, it is also true that African Americans, Latinas/os, and their political allies at specific moments in history have espoused ideas that have allowed them to practice *anti-imperialism* as a way of life. In the first half of the nineteenth century, this was accomplished in part through emancipatory internationalism, which developed as a mode of analysis often coupled with critiques of racial capitalism. Emancipatory internationalism was grounded in social movements both local and international in scope that viewed slavery as an aggressively imperial institution that grew by waging war on Native Americans, Mexicans, and others. This was a rejection of the idea, later referred to as "American exceptionalism," that the United States was uniquely democratic and served as an exemplar to other nations. Just the opposite was true, the *Frederick Douglass' Paper* opined: "He is strangely deluded who supposes this country, under the guidance of Whigs and Democrats, has reached the lowest point of oppression and debasement." The writer believed that it would take pressure from the outside to reform the culture of corruption and imperialism in the United States:

> In spite of the resistance of public sentiment, from the Seminole robbery and massacre, the conquest and purchase of Texas, the Mexican robbery, to the Compromise and the Fugitive Slave Law, those parties have dragged the country down, until the opposing force in the parties is all spent, and nothing but an external resistance can now prevent them from descending still to the lowest depths of dishonor, injustice and oppression.[42]

Frederick Douglass's ideas on slavery, racial capitalism, and emancipation were shaped by his youth as an enslaved worker in Baltimore. The booming port city was a key battleground for freedom and slavery in the antebellum decades. Given its proximity to Northern cities heavily invested in the South's infrastructure of credit, insurance, shipbuilding, and land speculation based on slavery, Baltimore became a key junction point for providing slave labor and commodities to New Orleans and other Southern ports. Enslaved workers were shipped from Baltimore to the burgeoning plantations of the Deep South, which supplied the majority of the world's cotton to Great Britain, France, and other

40   "Slavery," *Freedom's Journal* (November 30, 1827).
41   William Appleman Williams, *Empire as a Way of Life* (New York: Oxford University Press, 1980); Williams, "Empire as a Way of Life," *The Nation* (August 2–9, 1980): 104–19.
42   "What Is to Be Done?" *Frederick Douglass' Paper* (May 6, 1852).

industrializing nations.[43] Douglass recalled with despair how his youth had been shaped by the imperatives of the slave trade: "In the deep still darkness of midnight, I have been often aroused by the dead heavy footsteps, and the piteous cries of the chained gangs that passed our door. The anguish of my boyish heart was intense."[44]

At the same time, however, African Americans and their allies transformed Baltimore into a base of anti-slavery struggle.[45] Not long after Harriet Tubman escaped from an Eastern Shore slave labor camp to freedom, she made her way back to Maryland and helped lay the foundation for the Underground Railroad in Baltimore.[46] The ingenuity among free Blacks in providing sanctuary to escaped slaves was such that Baltimore's commercial elite despaired of ever being able to completely crush the Underground Railroad.[47] The Haitian Revolution, which culminated in the independence of Haiti in 1804, became a great source of inspiration to Black Baltimoreans. In April 1826, a group of enslaved African Americans on the slave-trading vessel *Decatur* bound for Georgia from Baltimore seized control of the ship.[48] After throwing the captain and first mate overboard, the insurrectionists ordered the surviving crew members to steer a course for Haiti and liberty. Unfortunately, the ship was soon boarded by the crew of a Yankee whaling vessel. The mutineers were seized and brought to New York for incarceration and trial.[49] Black Baltimore birthed and inspired generations of new abolitionists and freedom fighters including Benjamin Lundy, William Lloyd Garrison, Frances Ellen Watkins Harper, and many others. Writing as "A Coloured Baltimorean," William Watkins—Harper's

---

43   "Domestic Slave Trade," *National Anti-Slavery Standard* (July 17, 1845); Sven Beckert, *Empire of Cotton: A Global History* (New York: Knopf, 2014), 243; "A Bitter Inner Harbor Legacy: The Slave Trade," *Baltimore Sun* (July 12, 2000); "The Secret History of the Slave Trade [in Baltimore]," *Baltimore Sun* (June 20, 1999).

44   Frederick Douglass, *Frederick Douglass: Selected Speeches and Writings*, ed. Philip S. Foner (Chicago: Lawrence Hill Books, 1999[1950]), 196.

45   "Benjamin Lundy and His Times," *Baltimore Sun* (January 27, 1872). See also: Barbara J. Fields, *Slavery and Freedom on the Middle Ground* (New Haven: Yale University Press, 1984); Robert L. Hall, "Slave Resistance in Baltimore City and County, 1747–1790," *Maryland Historical Magazine* 84 (1989): 305–18; Christopher Phillips, *Freedom's Port: The African American Community of Baltimore, 1790–1860* (Urbana: University of Illinois Press, 1997).

46   "Underground Railroad Made Stops in Baltimore," *Baltimore Sun* (October 22, 1993).

47   "Twenty-Ninth Congress," *Baltimore Sun* (March 19, 1846). "Stampede Among the Slaves—The Underground Railroad," *Baltimore Sun* (October 27, 1849); "Opposition to the Underground Railroad," *Baltimore Sun* (October 29, 1849). Well into the twenty-first century, archaeologists continue to discover hidden tunnels, camouflaged cisterns, and secret compartments in church basements that harbored fugitive slaves in Baltimore and its environs.

48   See: *The Life, Travels, and Opinions of Benjamin Lundy: Including His Journeys* (Philadelphia: William D. Parish, 1847), 206–7; and Ralph Clayton, "Baltimore's Own Version of 'Amistad': Slave Revolt," *Baltimore Chronicle* (January 7, 1998), available at baltimorechronicle.com; Eric Robert Taylor, *If We Must Die: Shipboard Insurrections in the Era of the Atlantic Slave Trade* (Baton Rouge: Louisiana State University Press, 2006), 147–50.

49   Ralph Clayton, *Cash for Blood: The Baltimore to New Orleans Domestic Slave Trade* (Bowie, MD: Heritage Books, 2002).

adoptive father—penned a series of commentaries for *Freedom's Journal* beginning in the 1820s, predicting doom for the imperial nation that perpetuated
human servitude: "Slavery has destroyed kingdoms and empires, and what may
we not expect will happen to those religious communities in which this crying
evil is tolerated? The least evils that we can expect are disaffection and division."[50]

It was this spirit of resistance to slavery and racial capitalism that animated
a special public commemoration of the twenty-first anniversary of Haitian
independence in the summer of 1825, organized by African Americans in
Baltimore. Those assembled raised their glasses to offer a series of toasts in
honor of the Haitian Revolution, ending thus: "Washington, Toussaint, and
Bolivar—Unequalled in fame—the friends of mankind—the glorious advocates
of Liberty."[51] Free African Americans in Baltimore connected their embattled
liberties with the emancipation of their counterparts in Latin America and the
Caribbean. The toast promoted an understanding of the linkages between
movements for liberty throughout the entire Americas. Simon Bolívar was
admired by African Americans for his 1816 decrees which freed the enslaved
people fighting on behalf of the Third Republic of Venezuela against Spanish
colonialism. These declarations followed Bolívar's meeting with Haitian president Alexandre Pétion, who pledged military support to El Libertador contingent on his ending slavery.[52] In publicly exalting anti-slavery and anticolonial
icons in Haiti and Latin America—along with the obligatory nod to George
Washington—African Americans stressed their commitment to anti-imperialism as a way of life. This principle was the core curriculum of the Black Radical
Tradition that Frederick Douglass learned on his way to emancipation.

TOWARD A CONCLUSION

In a *Freedomways* essay published in 1964, Jack O'Dell described the histories of
slavery, the Anglo-American destruction of indigenous nations, and the invasion of Mexico (among other imperial interventions) as "the main path by
which the American power structure ascended to the position of a world power,
by the turn of the twentieth century."[53] The consequences of slavery imperialism
were devastating for the whole citizenry of the Americas. The analytical lens of

---

50   "Methodism and Slavery," *Freedom's Journal* (November 23, 1827).

51   "Haytien Independence," *The Genius of Universal Emancipation and Baltimore Courier*
(September 12, 1825).

52   Over the next century, African American communities continued to accord a place of
honor to Bolívar alongside heroes of Latin American, African, and Irish anticolonialism. See:
"William Whipper's Letters, No. II," *The Colored American* (February 20, 1841); "Gen. Antonio
Maceo," *The Freeman* (Indianapolis) (October 30, 1897); W. E. B. Du Bois, *The Negro* (Philadelphia:
University of Pennsylvania Press, 2001[1915]), 176, 182. For African American culture in
Baltimore, see: Fields, *Slavery and Freedom*; Hall, "Slave Resistance in Baltimore"; Phillips,
Freedom's Port.

53   Jack O'Dell, "Foundations of Racism in American Life," *Freedomways* 4, no. 4 (Fall 1964):
98–9.

emancipatory internationalism allowed Frederick Douglass to explain not only the disastrous US invasion of Mexico but also the origins of the American Civil War. In a speech he gave to an audience of Northerners in 1862, Douglass recounted how their nation's self-destructive foreign and domestic policies had driven Americans into fighting the bloodiest civil war in human history:

> We have bought Florida, waged war with friendly Seminoles, purchased Louisiana, annexed Texas, fought Mexico, trampled on the right of petition, abridged the freedom of debate, paid ten million to Texas upon a fraudulent claim, mobbed the Abolitionists, repealed the Missouri Compromise, winked at the accursed slave trade, helped to extend slavery, given slaveholders a larger share of all the offices and honors than we claimed for ourselves, paid their postage, supported the Government, persecuted free negroes, refused to recognize Hayti and Liberia, stained our souls by repeated compromises, borne with Southern bluster, allowed our ships to be robbed of their hardy sailors, defeated a central road to the Pacific, and have descended to the meanness and degradation of negro dogs, and hunted down the panting slave escaping from his tyrant master—all to make the South love us; and yet how stands our relations?[54]

Looking carefully at the ways that African American social movements—and thinkers rooted in those movements—in the nineteenth century interpreted epochal events such as the Mexican War of Independence, the US invasion of Mexico, and the Civil War allows us to better understand the trajectory of the Black Radical Tradition. The Mexican War of Independence, abolitionism, and other social movements gave Black thinkers deep insight into tactics for battling injustice, and allowed them to understand the common problems facing oppressed people in the Americas.[55] Emancipatory internationalism animated the thought of José Maria Morelos, Frederick Douglass, the Universal Negro Improvement Association, and many other Black radical organizations in the twentieth century as well.

In one of the signature statements of *Black Reconstruction,* W. E. B. Du Bois conceived of a global vision of freedom: "The emancipation of man is the emancipation of labor and the emancipation of labor is the freeing of that basic

---

54   "Speech of Frederick Douglass on the War," *Douglass Monthly,* February 1862.

55   We need much more research on the intimate relationships between freedom struggles in Mexico and the United States. Important works in this vein include: Gerald Horne, *Black and Brown: African Americans and the Mexican Revolution, 1910–1920* (New York: New York University Press, 2005); Christina L. Heatherton, *The Color Line and the Class Struggle: The Mexican Revolution and Convergences of Radical Internationalism, 1910–1946,* PhD diss., University of Southern California (2012); Bobby Vaughn and Ben Vinson III, "Unfinished Migrations: From the Mexican South to the American South—Impressions on Afro-Mexican Migration to North Carolina," in Darién J. Davis, ed., *Beyond Slavery: The Multilayered Legacy of Africans in Latin America and the Caribbean* (New York: Rowman & Littlefield, 2007), 223–45.

majority of workers who are yellow, brown and black."[56] We can now better understand that this new conception of freedom was situated in popular struggles for justice that spanned the Americas. Today, we have the opportunity to draw upon the wellsprings of the Black Radical Tradition to confront the brutality of racial capitalism "at home" and abroad.

56   W. E. B. Du Bois, *Black Reconstruction*, 15–16.

Chapter 10

Cedric J. Robinson's Meditation on Malcolm X's Black Internationalism and the Future of the Black Radical Tradition

Darryl C. Thomas

In recent years there has been a proliferation of studies focusing on the African diaspora, Global Africa, and what some refer to as Black internationalism, drawing attention to the interrelationships, interconnections, and linkages between Africa and its diasporas, including the diaspora of enslavement (both Eastern and the Black Atlantic and the diaspora of colonialism). Scholars are paying more attention to how the African American population has sought to influence international affairs, drawing attention to the plight of Ethiopia, Haiti, India, and other colonial zones during and after the Second World War. Moreover, African American interest in world politics can be traced back as far as the American Revolutionary War, the Haitian Revolution, and the abolition movement in the pre–Civil War era. New World Africans' interest in influencing international affairs took on new life when the United States established its overseas empire and Europe divided Africa into spheres of influence. At this critical juncture when much of the world came under the control of Europe or descendants of Europeans in the United States and elsewhere, African Americans developed a view of world affairs that drew connections between the discrimination they faced at home and the expansion of empire abroad.[1] Black internationalism, as this worldview will be called in this chapter, was an ideology that stressed the role of race and racism in world affairs and stressed observing the connections between racial capitalism and the color line in world affairs. This belief in the existence of a color scheme or hierarchy in global affairs served as the guiding theoretical framework for Black internationalism, which held that the victims of racial capitalism and imperialism—the world's so-called darker (non-European) races—shared a common interest in overthrowing white supremacy and creating a new world order based on social justice and racial equality. Black internationalism has provided African Americans with a comprehensive analysis of world affairs. This chapter will employ and contextualize the black internationalist framework and its contribution to the Black Radical Tradition. The demise of the Cold War conflict and the emergence of a new wave of globalization have spawned new approaches to

---

1 Marc Gallicchio, *The African American Encounter with Japan and China: Black Internationalism in Asia, 1895–1945* (Chapel Hill and London: University of North Carolina Press, 2000).

the production of knowledge. Malcolm X played a critical role in challenging the American/European narratives about civilization and global history. The role of African Studies, Black Studies, and Studies of African Diasporas has been critical to this new discourse. Cedric Robinson has been one of the unsung pioneers in this arena.

Until now, the Cold War conflict has been celebrated as the most significant postwar conflict between two imperial hegemonies because of the threat of nuclear annihilation, marginalizing all other interstate conflagrations. Cedric Robinson observes that it is now possible to conceptualize the Cold War era "as a historical sidebar to the struggles to obtain and vanquish racial domination."[2] Indeed, two of the most intensive sites of the Cold War were the United States and the Republic of South Africa. Contrary to the colossal cultural, political, technological, military, and propaganda industries contrived on behalf of the Cold War obsession over the past fifty years, the awe-inspiring and more lasting dualism has been what Frantz Fanon recognized as the racial order of colonial domination: "The cause is the consequence: you are rich because you are white: you are white because you are rich." From there he calculated that "it was not the *organization of production* but the *persistence and organization of oppression* which formed the primary social bases of revolutionary activities."[3] Furthermore, the West's political leaders ignored the crucial role of white supremacy in the imperial wars of the nineteenth century and the global wars of the twentieth, masked as they were beneath rhetoric of international conflict. Corporate and political elites/leaders ratcheted up the clash with the Soviet Union and China, providing them with an ideological apparatus with which to continue imperial and colonial "adventures" among darker peoples, and to keep in check democratic movements at home.[4]

MALCOLM X AND THE SEARCH FOR HIGHER GROUND

The spectacle of Barack Obama's election/re-election (2008 and 2012), including the festive inaugurations, reinforced the illusions of revitalized Black politics and a post-racial United States. Yet racialized stereotypes persist of thuggish Black males and Black welfare queens. One of the consequences of neoliberal/globalized US capitalism for many African Americans is a growing difference in life chances between poor and affluent Blacks—a divide, as Michael Dawson explains, that is beginning to be reflected in Black politics and in Black public opinion. Dawson contends that "the continuing weaknesses in black politics [make] it exceedingly difficult to address the material deprivations of poor black communities," let alone construct dynamic progressive movements in the United States. According to Dawson, Black politics must be reinvigorated by

---

2   Cedric J. Robinson, *Black Movements in America* (New York: Routledge, 1997), 134.
3   Frantz Fanon, *The Wretched of the Earth*, (New York: Grove Press, 2005[1965]), 22–3.
4   Ibid., 135.

rebuilding Black civil society and the "Black counter-public," as well as reestablishing independent Black political movements and organizations.[5]

Cedric Robinson also examined this dilemma in Black US politics from the slave insurrections of the sixteenth century to the Black power movements, outlining the emergence of two diverging Black political cultures of resistance and accommodation based on the radically different experiences of enslaved and free Blacks: "Long after free black workers had begun to sour on the new country," he writes, "the free Black middle classes remained enchanted by the possibility of achieving equality in America."[6] This included the development of a conservative sector in the aftermath of the Nixon, Reagan, and (first) Bush administrations and how it aided in the dismantling of liberal institutions such as the Civil Rights Commission. In contrast, African American women have been leaders in the Afro-Christianity that seethed underneath slavery and burst forth in its aftermath to renew the moral and ethical creed of deliverance. Black women produced both a gospel and a theology of community that still influence Black political culture.[7] Indeed, African American women have played a central role in the struggle for Black liberation, as Robinson demonstrates. Although much attention has been paid to nationalist organizations like the Nation of Islam, with its anti-white jargon, and to the decadence of Black youth gangs, the most significant, widespread, and influential institution among Blacks remains the Black church. Black Baptists, Pentecostalists, African Methodist Episcopalians and adherents of African Episcopal Zion dwarf Black Muslims in number. Here lies the bedrock of the community ethos that connects directly with the past while stretching into the future. "Without them," Robinson writes, "the inevitable uprisings are empty, episodic expressions of rage. With them it is always possible that the next Black social movement will obtain that distant land, and perhaps even transporting America with it."[8] It is this quest for Black liberation that compels Malcolm X to extend the boundaries of black internationalism into a force for universal freedom and human rights.

Using the framework of Robinson's Black Radical Tradition, let us examine Black Christian and Islamic Black Nationalist thought and the work of Marcus Garvey and the Universal Negro Improvement Association (UNIA) that together steered Malcolm X toward Black internationalism—a philosophy that included and engaged Third World populations inside and outside the United States. In the Black Radical Tradition, Malcolm represents the renegade Black Organic Intelligentsia within Black religion. One of the most critical tools in their toolkit, according to Robinson, was their use of "words":

---

5   Michael C. Dawson, *Not in Our Lifetimes: The Future of Black Politics* (Chicago: University of Chicago Press, 2011), ix–x.

6   Robinson, *Black Movements in America*, 51.

7   Ibid., 101.

8   Ibid., 153.

Words were their means of placement and significance, the implements for discovery and revelation. With words they might and did construct new meanings, new alternatives, new realities for themselves and others. But language, that is Western culture, was more than some recumbent artifact to be used or not as the intelligentsia saw fit. Its place in their lives had been established long before they found the means of mastering it. Indeed, they were themselves in part defined by those languages of rule and commerce.[9]

Malcolm X emerged as the master of delivering the words of Black liberation in both national and international contexts. He captured the voices and perspectives of the Black masses in a language that was clear and precise, defining what it meant to be free and to enjoy human dignity, autonomy, and unrestrained human rights.

DIFFERENT SHADES OF BLACK NATIONALISM

E. U. Esien-Udom defines the ideological landscape of Black nationalism in his influential work *Black Nationalism: A Search for an Identity in America*.[10] Starting with the post–World War I era until the 1960s, he identifies two basic streams of Black nationalism. The first, Islamic, is associated with the Moorish Science Temple and the Nation of Islam (NOI), while the second, more secular, is associated with the UNIA and similar organizations. The Moorish Temple of Science and the NOI considered Christianity the "white man's religion" and Islam the "Black man's religion"; Black Islamist nationalists adopted a Black Asiatic rather than a Negro American, African, or African diasporic identity. The Moorish Temple of Science and the NOI advocated Black separatism and employed vociferous rhetoric against whites, but did not engage in political activity or join social movements that directly confronted the American racial state. A careful reading of the literature of the Moorish Temple of Science renders their political objectives ambiguous at best, but the NOI clearly sought repatriation of African Americans back to Africa or the creation of an independent territory within the United States.[11]

Marcus Garvey's UNIA was both a secular and a religious movement that sought to transcend religious differences between Christianity, Judaism, Islam, and atheism. Most of its members were affiliated with the Christian Orthodox Church. Garvey Blackened key religious figures in Christianity, including Jesus, the Disciples, and the Virgin Mary, to convey that Black people should worship

---

9   Cedric J. Robinson, *Black Marxism: The Making of the Black Radical Tradition* (Chapel Hill: University of North Carolina Press, 2000), 183.

10   E. U. Esien-Udom, *Black Nationalism: A Search for Identity in America* (New York: Dell, 1969), 33–6.

11   Edward E. Curtis, *The Call of Bilal: Islam in the African Diaspora* (Chapel Hill: University of North Carolina Press, 2014).

a God that looked like them. The UNIA mobilized Black people across the United States on the basis of Black (racial) nationalism, with a focus on political and economic independence and ultimately seeking the creation of a Black empire based in Africa that would safeguard the interests of people there and in the African global diasporas. This empire would be structured around the European patriarchal and capitalist model of nation building through "science and religion."[12]

The fragile coalition between liberal and radical tendencies within the civil rights movement was shattered during the mid-1960s by the new wave of Black nationalism, and by the anger that had arisen with the measured and reformist political agenda of nonviolence and integration. "Black power" and Black nationalism introduced a passionate theoretical and tactical deliberation over the nature of racism and the future of Black politics in the United States, following the split in the NOI and the emergence of Malcolm X as the most visible spokesman for Black nationalism in the United States. The turn toward Black nationalism and Black power also coincided with President Lyndon Johnson's escalation of the Vietnam War, the emergence of a broad antiwar and anti-imperialist coalition, and a new phenomenon in US racial politics: Black-led, Black-based urban rebellions (that is, Black revolts), beginning in Harlem in 1964 and Watts in 1965 and culminating in Detroit and Newark in 1967.[13]

MALCOLM X AND THE GLOBALIZATION OF THE BLACK STRUGGLE

Malcolm X emerged as one of the most important leaders in the struggle against white supremacy and American/European imperialism, whether employed through colonialism, internal colonialism, neocolonialism, or the newer imperialism of Pax Americana and US-based multinational corporations. He continued the tradition of revolutionary Black nationalism initiated by David Walker, Henry Highland Garnett, Marcus Garvey, Claudia Jones, W. E. B. Du Bois, and Paul Robeson, among others, who linked the African American struggle for liberation with Third World struggles against colonialism, white supremacy at home and abroad, and racial capitalism. After Malcolm's departure from the NOI over his negative characterization of President Kennedy's assassination as "the chickens coming home to roost," he continued expanding his political philosophy to include complete self-determination and autonomy for African Americans and the right to self-defense by any means necessary, as well as unrestrained support for anticolonial and anti-imperialist battles in Africa, Asia,

---

12   Marcus Garvey, "African Fundamentalism," in Tony Martin, ed., *African Fundamentalism: A Literary and Cultural Anthology of Garvey's Harlem Renaissance* (Dover, MA: Majority Press, 1991), 4–6.

13   Michael Omi and Howard Winant, eds., *Racial Formation in the United States*, 3rd ed. (New York and London: Routledge, 2015), 82.

Latin America, and the Caribbean. At this juncture, Malcolm began conceptualizing the African American population as a colonial people and as a fundamental player in the global struggle against colonialism and racism. He made an invaluable contribution to Black internationalism, encouraging African Americans along with Latinos, Native Americans, and Asian Americans to wage twin battles against racism at home and racism abroad, in solidarity with Third World struggles against colonialism and American/European imperialism. He was critical in developing what Michael Dawson refers to as the "Black counterpublic,"[14] mobilizing African American public opinion against economic, political, cultural, and racial repression in Africa and the rest of the Third World. He was joined by a new generation of African Americans who cut their teeth on resistance to American empire at home and abroad through the civil rights and Black power movements.

Malcolm X was critical in converting the NOI from a small religious sect with no impact on the African American population to a major actor in the struggle for Black liberation. Indeed, he helped establish temples from Detroit to Harlem and Boston to Los Angeles. His organizational skills, charisma, and fiery intellectualism caught the attention of the FBI and other US intelligence agencies, just as Elijah Muhammad (leader of the NOI from 1934 until his death in 1975) had done previously. However, unlike Elijah Muhammad, Malcolm's religious consciousness had a distinct connection to Africa, which was rooted in his interest in Garveyism. Malcolm's African consciousness overlapped with the anticolonial movements that were sweeping the Third World.[15] In essence Malcolm employed the racial and religious theories and hypotheses of the NOI to analyze and interpret international relations; as a result his critique and condemnation of White America led to a criticism of European and American foreign policy.[16] He devoted a chapter in his autobiography to his growing disenchantment with the NOI over its refusal to take an active role in the work initiated by the civil rights movement against American racism. Malcolm concluded that it was inexcusable for the NOI to sit on the sidelines while the African American population was battling to transform the "Jim Crow" nation into a citadel of democracy and freedom:

> If I harbored any personal disappointment whatsoever, it was that privately I was
> convinced that our Nation could be an even greater force in the American black
> man's overall struggle—if we engaged in more action. By that I mean I thought
> privately that we should have amended, or relaxed, our general non-engagement
> policy. I felt that, whatever black people committed themselves, in the Little Rocks

---

14   Michael C. Dawson, *Black Visions: The Roots of Contemporary African-American Political Ideologies* (Chicago: University of Chicago Press, 2001), 44–84.

15   Mark Ledwidge, *Race and US Foreign Policy: The African American Foreign Affairs Network* (New York and London: Routledge, 2012), 140.

16   Ibid., 142.

and the Birmingham's and other places, militantly disciplined Muslims should also be there—for the entire world to see, and respect and discuss.[17]

Malcolm X was baptized into the radical Black nationalist tradition during his early youth. His parents were local officers in Marcus Garvey's UNIA. Later, his siblings recruited him into the NOI, which steered him from a life of crime to Black nationalism. After his departure from NOI, Malcolm developed practices and ideological positions that distinguished his perspectives from those of his nationalist predecessors, and took shape as Black internationalism. This evolution began while he was a spokesman for the NOI, when he developed an analysis of the impact of the Bandung Conference on the Third World and the struggle for Black liberation in the United States. "The stated position of Bandung," as Daulatzai writes, in light of US and Soviet political interference, "was a call to end colonialism and neocolonialism from European powers, the United States, and the Soviet Union and a vow to support the anticolonial struggles of countries still under the boot of colonialism and the eventual creation of what was called the Non-Aligned Movement."[18] Although journalist Carl Rowan, US congressman Adam Clayton Powell Jr., and writer Richard Wright did attend the Bandung Conference, many leading Black activists of the Left could not, due to political repression. The US government even revoked the passports of Paul Robeson and W. E. B. Du Bois. Nevertheless, Du Bois and Robeson sent telegrams to the delegates articulating their solidarity with the Bandung spirit.[19]

At this critical juncture, Malcolm X and the NOI defined all non-white people as Black, thus enlarging the global majority. Initially, Malcolm's response to the Bandung Conference was consistent with the NOI's prophetic tradition. Later, his position would be more nuanced, transcending the NOI to emphasize critical elements of Black internationalism:

> The time is past when the white world can exercise unilateral authority and control over the dark world. The independence and power of the dark world is on the increase; the dark world is rising in wealth, power, prestige, and influence. It is the rise of the dark world that is causing the fall of the white world.

As the white man loses his power to oppress and exploit the dark world, the white man's own wealth (power or "world") decreases . . . You and I were born at the turning point in history; we are witnessing the fulfillment of prophecy. Our present generation is witnessing the end of colonialism, Europeanism,

---

17   John Henrik Clarke, *Malcolm X: The Man and His Times* (Trenton, NJ: Africa World Press, 1992), xix–xx.

18   Sohail Daulatzai, *Black Star, Crescent Moon: The Muslim International and Black Freedom Beyond America* (Minneapolis and London: University of Minnesota Press, 2012), 25–6.

19   Ibid., 27.

Westernism, or "White-ism" . . . the end of white supremacy, the end of the white man's unjust rule.[20]

Malcolm made this observation during the era of decolonization in Africa and Asia, when the spirit of Bandung gave rise, for him, to the goal of worldwide revolution.

The theory and practice of Third World solidarity was based on the principle that the peoples of the Third World shared a common consciousness and common experiences of colonialism, no matter their geographical location. Predating the Cold War, it emerged from years of struggle for political, economic, and cultural independence within a global context of racial capitalism, invigorated by a shared interest in ending poverty and inequality.[21]

Indonesian President Sukarno, in his opening speech, outlined in bold relief the hopeful tone of this conference when he declared, "Let a New Asia and a New Africa Be Born." "The nations of Asia and Africa are no longer the tools and playthings" of Europe, the United States, and the Soviets, he argued.[22] Bandung represented more than a challenge by the "dark world" to the West. It promised a world order radically different from centuries of white power, colonialism, and capitalist control, and recognized that Western imperialism, despite its diverse variations, consistently maintained allegiance to a hierarchical racial structure.[23]

Malcolm also questioned the idea of American exceptionalism, linking Jim Crow segregation and racial terror in the United States to American empire-building abroad, a project that included the Cold War. Under the guise of "democracy" and "anti-communism," the United States was going to replace Europe as the imperial power in what Malcolm referred to as "benevolent colonialism" or "philanthropic imperialism."[24] In 1959, while an NOI spokesman, Malcolm made trips to the African and Arab world; was overwhelmingly affected by the assassination of Patrice Lumumba; convened a meeting with Fidel Castro in Harlem; supported Gamel Abdel Nasser of Egypt and his defiant stand against the British, French, and Israelis; and expressed support for the Mau Mau rebellion in Kenya and the Vietnamese victory at Dien Bien Phu.[25]

Malcolm departed from NOI in March 1964 and started his own organization, the Black nationalist Muslim Mosque Inc. (which attracted other NOI

---

20 This passage is from a speech Malcolm made in 1963 following the assassination of President John F. Kennedy.

21 Darryl C. Thomas, *The Theory and Practice of Third World Solidarity* (Westport and London: Praeger Publishers, 2001), 29–30.

22 Manning Marable and Vanessa Agard-Jones, eds., *Transnational Blackness: Navigating the Global Color Line* (New York: Palgrave Macmillan, 2008), 153; Daulatzai, *Black Star, Crescent Moon*, 26.

23 Ledwidge, *Race and US Foreign Policy*, 128.

24 Daulatzai, *Black Star, Crescent Moon*, 4.

25 Ibid., 5; Ledwidge, *Race and US Foreign Policy*, 142–5.

defectors) to provide the spiritual base for the moral rejuvenation of African American communities. He called for African Americans to control the economics and politics of the Black community and to reconstruct their African identity. His focus on armed self-defense when the federal government failed to provide protection of their human rights caught the attention of the FBI, Justice Department, State Department, Secret Service, CIA, and Military Intelligence. The goals of Muslim Mosque Inc. (MMI) were antagonistic to the interests of the US government, as Malcolm X focused the Black struggle on human rather than civil rights, preparing to charge the government with violating the human rights of African Americans. MMI also put forth a transnational and racial worldview calculated to convince African and Asian nations to petition the United Nations to intervene in US domestic affairs.[26] UN protocol prevented member states from interfering in each other's domestic affairs, which would include the domestic, civil rights issue of the treatment of African Americans. However, if framed as a "human rights" and thus international issue, the situation would fall under the jurisdiction of the UN Charter.[27] This strategy prompted surveillance of the organization by the FBI.

Starting in the 1960s, Malcolm X began questioning the theology of Elijah Muhammad, the NOI's refusal to become politically active, its politically and economically conservative programs (in the tradition of Booker T. Washington), and its patriarchal attitudes toward women. Later, he established the Organization of Afro-American Unity (OAAU) modeled on its African counterpart, the Organization of African Unity (OAU), to organize millions of non-Muslim African Americans into a militant organization that would act as a vanguard for Black liberation. The OAAU included South America, Central America, the Caribbean, and all of North America. For Malcolm X, globalizing the plight of the African American population would force the United States to be scrutinized and challenged by the Third World.

In mid-April 1964, Malcolm made a tour of the Middle East and Africa. King Faisal treated him as a foreign dignitary in Saudi Arabia and he was welcomed by state officials in Nigeria, Ghana, Morocco, and Algeria, receiving both acclaim for his work and empathy for the plight of African Americans. Malcolm also made a pilgrimage to Mecca, the shrine of orthodox Islam, where he encountered a fraternity among the multiracial pilgrims in sharp contrast to the racism of White America. These experiences confirmed Malcolm's discontent with the teachings of Elijah Muhammad and his embrace of Sunni Islam, enabling him to reject Elijah Muhammad's conception of whites as "devils" (and instead consider them "hypocrites") and paving the way for a possible alliance with the civil rights movement. Malcolm's conversations with Elijah Muhammad's sons Akbar and Wallace D. Muhammad before the trip had also

---

26   Ledwidge, *Race and US Foreign Policy*, 147; Louis A. DeCaro, *On the Side of My People: A Religious Life of Malcolm X* (New York and London: New York University Press, 1996), 195.

27   Daulatzai, *Black Star, Crescent Moon*, 38.

pushed him in this direction. The two sons, who had accompanied Malcolm on his pilgrimage, made it clear to their father upon their return to the US that his version of Islam was out of step with Islamic traditions. The NOI eventually split after Muhammad's death into two factions—one practicing NOI traditional doctrine under Minister Louis Farrakhan and the other practicing Sunni Islam.

Malcolm's tour also included an eighteen-week trip to Africa, where he met privately with the heads of state of Kenya, Egypt, Uganda, Nigeria, and Ghana to secure their support for charging the United States before the United Nations with violating the human rights of African Americans, just as the South African apartheid system had been charged. The US State Department and national security agencies were concerned about these meetings, as these states were pivotal to US Cold War interests in Africa as well as European and US economic interests. By the end of his trip, Malcolm had established a network of contacts in Egypt, Lebanon, Saudi Arabia, Nigeria, Ghana, Morocco, and Algeria. Nigerian Muslim students hailed him as "Omowale": the child who has come home. Malcolm returned to the United States as El-Hajj Malik El-Shabazz, totally transformed.

Malcolm's trip had convinced him that the African American community needed to broaden its scope, forcefully participating in the African and Third World liberation movement against the remaining vestiges of colonialism and imperialism. He believed the time was ripe for a radical vision of Pan-Africanism that encompassed Africa and its diaspora. He rejected the NOI's strategy of separatism and its members' penchant for machine idolatry and thirst for money and property[28] as mere imitations of their enemy within the circuits of racial capitalism. He called upon African Americans to adopt a theoretical framework and political practice that placed a premium on human dignity and freedom separate from the limitations of American and Western liberalism. His trip around the world had reinforced his belief that revolutionary Black nationalism was the political philosophy that would achieve Black liberation. Recalling a speech he had given after that trip:

> I was convinced that it was time for all Afro-Americans to join the world's Pan-Africanists. I said that physically we Afro-Americans might remain in America, fighting for our Constitutional rights, but that philosophically and culturally we Afro-Americans badly needed to "return" to Africa—and to develop a working unity in the framework of Pan-Africanism.[29]

Malcolm concluded that African Americans could achieve a psychological return to Africa as they gained self-determination and political and economic liberation from white domination in the United States.

---

28   John Henrik Clarke, *Africans at the Crossroads: Notes for an African World Revolution* (Trenton, NJ: Africa World Press, 1992), xxiii.

29   Malcolm X and Alex Haley, *The Autobiography of Malcolm X as Told to Alex Haley* (New York: Ballantine Books, 1964), 350.

On July 9, 1964, Malcolm left for another journey abroad to pursue his United Nations project. He flew to Cairo to attend the second meeting of the Organization of African Unity (OAU) as a representative of the OAAU.[30] He submitted an eight-page memorandum to the OAU in which he outlined the conditions of African Americans and appealed for support from the attendees for his petition against the US government to be presented before the United Nations. In the memorandum he declared that the human rights of African Americans were being violated daily:

> We beseech the independent African states to help us bring our problem before the United Nations, on the grounds that the United States government is morally incapable of protecting the lives and property of 22 million African Americans . . . In the interest of world peace and security, we beseech the heads of independent African states to recommend an immediate investigation into our problems by the United Nations Commission on Human Rights . . . We have been servants in America for over 300 years. We have a thorough knowledge of . . . Uncle Sam. Therefore you must heed our warning: Don't escape European colonialism . . . only to be enslaved by deceitful . . . American colonialism.[31]

As Mark Ledwidge notes, Malcolm had violated a mainstream convention: American citizens of any racial background usually avoided criticizing the United States on foreign soil. He had also developed a network capable of officially critiquing American foreign policy, encouraging the Afro-Asian bloc to use US racism against the United States to secure their own interests. More importantly, it was the first time African states had officially recognized their association and kinship with descendants of enslaved Africans shipped to the United States. Malcolm's efforts were not lost on the press, who chastised him for trying to ignite a global race war.[32] There were also rumors claiming that Malcolm X and the OAAU were receiving money from foreign sources.

Nevertheless, the OAU summit successfully passed a resolution recognizing the recent ratification of the 1964 Civil Rights Act by the US Congress, but acknowledging the continuation of racism in America and declaring that the member states were deeply disturbed by the mistreatment of people of African ancestry in the United States. Some member states also pledged support for Malcolm's efforts to prosecute the US for human rights violations before the United Nations. Malcolm's petition ultimately charged the US government with economic genocide, mental harm, murder, conspiracy, and complicity to commit genocide, declaring that in its treatment of African Americans, the US

---

30   James H. Cone, *Martin and Malcolm and America: A Dream or a Nightmare* (Maryknoll, NY: Orbis Books, 1991), 208. Sohail Daulatzai makes a similar observation in *Black Star, Crescent Moon*, 39.

31   Ledwidge, *Race and US Foreign Policy*, 148.

32   Ibid.

government had not only violated its own constitution, but also the Charter of the United Nations, the Universal Declaration of Human Rights, and the 1948 Draft Convention on the Prevention and Punishment of Genocide. Malcolm was echoing Du Bois's claim that the "Black condition in the United States is but a local phase of a global problem."

Malcolm was assassinated before the next United Nations session convened. Still, he had not only resurrected the memory of Africa in the African American community, but also identified the Black struggle with the African/Third World campaign against colonialism and imperialism in all forms, thus declaring that African Americans were a colonial people.

MALCOLM'S DISCOURSE WITH THE CIVIL RIGHTS MOVEMENT

Malcolm X's globalization of the Black struggle had a lasting impact on the youthful leadership of the Student Nonviolent Coordinating Committee (SNCC) and the Congress of Racial Equality (CORE). SNCC members had carved out a space for themselves as the most radical of the conventional civil rights organizations, confronting white supremacy with an independent and compelling dedication to social change. SNCC employed a collective approach to leadership that was inspired and directed by Ella Baker and that continued to evolve as the organization confronted the Southern white wall of resistance, including economic and political reprisals, violence, and brutality. When the strategies of nonviolence were considered ineffective, SNCC abandoned them for more a militant position, becoming an organization radically different from the one founded in 1960.[33] SNCC campaigns in the rural South, including in Alabama, Mississippi, and Georgia, played a key role in this gradual radicalization. After the 1964 Democratic Party Convention, when the Mississippi Freedom Democratic Party lost its bid to become the legitimate representative of the state of Mississippi, most SNCC activists concluded that simply exposing injustices would never convince the United States to eliminate racist practices.

After the convention, Black liberation rather than civil rights became the movement's primary focus. SNCC and MFDP activists, including Fannie Lou Hamer, Bob Moses, Donna Moses, Julian Bond, James Foreman, John Lewis, Ruby Doris Smith Robinson, and Prathia Hall Wynn made a trip to Guinea, which had just gained its independence from France, and met with the Guinean president, Sekou Toure. Harry Belafonte, a staunch supporter of SNCC, made the travel arrangements. The group was amazed to experience a country under Black leadership, whose people were proud of their indigenous culture and heritage, and felt a growing sense of identity with Africa.[34]

---

33   Michael LeMay, *The Perennial Struggle: Race, Ethnicity and Minority Group Relations in the United State*, 2nd ed. (Upper Saddle River, NJ: Prentice Hall, 2004), 215.

34   Belinda Robnett, *How Long? How Long?: African-American Women in the Struggle for Civil Rights* (New York: Oxford University Press, 1997), 173.

Following their trip to Guinea, SNCC began an internal debate over the fate of the organization. Malcolm X's perspective had gained credence and legitimacy among SNCC's leaders, who began to explore the work of Frantz Fanon, Amilcar Cabral, Fidel Castro, and other African and Third World theoreticians as well. Fannie Lou Hamer and the SNCC Freedom Singers appeared at the same rallies as Malcolm in December 1964. Malcolm himself had begun to connect Southern civil rights struggles with those in the North:

> America is Mississippi . . . There is no such thing as the South—it's America. If one room in your house is dirty, you've got a dirty house . . . You have authority over the whole house; the entire house is under your jurisdiction. And the mistake that you and I make is letting these *Northern* crackers shift the weight to the Southern crackers . . .
>
> The head of the Democratic Party is sitting in the White House . . . He could have opened up his mouth and had her seated. [Robert] Wagner, the mayor right here [in New York City], could have opened up his mouth and used his weight and had her seated. Don't be talking about some crackers down in Mississippi and Alabama and Georgia—all of them are playing the same game. Lyndon Johnson is the head of the Cracker Party.[35]

Malcolm continues by contextualizing Fannie Lou Hamer's story of oppression in gendered terms:

> No, we don't deserve to be recognized and respected as men as long as our women can be brutalized in the manner that this woman described, and nothing being done about it, but we sit around singing "We Shall Overcome."
>
> We need a Mau Mau [Kenya's Terrorist Mau Mau society led by Odinga Odinga]. If they don't want to deal with the Mississippi Freedom Democratic Party, then we'll give them something else to deal with. If they don't want to deal with the Student Nonviolent Committee, we have to give them an alternative. Never stick someone out there without an alternative.[36]

Robnett notes that Malcolm X's attitude toward women's participation in Black political movements began to change after his departure from the NOI and his increased interaction with the civil rights movement. Increasingly, Malcolm viewed Fannie Lou Hamer as the country's foremost freedom-fighting woman and claimed that

> you don't have to be a man to fight for freedom. All you have to do is be an intelligent human being. And automatically, your intelligence makes you want

---

35   Ibid., 175.
36   Ibid.

freedom so badly that you'll do anything, by any means necessary, to get that freedom.[37]

Malcolm X's dialogue and debate with the civil rights movement also influenced his ideological development toward secular Black nationalism. He saw the futility of the NOI's criticism of the civil rights movement without any program of tangible action that might contribute to Black liberation. He observed the men, women, and children who were prepared to put their lives on the line for freedom and liberation. And he recognized that many African Americans were not religiously inclined (which encouraged him to establish the secular Muslim Mosque Inc. and OAAU) and that the Harlem community of scholars and intellectuals who knew of the role of Arabs and Muslims in the slave trade with sub-Saharan Africa, which created the Eastern African Diaspora, was ambivalent toward Islam.[38] He had concluded that the NOI and the civil rights movement were still operating within the framework of American liberalism. Most leaders of the civil rights movement, including Bayard Rustin, Whitney Young, and Martin Luther King Jr., believed that Black Americans could achieve freedom if, through moral persuasion, they made White America hear their plea for justice.

President John F. Kennedy sought to quell the momentum of the 1963 March on Washington, attempting to discourage the civil rights leadership from going through with planned activities on August 28. Although Kennedy failed to dissuade them, the liberal financial backers of the civil rights movement took steps to unify Black civil rights leadership against militancy. Supported by the philanthropist Stephen Currier of the Taconic Foundation, the United Civil Rights Leadership Council was established to organize activities for the march, with $800,000 disseminated among all the major civil rights organizations, including SNCC. Through this act of co-optation, the Kennedy administration's goal of smothering radicalism was mostly achieved, though John Lewis, James Foreman, and other representatives of SNCC initially planned to demonstrate on the day of the March at the Justice Department, with Lewis delivering a speech criticizing the Kennedy administration and the federal government's neglect of the Black masses.[39] Despite some cracks in the unity of the civil rights coalition, however, the March on Washington remains a defining moment

37   Ibid.

38   See Edward E. Curtis, *The Call of Bilal: Islam in the African Diaspora* (Chapel Hill: University of North Carolina Press, 2014); Michael A. Gomez, *The Black Crescent: The Experience and Legacy of African Muslims in America* (New York: Cambridge University Press, 2005); Patrick Manning, *The African Diaspora: A History through Culture* (New York: Columbia University Press, 2009); and Robinson, *Black Marxism*.

39   Richard Benson, *Fighting for Our Place in the Sun: Malcolm X and the Radicalization of the Black Student Movement, 1960–1973* (New York, Bern, and Berlin: Peter Lang, 2015), 39.

in the movement's history and mobilized American public opinion in support of civil rights.[40]

A few months later, the principles championed by Martin Luther King Jr. and his constituents were tested by white violence in the South. The murder of four Black girls in a church bombing in Birmingham, Alabama, in the fall of 1963 angered the Black community, ignited a wave of disillusionment inside the civil rights movement, and caused many SNCC workers to question the use of nonviolence.[41] Malcolm X, who had been sharply critical of the March on Washington, encouraged African American leadership to return to the tradition of Black radicalism embedded in the community, rather than following the "talented tenth" of Black ministerial elites. This tradition directly opposed the cultural values promoted by the racial capitalist tradition and emphasized community, collective self-reliance, and shared decision-making processes. In line with these principles, Malcolm urged African Americans to develop independent political institutions that did not rely on financial support or leadership from outside the community. He encouraged them to look beyond Western liberalism toward Africa, the African diaspora, and the rest of the Third World, arguing that Black liberation was impossible without the liberation of other non-white people all over the world from oppression by the United States and other European powers.

Also in the Black Radical Tradition, Malcolm attacked the "Negro" as an invention who served as an apologist for the Atlantic slave trade and the divergent racial orders and racial regimes that evolved in its aftermath—an argument that was pivotal to the development of Africana, Black, Latino, Asian American, and Ethnic Studies. It created space for the emergence of Black power and Black consciousness and the expansion of the African American identity. Malcolm emphasized the importance of acquiring critical analytical skills through studying, analyzing, and excavating African, African American, and Third World history, particularly examples of systematic resistance to tyranny in the form of racial capitalism, colonialism, imperialism, globalization, and neoliberalism. This set the stage for one of his most significant contributions: Black internationalism.

Despite Malcolm X's assassination in 1965, critical aspects of his legacy endure in the development of several social movements. The Black Power movement, which he inspired, led to the development of the Revolutionary Action Movement (RAM), the Black Panther Party (BPP), the African Liberation Support Committee, the Pan African Liberation Support Committee, the Congress of African People, and TransAfrica, among other groups, and it transformed CORE and SNCC into Black Power advocates. These organizations operated from a wide spectrum of ideological perspectives but all sought to

40 Ibid., 39–40.
41 Ibid., 41–2.

influence US foreign policy, particularly from the mid-1960s to the 1990s. The Black Congressional Caucus also took on many initiatives aimed at fostering liberation and changing US foreign policy in Southern Africa. The anti-apartheid movement in the United States included university students, local and state officials, and ordinary citizens, and called for universities, municipalities, states, and multinational corporations to divest from apartheid South Africa. After the 1990s the forces of globalization and neoliberalism began to obstruct these activities, as Black communities have struggled to cope with deindustrialization, loss of meaningful employment, and gentrification in urban areas.[42]

It was the uprising popularly known as the Watts rebellion or insurrection, days after the passage of the 1965 Voting Rights Act, that influenced Dr. King's turn toward the radicalism of democratic socialism. The largest urban uprising in American history at the time, the revolt drew national and international attention as it appeared to contradict the American narrative of racial conciliation. King's advisors recommended that he denounce the rebellion along with the issues against which the protesters were rebelling; King, however, met with the insurrection's participants and stated in a press conference that the rebellion "was a class revolt of underprivileged against privilege"[43] by those whose material circumstances, notwithstanding the new legislation, were unchanged. King came to view American capitalism and US wealth distribution as ethically compromised and became a vocal advocate of democratic socialism, as well as an important ally to working people in the struggle against racism, militarism, and poverty.[44]

Despite his private respect for Malcolm X, King believed that violence was futile in addressing the political conflict and that nonviolence was tactically superior in achieving the goals of Black political movements. The Civil Rights Act of 1964 and the Voting Rights Act of 1965 were the pinnacle of the civil rights movement in the South, which had used mass mobilization, television coverage, appeals to American ideals, and the Cold War to redefine US race relations. Malcolm's assassination marked a new paradigm in US race relations, as the dismantling of the Jim Crow apparatus did little to alleviate the poverty, unemployment, and urban decay of American life in and outside of the South. Accordingly, 1965 witnessed significant race-related uprisings in Los Angeles, Detroit, and Chicago.[45]

---

42   See Michael L. Clemons, ed., *African Americans in Global Affairs: Contemporary Perspectives* (Boston: Northeastern University Press, 2010); Brenda Gayle Plummer, *In Search of Power: African Americans in the Era of Decolonization, 1956–1974* (New York: Cambridge University Press, 2013); and Ledwidge, *Race and US Foreign Policy*.

43   Jordan T. Camp, *Incarcerating the Crisis: Freedom Struggles and the Rise of the Neoliberal State* (Oakland, CA: University of California Press, 2016), 21.

44   Ibid.

45   Dayo F. Gore, Jeanne Theoharris, and Komozi Woodard Gore, eds., *Want To Start A Revolution? Radical Women in the Black Freedom Struggle* (New York and London: New York University Press, 2009), 131; Janet L. Abu-Lughod, *Race, Space, and Riots in Chicago, New York,*

In a similar vein, Dr. King's final years were filled with controversy as he departed from the quintessential tropes of the American Dream that had filled his speech at the March on Washington in 1963. Moving closer to Malcolm's critique of American power, King connected race, class, and imperialist tendencies of US racial capitalism to form a cross-cutting system of oppression. From 1965 to 1968, according to Ledwidge, King's emphasis shifted from condemning the racist policies of city and state governments in the South to combating de facto racism in the North and questioning capitalism and American involvement in Vietnam.[46] King argued that racism was an endemic feature of American society and that the United States was the foremost imperial power, arguing that American imperialism was fueled by economic greed and white supremacy. He motivated a radical revival in the freedom movement of materialist analysis and class interrogations, arguments considered during the Cold War era to fall outside of acceptable discourse.[47]

MALCOLM X AND THE MIDDLE EAST

Initially, Malcolm X's impact in the Middle East was modest. Since the 1990s, however, African Americans' interest in the region has intensified. The number of African Americans practicing Sunni Islam has steadily increased from over a hundred in the 1950s to well over 2.4 million since the 1990s, according to officials at the American Muslim Council. The growth in membership, partially due to Malcolm, can also be attributed to the growth in Muslim immigration since changes to immigration laws in 1965, as well as to an increase in interest in and knowledge of Islam and the Middle East by important sectors of the African American community. Sherman A. Jackson notes that US immigration law once rendered Muslim immigrants from the Middle East and Asia white, which meant that coming to the United States meant not simply a possibility for a better material life but a chance to participate in whiteness (the whiteness of colonial masters). But by the 1960s, American whiteness had become sanitized and vague, granting admission to Armenians, Greeks, Italians, Jews, and countless others, who then exerted a palpable homogenizing effect. Jackson observes that all Muslim immigrants understood (or soon learned to understand) the term "nigger," and took great pains to distance themselves from it. From the moment they entered the country, the American sociopolitical terrain almost guaranteed the deepening of any anti-Black prejudice that might have accompanied immigrant Muslims to their new home.[48] African American Muslims had

---

and Los Angeles (New York: Oxford University Press, 2007); and Ledwidge, Race and US Foreign Policy, 152.

46   Ledwidge, Race and US Foreign Policy, 152.

47   Camp, Incarcerating the Crisis, 22.

48   Sherman A. Jackson, Islam and the Blackamerican: Looking Toward the Third Resurrection (New York: Oxford University Press, 2005), 16.

preceded their immigrant co-religious by several centuries, yet found themselves unable to integrate and climb the socioeconomic ladder as quickly as the
new arrivals. Until now, the presumed race-blind discourse of historical/immi-
grant Islam showed itself to be helpless before, when not accommodating to,
American reality. Jackson contends that this would define the reality of most
immigrant Muslims until the events of September 11, 2001, which resulted in an
anti–immigrant Muslim backlash that carried noticeably racial implications. As
the "legal whiteness" of immigrant Muslims proves incapable of counteracting
the negative impressions of a newly acquired, post-9/11 "social whiteness," it
remains to be seen if they will join African American Muslims in what Jackson
refers to as a Third Resurrection, confronting white supremacy in the United
States without relapsing into prejudice or hiding behind empty clichés of
"Islamic" utopianism.[49]

After Malcolm's departure from the NOI, he continued to use race and
white supremacy as the dominant lenses through which to understand power in
the modern world. This was met with trepidation by some of the leaders and
organizations in the Muslim Third World, including in Egypt and Saudi Arabia.
Many assumed a universalist posture and opposed Malcolm's discourse on race,
believing that it fell outside Islamic analysis. Throughout his travels, Malcolm
challenged this line of thinking:

> Being one of 22 million oppressed Afro-Americans I can never overlook the miser-
> able plight of my people in America . . . I will never hesitate to let the entire world
> know the hell my people suffer from America's deceit and her hypocrisy as well as
> her oppression.[50]

Malcolm saw religious belief and antiracism not as mutually exclusive but as
deeply entangled. The struggle of Black people in the United States was a responsibility not just of the continent of Africa: "It must also be the concern and
moral responsibility of the entire Muslim world—if you hope to make the principles of the Quran a living reality."[51] Malcolm made it clear that if Muslim
internationalism hoped to become a major force for social change, it had to
incorporate global struggles against white supremacy and for Black liberation in
Africa and the African diaspora, including the African American struggle in the
United States.

The Israeli/Palestinian issue caught the attention of Malcolm X, as he
framed Zionism as a European strategy to divide the non-white world of Africa
and Asia. He also challenged the postwar support for Israel of many Black activists, including Ralph Bunche, who helped negotiate the creation of the state of

---

49   Ibid.

50   Daulatzai, *Black Star, Crescent Moon*, 5.

51   Louis A. DeCaro, *On the Side of My People: A Religious Life of Malcolm X* (New York and
London: New York University Press, 1996), 239.

Israel. He condemned these actors for undermining Black liberation at home and extending white supremacy and the subjugation of the Third World. He also contended that the French occupation of Algiers represented a police state and that police presence in Black communities in the United States, from Harlem to Detroit, amounted to the presence of an occupying army. The conditions that led Algerians to resort to terrorist-style tactics existed in every Black community.[52]

The growth and development of Afrocentrism, with its focus on Egypt and civilizations of the Nile Valley, has also increased African American interest in the Middle East. Many African American Christians have been influenced by the narratives of Exodus, slavery, and suffering, powerful tropes for connecting Biblical history to contemporary struggles around racism that link the Middle East to religious narratives of liberation and redemption. For a short time, the Congressional Black Caucus, Ambassador Andrew Young, and presidential candidate Jesse Jackson ventured into US–Middle Eastern foreign policy, but these actors have pivoted since the 1990s to addressing globalization and neoliberalism in post-racial America.

CONCLUSION: MALCOLM X AND THE BLACK RADICAL TRADITION

In 1964, Malcolm X's influential speech "the ballot versus the bullet" offered Black voters both a context and structure to comprehend how they should employ their vote effectively. At this critical juncture, Malcolm questioned the wholesale support of the Democratic Party by Blacks, particularly since Southern Democrats (he referred to them as Dixicrats) had control of Civil Rights legislation in Congress. According to Fredrick C. Harris, Malcolm was suspicious of white politicians and Blacks who were dependent upon the white party support. Malcolm believed that Blacks should control the politics and politicians in their communities.[53] Basically, Malcolm was calling on the Black community to hold politicians, both Black and white, accountable during and after each election cycle. Malcolm believed that the 1964 presidential election provided Blacks an opportunity to exercise their political independence and declared that the year offered a choice between "the ballot or the bullet." This was an ancillary warning that if Blacks did not receive their rights as citizens, they might turn to violence to express their discontent. Once Malcolm departed the NOI he created the OAAU to defend and promote the interests of Black Americans—the development of an independent, Black political force was the central mission of this organization.[54] Malcolm X's position was also captured in (SNCC leader and Civil Rights/Black Power activist) Stokely Carmichael and (political scientist) Charles V. Hamilton's book: *Black Power: The Politics of Liberation*. Carmichael

---

52   Daulatzai, *Black Star Crescent Moon*, 42–3.
53   Frederick C. Harris, *The Price of the Ticket* (New York: Oxford University Press, 2012), 4.
54   Ibid.

and Hamilton reinforced Malcolm's call for a Black politics revolving around independence and self-determination. For Carmichael and Hamilton, Black Power was not merely positioning Black faces into office, because Black visibility is not the same as Black power. They called for racial solidarity and urged blacks to be skeptical of casting their lot with one political party.[55]

Civil Rights activist Bayan Rustin was the architect of the coalition politics approach to Black politics. Rustin wrote a very influential essay, "From Protest to Politics: The Future of the Civil Rights Movement." He called on Civil Rights foot soldiers to become dependable voters of the Democratic Party. Rustin's confidence in the future of Black politics hinged on whether the contradictions of society could be resolved by a coalition of progressive forces becoming an effective political majority in the United States. Black voters answered Rustin's call to action in the mid-1960s creating a coalition that successfully passed civil rights reforms, laying the basis for Democrat Lyndon Johnson's landslide victory in 1964.[56] This coalition was composed of Blacks, labor unions, liberals, and religious groups. The struggle over the future of Black politics between Civil Rights leaders, Black Power activists, and Black politicians reached a fever pitch in 1972 at the first Black political convention in Gary, Indiana. The Congressional Black Caucus vowed to take a frontline position to focus on the interests of the Black community, setting the stage for the eventual election of Barack Obama in 2008. These events, along with the Black social movements, were responsible for ending African American invisibity from American politics.

The 2008 election of Barack Obama as the first African American US president resulted in the creation of the most powerful Black person in the history of civilization. Ali A. Mazrui has observed that, on the global stage and in the context of world history, Obama was far more powerful than Shaka Zulu in South Africa's history, Menelik II in Ethiopia's historical experience, Ramses II in the annals of ancient Egypt, and Julius Nyerere in postcolonial Tanzania. Equipped and endowed with the economic, military, and diplomatic power of the United States, Mazrui contends, Obama was more powerful than all those African makers of history added together.[57] Because Obama was the product of an interracial marriage, he had identity problems for a while. He knew he was half Kenyan, but for some time he was not sure if he was culturally African American. He became ideologically liberal and Democratic by party affiliation and identification—mainly because of his mother's influence. Obama immersed himself in African American history, studying the diverse approaches to achieving racial equality and what Hanes Walton and Robert C. Smith have framed as the quest for universal freedom (that is, the Fourteenth Amendment to the US constitution opening the doors of freedom to African Americans and all

---

55   Ibid., 5.
56   Ibid., 6.
57   Ali A. Mazrui and Lindah L. Mhando, *Julius Nyerere, Africa's Titan on a Global Stage: Perspectives from Arusha to Obama* (Durham, NC: Carolina Academic Press, 2012), 37.

regardless of race, religion, national origins, class, sex, gender, sexual preference, and so on).[58] Obama was acutely aware of Booker T. Washington's education, Black entrepreneurship, and limited freedom, and W. E. B. Du Bois's contention that the Black struggle should be led by what he called "the talented tenth," who would be the vanguard for Black struggle and wider opportunities. Du Bois, himself, was the first Black person to get a Ph.D. in Sociology at Harvard University. Barack Obama was also familiar with the legacy of Marcus Garvey, an immigrant from Jamaica who inspired millions of African Americans and people of African descent in both Africa and the Black diaspora. Garvey's solution to the Black problem was racial separatism and his back-to-Africa strategy, a kind of Black Zionism. He had great impact on the question of Black consciousness and Black dignity that manifested through various Black Islamic (the Moorish Temple of Science and the Nation of Islam, among others), Black Christian (the Church of the Black Madonna, for instance), Black nationalist, and cultural nationalist movements of the 1960s and 1970s, including the Black power movements. Garvey also influenced Malcolm X's ideas about Black Nationalism and Black Internationalism through his parents, who were activists in Garvey's UNIA. Garvey was convicted of using the mail to defraud the public and deported to the UK, where his last years were spent in poverty living in London.

Ultimately, Barack Obama was influenced by legacies of the Black struggle exemplified by Dr. Martin Luther King Jr. and Reverend Jesse Jackson. Their struggle was for the integration of Black Americans into a wider America without the rejection by Blacks of their unique separate identity. Both King and Jackson shared a goal that was not to create a post-racial America but to form a post-racism society. A post-racial America would seek to minimize racial consciousness and put a damper on things like racial pride in favor of a wider national identity, whereas a post-racism society would maintain racial consciousness and racial pride of each race, but abolish negative prejudice and stereotypes towards others and seek to end hostility between the races. The result would resemble the rainbow coalition Reverend Jackson called for. Mazrui states that, in the end, Obama's goal was not simply to end racism but to reduce racial consciousness and find the ideal racial balance as envisioned through the concept of the rainbow coalition. Obama's dream was for a non-racial rather than a multiracial America.[59] Nevertheless, the election of Barack Obama signalled the potential for dramatic demographic and political change as Euro-Americans are emerging as a new minority in the American political system.

The election and re-election of Barack Obama as the first American president of African descent, the growing importance of the African continent in the new

---

58   Hanes Walton, Jr. and Robert Smith, *American Politics and the African American Quest for Universal Freedom*, sixth edition (Pearson, 2015).

59   Ibid., 38.

scramble between the East (including China, India, and Russia) and the West (the United States, the European Union, and Japan) for oil and other vital minerals and commodities, and the pursuit of African land resources for farming by food production companies from the Middle East and Asia, place an enormous importance on Africans and their descendants as critical actors in the contemporary phase of global economic and political restructuring. In addition, new scholarship is establishing evidence of the dynamic roles of Africans and people of African descent in the development of American, European, and global civilization and history, as well as considering the implications of a growing Black/non-white populations in the United States and the emergence of white Americans as the new minority. Obama was the first American president to speak at the annual meeting of the African Union in Addis Abba, Ethiopia, in 2015, though he took the opportunity to tell African leaders to stop blaming colonialism and "Western oppression" for the continent's problems. Despite his familiarity with the anticolonial activities of Malcolm X and other Black activists, Obama's foreign policy, including the accelerated use of drones sanctioned by his administration, has not represented a departure from imperialist US foreign policy.

Samuel Huntington has identified "multiculturalism and diversity, the spread of Spanish as a second language, the adoption of Latino approaches to racial identity, and the assertion of group identity based on race, ethnicity, and gender"[60] as a domestic problem, while regretting how "new immigrants are altering US foreign policy in order to defend the interests of their original homelands."[61] Huntington also contends that, because of interest group politics in the United States, "foreign governments have greatly increased their efforts to affect American policies."[62]

The rise of Barack Obama and the inclusion of Condoleezza Rice and Colin Powell in the Bush administration, according to Ledwidge, reflect a greater involvement in the American political establishment by women, African Americans, and non-Christians. Huntington suggests the possibility of profound changes in US foreign policy, given that "non-whites have very different attitudes from those of the elites,"[63] who are predominantly white. Three models of identity might inform American foreign policy, according to Huntington. The first, called the cosmopolitan approach, entails a multicultural and linguistic pluralism of diverse worldviews according to which the United States could reshape its policies via the politics of diaspora and global forces. The imperial approach pushes the American empire to promote democracy and embed core US values in the global context, thereby reshaping the world in line with

---

60   Samuel P. Huntington, *Who Are We? The Challenge to American National Identity* (New York: Simon & Schuster, 2004).
61   Ibid., 285.
62   Ibid., 286.
63   Ibid., 314.

American mores and US interests. The nationalist approach is predicated on American exceptionalism and the preservation of Christianity and American "Anglo-Protestant culture."[64] Mark Ledwidge notes that this neoconservative model flirts with neo-racism and cultural and religious imperialism. Huntington's discussion anticipates both the prejudice and political tensions surrounding the presidency of Obama, which some American groups such as the Tea Party, the birthers, and racial conservatives saw as an assault on US racial, cultural, and political identity.[65] On March 11, 2016, Donald Trump had to cancel a campaign rally in Chicago, Illinois, because of clashes between his supporters and protesters opposing his use of language insulting to immigrants and minority populations. Trump's remarks on the campaign trail fall somewhere between the "imperial" and "nationalist" perspective.

Malcolm understood profoundly that racial capitalism and American/ Western liberalism could never produce genuine freedom and economic prosperity for the vast majority in Africa and the African diaspora. He recognized that the African American population would always be the proverbial outsider. The current system, whether we call it neoliberalism, global capital, or racial capitalism, was not designed to benefit Africans. Malcolm sought to inspire solidarity and collective action across national boundaries in order to combat white supremacy, the vestiges of colonialism, and imperialism. He insisted that African Americans were part of a global majority and should not constrict themselves politically to the domestic arena of the United States. Like Robinson after him, Malcolm resurrected a vast store of historical data on the resistance of Africans and people of African descent to enslavement.

Malcolm X belongs to Robinson's Black Radical Tradition, reached through religious and messianic Black nationalism. It was his interaction with Third World leaders and participants in the Bandung Conference that opened up a critical window into the "Dark World" and inspired him to fight against the imperialism embedded in US foreign policy. The fact that Euro-Americans are the new minority in American politics brings home the importance of Malcolm X's contributions to the Black Radical Tradition, as well as the global reach and deep archival excavation of Cedric Robinson, whose paradigm still resonates today. Robinson and Malcolm revealed the instability of racial regimes, and how they literally fall apart.

---

64   Ibid., 365.
65   Ledwidge, "Barack Obama," 72.

Part Three

Imagining the Future

Chapter 11

"It's Hard to Stop Rebels That Time Travel"

Democratic Living and the Radical Reimagining of Old Worlds[1]

H. L. T. Quan

When the great lord passes, the wise peasant bows deeply and silently farts.

—Ethiopian proverb

We don't look to be ruled!

—Barack Obama[2]

INTRODUCTION

Every field of inquiry, regardless of its ideological positioning, holds a set of questions which, more often than not, inform the deep structure of disciplinary thought, demarcating the thinkable from the unthinkable, the thought from the unthought.[3] Western philosophy, for instance, asks, What is the meaning of life? Or, what is the good life? Political scientists, on the other hand, ask, What is the ideal form of government? Or, how should we be governed? Indeed, political science seems particularly uninterested in how we should live or how we should be. Aside from freely casting judgment about why some lives matter more than others, political science as a field is singularly interested in how we shall be governed.[4] It is, therefore, ironic that the president of the United States, as the chief spokesperson for the American empire, drew attention in his rhetorical

1   Please note that a version of this essay was presented at the 2013 Historical Materialism Conference in London. I want to thank Gaye Theresa Johnson and Alex Lubin for their saintly patience and generous editorial support. I also want to acknowledge C. A. Griffith's endless suggestions and feedback. This essay remained 85 percent done for over eight months due to grief and heartbreak. I always imagined having the feedback of my friend and teacher of three decades, Cedric J. Robinson, before sending it to the editors. Even without the benefit of his review, I will always be in Cedric's debt.

2   US president Barack H. Obama at the Democratic National Convention (July 27, 2016).

3   See the work of Mohammed Arkoun, especially *Islam: To Reform or to Subvert*, 2nd ed. (London: Saqi, 2006), for an exposition and deep analysis of modern discursive investments and the many missed opportunities to explore the unthought, especially in Islamic studies.

4   In *The Terms of Order: Political Science and the Myth of Leadership* (Chapel Hill: University of North Carolina Press, 2016[1980]), Cedric J. Robinson suggests that an obsession with political leadership and political authority as order has governed much of Western social thought, especially American political science. See also the welcome reprint with an instructive foreword by Erica R. Edwards: Robinson, *The Terms of Order*.

flourishes to the very democratic impulse that his own government has sought to suppress, even if his administration inherited many of the structural mechanics from previous administrations. It is also remarkable that American political science, still largely informed by social contract and rational choice theories, almost always assumes that the people "consent" to be ruled. This, indeed, is the grand narrative of the fictitious social contract.[5] Classical social contract theorists, from Thomas Hobbes and John Locke to Jean-Jacques Rousseau and Immanuel Kant, however they differed in the specificities of their fiction, each conflated the transition to civil society with the desire to be ruled. Thus one could say that no other question concerns modern, political thought more than governability.

That singular obsession with how we shall be governed should be a cause of great concern, especially for those whom Sara Ahmed calls "willful subjects"[6]— those who do not look to be ruled, as well as those who actively refuse to be ruled, including making themselves unavailable for governing. Indeed, democratic living, as a way of collectivizing, concerns itself not with how we should be governed, but with how we should live and relate to one another.[7] In an era characterized by neoliberalism, wars, and empires, not to mention extreme wealth inequality, mass incarceration, police homicides, and deportations, livability may be predicated on democratic living, a praxis that can provide an alternative mode of being and of conducting critical social inquiries, especially about the future of Black radical thought and praxis.[8]

This essay builds on Cedric Robinson's critique in *The Terms of Order* of the political and political authority and revises James Scott's treatment of "the art of not being governed"[9] to draw attention to the multiple ways in which ordinary people and communities resist governing by state and non-state rule-making projects. Historically runaway slaves looked to the North Star not to be ruled by it, but to use its illumination as a guide to freedom. The practice of marronage is embodied democratic living (however momentarily) and the willful attempt to resist being governed. Through community

---

5   Charles W. Mills, *The Racial Contract* (Ithaca: Cornell University Press, 1997).

6   Here I am appropriating Ahmed's notion of a "willful subject," who refuses to be governed by normative notions of happiness or to be complicit with the existing social orders and dominions, implicitly rejecting a futurist happiness. Sara Ahmed, *Willful Subjects* (Durham and London: Duke University Press, 2014).

7   By democratic living, I am less concerned with democratic governance (or democracy with a capital D) and not at all with the Democrats (another capital D). Instead, I am concerned with the art of living democratically, even under tyrannical regimes, however these regimes are characterized.

8   While the Black Radical Tradition encompasses centuries of Black resistance against racial capitalism and hetero-patriarchal white supremacy throughout the modern world (see Cedric J. Robinson, *Black Marxism: The Making of the Black Radical Tradition* [London: Zed Press, 1983]), I am limiting my coverage of Black resistance to the United States for the purposes of this essay.

9   James C. Scott, *The Art of Not Being Governed: An Anarchist History of Upland Southeast Asia* (New Haven: Yale University Press, 2009).

building, where the terror and violence of racial capitalism and white supremacy were temporarily suspended, free men and women negotiated their own
terms of living, and in the process, negated the terms of order.[10] Following
Avery F. Gordon's suggestion that we need to "combine complex and acute
social analysis with a vision of how some people have lived and do live today
that is a model for how all of us could live," and Cedric Robinson's insistence
that marronage (flight and fugitivity) proves the existence of Black radical
consciousness and praxis, I look to the willful refusal to be governed as confirmation of democratic sensibility.[11] This sensibility, I argue, is an antidote to
the chronic state addiction that seems to affect many social and especially
political theorists, and provides an imperative for thinking about and learning
from Black radical thought and praxis.

A DETOUR: STATE ADDICTION AND UNGOVERNABILITY

Democratic living constitutes life forms that actively seek independence from
rule making. This ungovernability from below constantly threatens the unjust
peace of dominant orders, including settler colonialism, racial capitalism,
white supremacy, and hetero-patriarchy.[12] While contestations among the
elites are frequent, they do not represent ungoverning and are quite different
from the active refusal to be governed from below. The federal government
shutdown, out-of-control police and prison guards, and unregulated hyperspeculative finance, for instance, are not ungoverning at the top. Instead, they
are a form of governance that incites instability as a consequence of its incompetence and delinquency. In contrast, ungovernability from below represents
the inability of state and other dominions to assert control over subjects; the
ungovernable, therefore, are those individuals and communities that render
themselves unavailable for governing. In this way, the refusal to be governed
is at the core of popular resistance to all forms of dominions.[13]

---

10   Angela Y. Davis, *Women, Race, and Class* (New York: Vintage Books, 1983); Robinson,
Black Marxism and *Black Movements in America* (New York: Routledge, 1997); Deborah Gray
White, *Ar'n't I a Woman? Female Slaves in the Plantation South* (New York: W. W. Norton, 1985).
11   Avery Gordon, *Keeping Good Time: Reflections on Knowledge, Power, and People* (Boulder,
CO: Paradigm, 2004), 187; Robinson, *The Terms of Order* and *Black Movements in America*.
12   Even among those who study social movements and popular resistance, many are preoccupied with governing and rule making. Theorizing about governance and social protests thus
centers largely on the one hand on Foucault's exposition of "biopolitics" and "governmentality" to
get at the varying practices of governing and, on the other hand, the Hegelian and Marxian treatment of popular resistance as a dialectical response to structural domination and oppression.
Michel Foucault, Graham Burchell, Colin Gordon, and Peter Miller, *The Foucault Effect: Studies in
Governmentality: With Two Lectures by and an Interview with Michel Foucault* (London: Harvester
Wheatsheaf, 1991).
13   Building on Robinson's critique (*The Terms of Order*), elsewhere I have argued that this is
distinct from Western anarchism because the ungovernable seeks alternative to order, not necessarily an alternative order (H. L. T. Quan, "Emancipatory Social Inquiry: Democratic Anarchism
and the Robinsonian Method," *African Identities* 11, no. 2 (2013): 16.

The famed, British-trained, American political scientist Richard Rose famously stated, "Analytically, the concept of ungovernability is a nonsense."[14] Rose argued that, first, "the question is *not whether* we shall be governed *but how*," second, "ungovernability can only be a temporary phase of anarchy and of civil war,"[15] and, third, "for better or worse," being governed is a *natural* state, and being ungoverned is an *aberration* that needs to be corrected. This view naturalizes the idea of order and norms political authority as rational. Governability is thus ontological: we are the way we are governed, and being ungoverned is nonbeing. State evasion and other forms of avoidance of being governed are deviant behavior that necessitates disciplining, from reconditioning to total annihilation.

Ideationally then, the ungovernable has been conscripted as a problem-subject, and one that needs reform. Sociologists, for instance, often focus on problem-people and communities, those who have been normed and scaled as the gendered and/or racialized other. At one time or another, indigenous people, Arabs, Mexicans, Muslims, Africans, single women, and LBGTQ people have been among the "other," who have been thought of as problem people in need of being governed, tamed, subdued, and, in certain circumstances, annihilated altogether. It is presumed and argued that these ungovernable cannot be reasoned with; they are evil and will only understand the language of force.[16] Similarly, certain spaces, especially urban spaces, are seen as ungovernable. The West Side of Phoenix, Harlem, Cabrini Green, Watts, Detroit, large swaths of the Global South, and the entirety of the Third World are problem peoples and spaces because they are ungovernable, appearing together as a an entire cosmology, a fearsome Black planet. The poor, Black people of Ferguson, Chicago, East Los Angeles, and Harlem—and anywhere there are ungovernable lives—are problem subjects, especially in communities where Black lives matter. The rational choice that follow entails everything the capacious apparatuses and technologies of violence have to offer, including "evacuation," mass incarceration, deportation, tanks, guns, tear gas, and surveillance. In the aftermath of the killing of Michael Brown and the ensuing protests, Ferguson became an ungovernable problem-space, with the majority of its people and even its police force deemed troublesome. Former attorney general Eric Holder was regularly

---

14   Richard Rose, *Governing and "Ungovernability": A Sceptical Inquiry*, Center for the Study of Public Policy (Glasgow: University of Stratchlyde, 1977), 1.

15   Ibid.

16   Interestingly, in many of President Barack Obama's speeches about his approach to "global terrorism" and especially to ISIS, and (in constrast to his Republican opponents) despite his refusal to use the inflammatory language of "radical Islamic fundamentalism," he rarely strays from the essential narrative of the problem/ungovernable subject, frequently characterizing ISIS fighters and their sympathizers as fundamentally distinct from "us," even while explicitly acknowledging that they are "not an existentialist threat." "Remarks by President Obama and President Macri of Argentina in Joint Press Conference," The White House, Office of the Press Secretary (March 23, 2016), available at whitehouse.gov.

dispatched to troubled/ungovernable regions, enforcing coherence on the progressively implausible imperial narrative about American exceptionalism.[17] Then there is the frequent and increasingly amplified speechifying by the first Black president in defense of liberal democracies and their attendant ideologies, justifying the perpetual wars on the troublesome Middle East or South Asia or North Africa.

All the while, in political science, ungovernability scandalously continues to be dismissed as analytical nonsense. While the framing of the ungovernable is used, with great frequency and utility, to cast and organize people and lands, to justify and wage permanent wars and even genocide, in political science—the field tasked with helping us understand how we come by these policies—its mandarins persist in their views that ungovernability is conceptually nonsensical. This scandalous intent suggests an ideography that owes its pathos to and possessive investments on an epistemological ordering that relies on state addiction. This affliction is a pathology that renders its sufferers entirely dependent on the state for sensibility and intelligence. The symptoms are many and obvious: most prominent is the tendency to conflate government with governing, authority with leadership, and rule with submission.[18] State-centric analytics commit addicts to a certain notion of the state, even to the extent of the state becoming the very fiction that we fear.[19]

Take for instance the eminent architect of deconstructionism, Jacques Derrida, who conflated sovereignty with transcendence. According to Derrida, "sovereignty is in a certain manner un-historical, it is a contract made with a history contracting itself into the punctiform event of an exceptional decision without temporal and historical expansion. Thus sovereignty also withdraws itself from language."[20] So it is: timeless and outside of history; moreover, there is, "no sovereignty without violence, without the force of the stronger, the justification of which—as the right of the

---

17   Consistent with this narrative, Hillary Clinton's 2016 presidential campaign responded to the formidable challenge of her opponent thus: "We don't need to make America great again because America is already great!" For an examination of Obama's usage of "American exceptionalism," see Greg Jaffe, "Obama's New Patriotism: How Obama Has Used His Presidency to Redefine 'American Exceptionalism,'" *Washington Post* (June 3, 2015), available at washingtonpost.com.

18   Robinson, *The Terms of Order.*

19   The fear of a tyrannical, all-powerful state ironically does not seem to help analysts appreciate the many instances of failures by state actors. This is most apparent when critics of tyrannical regimes endow the state with such power and intelligence that they fail to seize on opportunities to expose the state's ever-present incompetence and delinquency. That both major political parties in the US failed miserably to contain internal dissents, individual grafts and collective ambitions, and so were unable to enforce discipline on the electoral pageantry that led to the elevation of an undiscipline, corrupt, political novice, in the form of Donald Trump as the nominal head of the American empire should, at a minimum, warrant some reflections on the presumed compentency and rationality of the state.

20   As cited in Friedrich Balke, "Derrida and Foucault on Sovereignty," *German Law Journal/ Special Issue: A Dedication to Jacques Derrida* 6, no. 1 (2005): 76.

strongest—consists in its power over everything."[21] The sovereign has power *over everything*, including life itself.

Rather than imagining the future in terms of democractic living, sensibilities, and formations of justice, state addicts leave us dependent on the state for means of expressions and terms of engagement. Their imaginary domains[22] are thus entirely dependent on the state's projections. The state's memory becomes our own memory. Just as Orlando Patterson's social death thesis fallaciously endows racial capitalism and white supremacy as cultural progenitors of Black life, so state analytics such as necropolitics[23] render life *sans* state, more often than not, chaotic, miserable and inauthentic.[24] Within the same frame of social death, as David Brion Davis has argued, Black enslaved people have "no legitimate, independent being, no place in the cosmos *except* as an instrument of [their] master's will."[25] Similarly, life *sans* state, as Hobbes declared in the *Leviathan*, is "evil, brutish and short."

Yet, empirically and intuitively, we know better. If rules are not about norms but about discovering new forms of life, as Giorgio Agamben argues in *The Highest Poverty*,[26] then, in thinking about the modern state and rule making, the ungovernable and ungovernability are theoretical spaces that can help us think about life and the politics of living wherein ordinary people and communities assert their own renderings of life and living rather than those of the state, capital and other dominions' terms of order. As suggested by the Ethiopian proverb, it is prudent to recognize those instances when subversion disguises itself as submission or obedience because those who are oppressed cannot always exchange "a slap for a slap, an insult for an insult," tear gas for tear gas.[27]

Just as sounds are not always heard and fights are not always open, in the shadow of the real and fictive narrations of governmentality and the awesome powers of the state, there have always lurked individuals and communities embodying governing's unsuccessful inscriptions *and* conscriptions. Individuals and communities remain frequently unscripted and unimpressed by the state, even as they live under constant surveillance and suppression. Life goes on,

---

21   Ibid.

22   Here I am appropriating Drucilla Cornell's concept of "the imaginary domain" to draw attention to the psychic space where differences and various social identities are formed and reworked, though I argue that space is not necessarily individualized or autonomous. That is to say, the imaginary domain can be porous, individual, and collective. Drucilla Cornell, *The Imaginary Domain: Abortion, Pornography and Sexual Harassment* (New York: Routledge, 1995).

23   On "necropolitics," see Archille Mbembe, "Necropolitics," *Public Culture* 15, no. 1 (2003): 11–40.

24   Orlando Patterson, *Slavery and Social Death: A Comparative Study* (Cambridge, MA: Harvard University Press, 1982).

25   David Brion Davis, *Inhuman Bondage: The Rise and Fall of Slavery in the New World* (New York: Oxford University Press, 2006), 31. Emphasis added.

26   Giorgio Agamben, *The Highest Poverty: Monastic Rules and Form-of-Life*, trans. Adam Kotsko (Stanford: Stanford University Press, 2013).

27   James C. Scott, *Domination and the Arts of Resistance: Hidden Transcripts* (New Haven: Yale University Press, 1990).

sometimes independently, all the while circumscribed by the so-called technologies of governing.[28] In short, the analytical problem with ungovernability is not about empirical verification, but about the epistemological investments in political order and a modern ontological commitment to governability.[29] This commitment to ruling conceals the fear of the ungovernable and ungovernablity from below. So even as we now understand that power is diffuse and relational (à la Foucault),[30] state addiction ensures that; the state remains at the fulcrum of our understanding of political power[31] and state reifification persists[32]—its

---

28 The state (through its bureaucratic, coercive, and cultural apparatuses) naturalizes its authority and rationalizes its containment of people and communities through mechanisms of violence and narratives of exceptional authority and dominions over life.

29 There are indeed instances of ungovernability from the top, but as pointed out earlier, ungovernability from the top cannot be equated with the absence of governing. For instance, it is not difficult to verify or controversial to assert that the hyperspeculative nature of today's financial system is, to a degree, ungovernable. It seems dubious however, to characterize the 2013 US federal government shutdown as ungoverning; though some have taken to describing the House of Representatives as ungovernable. I think this is so because there are many individuals within the state apparatus that explicitly adhere to a neoliberal ideology, so that the state in itself can be said to be governed by neoliberalism: Wendy Brown, *Undoing the Demos: Neoliberalism's Stealth Revolution* (London: Zone Books, 2015). Neoliberal state actors typically seek to dismantle whatever remnants are left of the social welfare contract so that ruling apparatuses appear to take on what Ruth Wilson Gilmore refers to as the antistate state form: Ruth Wilson Gilmore, "In the Shadow of the Shadow State," in INCITE! Women of Color Against Violence, ed., *The Revolution Will Not Be Funded: Beyond the Non-Profit Industrial Complex* (Cambridge, MA: South End Press, 2009), 41–52. The antistate antics displayed by many state actors are political theater and should not be confused with the absence of governing from the top. Take the 2013 federal government shutdown, for example. It was the Republican Congressional rebels that caused financial instability and social disruption, not the forces of Occupy Wall Street or organized labor. Plato understood this when he noted that social instability typically stems from the top. Moreover, and despite the fact that it was the circuit of financialism and its agents that harassed the Congressional rebels into finally ending the shutdown, we continue to speak of the "White House" and "Congress" as if they were not merely anthropomorphized actors on a much bigger stage. The frequent staging of populism by the Republican Party, including the anti-bank and anti–Wall Street varieties, can be similarly characterized as theater. It was also the threat of a financial default that ended the shutdown—a default that translated to potentially real instability in the financial markets and huge losses to bondholders and other investors. It certainly was not the disruption of domestic welfare provisions that ultimately halted the false rebels in their tracks. Indeed, there is little evidence that there was an absence of governing during the shutdown. Therefore, it is unintelligible to speak of the US government as ungoverning when its Treasury, Defense Department, and surveillance apparatuses did not cease operation at any moment during the entire "shutdown."

30 Or, as Rose and Miller put it: "Political power is exercise . . . through a profusion of shifting alliances between diverse authorities in projects to govern a multitude of faces of economic activity, social life and individual conduct." Nikolas S. Rose and Peter Miller, "Political Power Beyond the State: Problematics of Government," *British Journal of Sociology* 61 (2010): 272.

31 The problem is, as Foucault observed, that we have not succeeded in cutting off the king's head, even more than two centuries after monarchist absolutism went out of fashion. This is what Foucault called "the great trap" and what I call state addiction—the tendency to conflate all things powerful with the sovereign. Michel Foucault, *"Society Must Be Defended": Lectures at the Collège de France*, trans. David Macey (New York: Picador, 2003).

32 A focus on the "state of exception" and on "governmentality" and its corresponding apparatuses has fashioned this body of work, with the state continuing to signify the mightiest of all powers. A confluence of factors may explain this, namely: 1) the formalization of the US

promiscuous genealogy, its prodigious technologies, its capacious fantasies, and its monstrous realities.[33]

Within the context of an ever-growing global war on terror, the resurrection of works by the Nazi political theorist Carl Schmitt has granted little relief from our state addiction.[34] If anything, his intervention further ensures that the specter of the elusive state is finally vanquished. In its place is a state more capable than the technologies it possesses, more intelligible than the apparatuses it readied, and more autonomous than the subjects it has claimed.[35] Students of the Black Radical Tradition, however, are familiar with this phenomenon. Just as "every slave holder seeks to impress his slave with a belief in the boundlessness of slave territory, and of his own almost [limitless] power,"[36] so, too, it seems, is the case with other dominions, including discursive ones. It is also the case that slaves did run away, and many ran away successfully!

Because the state presupposes the ungovernable, it points to ungovernability as the reason for its existence and its capacious fantasies, justifying both, even as *its very existence produces insecurity*.[37] But life as we know it is quite complicated.[38] That we can speak of "governmentality"—as the conduct of statehood and a logic of governing—is precisely because *complex personhood* throws up ungovernability every time the state and other dominions mess with

---

"global war on terror"; 2) the rediscovery of Carl Schmitt's *Political Theology* and his critique of universal claims of rights for the "human"; and, 3) Foucault's work on biopolitics and governmentality (Foucault, *"Society Must Be Defended"*).

33 This reification, however unintended, is the reauthorization of the state as the center of governmental power.

34 Giorgio Agamben is credited with reigniting interest in the state and in Carl Schmitt's work at the start of the twenty-first century, especially in the power of the sovereign. In *Homo Sacer: Sovereign Power and Bare Life, Meridian* (Stanford, CA: Stanford University Press, 1998)—the first of a multivolume exposition on the sovereign—bare life is understood as life stripped of legal status, without rights, inhabiting the threshold of the juridico-political community. Schmitt was a jurist and theorist; his theory of the sovereign relies on the notion of the state of exception. He served as counsel for the Reich government in 1932, became a member of the Nazi Party in 1933, participated in the burning of books by Jewish authors, and called for more extensive purging of any works that embraced Jewish ideas. Also in 1933, Hermann Göring appointed Schmitt state councilor for Prussia. That same year, Schmitt became the president of the Union of National-Socialist Jurists, or the Nazi equivalent of the American Bar Association. As a professor at the University of Berlin, he was *the* Nazi intellectual—and his theoretical work served as the ideological foundation for Nazism and as justification for the autocratic state (*auctoritas*).

35 Schmitt's thesis grounds the exception for sovereignty in the Hobbesian presupposition of human nature and the exclusionary technologies of the global racial/sexual contracts. See Carole Pateman and Charles W. Mills, *Contract and Domination* (Cambridge, UK, and Malden, MA: Polity, 2007).

36 Frederick Douglass, *My Bondage and My Freedom* (New York: Dover Publications, 1969), 280.

37 Moments of partial consciousness that there is something beyond and perhaps more powerful than the state exist precisely not only because *life is just as much, if not more compelling than death*, but also because the concept of the state presupposes the concept of the ungovernable.

38 Avery Gordon, *Ghostly Matters: Haunting and the Sociological Imagination* (Minneapolis: University of Minnesota Press, 1997).

it. Population management is critical to the conduct of government precisely because the people have to be made into governable subjects. People have to be rendered governable because they are ungoverned as a precondition, and therefore are not legible to the state. It is not that our presence and complex personhood incite governing. Rather, governing incites its prodigious technologies as it encounters life *countering it* or *independent of it*. Governing is a possessively jealous beast!

So Rose, however famed he was, must be famously wrong! Throughout history, as noted, individuals and communities have always resisted modernity's state-building and rule-making projects. In addition to anti–state-building projects such as those by the hill peoples of *Zomia* (as documented by James Scott[39]), campaigns for bodily and community sovereignty, sometimes understood as forms of self-government, are well documented. These are often *in reaction to* or *in anticipation of* state-building and rule-making projects. Maroon societies are thus the embodiment of this refusal of rule making. James Scott characterizes the hill peoples as runaways and fugitives.[40] In addition to these state-evaders, however, there is the motley crew of rule-evaders who elude rules and rule making that are outside of the state's perogatives. Runaways, border-crossers, gender-benders, and general nonconformists are such examples of *failures of* or *resistance to* codified practices of governing. These legacies of resistance,[41] replete with women and men actively countering the many faces, structures, and technologies of violence, cruelty, and death, cannot be dismissed simply as nonsense. While we may never be able to completely escape state addiction and it would be foolish to stop interrogating the state altogether, *the state's memory, however, must not be our only memory*. Those who seek a more just present and future must, therefore, remain vigilantly skeptical of this affliction in order to recognize *how others live*, especially other genealogies and life forms that are independent of the imaginaries of the state and of capital.[42]

In *The Terms of Order*, Cedric Robinson calls for a social philosophy that rejects *the political* as an "ordering principle," maintaining that social order is folklore of the state, political order is an alien concept, and social leaders, more often than not, are "capricious, incompetent and mischievous."[43] To demystify social order is also to interrogate how in the West, the very idea of freedom is singularly wedded to the idea of an autonomous and rational individual, yet the collectivity always requires governing.[44] By pivoting to ungovernability instead

---

39 Scott, *The Art of Not Being Governed*.

40 Ibid., iv.

41 Short of anarchy or civil wars.

42 Gordon calls upon something "more powerful than skepticism" as a practical utopian standpoint, a necessary stance for livable life. *Keeping Good Time*, 205.

43 Robinson, *The Terms of Order*, 7, xi.

44 This is best encapsulated in Western anarchism, whose rejection of the state merely represents an "alternate order," not an "alternative to order." Ibid.

of the naturalness of the need to be governed, we expose the unnaturalness and illegitimacy of order.

People rendering themselves unavailable for governing trips up the system, more often than not, leading to crises of authority and further exposing elite incompetence and delinquencies.[45] Be it in Ferguson or Syria, the ungovernable withhold both consent and legitimation, and, in the process, render the state and its allies more transparently incompetent, brutal, and imperial. How many years has it been since the United States commenced bombing the Middle East? How long has patriarchy desired to tame the proverbial shrew? The ungovernable is thus an empirical verification of the ever-present democratic sensibility, belying the state's and its enablers' claims of intelligence, overwhelming force, and the power of exception,[46] not to mention the various economic, political, racial, or biological fantasies and life forgeries. As *midwives of civil strife*, the ungovernable are intent on impeding and negating the unjust peace of the organized practices that render subjects governable.

What Toni Morrison calls "rememory,"[47] particularly fugitive rememory, is a necessary tool in the evaders' and rebels' quest for wholeness, or what Robinson calls "the preservation of [an] ontological totality."[48] As Robinson insisted in *Black Movements in America*, running away and community building in the form of maroon societies are powerful counterexamples of the conceit of slavery—the claims of naturalness of people as property and the arrogant assumption that a people, any people, can be controlled, dominated totally. *Totalitarianism frequently fails for a reason.*

FLIGHT, FUGITIVITY, AND TIME TRAVELS

The act of running away, of building independent communities, is a catalogue of slavery as an unnatural political, economic, and moral ordering. Community building, rather than nation or state building, provides a way of knowing about forms of life outside the state and other dominions; marronage is thus a historical verification of life outside of the terms of slavery as a natural order.

Richard Price recorded that "for more than four centuries, the communities formed by . . . runaways dotted the fringes of plantation America, from Brazil to

---

45   The elevation of Donald Trump, who is perceived as unacceptable by most of the establishment, nevertheless failed to persuade the "unruly mass," especially as the majority of the (white) Republican electorate publically embraces the most virulent articulations of white nativism and bigotry, despite public disavowals by said establishment.

46   For an exposition on the awesome power of the national security state, see Giorgio Agamben, *State of Exception* (Chicago: University of Chicago Press, 2005).

47   In *Beloved*, Toni Morrison (New York: Knopf, 1987) introduced the concept of "rememory" as remembering memories. She suggests that the practice of deliberate recalling is part of a larger process of countering willful forgetting.

48   Robinson, *Black Marxism*, 243.

the southeastern United States, from Peru to the American Southwest."[49] Not only does the existence of these communities "dispel the myth of the docile slave" and embody the "antithesis of all that slavery stood for,"[50] it embarrassed plantation owners and historians alike, because their very existence defies what the enemies of Black people sought to achieve[51]—the annihilation of Black life and consciousness of a people who are unavailable for servitude and governing.[52] Even at the risk of severe and brutal punishments, such as having their Achilles tendons cut or being slowly roasted to death, by running away permanently and in the form of "repetitive [and] periodic truancy,"[53] these Black women and men revealed an idiom of resistance against those who sought to govern them totally.

Indeed, flight and fugitivity struck terror against slavery as an institution and a way of life.[54] At the height of slavery in the United States, white plantation owners were so frightful that they enlisted the medical establishment for help. Among those physicians, Samuel A. Cartwright invented a mental illness to explain the true cause of Black people running away from captivity. He called it "drapetomania," from the Greek terms "drapetes" (runaways) and "mania" (madness).[55] At the 1881 meeting of the Medical Association of Louisiana, Cartwright claimed that, for the most part, Black people are "very easily governed" and that drapetomania was simply "unknown to our medical authorities." The claim of an easily governed Black people harkened back to the view expressed by one Santo Domingo plantation owner in a letter that made its way to Paris on the eve of the Haitian Revolution in 1791: "The blacks are very

49 Richard Price, *Maroon Societies: Rebel Slave Communities in the Americas* (Baltimore: John Hopkins University, 1983), 1. The most significant example of marronage is the *Quilombo dos Palmares* in Brazil, where, for more than a century, an independent community of former slaves co-existed with and fought against first the Dutch and then the Portuguese slave plantocracies: Stuart B. Schwartz, *Slaves, Peasants, and Rebels: Reconsidering Brazilian Slavery* (Urbana: University of Illinois Press, 1992).

50 Price, *Maroon Societies*, 2.

51 Robinson, *Black Movements in America*.

52 Indeed, "individual fugitives banding together to create independent communities of their own . . . struck directly at the foundations of the plantation system" (Price, *Maroon Societies*, 2–3).

53 As Price explains: "Such communities stood out as an heroic challenge to white authority, and as the living proof of the existence of a slave consciousness that refused to be limited by the whites' conception or manipulation of it" (Ibid., 3).

54 Douglass captured well this fear when he argued against publicizing knowledge of the Underground Railroad. He explained it this way: "Such is my detestation of slavery that I would keep the merciless slaveholder ignorant of the means of flight adopted by the slave. He should be left to imagine himself surrounded by myriads of invisible tormentors, ever ready to snatch, from his eternal grasp, his trembling prey. In pursing his victim, let him be left to feel his way in the dark; let shades of darkness, commensurate with his crime, shut every ray of light from his pathway; and let him be made to feel, that, at every step he takes, with the hellish purpose of reducing a brother man to slavery, he is running the frightful risk of having his hot brains dashed out by an invisible hand" (Douglass, *My Bondage and My Freedom*, 324).

55 Samuel A. Cartwright, "Diseases and Peculiarities of the Negro Race," *Debow's Review* XI (1851).

obedient and will remain so always."[56] Cartwright himself was confident that drapetomania could be "entirely prevented," and prescribed "whipping the devil out of them" and removing both big toes to make running away impossible.

As Assata Shakur reminds us, "To become free, you have to be acutely aware of being a slave."[57] Rememory thus necessarily enlists fugitive history and is critical to becoming liberatory subjects. Flight and fugitivity are very much part of our social imaginary and contemporary repertoire of resistance. In 2003, Aaron Patterson received a full pardon for a wrongful death sentence in 1989. A group of teenage Black girls who had actively worked to free Patterson gave him tips about adjusting to life in Chicago in the twenty-first century (including how to deal with car alarms and cell phones). They also taught him the Harriet Tubman Code—it takes one to free one—to which members of the Prisoners of Conscience Committee, an organization co-founded by Fred Hampton Jr., adhere. Patterson joined the anti–death penalty campaign. Around the same time, Sophia Sorrentini, on her deathbed in Santurce, San Juan, the widow of the self-educated co-founder of the Socialist Party of Puerto Rico, claimed her identity as a "*Cimarrona*"—the Spanish term for a runaway slave. She made her children promise to preserve their family home as a "Cimmarona space," free and shared as part of the larger campaign against displacement and in living memory of Santurce as a free town.[58] This reclaiming of Santurce as free or the redeployment of the Harriet Tubman Code belongs to the practice of activating and enlisting fugitive rememories for campaigns of freedom and justice that rely on marronage as a tactic of liberation. In chains or in handcuffs, there seems to be an overwhelming urge to run away. Drapetomania, indeed!

Marronage in the twenty-first century takes myriad forms, including school truancy, gender nonconformity, border crossing, bench-warrant avoidance, and prison abolition. Remarkably, however, it also resembles marronage in the nineteenth, eighteenth, and seventeenth centuries. In other words, the propensity to run toward freedom and community building away from conditions of bondage has barely diminished within the context of persistent labor exploitation, hyper-surveillance and unending incarceration. As Kelley suggests, the desire to turn to flight and fugitivity (as a form of escapism) is familiar to Black radical imaginaries and especially when it shows up as a dimension of Afrofuturism—a hope, a wish for a Black futurity that is contradistinct from the present.[59] Ironically, recent studies on slavery and its

---

56   Eduardo Galeano and Mark Fried, *Children of the Days: A Calendar of Human History* (New York: Nation Books, 2013), 25.

57   Assata Shakur, *Assata: An Autobiography* (London: Zed Books, 1987), 262.

58   See the feature-length documentary *América's Home* (dirs. C. A. Griffith and H. L. T. Quan, QUAD Productions 2012).

59   Robin D. G. Kelley, *Freedom Dreams: The Black Radical Imagination* (Boston: Beacon Press, 2002).

contemporary afterlife[60] typically treat slavery as a past occurrence, a historical phenomenon, not a living, extant one.[61] Even those who have sought to learn from slavery's inheritance in order to interrogate its contemporary afterlife (e.g. mass incarceration), frequently treat slavery as a metaphor or, at best, an extended paraphrase (e.g., prison abolitionism).[62] Just as racism is still a thing, *however much we wish it away*, slavery remains with us today. Moreover, contemporary slavery is empirically proven to be much more than a metaphor, and the new Jim Crow, it turns out, is not very new at all. Much more than mass incarceration, it is also a systematic campaign of disenfranchisement, economic marginalization, and financial entrapment, including debt bondage and extreme social isolation.[63] So while the question "What does marronage look like in the twenty-first century?" can help us take stock of free towns, border crossing, gender bending, and other expressions of ungovernability, this same question requires another one: "What does twenty-first-century slavery look like?" Slavery in the twenty-first century, it turns out, is quite complicated.

It is not a small matter to note that our current world enslaves almost 30 million human beings.[64] Contemporary slavery takes the forms of human trafficking and forced labor, including debt bondage, forced marriages, and the sale of children. Some are born into slavery through hereditary rules, while others are captured, kidnapped, or kept for exploitation through financial entrapment. Some slaves are called bonded laborers, while others are called sex workers. Some slaves work in factories, others in nightclubs, the fields, or homes. Equally important, contemporary scenes of subjection include prevalent flight and fugitivity. For these women, men, and children, anti-slavery and abolitionism did not happen solely in

---

60   In the forms of Jim Crow, debt peonage, and mass incarceration, to name a few. Angela Y. Davis, *Are Prisons Obsolete?* (New York: Seven Stories Press, 2003); Douglas A. Blackmon, *Slavery by Another Name: The Re-enslavement of Black People in America from the Civil War to World War II* (New York: Doubleday, 2008); Michelle Alexander, *The New Jim Crow: Mass Incarceration in the Age of Colorblindness* (New York: New Press, 2010); Christina Sharpe, *In the Wake: On Blackness and Being* (Durham: Duke University Press, 2016).

61   Simone Browne's *Dark Matters: On the Surveillance of Blackness* (Durham: Duke University Press, 2015) is a wonderful exception. For Browne, dark souveillance is a continuous practice throughout the history of Black resistance. It is part of the larger praxis of fugitivity. Dark souveillance fundamentally subverts rule-making projects and renders Blackness illegible to the state and other forms of dominions.

62   Even in the critical work on mass incarceration, the prison industrial complex and prison abolitionism relies on slavery's afterlife (e.g., the convict lease system) to learn about slavery of a previous era, not of the current one. To be sure, this looking back is essential to both the theoretical production about prisons as a system and social praxis, as well as formulating critical resistance to mass incarceration.

63   W. E. B. Du Bois, *Black Reconstruction: A History of the Part Which Black Folk Played in the Attempt to Reconstruct Democracy in America, 1860–1880* (New York: Free Press, 1998[1935]); Davis, *Are Prisons Obsolete?* In *Black Reconstruction*, Du Bois was quite explicit about the failure of post-reconstruction reforms to abolish slavery as an economic, cultural, and political institution in total.

64   Official estimates list 29.8 million (*The Global Slavery Index 2013*, Walk Free Foundation, available at walkfreefoundation.org).

the past, and marronage is not a metaphor. Running away is an act of survival and of literally making oneself unavailable for servitude and governing.[65]

Just as slave narratives of the nineteenth century were critical to the anti-slavery movement, especially for the movement's most radical expressions, such as those by Frederick Douglass, Olaudah Equiano, and Sojourner Truth, contemporary slave narratives are essential to the formation of anti-slavery consciousness and politics, including the praxis and consciousness of flight and fugitivity. While a thorough sampling of such narratives is beyond the scope of this essay, the narratives of Roseline Odine and Christina Elangwe are instructive.[66] Collectively, they tell a story of two Cameroonian teenagers and former slaves in Washington, DC, in the first decade of the twenty-first century. When she came to the United States, Elangwe was seventeen, Odine only fourteen, dreaming of becoming a designer. Odine and Elangwe knew each other because their captors socialized in the same circles. Both had been tricked into coming to the United States with promises of education and babysitting jobs. As house slaves, Odine and Elangwe, rose at 5:30 in the morning and worked well into the night, without pay. Odine was enslaved for two and a half years, Elangwe for five. Their captors kept them from going to school, physically and verbally abused them, and performed indoctrination and mind control on them. Odine's male captor often sexually assaulted her. Elangwe was forbidden from speaking with her family in Cameroon. In Odine's own words:

> I think I was a slave. Because if I sit back sometimes and think about it and have a flashback, it was terrible. There were several nights and days that I would sit all by myself and think about things I could do with my sisters. How we used to play together. I would cry because I missed them, hoping that one day I would get together with them again. Everything, my dreams, just crushed down and I wasn't going to get it. I wasn't going to reach it . . .
>
> Whatever opportunity I had, Christina and I got together and talked about running.

So they turned toward freedom.[67] Odine escaped first. In the midst of one of her captor's abusive verbal attacks, she ran away:

> For some reason I wasn't thinking anymore—it was like my blood pressure was rising, my head was pumping inside. I had no shoes on, no jacket. I didn't think of anything, I just opened the door and ran out . . . [*She ran, fell, blacked out, then came to*

---

65   Gordon (*Keeping Good Time*) points to Toni Cade Bambara's utopian thought and suggests that part of being free is being "unavailable for servitude." I am extending this line of argument to include the refusal to be governed.

66   Kevin Bales and Zoe Trodd, *To Plead Our Own Cause: Personal Stories by Today's Slaves* (Ithaca: Cornell University Press, 2008).

67   Ibid., 145.

consciousness.] I kept telling myself, "That's it, that's it. I'm not going back in there. I'm not going back. That's it. I have nowhere to go, but one thing's for sure, I'm not going back.[68]

Odine then enlisted others to help her free Elangwe and another slave of Cameroonian descent in the Washington, DC, area. Clearly, the Harriet Tubman Code is alive in our nation's capital. In Elangwe's words:

> I was thinking about getting out but there was no way. I didn't know anybody, but I was just praying for one day to come when I could be free. I never knew when that day would be. I was just hoping and praying . . . I talked to Rosaline on the phone and cried and tried to figure out what to do. But there was no means. If we leave, where are we going to go? We didn't know anybody, so just had to stay there. Until one day [Rosaline] couldn't take it in there anymore, she had to run away. When she ran, she opened the door for all of us.[69]

Perhaps they suffered from drapetomania, or perhaps they were uninterested in state addiction or any form of governing! More than a century and a half ago, the runaway Frederick Douglass noted that running away promised a "deliverance from the evils and dangers of slavery."[70] Slavery's logic, however, requires flight and fugitivity be characterized as madness. Governing enablers and addicts must mark running away as madness so that they can dismiss ungovernability as nonsense. The alternative is to recognize that marronage is the embodiment of the refusal to be governed, to render oneself totally unavailable for servitude. The alternative is the recognition that being governed or being a slave, as Robinson understood,[71] is only *one* condition of our complex personhood. The alternative is the recognition that being ungoverned is *not* nonbeing. Rosaline Odine, Christina Elangwe, and countless slaves before them who ran away, in Douglass's words, "hated slavery, always, and the desire for freedom only needed a favorable breeze, to fan it into a blaze, at any moment."[72]

AN AFROFUTURIST PRELUDE TO TRAVELING

Janelle Monáe's "Q.U.E.E.N,"[73] featuring the queen of neo-soul herself, Erykah Badu, is an elegantly produced, Afrofuturistic, and ironic riff on the arrogance of the twenty-first-century carceral state's explicit intention to quell

---

68 Ibid., 149–50.
69 Ibid., 155–6.
70 Douglass, *My Bondage and My Freedom*, 279.
71 Robinson, *Black Marxism*.
72 Douglass, *My Bondage and My Freedom*, 273.
73 "Q.U.E.E.N," a neo-soul song, appears on Monáe's album *The Electric Lady* (2013) and was produced by Chuck Lightning, Nate Rocket, and Monáe. It was nominated for multiple awards, including the Soul Train Music Award for Best Dance Performance and the NAACP Image Award for Outstanding Song.

subversive, irresistible, and definitively Black music and culture. The music video is set in a post–twenty-first-century (un)reality where Monáe, members of the group Wondaland, and her "dangerous accomplice, Badoulda Oblongata"[74] (Badu) have been locked in a stark, walk-through diorama/gallery space by the Metropolis Ministry of Droids. We are informed by the Ministry that this so-called Living Museum is where "legendary rebels from throughout history have been frozen in suspended animation." The embodiment of the Ministry appears via a small monitor and confidently claims in her posh British accent (of course it's British!): "It's hard to stop rebels that time travel; but we at the Time Council pride ourselves on doing just that!" The lyrics and music video, which had over 16 million views as of December 2016, disrupt this conceit through "songs, emotions, pictures, and works of art," the very things that the Ministry failed to contain in suspended animation. Characteristics of Monáe's and Wondaland's brilliant use of ironic gender- and culture-bending mélange of historical iconographies, "Q.U.E.E.N" is visually stunning. It features a bold, iconic palate of black and white stripes, plaids and solid clothes, shoes and walls, and almost entirely Black people. Touches of red are reserved for Monáe's lipstick and crocheted alien sash, as well as the single red line from forehead to chin of Badu's Wodaabe/Bororo male–inspired face paint. Gold is limited to five items that conjure Afrocentricity and womanist power: Badu's armor-like arm cuff and alternating lion-like mane and bone-straight bob; Monáe's square earrings and a white skull with a single, sharp gold incisor that serves as the needle for the "Q.U.E.E.N" LP. The tune's get-up-and-dance groove and call-and-response lyrics are layered in an infectious R&B beat that suggest a dance tune meant for leaving your troubles on the floor. Yet, for the majority of the video, Monáe appears in elegant sci-fi-meets-*Emperor-Jones* militaristic garb, and this dichotomy is quite intentional. Later, in full James Bond mode complete with silhouette, dual spotlights against a white backdrop, flattering lighting, and with a bespoke tuxedo, Monáe appears and her lyrics turn explicitly politically and culturally provocative, if not outright revolutionary:

> Are we a lost generation of our people?
> Add us to equations but they'll never make us equal . . .
>
> They keep us underground working hard for the greedy
> But when it's time to pay they turn around and call us needy
> My crown too heavy like the Queen Nefertiti
> Gimme back my pyramid, I'm trying to free Kansas City.

---

74   Clearly this is a riff on the medulla oblongata, a portion of the hindbrain that is responsible for autonomic functions and relaying messages between the brain and the spinal cord. So presumably for the Ministry, Badu is genetically predisposed to be baaaad! Or badly subversive.

Key artistic interventions—from the opening voice-over that places this imaginary in the future, with Monáe, Badu, and Wondaland members as rebels captured in suspended animation in this diorama/prison *sans* walls—show the foolishness of those who believe that uprisings are one-time events, or that the powerful elites can contain rebels. Consistent with the theme of rememory, Monáe, even in suspended animation, is impeccably coiffed, super fashionable, and seated on a white chair at a white table, about to sip tea while listening to two Wondaland members who were frozen as they performed (for whom?) wearing loincloths and smeared in white clay. Was she in this position before capture, or was she repositioned for eternity? The two young Black women who enter the sterile museum smirk at the Ministry's claim and place *their* LP on the turntable; just like that, and despite the professed power of those who imprisoned the rebels, it only takes a little bravery and a single song to disrupt the Ministry's conceit. As the song begins to play, on the LP, a fly—out of place in this setting—lands on Monáe's hand. She blinks. She blinks faster. Moments later, the two young rebels tie up the security guard, Wondaland comes to life, and even the stuffy art patrons can't help but dance because, as the chorus tells us, "the booty don't lie." All the while, Monáe insistently asks: "Hey sister, am I good enough for your heaven? Say, will your God accept me in my black and white? Will he approve the way I'm made? Or, should I reprogram the program and get down?" After a Wondaland member (previously imprisoned in Plexiglas) is freed, he takes the manual typewriter from the exhibit and types over and over again: "I will create and destroy ten art movements in ten years." Soon after, Badu and Monáe instruct the rebels and anyone else listening:

> Baby, here comes the freedom song
> Too strong we moving on
> Baby this melody
> Will show you another way
> Been tryin' for far too long
> Come home and sing your song
> But you gotta testify

Such radical performativity is a necessary part of the Black Radical Tradition, wherein the rematerialization of the "ontological totality" of Blackness requires the blending and bending of gender/sex/race structures and meanings.[75] Indeed, there is no question that Janelle Monáe is one of the most astute artists and cultural workers of her generation,[76] and "Q.U.E.E.N" merely

---

75   Robinson, *Black Marxism*; Fred Moten, *In the Break: The Aesthetics of the Black Radical Tradition* (Minneapolis: University of Minnesota Press, 2003).

76   I am grateful to Erica R. Edwards for insisting, nearly a decade ago, that I "need to check out" Monáe's work.

cements her status as one of the many Black artists in the long tradition of what Fred Moten calls "the modes of radical performativity," where "blackness marks simultaneously both the performance of the object and performance of [Black] humanity."[77] "Q.U.E.E.N" provocatively places Black aesthetics "in the break," insofar as it posits the possibility of radical experimentation in which the "phonic substance" reconstructs Blackness as "a special site and resources for a task of articulation where immanence is structured by an irreducibly improvisatory exteriority that can occasion something very much like sadness and something very much like devilish enjoyment."[78]

But it is Monáe's signatory and visceral call to arms "Hell You Talmbout" that functions as a primal scream of Black Lives Matter's protest anthem against the epidemic of police murders, where we are *required* to Say Their Names! To simple, syncopated, electronic drumbeats, we are asked, "Hell you talmabout?" followed by the litany of names—"Walter Scott, say his name! Jerame Reid, say his name! Philip White, say his name! Eric Garner, say his name! . . . Aiyana Jones, say her name! Sandra Bland, say her name!" From Emmett Till and Amadou Diallo to Trayvon Martin and Miriam Carey, Monáe and her fellow Wondaland artists implore us to Say Their Names! In doing so, they/us take part in not only recalling our dead but also turning the vulgarity and violence of subjection into defiant acts of mourning and the necessity of resistance that follows. The fact that these men and women, frequently much too young to die, are grievable[79] and their ghosts are necessarily haunting, belies post-racial fantasies at the same time that they expose, at best, the legal impotence of the so-called justice system.[80]

---

77   Moten, *In the Break*, 2.

78   Ibid., 255.

79   In *Precarious Life*, Judith Butler (*Precarious Life: The Powers of Mourning and Violence* [New York: Verso, 2004]) astutely observes: "The differential allocation of grievability that decides what kind of subject is and must be grieved, which kind of subject must not, operates to produce and maintain certain exclusionary conceptions of who is normatively human: what counts as a livable life and a grievable death?" While this consideration of grievability is within the context of the war dead, Butler's observation is cogent here insofar as Black people who are killed, especially by the police, are nearly always perceived as not deserving of public mourning and retributive or reparative justice, as evident by the majority of officers who killed who are either not charged or not convicted of any wrongdoing (Naomi Zack, *White Privilege and Black Rights: The Injustice of US Police Racial Profiling and Homicide* [Lanham, MD: Rowman & Littlefield, 2015]). For further information on police homicides, especially of unarmed Black and brown people, see updated compilations by *The Guardian* (Jon Swaine, Oliver Laughland, and Jamiles Lartey, "The Counted: People Killed by Police in the US," available at theguardian.com), *The Washington Post* (Kimberly Kindy, Marcy Fisher, Julie Tate, and Jennifer Jenkins, "A Year of Reckoning: Police Fatally Shoot Nearly 1,000," available at washingtonpost.com), and, the Mapping Police Violence project (available at mappingpoliceviolence.org).

80   In a remarkable reflection on the epidemic of police homicides of Black people in the United States, the philosopher Naomi Zack (*White Privilege and Black Rights*) argues that because "police racial profiling and homicide have been found to be bounded by law, individual misinformation, distorted cultural association of crime and race, and the legacies of earlier injustice" (93), not having to worry about police killing is less about white privilege and more about

From art and architecture to ARTs (assisted reproductive technologies) and AI (artificial intelligence), to posthumanist ideography, futurist sensibilities frequently mask their fascist origins. As a historical phenomenon, futurism refers to an artistic and social movement that can be traced to early-twentieth-century modernism in Italy. As a social phenomenon, futurism can be understood as a belief in the future. Artistically, sociologically, and anthropologically, futurism emphasizes transformation rooted in the present world. In its modernist form, futurism almost always emphasizes technology, youth, and urbanity. While many scholars have credited Italian poet and propagandist Filippo Tommaso Marinetti's *The Founding and Manifesto of Futurism* with launching futurism, few dig into Marinetti's deep commitment to fascism.[81] Published in 1909, the *Manifesto* conflates modernity with futurist society, offering a nationalist defense of Italy as a significant cultural actor and producer. It rejects the past as primitive and glorifies a technocratically advanced modernity, celebrating machinery, speed, industry, youth, masculinity, and violence. Indeed, it declares that "we will glorify war—the world's only hygiene—militarism, patriotism, the destructive gesture of freedom-bringers, beautiful ideas worth dying for, and scorn for women."[82] Its explicit reification of war and rejection of liberal pluralism lent coherence to the emergent fascist ideological formations, including the Futurist Political Party, which later became part of the larger Italian Fascist Party. Marinetti would become one of the chief architects of Italian fascist politics, and in 1919, with Alceste De Ambris, he would co-author *The Fascist Manifesto* (1919), the first blueprint of Italian fascism.[83]

In contradistinction to Western futurism, Afrofuturism is explicitly antifascist insofar as it provides an imaginary domain for radical democratic politics and life-forms outside of white supremacy, racial capitalism, and hetero-patriarchy. As Robin D. G. Kelley points out in *Freedom Dreams*, both space travel and fugitivity have prefigured prominently in Afrofuturist cultural productions. Afrofuturism, as emblematic of radical performativity and freedom struggles, therefore, promises future imaginings that can "transport us to another place, compel us to relive horrors, and more importantly enable us to imagine a new society."[84] Time travel, especially looking to the past for rememories of resistance in order to reimagine a just future, is thus radically different from a Western

---

Black people's rights. Therefore, we need an "applicative justice [that can] bring the legal treatments of black people with the legal treatments of white people beyond written law, into real life practice" (95). Until then, "simply reiterating how whites are 'privileged' is not an effective response" for academics or activists.

81   For further information, consult Anne Bowler's informative essay "Politics as Art: Italian Futurism and Fascism," *Theory and Society* 20, no. 6 (December 1991): 763–94.

82   Filippo Tommaso Marinetti, "The Founding and Manifesto of Futurism," in Lawrence Rainey, Christine Poggi, and Laura Wittman, eds., *Futurism: An Anthology* (New Haven: Yale University Press, 2009), 49–53.

83   For an English translation of *The Fascist Manifesto*, see conservapedia.com.

84   Kelley, *Freedom Dreams*, 9.

futurist fantasy in which Black cosmologies, Black epistemologies, and Black life world have been disappeared or merely acquired a functionary status of an appenditure. More critically and as Susanna M. Morris points out in "Black Girls Are from the Future," there is a distinct tradition of black feminist Afrofuturism that "trangressively revises" mainstream icons and troubles "normative notions of race, fantasy, and power."[85] Black feminist Afrofuturism thus grounds its imaginary domains within the larger intersectional matrix of race/gender/sexuality, even as it mixes and unsettles that same matrix while rebelliously time-traveling into a fugitive past.

As signs of declining US hegemonic dominion are everywhere, especially in various theaters of war,[86] Americans are treated to the elevation of Donald Trump, a proto-fascist whose administration-in-waiting is mostly staffed with generals, multimillionaires, and billionaires, some of whom are also political hacks and white supremacists.[87] It is within the context of our contemporary neoliberal antidemocracy[88] that we must consider and constantly retool various formations of Black radical consciousness and praxes, including Afrofuturism,

---

85   Susana M. Morris, "Black Girls Are from the Future: Afrofuturist Feminism in Octavia E. Butler's *Fledgling*," *Women's Studies Quarterly* 40, nos. 3 and 4 (2012): 148–9.

86   Current arms conflicts include, in alphabetical order: Afghanistan, Iraq, Libya, Nigeria, Pakistan, Somalia, Syria, and Yemen. According to Nick Turse of *The Nation*, this list does not include the various operations by US Special Operation Command (SOCOM), which has special operation forces (SOFs) in 134 countries for the purpose of combat, special missions, or advising and training: "America's Secret War in 134 Countries," *The Nation* (January 16, 2014), available at thenation.com.

87   I am not alone in characterizing the incoming US president as a proto-fascist. Ironically, some of the most decisive assertions have come from neoconservatives. Among them, Robert Kagan, a senior fellow at the Brookings Institution, is most insightful in his analysis of the abject failure of the Republican Party to reject its own presidential nominee. As he warns in the May 18, 2016 column: "This is how fascism comes to America, not with jackboots and salutes (although there have been salutes, and a whiff of violence) but with a television huckster, a phony billionaire, a textbook egomaniac 'tapping into' popular resentments and insecurities, and with an entire national political party—out of ambition or blind party loyalty, or simply out of fear—falling into line behind him" (Robert Kagan, "This Is How Fascism Comes to America," *Washington Post* [May 18, 2016], available at washingtonpost.com). Unlike Kagan and other neoconservatives, I take a cue from Oliver Cromwell Cox (1964) when he suggested that fascism is not alien to or deviant from the US brand of capitalist democracy. Cox explained that fascists are the "capitalists and their sympathizers who have achieved political class consciousness [and] have become organized" as a class against workers in defense of capitalism (as cited in H. L. T. Quan, *Growth Against Democracy: Savage Developmentalism in the Modern World* [Lanham, MD: Lexington Books, 2012], 195). The fact that the nominally civilian administration in waiting is utterly reliant on the sensibilities and interests of generals and extremely wealthy corporate representatives suggests an intentional coupling of militarist and capitalist ideologies, not uncommon in many fascist regimes.

88   Elsewhere in my work, I use the term "savage developmentalism" to characterize key features of such a regime. I define savage developmentalism as the overarching logic of modern economic thought and developmental programs that rely on expansionism, order, and antidemocracy; and, the consequences of which necessarily entail a great deal of violence, cruelty, and dehumanization. For further reference, see Quan, *Growth Against Democracy*. See also Brown, *Undoing the Demos* for neoliberalism's "stealth revolution" against democracy.

as necessary antidotes to messianic billionairism[89] and futurist racial fantasies, and as an affirmation of life, dignity, and the pursuit of wholeness. When an epidemic of police killings and white vigilante violence against Black and brown people, the dismemberment of communities of color, and the permanent installation of the national security state sustained by total surveillance, a militarized police force, and mass incarceration are the main preoccupations of daily life, one wonders why all of us, as "willful subjects," have not time traveled sooner or more frequently, all the while awaiting for that favorable breeze, or for the fire next time.

---

89 See, for instance, the many millionaires and billionaires who are deemed worthy of holding public offices simply because they are "successful," or nearly two decades worth of Hollywood movies about wealthy superheroes (e.g., Batman, Iron Man), not to mention episodic television shows featuring billionaire saviors.

Chapter 12

The Bruise Blues

Avery F. Gordon

This essay emerged out of conversations I routinely have about politics and images, or about the political and the aesthetic in the art world and in the movement to abolish prisons and policing, two different social worlds in which I work. It might be read as a field report by a politically engaged radical critic, providing a couple of useful notes for those similarly engaged with these specific questions of visual culture. By "politically engaged radical critic," I refer to the description provided years ago by the anarchist writer Chuck Morse when introducing an interview he had done with Cedric J. Robinson, whom he thought exemplary. It is an eloquently articulated instruction. Morse writes:

> It is the task of the radical critic to illuminate what is repressed and excluded by the basic mechanisms of a given social order. It is the task of the *politically engaged* radical critic to *side* with the excluded and repressed: to develop insights gained in confrontation with injustice, to nourish cultures of resistance, and to help define the means with which society can be rendered adequate to the full breadth of human potentialities.[1]

In these conversations, some of which are public and some of which are not, the question, always urgent, of the representation of violence figures prominently. The specific figures vary, of course, depending on the moment. Recently, in addition to discussions about the highly mediated pictures of the desperate refugee, a problematic and decontextualized image of refuge and fugitivity deserving of greater attention,[2] the focus is on Black Lives Matter, on the renewed popular attention to police violence and anti-Black racism, and on what this moment of ferment means now and might portend for the future. In these conversations, the youthful or newly converted enthusiasm for the struggle and for the possibility of change "now that we know," to quote Ruth Wilson Gilmore, is inspiring. At the same time, the seasoned and the elders are also

---

1 Chuck Morse, "Capitalism, Marxism, and the Black Radical Tradition: An Interview with Cedric Robinson," *Perspectives on Anarchist Theory* 3, no. 1 (Spring 1999).

2 See Berlin filmmaker Philip Scheffner's new film *Havarie* (2016), an extraordinarily powerful and visually experimental treatment of thirteen Algerian men floating in a rubber dinghy in the Mediterranean Sea, awaiting the arrival of the Spanish Coast Guard. See Avery F. Gordon, "Keeping Eye Contact," Berlinale Forum 2016, available at arsenal-berlin.de/fileadmin/user_upload/forum/pdf2016/forum_englisch/E_Havarie.pdf.

frustrated sometimes at both the historiography embedded in "now," as in "only now?!?," and at the comprehension or political epistemology embedded in "know," as in, to quote Gilmore again, "know what?" In these conversations, important questions of political consciousness are being raised, including the routes, visual and otherwise, by which "the relationship between existential consciousness and truth systems" are disturbed and activated to abolitionist ends.[3] These spirited conversations inevitably take us to the heart of how racial regimes operate and the conditions under which they change and might be abolished. To quote Cedric J. Robinson on his generative concept, explicitly elaborated in the context of cinema:

> Racial regimes are constructed social systems in which race is proposed as a justifi-
> cation for the relations of power. While necessarily articulated with accruals of
> power, the covering conceit of a racial regime is a makeshift patchwork masquerad-
> ing as memory and the immutable. Nevertheless, racial regimes do possess history,
> that is, discernible origins and mechanisms of assembly. But racial regimes are
> unrelentingly hostile to their exhibition. This antipathy exists because a discovera-
> ble history is incompatible with a racial regime and from the realization that, para-
> doxically, so are its social relations. One threatens the authority and the other saps
> the vitality of racial regimes. Each undermines the founding myths. The archaeo-
> logical imprint of human agency radically alienates the histories of racial regimes
> from their own claims of naturalism. Employing mythic discourses, racial regimes
> are commonly masqueraded as natural orderings, inevitable creations of collective
> anxieties prompted by threatening encounters with difference. Yet they are actually
> contrivances, designed and delegated by interested cultural and social powers with
> the wherewithal sufficient to commission their imaginings, manufacture, and
> maintenance. This latter industry is of some singular importance, since racial
> regimes tend to wear thin over time.[4]

In what follows, and with these conversations in mind, I respond to an exhibition consisting of three commissioned works by African American artist Glenn
Ligon titled "Call and Response", which was on display at Camden Arts Centre
in London, from October 10, 2014 to January 11, 2015.[5] This response initially
emerged out of a panel discussion in which Camden Arts Centre curator Nisha
Matthews asked artist and filmmaker John Akomfrah, legal scholar and anti-
police violence activist Eddie Bruce-Jones, art curator Gilane Tawadros, and me

---

3   Cedric J. Robinson, *The Terms of Order: Political Science and the Myth of Leadership* (Chapel
Hill: University of North Carolina Press, 2016), 214.
4   Cedric J. Robinson, *Forgeries of Memory and Meaning: Blacks and the Regimes of Race in
American Theater and Film before World War II* (Chapel Hill: University of North Carolina Press,
2007), xii—xiii.
5   See Camden Art Centre's website for a description and images of the exhibition, available at
camdenartscentre.org.

to address Ligon's work in the context of "postracial futures and how we might keep alive utopian ideals of living together better ... in an age haunted by a history of racial oppression."[6]

Two of the component works of the exhibition—*Untitled (Bruise/Blues)* and *Come Out #4 and #5*—reference a case of police brutality. Combining the two works in a single exhibition put additional pressure on the already complex and contentious terms "post-racial" and "utopian" that launched the discussion. For many, of course, the term "post-racial" functions less as a desirable utopian ideal and more as a regulatory fiction: one that mystifies the existence and origins of racism and racial inequalities; that reproduces whiteness by making it the unspoken norm of the two most commonly accepted forms of post-raciality— colorblindness and diversity or corporate multiculturalism; and that justifies historical amnesia and its accompanying sanctioned ignorance. By the latter I refer, for example, to the general state of surprise in the United States and Europe at the killing of Michael Brown in Ferguson, Missouri, on August 9, 2014, and at the routine tactical behavior of urban police forces and the judicial system, which authorizes and protects them. I emphasize the word "routine." Eric Garner died on July 17, 2014, from a chokehold. John Crawford III was shot to death by police officer Sean Williams in a Walmart store near Dayton, Ohio, on August 5, 2014, for holding an air rifle in the store. Akai Gurley died in Brooklyn after he was shot by police officer Peter Liang on November 20, 2014, in the stairwell of a public housing project. Tamir Rice died in Cleveland on November 23, 2014, the day after he was shot by police officer Timothy Loehmann, accompanied by his partner, Frank Garmback. Tanisha Anderson was also killed in police custody in Cleveland in November 2014. Yvette Smith was killed by police on February 16, 2014, opening her front door in Texas. In 2014, after NYPD officer Daniel Pantaleo was not indicted for killing Eric Garner, the NAACP Legal Defense Fund tweeted the names of seventy-six unarmed men and women killed in police custody since the 1999 death of Amadou Diallo in New York City. *The Guardian* counted 1,140 people killed by the police in the United States in 2015, 578 of whom were white. As of the end of February 2016, we can add another 167 individuals.[7]

---

6   Personal correspondence from Nisha Matthews, whom I thank for inviting me to participate in the panel on January 10, 2015, and for prompting the writing of this piece. These ideas were further developed for Ruth Wilson Gilmore's session on violence and the problem of the visual at the CASAR Annual Conference held at the American University of Beirut in January 2016.

7   Rich Juzwiak and Aleksander Chan, "Unarmed People of Color Killed by Police, 1999– 2014," Gawker (December 8, 2014), available at gawker.com and at huffingtonpost.com; Jon Swaine, Oliver Laughland, and Jamiles Lartey, "The Counted: People Killed by Police in the US," available at theguardian.com. *The Guardian* began its project because the US government has no comprehensive record of people killed by the police and other law enforcement agencies.

1. POLICE POWER

Glenn Ligon draws on Steve Reich's 1966 sound composition *Come Out* in two of the three works in the exhibition "Call and Response." Reich's piece was, in turn, based on the voice of Daniel Hamm, one of six youths arrested for murder in 1964. When James Baldwin wrote a story for *The Nation* in 1966 about the beatings and arrests that took place on April 17, 1964, he began his story not with Wallace Baker, Willie Craig, Ronald Felder, Daniel Hamm, Robert Rice, and Walter Thomas, known at the time as the Harlem 6, but with an account of what happened earlier in the day to Frank Stafford, a thirty-one-year-old sales-man arrested and beaten badly by the police (he lost an eye); Fecundo Acion, a forty-seven-year-old Puerto Rican sailor; and two unnamed others who were picked up and celled together.[8] In 1964 or 2017, even before we get to the names on everyone's mind at the ever-repeating moment, there are always the ones who came before. Baldwin, too, wonders how anyone could be "astonished" or "bewildered" that three months later, on July 16, 1964, a white policeman named Thomas Gilligan shot and killed James Powell, a fifteen-year-old African American boy, in front of his friends, prompting a rebellion and spilling, as Baldwin puts it, "the overflowed unimaginably bitter cup."

The violence of racial regimes is axiomatic whether we are talking about the taken-for-granted social divisions and economic stratifications produced by racial capitalism or whether we are talking about the harassed everyday life of young people of color, especially in cities where, as Daniel Hamm said back in 1964: "They don't want us—period!" The violence of racial regimes is self-evident whether we are talking about the systems of mass imprisonment that are used to manage surplus, disposable, and politically troublesome populations, or whether we are talking about the individuals, communities, and cultures vulnerable to intellectual trivialization and the continuum that runs from genocide to phased-in obsolescence. It takes enormous work by states, corporations, media and educational systems, civil society organizations, and individuals to keep racial regimes going and to transform them since they are, to quote Robinson, "forgeries of memory and meaning," and thus, despite appearances, fragile and always in danger of breaking apart.[9]

---

8 James Baldwin, "A Report from Occupied Territory," *The Nation* (July 11, 1966).

9 "The degeneration of racial regimes occurs with some frequency for two reasons. First, apparent difference in identity is an attempt to mask shared identities ... A second source of regime entropy ensues from the fact that because the regimes are cultural artifices, which catalog only fragments of the real, they inevitably generate fugitive, unaccounted-for elements of reality. Abraham Lincoln's insistence that fugitive slaves were "contraband" (in effect, property which had illegally seized itself) did not prepare the president for their role in subverting his war aims. Lincoln believed reuniting the nation did not require the abolition of human property. As fugitives, troops, and sailors, that same property disabused him of his delusional political program. This was an instance of what Hegel termed the negation of the negation, flawed or delinquent comprehension colliding with the real." Robinson, *Forgeries of Memory and Meaning*, xiii–xiv.

Police power or the power to police is a crucial element in that work. By police power, I don't mean only police officers or police departments and their more spectacular violence. Police power is a mode of governance, the discretionary power to dispose of present threats to the social order and to avert future dangers to it. The responsibility of the power for the future is important—predicting dangerousness is one of its main functions. Police power is always anticipatory in this sense, and its seventeenth- and eighteenth-century European theorists viewed it as a means to achieve the political ideal of a harmonious state, its interior affairs all in good order. Settler colonial regimes have been especially propitious laboratories for the development of a police power capable of effectively expropriating and protecting private property, including racial property such as whiteness, and protecting social order, as the case of the United States demonstrates clearly. In the antebellum United States, police power was an explicitly racial privilege. The state did not, in fact, hold a monopoly on the use of force, thus the right of slave owners and their deputies, such as slave patrols and labor overseers, to police at will and to usurp the judicial power to punish. In principle, police power defers or cedes the power to punish to the judge, although this principle, constitutional in nature, has a rather checkered history and one could argue that the prison, which concentrates police power, mocks the very principle itself.[10]

In the United States, this history has been passed down as the specific right of white property owners to exercise police power when threatened, colloquially known today as "Stand Your Ground." As is well known, "line in the sand" and "the castle doctrine" were the legal grounds for the acquittal of George Zimmerman for killing Trayvon Martin; the genealogy of those legal rights is to be found in the post–Civil War history of the Black Codes, convict leasing, and lynching. Whether the individual right to bear arms is constitutional precedent or merely a practical requirement for exercising police power is a question for a legal scholar to answer. Political history suggests that the insistence on the right to bear arms is usually in the service of a struggle over the exercise of police power. This was the case in the American Revolution against the British. And it was the position of the Black Panther Party, made explicit on May 2, 1967, when several members of the party attempted to enter the California State Capitol building to oppose passage of the Mulford Bill, which had been designed to

---

10   See Nikhil Pal Singh, "The Whiteness of Police," *American Quarterly* (2014): 1091–9; Pasquale Pasquino, "Theatrum Politicum: The Geneaology of Capital—Police and the State of Prosperity" in Graham Burchell, Colin Gordon, and Peter Miller, eds., *The Foucault Effect: Studies in Governmentality* (London: Harvester Wheatsheaf, 1991); George S. Rigakos, John L. McMullan, Joshua Johnson, and Guilden Ozcan, eds., *A General Police System: Political Economy and Security in the Age of Enlightenment* (Ottawa: Red Quill Books, 2009); Mark Neocleous, *The Fabrication of Social Order: A Critical Theory of Police Power* (London: Pluto Press, 2000); Bryan Wagner, *Disturbing the Peace: Black Culture and the Police Power after Slavery* (Cambridge, MA: Harvard University Press, 2009); Markus Dirk Dubber, *The Police Power: Patriarchy and the Foundations of American Government* (New York: Columbia University Press, 2005).

effectively end the Panther Police Patrols. Unable to enter the building, they were famously photographed holding their weapons on the steps of the Capitol building in advance of issuing a statement to this effect.[11]

More generally, this history has been passed down as the restricted authority to determine what and who is a threat to the terms of order—in other words, to create crimes and criminals. Of course, Black people are not, by any means, the only object of such condemnation, to use Khalil Gibran Muhammad's apt word, though they are rarely exempt from it.[12] Here, I note that police departments obviously do the bidding of other masters—Baldwin rightly called them the "hired enemies" of urban communities of color—and the price they charge is exemption from being policed, which they receive, save in those exceptional situations in which to save police power an individual police officer might need to be sacrificed. It's for this reason that Nikhil Pal Singh uses the phrase "the whiteness of police" in his seminal article, whiteness signifying here not the ethnicity of the individual members of police forces, but the status that confers immunity from criminalization.[13]

These are complex issues. Here, I would like to emphasize the extent to which police power does the work of racial ordering that the state has formally outlawed in a post–civil rights or multicultural context in which we are, as the commonsense goes, post-racial, the definitive proof being, in the United States, the presidency of Barack Obama. I emphasize this for two reasons. One reason is the obvious implication that before we get to post-racial in any meaningful sense, we need first to understand the extent to which racism operates precisely through the presumption that it no longer really exists; criminalization, particularly given the elasticity that the notion of security has acquired, is not the only means by which this presumption is reproduced, but it is a crucial and highly flexible one. The second reason is the further implication that any meaningful notion of the utopian must address this condition or at least emerge in relation to it.

2. BRUISE BLUES

If we define the utopian not as it is commonly defined—as a homogeneous perfect future no-place—but rather as a standpoint for living in the here and now, then we might find meaningful instances of it in the history of social

---

11   To watch Bobby Seale deliver BPP Executive Mandate No. 1 outside the lawn of the California statehouse, see pbs.org/hueypnewton/actions/actions_capitolmarch.html. On the American Revolution, see Woody Holton, *Forced Founders: Indians, Debtors, Slaves, and the Making of the American Revolution in Virginia* (Chapel Hill: University of North Carolina Press, 1999).

12   Khalil Gibran Muhammad, *The Condemnation of Blackness: Race, Crime, and the Making of Modern Urban America* (Cambridge, MA: Harvard University Press, 2011).

13   Singh, "The Whiteness of Police."

struggle.[14] In the US Black Radical Tradition, the history of social struggle is, for obvious reasons, bound up with slavery and its afterlife, in which police power, unrelenting, is a continuous object of attention. In this context, the framework of abolitionism has political resonance, not as formal emancipation or liberal legal rights, but as what the writer Toni Cade Bambara described as being "unavailable for servitude" in the broadest sense of servility and availability. This struggle or process aims to establish the conditions of possibility for a free life for all, without misery or oppression. For abolitionists today, one of our most urgent demands is the abolition of police power in all its dramatic and routine manifestations. To view this demand as a political exigency and not "merely utopian" in the dismissive sense is exactly the kind of utopianism that radical abolitionists have historically modeled.

This kind of utopianism has many sources, one of which the late social geographer Clyde Woods called a "blues epistemology," by which he meant that "longstanding African American working class tradition of explaining reality and change."[15] Woods found its "trunk" in the Mississippi delta where the blues originated in plantation life to sound out its burdens and pains and simultaneously to "construct a vision of a non-oppressive society."[16] The both/and is distinctive to this praxis. For Woods, a blues epistemology "bridges the gap between the blues as a widely recognized aesthetic tradition and the blues as a radical theory of social and economic development and change."[17] It is an epistemology with "multiple roots and branches," an "evolving complex of explanation and action that provides support for [sometimes conflicting] traditions of resistance, affirmation and confirmation."[18]

A blues epistemology is signaled in Ligon's *Untitled (Bruise/Blues)*, two blue neon signs that correct Daniel Hamm's slip of the tongue when he explained what he did to get the police to take him to the hospital for treatment when they refused: "I had to like open the bruise up and let some of the blues blood come out to show them." Bruise blues or blues blood: from a certain point of view, the slippage is a recognizable improvisational phrasing. It can easily be picked up and passed on to the next player. Reich's thirteen-minute sound composition performed originally at a benefit for the retrial of the Harlem 6, pushes this sentence to the point of utter collapse, where the rhythmic and narrative structure of a blues song or a blues

---

14   See Avery F. Gordon, "Some Thoughts on the Utopian," "Something More Powerful Than Skepticism" (on Toni Cade Bambara), and "An Anthropology of Marxism" (on Cedric J. Robinson) in *Keeping Good Time: Reflections on Knowledge, Power, and People* (Boulder, CO: Paradigm, 2004), and Avery F. Gordon, *The Hawthorn Archive: Letters from the Utopian Margins* (New York: Fordham University Press, 2017).

15   Clyde Woods, *Development Arrested: The Blues and Plantation Power in the Mississippi Delta* (London: Verso, 1998), 16.

16   Ibid, 39.

17   Ibid., 20.

18   Ibid., 27. See Angela Y. Davis, *Blues Legacies and Black Feminism: Gertrude "Ma" Rainey, Bessie Smith, and Billie Holiday* (New York: Vintage Books, 1999).

theory is dissolved and one hears, if one can listen that long, only the echo of the original bruising.[19] *Come out to show them come o*

3. COME OUT AND SHOW THEM!

The abstraction works differently in *Come Out #4 and #5* and its monumental silence makes it seem more like a memorial. Substituting the phrase "come out to show them" for the roll call of the names of the dead usually displayed by war memorials, *Come Out* avoids the common and limiting presumption that only the dead can adequately represent the violence of police power and also avoids presuming that what happened is singular and safely in the past. *Come Out*, carrying its blues epistemology, presents us with refraining and shadow: the repetition of the phrase as singular incident such that it appears as density, structure, pattern; the shadowing of the phrase as multiple voices, some bright and loud, some inaudible, blacked-out. Repetition, shadow, and the call to future action: COME OUT AND SHOW THEM!

4. PRESENCE UNDER PRESSURE

Show them what? Possibly what's living and breathing in the blind field that racial profiling presumes and produces. Perhaps because I started with *Bruise/ Blues* and had just come out of what I experienced as a memorial to the Harlem 6, I was predisposed to see *Live*, Ligon's multi-channel video work that removes the sound and disarticulates Richard Pryor's 1982 performance *Live on the Sunset Strip*, as the third response to the call of the same event.[20] I found it a surprisingly beautiful rebuke to the criminal anthropology that underwrites police power today and whose origins are in nineteenth-century racial science.

---

19   Reich's *Come Out* can be found on YouTube.

20   This is not an unreasonable response, given Ligon's work and the making of *Live* for an exhibition with two major works in relation to the Harlem 6. But it is also an analytic stretch. Glenn Ligon has had a long engagement with Richard Pryor, including a series of neon color paintings made in 2004 that consist of words taken from Pryor's standup routines, and thus there is another context for interpretation I ignore here.

Without the space here to elaborate, suffice to say that criminal anthropology's most well-known inventors, such as Cesare Lombroso, found in their ethnology colleagues' research into the racial ordering of Western civilization support for their belief that the criminal, in whom Lombroso found traces of the "apish atavism" of our primitive past, was a distinct and inferior race of men and women. The implications of this scientific belief in innate criminality are significant for understanding the extent to which criminalization is a form of racialization. Race, in the sociological and commonsense way we tend to use it, not only explains who is most likely to become a criminal—that is, who is most likely to be criminalized—it also describes what the criminal becomes, that is to say, a specific race of men and women. Or, to put it another way, police power produces race—it is a medium of racialized statecraft—as much as it relies on already existing racial categories. Natural-born criminals were imminently classifiable and thus logical subjects for surveillance: Lombroso and the early criminal anthropologists were convinced they could identify a member of the criminal race by certain visual signs or stigmata, such as longer arms, woolly hair, precocious wrinkles, excessive hand gestures, or the use of unintelligible argot. Lombroso was especially obsessed with prostitutes and anarchists.[21]

In the case of African Americans, the double racialization has been ascriptive.[22] African Americans are treated as a criminal race, whose ontology—what they were, what they are, what they could be—is reduced to its essential criminality, their supposed basic nature. This is one reason why criminal profiling is more or less the same as racial profiling, a brutal reduction of human differences into the evident visual stigmata of the body of the known criminal, a threat to the order of things. This is also one reason why all attempts to deal with police power—from stop and search to arrest to imprisonment—as if it were possible to reform it by eliminating its "abuses" of the "innocent"—is a trap and will fail. The ideological legitimacy of police power rests on its claim to make the distinction between innocent and guilty accurately, fairly, and justly, notwithstanding the fact that the whole history of crime belies this claim. Abolition starts elsewhere, politically, culturally, aesthetically.[23]

---

21   On criminal anthropology and race-making, see Avery F. Gordon, "'I'm Already in a Sort of Tomb': A Reply to Philip Scheffner's *The Halfmoon Files*," *South Atlantic Quarterly* 110, no. 1 (Winter 2011): 121–54.

22   It has also been predictive to the extent that in the United States especially, the criminalization of Black people operates like a kind of laboratory for experimentation in procedure, legitimation, and management, thus enabling application to other groups.

23   Here the work of groups such as Critical Resistance and INCITE! Women of Color Against Violence are crucial for leading the way in finding alternative languages and practices to policing and incarceration. See, for example, Critical Resistance's Abolitionist Toolkit at criticalresistance.org and INCITE!'s Anti–Police Brutality Palm Card available at incite-national.org. See also Beth E. Richie, *Arrested Justice: Black Women, Violence and America's Prison Nation* (New York: New York University Press, 2012) and Sarah Lamble, "Transforming Carceral Logics: 10 Reasons to Dismantle the Prison Industrial Complex Through Queer/Trans Analysis and Action" in Eric A. Stanley and Nat Smith, eds. *Captive Genders: Trans Embodiment and the Prison Industrial Complex* (Oakland, CA: AK Press, 2011).

There's a certain erotic feeling in watching Pryor's body in the dark with the sound off, especially watching him touch himself in that repetitive gesture where he moves his hand quickly back and forth from heart to crotch, which lends to the repetition of the phrase—"come out come out come out to show them"—a different meaning and complicates the heterosexual masculinity Pryor is famous for performing. The memorial is cold, this room is warmer. I'm remembering having seen this performance before or parts of it seem familiar, something is coming back to me. I'm loving those fabulous gold shoes set off by the yellow rosebud in the pocket of the red/orange suit, out-of-fashion color jumping up all over the place not as skin but as pure provocation to the self-determination of blaxploitation. I'm watching intently Pryor's expressive face, full of frowns, rarely smiling, like a professor. You'd never know he was telling jokes unless you already knew or caught the funky chicken dance moves when even he can't stop himself from laughing at himself, at you, at us. I'm caught up in those moments when lip-reading, I can hear his voice: angry—"bullshit"; showing off—"motherfucker"; concluding the riff—"alright"; taking the piss—"holy shit!" I'm moved profoundly by the beauty of Pryor's hands constantly fluttering here and there, etching an elaborate sign language, a poetry of call and response without spoken words, which reminds me of James Drake's equally moving video installation *Tongue-Cut-Sparrows*. (Drake's 1998 work is based on the sign language women used to communicate with the men inside the El Paso County Detention Facility, who were almost entirely Latino immigrants serving time for violations of immigration rules. Drake had seen the women and asked them if he could film them and if they would select a piece of literature and sign it to the men inside. They agreed.) The performance ends when Pryor steadies his fluttering hands, reaches into his pocket to light a cigarette, and raises his fist.

In that room, surrounded by the celebrity famous for his critical and uncompromising words, now cut into scenes of silent gestures, the unique individual performer transformed into a set of disarticulated visual signs, the effect is exactly the opposite of the reductionism and dehumanization of the racial profiling Pryor understood all too well. Rather, there's an exquisite delicacy of touch and being, what Bennett Simpson described as "the gritty particularity of presence under pressure."[24] Something we might just call respect, in the capacious Zapatista sense of dignity, which is how the film *Live on the Sunset Strip* ends, credits rolling, with Aretha Franklin singing her famous standard of the same name.[25]

---

24   Evident, he thought, in Ligon's Pryor paintings. See Simpson, "Pryor Versions."

25   We might also see respect in the fact that *Live* begins and ends with the film *Live on the Sunset Strip* shown in its integrity on all seven screens, which enables the artist and the viewer who watches the entire installation to credit the makers of the film. It also reminds us that in the beginning and in the end there is a whole person before the cuts.

5. WE ARE THE ONES WE'RE WAITING FOR

The Black Radical Tradition brings to the now ubiquitous images of the police killings of Black men and women something much more than ahistorical calls to reform police departments. It brings the history and ongoing struggle against racial capitalism and the requirement to specify the nature of the radical thought that is adequate to confront what Cedric J. Robinson once called "the nastiness" that is everywhere too evident today. "The Black Radical Tradition," Robinson wrote, "was an accretion over generations of collective intelligence gathered from struggle."[26] This collective intelligence harbored a critique of an entire civilization or way of life. In Robinson's hands, it presumed a commitment to a politics in which the struggle to transform the world as we know it takes place through means that embody the alternative values, practices, and institutional formats we desire and for which we bother to struggle. As Robinson never ceased to remind us, this tradition is as much an invention as it was a discovery of something already there and fully formed, even if part of the struggle was to make it obvious that living and breathing in the enlightened civilization's blind field was precisely that collective intelligence at work. The Black Radical Internationalist Tradition, to appropriate Barbara Ransby's naming, is a living tradition, a moving tradition, that changes and takes shape as it opposes and negates racial, class, and gender regimes that themselves mutate, including police power. While marronage might be its first principle, one of the key watchwords of this tradition is movement.[27]

In the movement to abolish police power and the carceral state, abolition feminism has grounded a radical imaginary that keeps the tradition moving. Abolition feminism is not a sub-program or an identity; it is a methodology and a practice, a way of seeing, thinking, and acting that above all makes connections. Abolition feminism makes analytical connections between seemingly disparate institutions, functionalities, and technologies of power and domination—imprisonment and debt, for example—and political connections between seemingly unrelated oppositional and resistant struggles—opposition to racialized policing in the United States and Palestinian self-determination, for example. And abolition feminism makes human connections—solidarity—between seemingly divided and disconnected peoples and places—landless people and deserting soldiers, for example. As a methodology, abolition feminism treats

---

26   Cedric J. Robinson, *Black Marxism: The Making of the Black Radical Tradition* (Chapel Hill: University of North Carolina Press, 2000[1983]), xxx.

27   At the conference "Confronting Racial Capitalism: The Black Radical Tradition and Cultures of Liberation" held at the CUNY Graduate Center on November 20–1, 2014, and organized by Jordan Camp, Christina Heatherton, and Ruth Wilson Gilmore, the "Black Radical Internationalist Tradition" was the term Barbara Ransby used in her presentation to signify and distinguish the specific standpoint represented there and among most of the contributors to this volume. At that conference, Cedric Robinson nominated the word "ideology" as the tradition's key watchword. He said, "It's not experience that frames our conduct but ideology."

race, gender, and sexuality as "forgeries of memory and meaning," that is to say, as interlocking and normalizing constructs that are unsustainable fabrications and thus whose natural history is always literally falling apart. And abolition feminism embodies a way of being, working, and living—a version of the personal as political—that tries to be better than the petty ambitions, narcissism, and sectarianism that characterize too much political culture today. This feminism has a steady and sturdy moral compass that easily crosses national and nationalist borders, if it is not self-consciously internationalist, and which it uses as a guide while building the social, economic, and political infrastructure that makes a life without slavery, exploitation, confinement, and repressive normalization possible for all.

This is the picture or the image of the radical abolitionist practice and the future it brings. It is not in the image of our being smashed up the side of the head or shot to death by the police. At the 2003 World Social Forum in Porto Alegre, Brazil, Danny Glover ended his public testimonial with these words:

> June Jordan said that we are the ones we are waiting for. There's no one else but us. Myself, you, none of us are absolved of this responsibility. We are not Gods, but we are many. Since we are not Gods, we can be great and we can be a great many.

In his perhaps least read book, *An Anthropology of Marxism*, Cedric J. Robinson reclaimed socialism for all those whom Marxism had excluded from its history and its future, including heretical women, slaves, peasants, nonindustrial workers, and intellectuals, on the grounds that "a socialist discourse is an irrepressible response to social injustice."[28] Robinson found confirmation for these grounds not in "the fractious and weaker allegiances of class" but rather in a kind of divine agency. This divine agency is not a God, but, like June Jordan's great many, it carries the power of the "history and the persistence of the human spirit" in the face of "domination and oppression."[29] As we face the challenge of realizing the political and aesthetic representation of this audacious power, we can draw on the great work and legacy of the Black Radical Tradition and Cedric J. Robinson's crucial contributions to its inventions.

---

28   Cedric J. Robinson, *An Anthropology of Marxism* (Aldershot: Ashgate Publishing, 2001), 157.

29   Ibid.

Chapter 13

"The People Who Keep on Going"

A Listening Party, Vol. I

Shana L. Redmond and Kwame M. Phillips

I tried to write poems like the songs they sang on Seventh Street—
gay songs, because you had to be gay or die;
sad songs, because you couldn't help being sad sometimes.
But, gay or sad, you kept on living and you kept on going.
Their songs—those of Seventh Street—
had the pulse beat of the people who keep on going.

— Langston Hughes, *The Big Sea* [1]

What do you hear when we say "Black Radical Tradition"? Do you hear Fela's sax as it cries after his mother's murder? The defiant tremolo of Marian Anderson's mezzo or the callouses on the fingertips of Sister Rosetta? Do you hear the claves of Havana, the tambourines of Rio de Janeiro, and the boom-bap machines of the Bronx in the same song, the same measure? What about the vectors of language—Xhosa, Portuguese, and Patois—sung across the Atlantic, the Mediterranean, and the Pacific, in every direction? Do you hear the "accretion, over generations, of collective intelligence gathered from struggle"[2]?

If you knew, you'd listen. The tradition is brilliantly displayed and imagined and practiced anew through sound; Robinson hints at this fact, encouraging readers of *Black Marxism* to "examine how the tradition insinuated itself . . . into the blues composed by Rainey and all the women named Smith."[3] Indeed, Ma and Clara, Bessie, Trixie, Laura, and Mamie carried dangerous knowledges with them that altered the course of popular culture and challenged the overdetermined nature of Black social consciousness.[4] What follows is a listening party—a preliminary opportunity to hear the long genealogies of the tradition by way of a method that complicates and enlivens its histories, exposing its roots and carrying them forward as sample, metaphor, and trace throughout our shared "changing same."[5] This playlist is a guided meditation from keepers of the tradition who, with horns and machines and keys and voice, assist us in understanding how music creates "a

---

1 Langston Hughes, *The Big Sea* (New York: Knopf, 1940).
2 Cedric J. Robinson, *Black Marxism* (Chapel Hill: University of North Carolina, 1983), xxx.
3 Ibid., xxxii.
4 Angela Y. Davis, *Blues Legacies and Black Feminism* (New York: Pantheon, 1998).
5 Amiri Baraka, *Black Music* (New York: W. Morrow, 1967).

world of pleasure, not just to escape the everyday brutalities of capitalism, patriarchy, and white supremacy, but to build community, establish fellowship, play and laugh, and plant seeds for a different way of living, a different way of hearing."[6]

These are the liner notes for a hypothesis in wax—the inadequate words that trail behind sound's experiments of desire, hope, and ambition. It is a people's songbook, a soundtrack to the improvisational life and living of Blackness under the control of white supremacy. This is an effort to pull forward and give a name to what our bodies tell us with every needle drop, to hold tight that which combines individual voice and people's rebellion, to play together in the porous force field that incubates new knowledge and launches our freedom dreams. Our hope is to relay the diaspora meters that shake and raise the earth to move the feet of millions and expose its historical spine from the drum to the drum machine.

Inspired by the revelations and revolutions of Cedric Robinson's oeuvre, these songs were mined from the layers of twentieth-century Black thought and practice that animate our relationship to the past, present, and future conjunctures of our living. As the "Vol. I" in the chapter title suggests, this soundscape is not exhaustive. It is, in many respects, speculative in its curation of approaches, voices, local and diasporic conditions and beliefs. It is a repetitive introduction to the sound of a global Seventh Street that trembles with the "pulse beat of the people who keep on going."

Track List:

> Max Roach ft. Abbey Lincoln, "Freedom Day" (1960)
> Syl Johnson, "Is It Because I'm Black?" (1967)
> Hank Ballard, "Blackenized" (1969)
> Derrick Harriott, "Message from a Black Man" (1970)
> Miriam Makeba, "KwaZulu (In the Land of the Zulus)" (1965)
> Cipher J.E.W.E.L.S, "2000 Years" (2002)
> THEESatisfaction, "On What It Means to Be Black" (2010)
> OCnotes, "Radio Nat Turner" (2014)
> Kendrick Lamar, "Alright" (2015)
> Death, "Politicians in My Eyes" (1976)
> Dennis Brown, "Revolution" (1983)
> Janelle Monáe and Wondaland, "Hell You Talmbout" (2015)
> Ray Angry ft. Nadia Washington & Chris Potter, "Celebration of Life Suite: Awareness & Revolution" (2015)
> D'Angelo and the Vanguard, "The Charade" (2014)
> Thundercat ft. Mono/Poly, "Paris" (2015)

We start with the drum.

---

6 Robin D. G. Kelley, *Freedom Dreams* (Boston: Beacon Press, 2002), 11.

MAX ROACH FT. ABBEY LINCOLN, "FREEDOM DAY" (1960)

A single cymbal introduces a grand historical symbol. We enter our sound world in 1960 but it's really 1863. We start here as a commemoration of emancipation, a remembrance of liberty. The horns signify a grandeur; the drums signal a call to attention. The Emancipation Proclamation, nearly a century old when we lean in to listen, is the ongoing conjecture—an imperfect conclusion grounded by rumor. "Whisper, listen. Whisper, listen. Whispers say we're free." Recalling the slow delivery of the news that the Civil War had ended, the caution of the song exists in the space between President Lincoln's issuance of the Emancipation Proclamation on January 1, 1863, and Union general Gordon Granger's declaration on June 19, 1865, of "General Order Number 3," confirming the total emancipation of enslaved Africans in the United States. Freedom Day is not a lived reality; it is whispered hearsay, barely conceivable or believable. Abbey Lincoln's steady, stately vocal cadence in "Freedom Day" works against the quick dexterity of Max Roach (drums), James Schenk (bass), Walter Benton (tenor saxophone), Booker Little (trumpet), and Julian Priester (trombone). She slows the listener's excited gait in pursuit of the other musicians, causing us to drag, ever so slightly. Caution is her order in recognition of the ellipses and question marks that punctuate her narrative: "Can it really be?" This hesitation and inquiry was intended; according to Roach, "[Oscar Brown, Jr. and I] never could finish [the project]. It [still] isn't finished." The incompleteness of the *Freedom Now Suite* was not due to an artistic, or even a personality, dispute; its status—in progress—has to do with the very nature of Black (un)freedom. As Roach argued, "We don't really understand what it really is to be free."[7] The "dilemma or double bind of freedom,"[8] which is so often marked dialectically, was not posed first by the conditions of enslavement but rather by the historical consciousness that Africans brought with them across the Atlantic; "after all it had been as an emergent African people and not as slaves that Black men and women had opposed enslavement."[9]

Freedom then, as Nelson Mandela taught, is not an event but a process. Here, again, the ellipses of Lincoln's vocal fade tapped out on Roach's hi-hat. The caution of Lincoln's restrained exaltation gives way to the frantic drums and trumpet of Roach and Little, evoking more urgency than celebration, as if the "shackle 'n chains" have been thrown away but the path towards true liberation dimmed and the way hidden. Icon Frederick Douglass, who himself tested the limits of freedom as policy and practice, made his own fateful advances toward freedom more than once. Freedom Day is not an end point; it is where we begin, a false dawn, an unfulfilled covenant. It would take another four years after the

---

7   Ingrid Monson, "Jazz Articles: Revisited! The Freedom Now Suite," *JazzTimes* (September 2001), available at jazztimes.com.

8   Saidiya V. Hartman, *Scenes of Subjection: Terror, Slavery, and Self-Making in Nineteenth-Century America* (New York: Oxford University Press, 1997), 115.

9   Robinson, *Black Marxism*, 170–1.

release of the *Freedom Now Suite* before the Civil Rights Act of 1964 would pass employment discrimination law to allow Black Americans a measure of protection in their efforts to "earn [their] pay," and a further year before the United States Congress would pass the Voting Rights Act of 1965, giving greater assurance to being "free to vote." Lincoln's repetition—"Slave no longer. Slave no longer. This is Freedom Day"—is the mirror of sound for Douglass' and others' countless attempts at flight, and accelerates the declarative sentence from a plea to an assertion of subjectivity. "Freedom Day" is a meditation on the possibility for emancipation that is announced in the rumor of US policy and practice.

SYL JOHNSON, "IS IT BECAUSE I'M BLACK?" (1967)

Questions of political and socioeconomic power are further explored by Syl Johnson. Chicago-based soul producer James L. "Jimmy" Jones and his accompanying band The Pieces of Peace provide a fitting minor-keyed, blues-inspired soul groove to Johnson's mournful invocation. Johnson begins poetically, embodying his shared pain in his skin, his bones, and his soul: "The dark brown shades of my skin / only add colour to my tears / That splash against my hollow bones / that rocks my soul." The evidence of a peaceful transition to freedom is troubled and questioned by Johnson, whose "false dreams" never came true. It's unclear if his/our dreaming was deferred, à la Hughes, or forestalled; survival and death are his options and both appear to carry equal likelihood. Johnson exposes a growing consciousness and recognition that something fundamental was set against the race: "Something is holding me back. Is it because I'm black?" That last question is simple, but reflects a much deeper inquiry into race and its connection to poverty, oppression, identity, and ultimately mortality.

Three decades later and an ocean away, this sorrowful question is made into satire—"is it cos I is black?"—by Cambridge-educated white British comedian Sacha Baron Cohen, through his ignorant, wannabe Black, misogynist character Ali G. Here it becomes a comic catchphrase, "one more surreal jingle for the playground," spoofing racial appropriation fifteen years before Rachel Dolezal was revealed to the world. Here it becomes "a line that bigots use to taunt someone who has complained about racial discrimination."[10] But for Syl Johnson and his kind who know the feel of racial oppression, there is no laughter. It is not a phrase that is carelessly used, only to be equally carelessly tossed aside as an affront to an American ideal that requires pulling oneself up by the bootstraps. Rather, in asking "Will I survive, or will I die?" Johnson begs a fundamental, time-worn question of this US democracy. By the second half of the song, listeners are absorbed in the two-step groove and Johnson's questions give way to assertions that reveal that he's known the answers all along: "You keep holding me back . . . Keep on picking on me." The opposing force to Black advance is

10 "Is It Cos I Is Black?," *The Guardian* (January 12, 2000), available at theguardian.com.

white supremacy, which can only be combatted through recognition and collective acts of Black togetherness: "If you have white-like brown skin and a high yeller, / you're still Black, / so we all got to stick together right now."

HANK BALLARD, "BLACKENIZED" (1969)

Here the playlist shifts from a Du Boisian sorrow song to a movement ballad, demonstrating the didactic power of Black music. The hidden downbeat, heavy bass, and sharp guitar of Hank Ballard's funky "Blackenized" is the sound of Detroit, Washington, DC, and Harlem at the transition from nonviolence to armed militancy in Black movement struggle. It should come as no surprise that the song was written and produced by the "Godfather of Soul," James Brown, in 1969. Brown's work with Ballard in the late '60s helped to revitalize the latter's career and return him to the charts after half a decade of absence. By this point he joined the ranks of musicians such as Nina Simone and Donny Hathaway, who explicitly linked their music to people's movements and understood the stage as an extension of the streets. No longer "Negroes and colored people," this vanguard was pushing the aesthetic and political limits of Blackness by drawing attention to internal dynamics within the Black community, pointing out the existent conditions (Hathaway's "The Ghetto") as well as the indigenous visions yet unfulfilled (Simone's "To Be Young, Gifted and Black").

Ballard's contribution to this unfolding worldview was a verb—Blackenized—which included beliefs, politics, and style. As if directly answering Syl Johnson, Ballard sings that jive fellas "been leaning on others" and argues that recognition and respect for African-descended people will only come from being Blackenized. Not content with pointing fingers elsewhere, Ballard starts at home, demanding that the (Black) listener "find yourself and do your own thing." He's willing to document his own evolution as an example: "Took me a long time to cut my hair. / Reason why? I wasn't aware." While it may seem trivial, hair is socialized, as cultural studies scholar Kobena Mercer argues, making it an important act of identification and contestation. Black hairstyles like the Afro and dreadlocks "are a medium of significant statements about self and society and the codes of value that bind them or do not."[11] Blackenization is concerned with the politics of beauty—politics that need first to be articulated, demonstrated, and preserved for us, by us. Ballard displaces the emphasis on reforming the external world in favor of inciting a mental and physical revolution *within* Blackness. This revolution includes usurping language and fundamentally destabilizing empirical order; "Blackenized ain't in the dictionary but today it's so necessary." These new vocabularies are Soul lessons and internal communiqués, evidence of "the continuing development of a collective consciousness informed by the historical struggles for liberation and motivated

---

11   Ken Gelder and Sarah Thornton, *The Subcultures Reader* (London: Routledge, 1997), 420.

by the shared sense of obligation to preserve the collective being, the ontological totality."[12]

DERRICK HARRIOTT, "MESSAGE FROM A BLACK MAN" (1970)

The relative rapidity of our progress toward "we" through this playlist is intentional. So too is its focus, thus far, on how people who identify with one another work toward unison, even if under tension and across many miles. If the previous songs are messages inside of and accountable to the Black community through their questions, concerns, and methods of identification, then Derrick Harriott's cover of "Message from a Black Man" represents an external communication to an oppressive global whiteness. From his location in Babylon, he outlines what those throughout the Black Atlantic world have articulated for many generations: that color is not a system of value. Like Johnson, Harriott understands how disadvantage has been linked to racial categorization ("Yes, my skin is Black, / but that's no reason to hold me back"), however he insists that wider society "think about it" again and again in order to recognize, as he states definitively, "Black is a color, just like white. Tell me how can a color determine whether wrong or right?"

This challenge to white supremacy was first sung by the Temptations. Recorded in 1969 for their album *Puzzle People*, the original six-minute song is slower paced than the Harriott version, which is a reggae cover indicative of a diasporic transmission of radical thought and camaraderie. Within ten seconds, listeners know that they are hearing the Caribbean. The revision of the production—with stronger rhythm guitar and emphasis on the upbeat—forces us to travel and differently adjust our bodies to what are otherwise familiar conditions and language. In interpolating James Brown's "say it loud" into the lyrics, Black pride is no longer a whisper, nor is it nationally bound. It is a vocal assertion of self-possession and a diasporic rallying call, even as it is mixed with language that reinforces a liberal rights tradition: "I have wants and desires just like you. / So move aside 'cause I am comin' through." Harriott proved that the African-descended stood on higher moral and ethical ground as the stewards of civilization, and forecasted for those who believed otherwise that they would need to "confront [the] political reality of movement"[13]: "No matter how hard you try, you can't stop me now."

MIRIAM MAKEBA, "KWAZULU (IN THE LAND OF THE ZULUS)" (1965)

"KwaZulu (In the Land of the Zulus)" continues to assert Blackness as a coherent worldview, this time in the Zulu language of Miriam Makeba who, in the

---

12   Robinson, *Black Marxism*, 171.
13   Ibid., 291.

South African folk tradition, tells a Xhosa story against the backdrop of contemporary apartheid. By the time of the song's release in 1965 as part of the collaborative, Grammy-award–winning album *An Evening with Belafonte/Makeba*, with entertainer and civil rights activist Harry Belafonte (himself a folk griot of renown), Makeba had long campaigned against her homeland's apartheid system and, as a result, had her passport revoked in 1960 and her citizenship and right to return revoked in 1963.[14] "KwaZulu" operates solidly inside of an African oral tradition in which new meaning is imbued to songs with each performance, translation, and hearing. As Makeba understood, "Folks songs in Africa are a repository of history."[15] It also belongs to an oral tradition of women's songs that have been used as forms of social discourse and protest.[16] In her unique interpretation, Makeba's call and response invites a collective reclamation of space within Black South African history, which is epistemological, social, and proprietary. She sings, "I won't go to KwaZulu. / That's where mom and dad died."[17] Her choice of no return is significant for African diaspora histories: it upends the diaspora fixation with return to a homeland, instead suggesting that there are other ways in which African peoples make a "place" for themselves elsewhere. Especially in the context of the heavily policed apartheid South Africa, in which pass books and curfews ruled state-sanctioned mobility, for Makeba to say that she would not go somewhere is a departure from expectations regarding the dutiful colonial subject. Makeba's exiled position outside of South Africa, but visible position on the international stage and access to the Western recording industry, adds an invitation to the world to pay attention to her choices and to question why she acts as she does.

Makeba's heart is also a terrain of struggle in "KwaZulu." While the male chorus backs *her* voice, she establishes her independence, boldly asserting that she will determine who, if anyone, will share her intimate life. "I won't find a lover among the Zulus," she sings. "No, I'll find one among the Bhacas." The song could be read as a protest against Zulu domination, but, in the context of apartheid South Africa, its tone and usability are adjusted, taking on new power and meaning. The land of the Zulus of 1825 was a dominant force and one of the most powerful kingdoms in southern Africa. The land of the Zulus of 1965 was a *Bantustan*, one of ten Black "independent" South African territories forcibly segregated along ethnic lines, stripped of rights to citizenship, and populated by masses of displaced Black South Africans, many of whom had never resided in their identified "homeland."[18] Established under the apartheid system by then

14   Emmanuel Kwaku Akyeampong and Henry Louis Gates, *Dictionary of African Biography* (Oxford: Oxford University Press, 2012), 54.

15   Miriam Makeba, Jonas Gwangwa, and E. John Miller, *The World of African Song* (Chicago: Quadrangle Books, 1971), 11.

16   Nompumelelo Zondi, "Bahlabelelelani: Why Do They Sing? Gender and Power in Contemporary Women's Songs," PhD diss., University of KwaZulu-Natal (2008).

17   Translation by Zanele Netshapapame.

18   John Western, "A Divided City: Cape Town," *Political Geography* 21, no. 5 (2002): 711–16.

prime minister Hendrik Verwoerd—who was also beautifully exposed by Makeba on *Evening*—the policy of "separate development" was justified as "not a policy of discrimination on the grounds of race or color, but a policy of differentiation on the ground of nationhood, of different nations, granting to each self-determination within the borders of their homelands."[19] "I'll never go to the land of the Zulus," then, is more than a response to intertribal histories; it is a meta-argument in a native tongue for the right to live and love without fear or coercion, sung in an ebullient tone that disguises its sharp analysis and condemnation of the settler state as a strategy of dissemination and protection. It is a song from a woman and world citizen who refuses to be silenced, even in exile.

CIPHER J.E.W.E.L.S, "2000 YEARS" (2002)

"2000 Years" (2002) is a historical genealogy and recovery project that eschews linear temporalities in favor of compelling juxtapositions by Afro-British emcee Cipher J.E.W.E.L.S. The somber jazz horn leads us to the drum machine break and the provocation, "How would you feel if everything around you came from something that you made? From pyramids to projects . . . you the father of all?" Cipher's queries continue in the thematic unearthing and reclamation of historical truths and speak to the "love and theft" of Eric Lott's description, in which Europeans literally play in their fears of Blackness. Cipher details how cultural appropriation by Europeans and their descendents swallows Black culture but spits at Blackness, summing it up with: "The father of all turned into the footstool of the world." Descendancy and kinship claims are prominent within Black theologies and philosophies, including the Five Percent Nation, which began as an offshoot of the Nation of Islam and believes that they (the 5 percent) are the keepers and translators of a supreme, liberatory truth. The Five Percenter ideology espoused in Cipher's lyrics again speaks to the power of the diaspora to carry trace histories of Black radicalism. More than anything, though, and akin to Robinson's scholarship, "2000 Years" revolts, reclaims, and recenters Black history as critical to human civilization. "Without me there would be no you," states Cipher, fundamentally reorienting the "Western" historical compass and refusing liberal incorporative models.

In Cipher's narrative, there is no disconnect between the ancient world and the one that contemporary listeners have inherited. The violence remains, as does the collective consciousness of what Africa and its descendents have brought to the evolution of world culture. Cipher reminds us that Black bodies imagined and built world architecture and that the great gods of Egypt are carried with us in some of hip-hop's most revered emcees, including Ol' Dirty Bastard of the Wu Tang Clan and the legendary Rakim. He reminds us that 2,000 years ago, Jesus

---

19   Bantu Affairs Committee, *Second Report from the Sessional Committee on Bantu Affairs* (1968).

was educated in Kushite philosophy and that "Newton was new when Imhotep was old." The sample of Erykah Badu's voice on loop in the background singing, "On and on and on and on" (from 1997's "On and On") binds these histories of exclusion and excellence that are untethered to historical orthodoxy.

THEESATISFACTION, "ON WHAT IT MEANS TO BE BLACK" (2010)

Stasia "Stas" Irons and Catherine "Cat" Harris-White fuse avant-garde stream of consciousness hip-hop and neo-soul to form a futuristic soundscape that affirms Blackness as intoxicating and transcendent, embodying "earth, winds, and fires," as well as "Afro-Sheen and cornrow, dread I, tambourines and handclaps and cries." Soaring heights—"I'm so high on what it means to be Black"—and later descent toward the "golden path" is the choreography of THEESatisfaction's "On What It Means to Be Black," which briefly models the myth-power that underwrites Black radical histories. It is through culture that the significance of the mystical in Black communities is best understood. In his canonical study of slave culture, historian Lawrence Levine investigates spirituals and other folk-tales of the eighteenth and nineteenth centuries. In them one hears the histories and hopes of the enslaved but, according to Levine, they remain of a certain variety and style. "Frequently told stories" of flying Africans had a didactic qual-ity in excess of pure fantasy; in some tales, the Africans "delayed their escape until they could teach their American-born relatives and friends the power of flight as well."[20] This lesson suggests that the difference between African-born and American-born African-descended people was not a respected truth or condition of division, as all shared in the strategies of fugitivity that made for fantastic tales and even more fantastic realities.

Variations of flying and flight, higher and height—"I am flier than fly can fly. / My flag is higher than high"—mark THEESatisfaction's elevation and perspective, which is a project of constant consciousness-raising that Robinson argues was of central significance to Richard Wright. Alternative sight lines made possible other ways of living and understanding Blackness. In "Carrying the Run-Aways"—a story in the appropriately titled collection of Black folktales *The People Could Fly*—the narrator describes his panicked late-night trips across the river to Ripley, where he would deliver enslaved people to their freedom. The fateful initial trip exposed how penetrating the psychological hold of captiv-ity could be: "Now, I had heard about the other side of the river from the other slaves. But I thought it was just like the side where we lived on the plantation. I thought there were slaves and masters over there, too, and overseers and rawhide whips they used on us. That's why I was so scared."[21] The peculiar institution

---

20   Lawrence W. Levine, *Black Culture and Black Consciousness* (New York: Oxford University Press, 1977), 87.

21   Virginia Hamilton, Leo Dillon, and Diane Dillon, *The People Could Fly* (New York: Knopf, 1985), 142.

worked to stunt the imaginations of the enslaved, to "keep the body [but] take the mind,"[22] to ensure that any flight, however physically possible, would always be compromised and prone to being second-guessed by the fugitive property. THEESatisfaction, however, rises above the plantation and works against any circumstantial evidence that "*Blacks became slaves*" at all, ever,[23] announcing through their wordplay and from their height above our daily terrain ("I heard that I could out-higher a bird, a bee, a fly/ I am highered 'cause I'm so high") that another vantage point was always in view and operable for the task of freedom.

OCNOTES, "RADIO NAT TURNER" (2014)

Now that we've reached an appropriate altitude, let's check our devices. Is the radio tuned? Is the clock right? The electro-funk of OCnotes returns us to the nineteenth century and to the rebellion—"Blacker than your midnight"—that so frightened white Southerners that Black captives in neighboring states were executed under suspicion of collusion. Nat Turner, who was described by members of his community as a prophet, led his 1831 uprising after seeing visions and signs in the skies, forests, and crops. This icon of slavery historiography is reimagined by conceptual musician OCnotes as a vibration that organizes our relationship to techno-history over the airwaves. "Radio Nat Turner" thinks of rural Virginia but sounds like Chicago. The deep house composition lands heavy in the middle ear and infuses the song with other rebellious elements from the original queer, urban undergrounds that gave birth to the form. As a part of Black Weirdo—a cultural and musical movement created by THEESatisfaction—Otis Calvin III (aka OCnotes) says of his work, "I get to stir people's souls up with my tunes and get people free for a minute." Calvin's "free" is reflected in the lore of the song's namesake, whose rebellion against slavery— though lasting only a few days—involved dozens of captives and was one of the few instances of mass violence under enslavement. Turner's knowledge of signs and mystical systems allowed him to join those who "lived on their terms, they died on their terms, they obtained freedom on their terms. These were the terms that these African peasants and farmers had brought with them to their captivity. They were also the only terms in which their freedom could be acquired."[24]

"Owning your identity and representing your own truth"[25] is the motivation for OCnotes's rejection of society's ambition and rules of respectability. He is aware of the structures that circumscribe his energies and dreams—he simply refuses to be defined by them or to accord to those at the top of the pyramid the power that they request: "I don't need your pity. / I don't want your life. / I see

22 *The Great Debaters* [film], dir. Denzel Washington (USA: Weinstein Company, 2007).

23 Robinson, *Black Marxism*, 124. Emphasis in original.

24 Robinson, *Black Marxism*, 170.

25 Alexa Teodoro, "OCnotes on Why Black Weirdo Matters," *Seattle Weekly* (February 17, 2015), available at seattleweekly.com.

you got privilege. / I'm doin' alright." He follows in a long tradition of disruption to and critical denial of a "Western" culturo-intellectual project: "Radio Nat Turner" mobilizes music as a historical register that rejects outside definition and continues the long movement away from expressing humanity in terms of a consolidated whiteness. The character of a musical Nat Turner is steeped in vision, sacrifice, and rebellion, and it is in this space of possibility that the radio and developing technologies provide an increasingly digital diaspora with a laboratory for cultural experimentation. OCnotes exhibits an Afrofuturism grounded by musical composition that, according to an online profiler, "places us closer to our ancestors and our future selves."[26] Eventually the vocal fades into the beat and nothing else is heard but unintelligible chanting as the notes of a discordant synthesizer play, widening our listening horizons and leading us back to the heavy bass pulse, back to rhythm.

KENDRICK LAMAR, "ALRIGHT" (2015)

The indefatigable nature of Blackness—as identity and project—touches down and finds fertile ground in Compton, California, where we hear the play-by-play of the city streets hot with energy and exchange. With his doo-wop and jazz horns to guide him, the oracle of hip-hop Kendrick Lamar opens his anthem "Alright" by extending the sounds of Sofia from *The Color Purple*, saying: "Alls my life I has to fight, nigga." Like OCnotes, Lamar is cool—"alright," as they both state—demonstrating not acquiescence but resolve even as his conditions have led him to "the preacher's door." This search for both answers and peace has encouraged African-descended peoples to travel abroad and the same is true for Lamar. His approach to "Alright" was deeply influenced by a trip to South Africa, during which he witnessed conditions that put his own in perspective. This is not to say that he was willing to sacrifice his reality for those abroad. The arresting optics of "Alright," shot in both Los Angeles and Oakland, are gritty in their depiction of Black life in 2015 and pay particularly rapt attention to the overwhelming police presence in Black communities. Within one minute of the six minutes and fifty-four seconds of the production, we see the public surveillance arm of the state—the police—as a backdrop to the unfolding events. It is the sound of a discharged police-issued gun that officially launches the song's prelude, which samples an alternative production and shows Lamar in a car with three other young Black men, rhyming to a head-nodding beat. After six bars the camera pulls back to reveal that the car has no wheels and is being carried and moved forward by four police officers, one at each wheel well. They carry him as obedient servants would carry a king, stepping heavy with each burdened advance, eyes straight ahead. From there the squealing tires of a

---

26 "Black Weirdo of the Week 3: OCnotes," *Black Weirdo* (February 25, 2014), available at uniquenoir.tumblr.com.

donut-spinning muscle car introduce us to the anticipated track and the fact that Lamar too can fly.

The video's representation of police violence—including Lamar's shooting at the very end—concretizes the "real" in the mystical realism of "Alright" and ensures that his insistence ("we gon' be alright") is measured not against pure fantasy but in a complex field of power relations. The assurance that we'll be "alright" is based not on a faith in things unseen, nor in the mediated democracy that Fred Moten reminds us is fraught (for "every element that intervenes between the commons and authority carries with it a danger for the democracy to come; every idea and procedure that limits or circumscribes common participation is, similarly, a danger"[27]) but rather in a collective sensibility and knowledge of the world as it currently exists: "When you know we been hurt been down before, nigga. / When our pride was low, lookin' at the world like 'Where do we go?,' nigga. / And we hate po-po, when they kill us dead in the streets fa sho, nigga. / I'm at the preacher's door, my knees gettin' weak and my gun might blow but we gon' be alright." Lamar's song is described by critics as "an ebulliently simple five-syllable refrain [that has] soundtracked a movement . . . [a] holistic sentiment as a siren against innumerable injustices."[28] His documentation is active and archival; contrary to the opinions of critics, a song that references Alice Walker in its first lines is not about forgetting reality. A song that has come to resonate with a broad Black Lives Matter coalition and is used as a modern anthem against police brutality and systematic oppression is not about forgetting reality.[29] The hope that Lamar conveys in this song is not a means of overlooking; rather it is a verb—an action—requiring that one recognize injustice and wilfully declare it inferior. His speech to his listeners—"Do you hear me? / Do you feel me? / We gon' be alright"—is the call-and-response tradition that prophetically but insistently affirms the futures ahead.

DEATH, "POLITICIANS IN MY EYES" (1976)

The dangerous democracy that Moten describes and Lamar shows is given a spectacular hearing in "Politicians in My Eyes" by the metal band Death. Emerging from Detroit, the music and the band's name would prove to be prophetic. Indeed, "Scrappy, snarly, epic in scope, and burnt with intensity, Death sounded like nothing else on the planet in 1973 and '74," a moment that predated the punk icons the Ramones and the Clash.[30] In the 1960s and '70s their

27 Quoted in Bruce Burgett and Glenn Hendler, *Keywords for American Cultural Studies* (New York: New York University Press, 2007), 73.

28 Matthew Schnipper, "Staff Lists: The 100 Best Tracks of 2015," *Pitchfork* (December 14, 2015), available at pitchfork.com.

29 "Activists Chant Kendrick Lamar's 'Alright' in Protest at Police Harassment," FACT (July 9, 2015), available at factmag.com.

30 Chris Barsanti, "Don't Call Them Proto-Punk: A Band Called Death," *Popmatters* (July 3, 2013), available at popmatters.com.

birthplace was a thriving metropolis, a top-ten largest city, and known as "The Arsenal of Democracy," but its rapid infrastructural atrophy in the decades to follow is legendary.[31] The song "Politicians in My Eyes" is a fitting and necessary indictment of political mismanagement and corruption, whether set against the backdrop of the mid-70s or the modern 2000s.[32] The music fluctuates between frenetic anger and anguished imploring, and is both accusatory and questioning. It lays the blame for the unfulfilled promises of the state squarely on the shoulders of power's representatives, who are happy to reach out and shake hands, "wearing false smiles," all while stepping on the people. "They could care less about you, they could care less about me," the band sings, "as long as they are to end the place that they want to be." The song ends with an extended instrumental section that is equal parts funereal and fierce, perfectly meshing rock and blues, to accent the final lyric: "Politicians tell me why can't you hear the people cry?"

The Hackney brothers—David, Bobby, and Dannis—are now considered visionaries, but in 1975, when the three self-taught musicians recorded a seven-song session at United Sound Studios for Columbia Records president Clive Davis, they were asked to change precisely that which made them unprecedented. Though originally called Rock Fire Funk Express and known for playing traditional rhythm and blues, guitarist David—moved by the musical influences of Alice Cooper and the Who, as well as by the spirit of their preacher father's Baptist teachings—persuaded his brothers to change the band's musical direction to rock. The DIY band who used to play gigs in their garage and disturb their neighbors with their "white boy music" also took on the provocative moniker Death—a term that David hoped to spin "from the negative to the positive."[33] Failing to understand—unlike so many Afro-diasporic cultures—that death is not final, Davis deemed the name commercially unviable and when David refused to compromise his vision, Davis withdrew his support. As a result, the music of this pioneering band went unreleased for over three decades. Like so much of Black music, however, it would gain another life as inspiration for new musicians and new sounds.

DENNIS BROWN, "REVOLUTION" (1983)

Though no stranger to socially conscious music (1977's cover of Earl 16's "Malcolm X" being a notable example), Dennis Brown—dubbed by Bob Marley

31   By 2010, Detroit's population was less than half what it had been fifty years prior (*Detroit's Financial Crisis* [Detroit: State of Michigan, 2013], available at michigan.gov/documents/detroit-cantwait/DetroitFactSheet_412909_7.pdf).

32   Plagued by the decline of the automobile industry, urban decay, unemployment, and poverty, Detroit became the largest American city to file for Chapter 9 bankruptcy protection in 2013 and has come to be known as a "ghost town" ("Detroit: Now A Ghost Town," *Time* [2009], available at content.time.com).

33   Stephen Thompson, "Death: A '70s Rock Trailblazer, Reborn," NPR (March 17, 2010), available at npr.org.

as the "Crown Prince of Reggae"—is noted more for his contributions to the Lovers Rock genre of reggae and his Rastafari-influenced content than for politically charged messages. But his 1983 hit "Revolution" finds him at his most radical, asking his audience, "Are you ready to stand up and fight the right revolution?" It is a battle cry, summed up by the absence of a chorus, instead replaced by a continued wailing chant, as if summoning ancestral strength to embolden a revolutionary spirit to fight "against downpression."[34] Without the mooring of a chorus to return to, we can only move forward, creating new sounds and strategies in our quest to "live forever." War metaphors continue in both the lyrics and the music. Brown asks, "Are you ready to stand up and fight it just like soldiers?" while the bass of Robert "Robbie" Shakespeare—one half of legendary Jamaican production team Sly and Robbie—keeps time like a march to battle in which "many are called [but] few are chosen."

Rasta traditions ground Brown's politics. De Albuquerque[35] and Chevannes[36] both argue for Rastafari as a revolutionary, millenarian movement, rooted in the fundamental belief that a major transformation of society is necessary and imminent. As Walter Rodney would state, "The only great men among the unfree and the oppressed are those who struggle to destroy the oppressor."[37] "Revolution" marks Brown's contribution to that struggle. His marching orders are simple: fight (for the right), live (forever), love (each other). Here love is revolutionary and Brown shares in that belief with comrades all over the world—surrealists and utopianists alike. Indeed, Robin Kelley argues that "freedom and love may be the most revolutionary ideas available to us"[38] and the placement of love at the end of Brown's cue suggests that it may be the pinnacle of liberation action. This emphasis is not a surprise given Brown's prominence within Lovers Rock; that the form is heard in a song organized around the idea and practice of revolution, which is so often attached to violence and bloodshed, however, offers a significant revision to the masculinist historiographies of war and empire in Western societies. The history of marronage in Jamaica—with a cast of characters inclusive of the Obeah mystics who later influenced the Rastafarians—plays a crucial role in New World resistance. It is that radical practice of intimacy and sacrifice for the good of the whole that allows for the dream and possibility of revolution.

---

34 In a further example of language transformation, "downpression" is the Rastafarian term for "oppression," which is used because oppression holds you down, rather than lifts you up, where "up" and "opp" are homophonic prefixes.

35 Klaus De Albuquerque, *Millenarian Movements and the Politics of Liberation* (Ann Arbor: University Microfilms International, 1977).

36 Barry Chevannes, "Rastafari: Towards a New Approach," *New West Indian Guide / Nieuwe West-Indische Gids* 64, nos. 3–4 (1990): 127–48.

37 Walter Rodney, A. M. Babu, and Vincent Harding, *How Europe Underdeveloped Africa* (Washington, DC: Howard University Press, 1981 [1972]), 131.

38 Kelley, *Freedom Dreams*, 11.

JANELLE MONÁE AND WONDALAND, "HELL YOU TALMBOUT" (2015)

There are few sounds as distinctive as a drum line. Though often associated with the military, the form is best represented in the United States by historically black colleges and universities whose formations are fantastically displayed at sporting events and rallies. The snaps of the snare and boom of the bass represent the US South, home of Civil War and civil rights battles. These histories are inside of "Hell You Talmbout," a standout political track by the Wondaland Records collective and its resident android-leader, Janelle Monáe. In its original form, "Hell You Talmbout" was a bonus track on the deluxe edition of *The Electric Lady* album released in 2013. On it Monáe sings about the everyday struggles of living in the inner city. Two years later the song was reborn as a protest anthem, with Monáe and members of the Wondaland collective each crying out the name of a Black person felled by the many manifestations of institutional racism and imploring the audience to say their names. Fusing the "heavy, intense martial drums" of the marching band tradition with the call-and-response motif adopted by the gospel tradition of the Black church, the composition is as simple as it is devastatingly powerful, making it tailor-made for organized movement.[39]

Though she previously claimed to "not [be] into politics actually," Monáe has since maintained that the job of an artist "is to be the voice, your job is to bring awareness, your job is to be a rebel, your job is to start a revolution."[40] "Hell You Talmbout" has started to do that work in the streets, from marches to demonstrations at presidential campaign fundraisers. It is a grounded, material intervention from an artist otherwise known for her Afrofuturist psychedelia. Steeped in history and violence, the song is also affirming of life and humanity, even in death, by allowing the names of the deceased to be spoken and remembered. The inventory of lives lost takes form in a roll call that connects seemingly disparate acts of anti-Black violence; through that, it conjoins the long histories of racism that continue to make African-descended peoples more vulnerable than others to disadvantage and death. According to Monáe:

> This song is a vessel. It carries the unbearable anguish of millions. We recorded it to channel the pain, fear, and trauma caused by the ongoing slaughter of our brothers and sisters. We recorded it to challenge the indifference, disregard, and negligence of all who remain quiet about this issue. Silence is our enemy. Sound is our weapon.

---

39   Aisha Harris, "Janelle Monáe Brings a Powerful New Protest Song to the Black Lives Matter Movement," *Slate* (August 14, 2015), available at slate.com.

40   "Rnb Sensation Janelle Monáe Is Here Because We Need Her," *Evening Standard* (July 4, 2011), available at standard.co.uk.

They say a question lives forever until it gets the answer it deserves . . . Won't you say their names?[41]

Weaponized thus, Monáe and others raise the names of Walter Scott, Eric Garner, Trayvon Martin, Sean Bell, Freddie Gray, Aiyana Jones, Sandra Bland, Kimani Gray, John Crawford, Michael Brown, Miriam Carey, Emmett Till, Amadou Diallo, and others as a way to honor them and the collectives online and off who, through social media and in-person protests, bring attention to the scale of violence facing Black women and men. Wondaland's contribution, however, is an intervention in that it takes the written word and transforms it into something altogether different, turning communication into communion by again displaying Black music as a unique, nonliterate (though not uneducated), and mobile platform with powers well beyond 140 characters.

RAY ANGRY FT. NADIA WASHINGTON & CHRIS POTTER, "CELEBRATION OF LIFE SUITE: AWARENESS & REVOLUTION" (2015)

The soundscape of this incomplete listening party suggests the arc of movement cultures, from quiet and inquisitive to raucous and spectacular, back to introspection and those moments in which we allow ourselves to be vulnerable, to feel, to re-center our energies and ambitions. Though it reorients the anger behind "Hell You Talmbout," "Celebration of Life: Awareness & Revolution" is no less passionate in its articulations of subjecthood and purpose. "It's basically about the evolution of life," composer and pianist Ray Angry explains. In "Awareness & Revolution"—the first movement of the two-part suite—Angry's solo piano builds to incorporate the sounds of Nadia Washington's soulful vocal line, which vacillates between the piano keys and Chris Potter's saxophone, calling the listener to recognize "the light from deep within" those most marginalized and violated. We raise our glasses to them, to us; "Here is to life," she sings in defiant celebration. Then an escalation toward the explosion of Potter's sax solo springs and leaps to center stage in a joyous choreography of Black experience. Potter then retreats, leaving Angry and Washington who return the piece to a sense of serenity, as if beginning again—charting the seasons of revolution and regeneration, blossoming anew like Tupac Shakur's rose that grew from a crack in the concrete, learning to breathe fresh air.

A moment of celebration, not just for good times but also for those that aren't. To hold and cherish what we know and feel at the moment in which we know and feel it is also on our spectrum of freedom.

---

41 Janelle Monáe, "Hell You Talmbout" [image] (2015), available at instagram.com/p/6VNc3hn_m1.

Here is to life in the wake of nine murders in a Charleston, South Carolina, church. Here is to life for each unarmed citizen brave enough to risk life to look riot police in the eye. Here is to life for little children, all of whom deserve the chance to see life's milestones, tell their stories, and touch the world without having their promise interrupted by a bullet—intentional or errant. Here is to life, as each musician sees fit to breathe it back into the populace. Here is to every revolution—in the streets and on wax, thick with the brutal honesty and abiding love necessary to break down walls, reveal the light and heal the world from within.[42]

Add this to the dictionary of Black liberation: celebration, a strategy of remembrance and joy that holds within it the opportunity to be in the moment and to know, without fear, that one is there.

D'ANGELO AND THE VANGUARD, "THE CHARADE" (2014)

The critical need for enjoyment is reinforced in the turn to D'Angelo, whose return to the stage in 2015 included new musicians (known as the Vanguard) and a powerful single, "The Charade." Channeling Prince and Sly Stone, the production—replete with walking bass line, simultaneous backup harmonies, and sonic interplay between the boom of the drum and punctuated clapping— quickly ushers listeners into a fast-paced accounting of contemporary Black life. Performed in the wake of an eruption of political demonstrations and organizing in Ferguson, Missouri, "The Charade" recounts the dispossession of post–civil rights generations and challenges the approaches used to respond to it. The dynamics of (Black) petition and (white) response are shown by D'Angelo as a failed equation of advance: "All we wanted was a chance to talk. / 'Stead we only got outlined in chalk." Despite the "many miles we've walked," there remains a fundamental distance between the dream and its realization. D'Angelo hints at histories of uplift and the iconography of Booker T. Washington when he mentions the veil that has been lifted from our eyes. It is with this sightedness that the truth of the nation's charade is revealed ("at the end of the day").

Sounding like a funk-driven dirge, D'Angelo's often obscured vocals, along with his play on guitar and piano, ?uestlove on drums, and Pino Palladino on bass create a harmonious collage of noise that in its complexity adds a rich texture to Black experience. Fifteen years prior, on "Devil's Pie," D'Angelo would sing, "Ain't no justice / It's just us / Ashes to ashes / Dust to dust," lamenting the economic injustice that feeds impoverished materialism. Fifteen years later, social inequities conjured "The Charade" for the world, having hinted at existence in Internet leaks and sporadic live performances. Fifteen years later, 400

---

42   Karas Lamb, "Ray Angry Stirs Revolution with 'Celebration of Life Suite,'" *Revive Music* (August 24, 2015), available at revive-music.com.

years later, there's still no justice, it's still just us, and dust to dust is ritually enforced upon Black bodies by policing and vigilantism, the prison industrial complex, health disparities, and poisoned Flint, Michigan, water. With these lingering oppressions still in view, we might consider the past tense of the repeated ending of "The Charade" ("All we *wanted* was a chance to talk") as a provocation to leave that tactic there—in the past—and imagine something new.

THUNDERCAT FT. MONO/POLY, "PARIS" (2015)

Imaginaries are a fitting place to pause—not end—our excursions of the ear and mind. The progeny of bassist and composer Thundercat and collaborating producer Mono/Poly, "Paris" is an experimental expatriation. Like Langston Hughes, Richard Wright, Josephine Baker, and James Baldwin before him, Thundercat traveled across the Atlantic in search of . . . a sound? Sentience? Both are embedded in "Paris," which speaks to the listener even in the absence of words. Experimental and computer-generated musical forms "represent the particular ideas of their creators," according to scholar-musician George Lewis.[43] As he argues, "'Sound' becomes identifiable, not with timbre alone, but with the expression of personality, the assertion of agency, the assumption of responsibility and an encounter with history, memory and identity."[44] The identifiable quality of Black music-making, then, is about literacy not in language or composition, but in its aesthetic and affective qualities, as well as its use. These are the metrics of discernable value that exist outside of the marketplace and the formalism of Western knowledge, and this is where Black music makes its greatest interventions and becomes a tool for liberation.

Thundercat's work as a solo artist as well as a collaborator with Terrace Martin, Kendrick Lamar, Flying Lotus, and others produces a compelling matrix of feeling. Composed as a response to the November 2015 attacks in the City of Light, "Paris" is an offering and a moment of recognition from a uniquely Black musical perspective. It is a digital vigil and a memorial not only to current tragedy, but to the former glories of lived freedom. As expat Baldwin believed, "African-Americans discover in Paris the terms by which they can define themselves. It's the freedom to work beyond the assumptions of what we can and can't do as African-Americans. It's a different rhythm and pace. We can imagine ourselves in new ways in that space."[45] Thundercat imagines and composes Blackness differently and uses music as the method of its exploration and exposition. To Baldwin's freedom, "Paris" offers a prayer bell and an ethereal murmur

---

43 George Lewis, "Too Many Notes: Computers, Complexity and Cultures in *Voyager*," *Leonardo Music Journal* 10 (2000): 33–9.

44 Ibid., 33, 37.

45 Maureen Jenkins, "African-Americans in Paris: 'It's Always Been About Freedom for Us,'" CNN (February 26, 2013), available at edition.cnn.com.

that "rises up and mellows almost instantly as a lyrical bass melody says its piece and fades away."[46] Yet even in silence it is not gone. It remains as a faint vibration that we carry into the next encounter, the next challenge, the next dream. All these notes we keep and consolidate as evidence of our knowing and as a resource in the composition of our next magnificent song.

---

46   Philip Sherburne, "Thundercat: 'Paris,'" *Pitchfork* (November 18, 2015), available at pitch-fork.com.

Chapter 14

Abolition Geography and the Problem of Innocence

Ruth Wilson Gilmore[1]

We were trying to find language to make sense of a time before whatever came after.
—China Miéville, *Embassytown* [2]

1. MONEY

Loot. Pay. Wage. Profit. Interest. Tax. Rent. Accumulation. Extraction. Colonialism. Imperialism.

The modern prison is a central but by no means singularly defining institution of carceral geographies in the United States and beyond, geographies that signify regional accumulation strategies and upheavals, immensities and fragmentations, that reconstitute in space-time (even if geometrically the coordinates are unchanged) to run another round of accumulation.

Prison rose in tandem with a world-historical transition in the role of money in everyday life. In retrospect, the transformation looks just like a flip. From having been, as for most people it continues to be, a *means* to move stored energy between sellers and buyers of desired objects, money became the desirable *end*, not for hoarders' and misers' erotic caresses, but to touch differently and not for too long—to enliven through pressing into imperative motion irregular but perpetual cycles of transformation to make money more. Capitalism: never not racial, including in rural England, or anywhere in Europe for that matter, where, as Cedric Robinson teaches us, hierarchies among people whose descendants might all have become white depended for their structure on group-differentiated vulnerability to premature death, exploited by elites, as part of all equally exploitable nature-as-other, to justify inequality at the end of the day, and next morning as well.

Racial capitalism: a mode of production developed in agriculture, improved by enclosure in the Old World, and captive land and labor in the Americas,

---

1 Versions of this lecture were delivered at the twenty-ninth annual Sojourner Truth Lecture for the Department of Africana Studies of the Claremont Colleges (September 2014); Confronting Racial Capitalism: A Conference in Honor of Cedric Robinson at the CUNY Graduate Center (November 2014); the Antipode Institute for Geographies of Justice, Women's Gaol, Johannesburg (July 2015); the American Studies Association (October 2015); and the biannual conference of the Center for American Studies and Research at the American University of Beirut (January 2016). The author is grateful to the editors of this volume and to many interlocutors for encouraging criticism.

2 China Miéville, *Embassytown* (New York: Del Rey, 2011), 191.

perfected in slavery's time-motion field-factory choreography, its imperative forged on the anvils of imperial war-making monarchs, and the peers who had to ante up taxes—in cash not kind—so the sovereign might arm increasingly centralized and regularized militaries who became less able to pay themselves, as they had in the past, by looting at each battle's end. Not that they stopped looting later or now.

Nor did the pay packet come all at once: in the United States many nineteenth-century citizen-soldiers went to their graves still waiting to be paid for having killed or agreed to kill Native Americans or French or their proxies. The compensation took the form of something that could be transformed into something else: either title to looted land—an honor for the vast "herrenvolk peerage" of enfranchised white men—land, a good that can't be moved though a deed can be pocketed or sold or borrowed against or seized for a lien—in other words turned into money; and if not a title a pension, an entitlement paid out regularly as money to ease one's golden years.

Indeed, modern prisons were born alongside, and grew up with, the United States of America. Penitentiaries established state-making at the margin of the early republic, whose every founding document recapitulated free as against other, imported as against immigrated, to clarify that sweeping ideals of defense and general welfare, long before the Thirteenth Amendment, had no universal remit but rather defined in the earliest pages who was in and who out.

Then, as now, competing concepts of freedom shaped planetary movement of people and relationships. Like lives, early sentences were short, absorbing one by one people who wouldn't toe their assigned or presumed line, play their part, hit their mark, in racial capitalism's dramatically scaled cycles of place-making—including all of chattel slavery, imperialism, settler colonialism, resource extraction, infrastructural coordination, urban industrialization, regional development, and the financialization of everything.

Racial capitalism's extensive and intensive animating force, its contradictory consciousness, its means to turn objects and desires into money is people in the prime of life or younger, people who make, move, grow, and care for things and other people.

Who then was or is out of place? Unfree people who sold things they made or grew on the side, hiding the money in an emancipation pot. People who couldn't say where they work, or prove that they are free, or show a ticket or a pass, a document to save their skin, or save themselves from the narrative that their skin, stretched in particular ways across muscles and bones, seemed or seems to suggest something about where they shouldn't be—caught.

Racial capitalism's imperative requires all kinds of scheming, including hard work by elites and their compradors in the overlapping and interlocking space-economies of the planet's surface. They build and dismantle and refigure states, moving capacity into and out of the public realm. And they think very hard about money on the move. In the contemporary world, when product and profit cycles turn faster and faster, with racial capitalism ever less patient with any friction on money-flow, sticking resources in prisons whence they might not emerge on time and of the quality required isn't all that attractive, even though the cages are full of millions of people in the prime of life.

We used to think that in the United States, contemporary mass un-freedom, racially organized, must be a recapitulation of slavery's money-making scheme. But if these massive carceral institutions, weighted like cities, are not factories and service centers, then where's the profit, the surplus money at the end of the day? Today's prisons are extractive. What does that mean? It means prisons enable money to move because of the enforced *inactivity* of people locked in them. It means people extracted from communities, and people returned to communities but not entitled to be of them, enable the circulation of money on rapid cycles. What's extracted from the extracted is *the* resource of life—time.

If we think about this dynamic through the politics of scale, understanding bodies as places, then criminalization transforms individuals into tiny territories primed for extractive activity to unfold—extracting and extracting again *time* from the territories of selves. This process opens a hole in a life, furthering, perhaps to our surprise, the annihilation of space by time. A stolen and corrupted social wage flies through that time-hole to prison employees' paychecks. To vendors. To utility companies. To contractors. To debt service. The cash takes many final forms: wages, interest, rent, and sometimes profit. But more to the point, the extractive process brings the mechanics of contemporary imperialism to mind: extraction, in money form, from direct producers whose communities are destabilized too. But money, too, gives us some insight into the enormity of the possible inhabitants and makers of abolition geographies—abolition geography, the antagonistic contradiction of carceral geographies, forms an interlocking pattern across the terrain of racial capitalism. We see it.

2. ABOLITION GEOGRAPHY

Abolition geography starts from the homely premise that freedom is a place. Place-making is normal human activity: we figure out how to combine people, and land, and other resources with our social capacity to organize ourselves in a variety of ways, whether to stay put or to go wandering. Each of these factors—people, land, other resources, social capacity—comes in a number of types, all of which determine but do not define what can or should be done. Working outward and downward from this basic premise, abolitionist *critique* concerns itself with the greatest and least detail of these arrangements of people and resources and land over time. It shows how relationships of un-freedom consolidate and stretch, but not for the purpose of documenting misery. Rather, the point is not only to identify central contradictions—inherent vices—in regimes of dispossession, but also, urgently, to show how radical consciousness in action resolves into liberated life-ways, however provisional, present and past. Indeed, the radical tradition from which abolition geography draws meaning and method goes back in time-space not in order to abolish history, but rather to find alternatives to the despairing sense that so much change, in retrospect, seems only ever to have been displacement and redistribution of human sacrifice. If unfinished liberation is the still-to-be-achieved work of abolition, then at bottom what is to be abolished isn't the past or its present ghost, but rather the processes of hierarchy, dispossession, and exclusion that congeal in and as group-differentiated vulnerability to premature death.

Everyone was surprised in May 2011 when the notoriously pro-*states'-rights* Supreme Court of the United States (SCOTUS) upheld a lower court order that the California Department of Corrections and Rehabilitation reduce the number of people held in then-current stock of adult prisons and camps. SCOTUS affirmed a lower court's opinion that the Golden State could not "build its way out" of constitutional violations so severe they could be measured in premature, which is to say preventable, death: averaging one per week, every week, for decades, due to well-documented medical neglect.

The decision, although a victory, did not mark a clear turn away from nearly forty years of life-shortening mass criminalization, even though five judges recognized the accumulated catastrophe of premature death happening to the people whom most Americans of all races, genders, and ages have learned to abhor and ignore. And yet, in the context of the global war on terror coupled with domestic wars on vulnerable people, we know that challenges to murderous outrage (torture, drone strikes, police killings, poisoned water) readily dissolve into frenzied analytical activity that produces fresh justification, cancelling out prohibitions by the combined force of applied violence, revised legal reasoning, and lengthy commission reports. In the wake of scandal and demand for prison reform, the ruthless principles and procedures of criminalization remain intact, noisily tweaked at the margin but ever hardening at the center where most people in prison languish: average sentences, average conditions, average cages, average charges, average misery. In other words, against the scandal of documented deliberate neglect, criminalization remains a complicated means and process to achieve a simple thing: to enclose people in situations where they are expected, and in many ways compelled, to sicken and so die.

The processes contributing to both the development and epochal ordinariness of mass criminalization have been the focus of research, action, advocacy, and other forms of study trying to make sense of experience. A general but not exhaustive summary goes like this: In the United States, the multi-decade crisis-riven political economy threw off surpluses that became prison expansion's basic factors: land, people, money-capital, and state capacity. The elements of "the prison fix" neither automatically nor necessarily combined into extensive carceral geographies. Rather, an enormously complicated people-, income-, and asset-rich political economy made a relatively sudden turn and repurposed acres, redirected the social wage, used public debt, and serially removed thousands and thousands and thousands and thousands and thousands and thousands and thousands and thousands of modestly educated people from households and communities.

As we can see, something changed. Therefore, instead of imagining the persistent reiteration of static relations, it might be more powerful to analyze relationship dynamics that extend beyond obvious conceptual or spatial boundaries, and then decide what a particular form, old or new, is made of, by trying to make it into something else. This—making something into something else—is what negation is. To do so is to wonder about a form's present, future-shaping design—something we can discern from the evidence of its constitutive patterns, without being beguiled or distracted by social ancestors we perceive, reasonably or emotionally, in the form's features. (I'll come back to ancestors in a few pages.) To think this way is to think deductively (there are forms) and inductively (interlocking patterns reveal generalities which might or might not be structural). I suppose I became a geographer because this kind of back and forth is what we do, trying to see and explain the formalities and improvisations of place-making, which are shaped by human/environmental relationships of dependency—the coupling or connection of power with difference—and sometimes but not inevitably interrupted by preventable fatalities. Deliberately propagated fatalities, and the forms and patterns that coalesce into premature death, reveal human sacrifice as an organizing principle, or perhaps more precisely as an unprincipled form of organizing, which returns us to racial capitalism and the role of criminalization in it.

The prolific advocacy-shaping efforts to foster anti-prison awareness and action partially reveals, campaign by campaign, bits of mass incarceration's breath-taking structure. The selection and arrangement of categories inspiring sustained action ironically tends to legitimize the system as such by focusing on how it's specifically harmful to youth, women, parents, mothers, men, gender nonconforming people, the aged or infirm, or how it's the outcome of the war on drugs, stop and frisk, racism, privatization, and so forth. And yet, the extraction of time from each territory-body specifically and viscerally changes lives elsewhere—partners, children, communities, movements, the possibility of freedom. At the same time, the particular also implies entire historical geographies in constant churn. For some examples think: gentrification. Auto or steel manufacturing. Coal mining. Gold mining. Conflict minerals. Fracking. New shipping technologies. Robotics. Commodity chains. Finance capital. The challenge is to keep the entirety of carceral geographies—rather than only their prison or even law-enforcement aspects—connected, without collapsing or reducing various aspects into each other. Any category or system has many dimensions, necessitating analytical stretch in order to perceive the material world in a variety of overlapping and interlocking totalities. This basic imperative requires more in the way of self-critical consciousness than additional data (we already have too much): although what's real matters absolutely, the experience of it will never automatically reveal how and why negation (the thorough reworking of materiality and consciousness) sometimes succeeds.

Worldwide today, wherever inequality is deepest, the use of prison as a catchall solution to social problems prevails—nowhere as extensively as in the United States, led by California. Ideologically, which is to say in thought *and* everyday culture, the expression and normalization of the twin processes of centralization and devolution—patterned as they are by the sensibility of permanent crisis—shape structures of feeling and therefore, to a great extent, socially determine the apparent range of available oppositional options. In other words, the doctrine of devolution results in a constantly fragmenting array of centers of struggle and objects of antagonism for people who seek equal protection, to say nothing of opportunity. In crisis, in resistance, in opposition: To whom, at whom, against whom does one carry one's petition or raise one's fist?

Devolution is partition, sometimes provisional, sometimes more secure. Its normalizing capacities are profound, patterning political imagination and thus contouring attacks on the carceral form. As a result, many such attacks exhibit trends which, not surprisingly, coalesce tightly around specific categories: policing, immigration, terrorism, budget activism, injunctions, sexuality, gender, age, premature death, parenthood, privatization, formerly and currently incarcerated people, public sector unions, devalued labor, and (relative) innocence. Racism both connects and differentiates how these categories cohere in both radical and reformist policy prescriptions—in other words, how people, and here I cite Peter Linebaugh's exquisite phrase, "pierce the future for hope." Insofar as policies are a script for the future, they must be sharp, a quality often confused with excessive narrowness—something devolution's inherent patterning encourages to a fault. As A. Sivanandan teaches, while economics determine, the politics of race define techniques and understanding, even though racial categories and hierarchies—at any moment solid—are not set in concrete. If, as Stuart Hall argued back in the late 1970s, race is the modality through which class is lived, then mass incarceration is *class* war.

And yet, breadth carries analytical and organizational challenges as well. It's not news that we find the answers to the questions we ask. What then might the most adequate general term or terms be that usefully gather together for scrutiny and action such a disparate yet connected range of categories, relationships, and processes as those conjoined by mass criminalization and incarceration? Twenty years ago, the abolitionist organization Critical Resistance came into being, taking as its surname "Beyond the Prison Industrial Complex." The experimental purpose of the term "prison industrial complex" was to provoke as wide as possible a range of understandings of the socio-spatial relationships out of which mass incarceration is made by using as a flexible template the military industrial complex—its whole historical geography, and political economy, and demography, and intellectual and technical practitioners, theorists, policy wonks, boosters, and parasites, all who participated in, benefitted from, or were passed over or disorganized by the Department of War's transformative restructuring into the Pentagon.

In other words, we meant prison industrial complex (PIC) to be as conceptually expansive as our object of analysis and struggle. But I think in too many cases its effect has been to shrivel—atrophy, really, rather than to spread out—imaginative understanding of the system's apparently boundless boundary-making. As a result, researchers spend too much time either proving trivial things or beating back hostile critiques, and activists devote immense resources to fighting scandals rather than sources. And yet there is a PIC. So it has occurred to me, as a remedial project, to provisionally call the PIC by another name—one I gave to a course I developed in 1999 and taught for half a decade at Berkeley—the somewhat more generic "carceral geographies." The purpose here is to renovate and make critical what *abolition* is all about. Indeed, abolition geography is carceral geography's antagonistic contradiction.

I will return to this point at the end, but here—as you who know me will expect—I will remind us that, in the archival record of self-organization and world-making activity among the Black people of the South under Reconstruction, the great communist W. E. B. Du Bois *saw* places people made—abolition geographies—under the participatory political umbrella of what he called "abolition democracy." (Thulani Davis has most recently and exquisitely elaborated this work through tracing its expansion and contraction across space-time.) People didn't make what they made from nothing—destitute though the millions were as a result of the great effort to strike, free themselves, and establish a new social order. They brought things with them—sensibilities, dependencies, talents, indeed a complement of consciousness and capacity Cedric Robinson termed an "ontological totality"—to make where they were into places they wished to be. And yet they left abundant evidence showing how freedom is not simply the absence of enslavement as a legal and property form. Rather, the undoing of bondage—abolition—is quite literally to change places: to destroy the geography of slavery by mixing their labor with the external world to change the world and thereby themselves—as it were, habitation as nature—even if geometrically speaking they hadn't moved far at all.

Such Reconstruction place-making negated the negation constituted as and by bondage, and while nobody fully inhabits its direct socio-spatial lineage because of the counterrevolution of property, the consciousness remains in political, expressive, and organizational culture if we look and listen. (Indeed, 2015 is the 100th anniversary of *The Birth of a Nation*—a tale that made the wages of whiteness not only desirable but in many senses obligatory.) What particularly concerns us here is a general point: to enhance their ability to extract value from labor and land, elites fashion political, economic, and cultural institutions using ideologies and methods acquired locally, nationally, and internationally. They build states. Tweak them. Aggrandize and devolve them.

Promote and deflate explanatory and justificatory explanations of why things should either be otherwise or as they are. But even in the throes of periodic abandonment, elites rely on structures of order and significance that the anarchy of racial capitalism can never guarantee. Further, as the actual experience of the Negro during the Civil War and Reconstruction shows, non-elites are never passive pawns. Ordinary people, in changing diversity, figure out how to stretch or diminish social and spatial forms to create room for their lives. Signs and traces of abolition geographies abound, even in their fragility.

Gaza and the West Bank: During the first intifada (1987–93) popular committees throughout the territories organized an astonishing array of institutions that would constitute the outline of an infrastructure for postcolonial Palestine. The projects included health clinics, schools, shops, food growing and processing capacities, and clothing factories. The people who organized and worked in these places discussed the work as partial although necessary to liberation, and requiring persistent work on consciousness through imaginative education, training, and other programs. For example, some of the women who worked in food processing discussed how the revolution-in-progress could not be sustained unless patriarchy and paternalism became as unacceptable and unthinkable as occupation. The work in popular education depended on stretching awareness from the particular (an inoculation, an irrigation ditch, an electrically powered machine) to the general requirements for the ad hoc abolition geographies of that time-space to become and become again sustained through conscious action.

Domestic Violence: Carceral feminism has failed to end violence against women or domestic violence in general, although sometimes law enforcement intervention makes time and space for people to figure out alternatives. So, INCITE! Women of Color against Violence and many other people organized in a variety of ways around the world have tried to figure out how to make that time-space in the context of household or community building rather than criminalization. The idea here is rather than punish violence better or faster, to end violence by changing the social relationships in which it occurs. As a result, as the Story Telling Organizing Project demonstrates, people around the world have devised many approaches to stopping the central problem—violence—without using violence to achieve successful change, involving friends, neighbors, wider communities, and different strategies.

Decolonial education: Sónia Vaz Borges's 2016 PhD thesis on the liberation schools established by the anticolonial forces during the Guinea-Bissau thirteen-year liberation war shows the intricate interrelation of place-making, space-changing activities. Educated to be a member of the Portuguese state's overseas professional managerial class, Amilcar Cabral's role in the development of revolutionary consciousness drew in part from his training as an agronomist. Having walked the land of G-B and CV to evaluate problems and solutions for soil productivity, he also got to know the people who lived on and worked that land. The PAIGC created a curriculum for alphabetical, practical, and political literacy, wrote textbooks, and trained soldiers to become teachers. The schools, built and staffed as soon as possible after expulsion of the colonial military in each region of the country, articulated possible futures for localities and beyond, with particular emphasis on Pan-African and Third World connection.

Oakland anti-gang injunctions: The range of concrete control exercised by the criminal justice system doesn't stop at the system's border. Rather, local administrators can use civil law to extend prison's total-institution regime to households and communities, while employers can discriminate at will against the 65 million or more people in the United States who are documented not to work because of felony convictions. In Oakland, a coalition of formerly incarcerated people, several social and economic justice organizations, family members, and others launched a campaign to compel the city government to cancel an established injunction zone and not establish more planned zones. In a zone, people named in the injunction and the places they live and frequent have no barriers to police questioning and searches. Further, household members become involuntary deputies, expected to enforce injunction terms or get into trouble themselves. Transforming the zone into an abolition geography required transforming consciousness, as officially and locally mocked and reviled individuals had to develop their persuasive power both at city hall and in the streets and empty lots where they built community and trust through extraordinary commitment to ordinary things: creating a garden and a mural. Being the first to respond in times of trouble. Leading by following. Curiously, people not afraid to die had to demonstrate in altogether novel contexts their fearlessness anew.

3. THE PROBLEM OF INNOCENCE

I noted earlier that many advocates for people in prison and the communities they come from have taken a perilous route by arguing why certain kinds of people or places suffer in special ways when it comes to criminalization or the cage. Thus, the argument goes, prisons are designed for men, and are therefore bad for women. Prisons are designed for healthy young men, and are therefore bad for the aged and the infirm. Prisons are designed for adults and are therefore bad for youth. Prisons separate people from their families and are therefore bad for mothers who have frontline responsibility for family cohesion and reproductive labor. Prisons are based in a rigid two-gender system and are therefore bad for people who are transgender and gender nonconforming. Prisons are cages and people who didn't hurt anybody should not be in cages.

Now this does not exhaust the litany of who shouldn't be in prison, but what it does do is two things. First, it establishes as a hard fact that some people should be in cages, and only against this desirability or inevitability might some change occur. And it does so by distinguishing degrees of innocence such that there are people, inevitably, who will become permanently not innocent, no matter what they do or say. The structure of feeling that shapes the innocence defense narrative is not hard to understand: after all, if criminalization is all about identifying the guilty, within *its* prevailing logic it's reasonable to imagine the path to undoing it must be to discover the wrongly condemned.

The insistence on finding innocents among the convicted or killed both projects and derives energy from all the various "should not be in cages" categories, such as those I listed above. But it also invokes, with stupefying historical imprecision, a cavalcade of other innocents to emphasize the wrongness of some aspect of mass incarceration. In particular, many carry on as if mass incarceration were the means to assign inherited duty for some set of uncompensated tasks because of what our ancestors were violently compelled to do. It's a reasonable belief given the historical facts of convict leasing and chain gangs that once upon a time were widespread. However, since half of the people locked up are not, or not obviously, descendants of racial chattel slavery, the problem demands a different explanation and therefore different politics. This does not mean that the lineage of abolition extending through chattel slavery is not robust enough to form at least part of the platform for ending mass incarceration in general. However, as it stands, to achieve significance, the uncritical extension of a partial past to explain a different present demands a sentimental political assertion that depends on the figure of a laboring victim whose narrative arc—whose structure of feeling—is fixed, and therefore susceptible to rehabilitation—or expungement—into relative innocence. The turn to innocence frightens in its desperate effort to replenish the void left by various assaults, calculated and cynical, on universalism on the one hand and rights on the other. If there are no universal rights, then what differentiated category might provide some canopy for the vulnerable? In my view, the proponents of innocence are trying to make such a shelter, but its shadow line or curtilage—like that "legally" demarcating people drone-murdered or renditioned by the United States abroad—can and does move, expunging the very innocence earlier achieved through expungement. In other words, dialectics requires us to recognize that the negation of the negation is always abundantly possible *and* hasn't a fixed direction or secure end. It can change direction, and thereby not revive old history but calibrate power differentials anew.

Consider this: a contemporary development in the relative innocence patrol, highlighted by the Supreme Court decision but not born of it, is toward the phenomenal spread of both saturation policing (stop and frisk; broken windows; and various types of so-called "community policing"), and its new formation (which echoes some Second Klan practices): carceral or police humanitarianism. One of the results of contemporary racial capitalism's relent-lessly restructured state-institutional capacities, and the discourses and prac-tices that combine to enliven them, is "the anti-state state"—governmental capacity dominated by mainstream parties and policies that achieve power on the platform that states are bad and should shrink. Mass incarceration might seem inconsistent with something named the anti-state state. I think, to the contrary, mass incarceration is its bedrock. In other words, the dominant trend that goes hand-in-hand with mass incarceration is devolution—the off-loading to increasingly local state and non-state institutions of the responsibility for thinning social welfare provision. At the same time, increased centralization (the strong executive) belies one of democracy's contemporary delusions—the notion that more local is somehow more participatory.

Carceral/police humanitarianism is a domestic counterinsurgency program spreading rapidly throughout the United States and abroad. Like mass incar-ceration, this humanitarianism is a feature of what I've long called the anti-state state: a dynamic pattern among the patterns shifting and reconsolidating the anti-state state form, dispensing, to riff on Du Bois, the wages of relative inno-cence to achieve a new round of anti-state state building. It's not new, but now altogether notable in the general landscape of exclude and define, capture and reward. This too is part of devolution, and more aggrandizing of police organi-zations coupled with not-for-profit and state-linked partners to identify and attend to the (relatively) innocent victims of too much policing and prison—sometimes formerly incarcerated people, sometimes their families, sometimes their neighborhoods. Police humanitarianism targets vulnerable people with goods and services that in fact everybody needs—especially everybody who is poor. But the door opens only by way of collaboration with the very practices that sustain carceral geographies, thereby undermining and destroying so many lives across generations, in the first place.

We have already seen that innocence is not secure, and it's a mystery why it ever seemed reliable. And while nothing in this life is secure, sitting down to make common cause with the intellectual authors and social agents who unleashed and manage the scourge of organized abandonment—highlighting for the present discussion the organized violence on which it depends—puts into starkest terms the peril of the innocence defense.

Let's think about this problem in another way: While all those who benefit-ted from chattel slavery on both sides of the Atlantic, and from all the forms of slavery that preceded and intersected with and since have followed it, are responsible for vicious injustices against individuals and humanity, to prove the innocence of those who have been or are enslaved for any purpose ought to play no role in the redress of slavery. In his controversial but indispensible *Slavery and Social Death*, Orlando Patterson notes that the power to kill is a precondi-tion for the power of "violent domination, natal alienation, and general dishonor." The power to put humans in cages also derives from the power to kill—not only by way of the ritualized punishment of the death penalty, but also by life sentences, as well as the ritual of serially excused police killings that transformed #BlackLivesMatter from a lament to a movement. Patterson gives us the elegant turn of phrase that helps us, sadly, wrap our minds around the continuum of killing to keeping: "One fell because he was the enemy; the other became the enemy because he had fallen." Human sacrifice rather than innocence is the central problem that organizes the carceral geographies of the prison industrial complex. Indeed, for abolition, to insist on innocence is to surrender politically because "innocence" evades a problem abolition is compelled to confront: how to diminish and remedy harm as against finding better forms of punishment. To make what I'm discussing a bit more explicit, I turn to the words of the great armed thief and spy Harriet Tubman. She told this story:

> I knew of a man who was sent to the State Prison for twenty-five years. All these years he was always thinking of his home, and counting the time till he should be free. The years roll on, the time of imprisonment is over, the man is free. He leaves the prison gates, he makes his way to the old home, but his old home is not there. The house in which he had dwelt in his childhood had been torn down, and a new one had been put in its place; his family were gone, their very name was forgotten, there was no one to take him by the hand to welcome him back to life.

> So it was with me. I had crossed the line of which I had so long been dreaming. I was free, but there was no one to welcome me to the land of freedom, I was a stranger in a strange land, and my home after all was down in the old cabin quarter, with the old folks and my brothers and sisters. But to this solemn resolution I came; I was free, and they should be free also; I would make a home for them.

4. INFRASTRUCTURE OF FEELING

W. E. B. Du Bois interviewed Harriet Tubman late in her life. For a while in the mid-twentieth century, a small but rather raucous scholarly competition developed to "prove" how many (which is to say how *few*) people Tubman helped "keep moving" along the Underground Railroad. By contrast, Harvard- and Humboldt-trained historian and sociologist Du Bois, a numbers guy if ever there was one, said hundreds. Then thousands! Why? Did he just get sloppy? Or did he begin to see how abolition geographies are made, on the ground, everywhere along the route—the time-route as well as the space-route. Indeed, was he able to redo in *Black Reconstruction in America* his earlier research on the Freedman's Bureau because of the insights—truly visionary—he gained from talking with the ancient Tubman? It's here that I think the concept "infrastructure of feeling" might help us think about the development and perpetuation of abolition geographies, and how such geographies tend toward, even if they don't wholly achieve, the negation of the negation of the overlapping and interlocking carceral geographies of which the PIC is an exemplar while absolutely non-exhaustive, as the examples of abolition geographies show.

Raymond Williams argued more than fifty years ago that each age has its own "structure of feeling," a narrative structure for understanding the dynamic material limits to the possibility of change. Paul Gilroy and many others have engaged Williams's thinking, and shown that necessarily ages and places have multiple structures of feeling, which are dialectical rather than merely contemporaneous. Williams went on to explain how we might best understand tradition as an accumulation of structures of feeling—that gather not by chance, nor through a natural process that would seem like a drift or tide, but rather by way of what he calls "the selection and reselection of ancestors." In this, Williams disavows the fixity of either culture or biology, discovering in perpetuation how even the least coherent aspects of human consciousness—feelings—have dynamically substantive shape.

The Black Radical Tradition is a constantly evolving accumulation of structures of feeling whose individual and collective narrative arcs persistently tend toward freedom. It is a way of mindful action that is constantly renewed and refreshed over time but maintains strength, speed, stamina, agility, flexibility, balance. The great explosions and distortions of modernity put into motion—and constant interaction—already existing as well as novel understandings of difference, possession, dependence, abundance. As a result, the selection and reselection of ancestors is itself part of the radical process of finding anywhere—if not everywhere—in political practice and analytical habit, lived expressions (including opacities) of unbounded participatory openness.

What underlies such accumulation? What is the productive capacity of visionary or crisis-driven or even exhaustion-provoked reselection? The best I can offer, until something better comes along, is what I've called for many years the "infrastructure of feeling." In the material world, infrastructure underlies productivity—it speeds some processes and slows down others, setting agendas, producing isolation, enabling cooperation. The infrastructure of feeling is material too, in the sense that ideology becomes material as do the actions that feelings enable or constrain. The infrastructure of feeling is then consciousness-foundation, sturdy but not static, that viscerally underlies our capacity to select, to recognize possibility as we select and reselect liberatory lineages—in a lifetime, as Du Bois and Tubman exemplify, as well as between and across generations. What matters—what materializes—are lively re-articulations and surprising combinations. If, then, the structures of feeling for the Black Radical Tradition are, age upon age, shaped by energetically expectant consciousness of and direction toward unboundedness, then the tradition is, inexactly, movement away from partition and exclusion—indeed, its inverse.

5. UNBOUNDEDNESS, AGAINST CONCLUSION

Thus, abolition geography—how and to what end people make freedom provisionally, imperatively, as they imagine *home* against the disintegrating grind of partition and repartition through which racial capitalism perpetuates the means of its own valorization. Abolition geography and the methods adequate to it (for making, finding, and understanding) elaborate the spatial—which is to say the human-environment processes—of Du Bois's and Davis's abolition democracy. Abolition geography is capacious (it isn't only by, for, or about Black people) and specific (it's a guide to action for both understanding and rethinking how we combine our labor with each other and the earth). Abolition geography takes feeling and agency to be constitutive of, no less than constrained by, structure. In other words, it's a way of studying, and of doing political organizing, and of being in the world, and of worlding ourselves.

Put another way, abolition geography requires challenging the normative presumption that territory and liberation are at once alienable and exclusive—that they should be partitionable by sales, documents, or walls. Rather, by seizing the particular capacities we have, and repeating ourselves—trying, as C. L. R. James wrote about the run-up to revolutions, trying every little thing, going and going again—we will, because we do, change ourselves and the external world. Even under extreme constraint.

A last story: in the 1970s, the California Department of Corrections (CDC) decided to reorganize the social and spatial world of people in prison in response to both reformist and radical mobilization. Evidence shows that the CDC experimented with a variety of disruptive schemes to end the solidarity that had arisen among its diverse (although then mostly white) population in the prisons for men. Cooperation, forged in study groups and other consciousness-raising activities, had resulted in both significant victories in federal courts over conditions of confinement, and deadly retaliation against guards who had been killing prisoners with impunity. In spite of twenty years of Washington, DC, rule-making forbidding, among other things, segregation, failure to advise of rights, lack of due process, and extrajudicial punishment, the CDC decided to segregate prisoners into racial, ethnic, and regional groups labeled gangs, to remand some of them to indefinite solitary confinement, and to restrict the end of punishment to three actions: snitch, parole, or die. To reify the system as the built environment, the CDC created two prisons for men and one for women with high-tech Security Housing Units (SHU—a prison within a prison). The history of SHUs has yet to be fully told; it is indisputable that they induce mental and physical illness, which can lead to suicide or other forms of premature, preventable death. Indeed, the United Nations defines solitary confinement in excess of fourteen days as torture.

The people locked in the Pelican Bay State Prison SHU, some from the day it opened, on December 10, 1989, might or might not have done what they were convicted of in court; their innocence doesn't matter. For many years lawyers and others have worked with people in the SHU trying to discover the way out, not picking and choosing whom to aid, but interviewing any willing subject about conditions of confinement and struggling to devise a general plan. Activists created handbooks and websites, lobbied the legislature, testified to administrative law judges, devised lawsuits, held workshops, organized with family members, and otherwise sought to bring the SHU scourge to light. (In 1998, at a hearing into the cover-up of seven SHU prisoners shot dead by guards, a producer for Mike Wallace's *60 Minutes* asked: "Tell me why to care about these guys." "Do you care about justice?" "Of course. But the audience needs to care about people. Why should they care?")

The department absolves itself of breaking laws and violating court decrees by insisting that the gangs it fostered run the prisons and the streets. After almost forty years of people churning through the expanded CDC, it's impossible that there's no stretch or resonance across the prison walls. SHU placement mixes people from ascriptive (what the CDC says) and assertive (what the prisoners themselves say) free-world social geographies in order to minimize the possibility of solidarity among people who, the circular logic goes, are enemies or they wouldn't be in the SHU. They can't see or touch one another, but across the din of television sets and the machine-noise of prisons they can talk, debate, discuss. And while race is not the SHU's only organizing factor, race is the summary term that ordinary people, inside and out, use to name the divisions. For many years some of the most active SHU residents debated racism versus racialism, first embracing and then challenging a variety of supremacies, while for years continuing to accept the structure of feeling that keeps race constant as naturally endowed or culturally preferable.

People make abolition geographies from what they have; changing awareness can radically revise understanding of what can be done with available materials. It's clear that the SHU, in calculated opposition to 1970s Soledad or San Quentin or Attica, thins social resources to the breaking point. But what breaks? In many cases the persons locked up. But consciousness can break into a different dimension, shedding commonsense understandings of being and solidarity, identity and change. A negation of violence through violence is possible, which returns us to the territory of selves invoked in the opening pages of this discussion. Even in a total institution sovereignty is contradictory, as resistance to torture demonstrates. The regime—its intellectual authors and social agents, its buildings and rules—tortures captives one by one. They can turn on the regime through shifting the object of torture into the subject of history by way of hunger strikes. Participating individuals turn the violence of torture against itself, not by making it not-violent but rather by intentionally repurposing vulnerability to premature death as a totality to be reckoned with, held together by skin.

The first strike, whose organizers represented all of the alleged prison gangs, sent its demands upward to the CDC, asking for modest improvements for all SHU dwellers' experience and fate: better food, improved visitation, and some way to contest SHU sentences based in evidence rather than system-aggrandizement. People in many non-SHU prisons joined the strike in solidarity, and one died. The CDC offered to negotiate; the strike ended. Nothing changed.

A second strike erupted, well-covered both by the ever-active in-prison grapevine, and the organizing collective's free world support infrastructure. In the context of the Supreme Court decision concerning medical neglect, and uprisings in many parts of the planet—North Africa, West Asia, South Africa, the streets of the United States—the demands took a new direction, against the partitions that, especially in the contemporary era, normalize devolved imaginations and shrunken affinities when expansiveness seems absolutely necessary. The collective sent its demands out, horizontally as it were, to their constituent communities inside and out, calling for an end to the hostilities among the races. Although some people interpret the call as "Black–brown solidarity," the collective's documents are radical and all-encompassing, leaving no group out. The call has a history as old as modernity, however anachronistic contemporary labels might be.

The racial in racial capitalism isn't secondary, nor did it originate in color or intercontinental conflict, but rather always group-differentiation to premature death. Capitalism requires inequality and racism enshrines it. The PBSP collective, hidden from each other, experiencing at once the torture of isolation and the extraction of time, refigured their world, however tentatively, into an abolition geography by finding an infrastructure of feeling on which they could rework their experience and understanding of possibility by way of renovated consciousness. The fiction of race projects a peculiar animation of the human body, and people take to the streets in opposition to its real and deadly effects. And in the end, as the relations of racial capitalism take it out of people's hides, the contradiction of skin becomes clearer. Skin, our largest organ, vulnerable to all ambient toxins, at the end, is all we have to hold us together, no matter how much it seems to keep us apart.

Chapter 15

An Interview on the Futures of Black Radicalism

Angela Davis, interview by Gaye Theresa Johnson and Alex Lubin

In your scholarship you have focused on prison abolitionism, Black feminism, popular culture and the blues, and Black internationalism with a focus on Palestine. Taken together, how does this work draw inspiration from, and perhaps move forward, the Black Radical Tradition?

Cedric Robinson challenged us to think about the role of Black radical theorists and activists in shaping social and cultural histories that inspire us to link our ideas and our political practices to deep critiques of racial capitalism. I am glad that he lived long enough to get a sense of how younger generations of scholars and activists have begun to take up his notion of a Black Radical Tradition. In *Black Marxism*, he developed an important genealogy that pivoted around the work of C. L. R. James, W. E. B. Du Bois, and Richard Wright. If one looks at his work as a whole, including *Black Movements in America* and *The Anthropology of Marxism*, as H. L. T. Quan has pointed out, we cannot fail to apprehend how central women have been to the forging of a Black Radical Tradition. Quan writes that when asked about why there is such an enormous focus on the role of women and resistance in his body of work, Robinson replies, "Why not? All resistance, in effect, manifests in gender, manifests as gender. Gender is indeed both a language of oppression [and] a language of resistance."[1]

I have learned a great deal from Cedric Robinson regarding the uses of history: ways of theorizing history—or allowing it to theorize itself—that are crucial to our understanding of the present and to our ability to collectively envisage a more habitable future. Cedric has argued that his remarkable excavations of history emanate from the positing of political objectives in the present. I have felt a kinship with his approach since I first read *Black Marxism*. My first published article—written while I was in jail—which focused on Black women and slavery was, in fact, an effort to refute the damaging, yet increasingly popular, discourse of the Black matriarchy, as represented through official government reports as well as through generalized masculinist ideas (such as the necessity of gender-based leadership hierarchies designed to guarantee Black male dominance) circulating within the Black movement in the late 1960s and

---

1 Interview with Cedric Robinson by H. L. T. Quan, quoted in Quan, "Geniuses of Resistance: Feminist Consciousness and the Black Radical Tradition," *Race and Class* 47, no. 2 (October 2005): 47.

early 1970s. Although this is not how I was thinking about my work at that time, I certainly would not hesitate today to link that research to the effort to make a Black radical, thus feminist, tradition more visible.

The new field formation—critical prison studies and its explicitly abolitionist framework—situates itself within the Black Radical Tradition, both through its acknowledged genealogical relation to the period in US history we refer to as Radical Reconstruction and, of course, through its relation both to the work of W. E. B. Du Bois and to historical Black feminism. The work of Sarah Haley, Kelly Lytle Hernandez, and an exciting new generation of scholars, by linking their valuable research with their principled activism, is helping to revitalize the Black Radical Tradition.

With every generation of antiracist activism, it seems, narrow Black nationalism returns phoenix-like to claim our movements' allegiance. Cedric's work was inspired, in part, by his desire to respond to the narrow Black nationalism of the era of his (and my) youth. It is, of course, extremely frustrating to witness the resurgence of modes of nationalism that are not only counterproductive, but contravene what should be our goal: Black, and thus human, flourishing. At the same time it is thoroughly exciting to witness the ways new youth formations— Black Lives Matter, BYP100, the Dream Defenders—are helping to shape a new Black feminist-inflected internationalism that highlights the value of queer theories and practices.

What is your assessment of the Black Lives Matter movement, particularly in light of your participation in the Black Panther Party during the 1970s? Does Black Lives Matter, in your view, have a sufficient analysis and theory of freedom? Do you see any similarities between the BPP and BLM movement?

As we consider the relation between the Black Panther Party and the contemporary Black Lives Matter movement, it feels like the decades and generations that separate one from the other create a certain incommensurability that is a consequence of all the economic, political, cultural, and technological changes that make this contemporary moment so different in many important respects from the late 1960s. But perhaps we should seek connections between the two movements that are revealed not so much in the similarities, but rather in their radical differences.

The BPP emerged as a response to the police occupation of Oakland, California, and Black urban communities across the country. It was an absolutely brilliant move on the part of Huey Newton and Bobby Seale to patrol the neighborhood with guns and law books, in other words, to "police the police." At the same time this strategy—admittedly also inspired by the emergence of guerrilla struggles in Cuba, liberation armies in southern Africa and the Middle East, and the successful resistance offered by the National Liberation Front in

Vietnam—in retrospect, reflected a failure to recognize, as Audre Lorde put it, that "the master's tools will never dismantle the master's house." In other words, the use of guns—even though primarily as symbols of resistance—conveyed the message that the police could be challenged effectively by relying on explicit policing strategies.

A hashtag developed by Patrisse Cullors, Alicia Garza, and Opal Tometi in the aftermath of the vigilante killing of Trayvon Martin, #BlackLivesMatter began to transform into a network as a direct response to the rising protests in Ferguson, Missouri, which manifested a collective desire to demand justice for Mike Brown and for all of the Black lives sacrificed on the altar of racist police terror. In asking us to radically resist the racist violence at the very heart of policing structures and strategies, Black Lives Matter early on recognized that we would have to place the demand to demilitarize the police at the center of our efforts to move toward a more critical and more collective mode of justice. Ultimately linked to an approach that calls for the abolition of policing as we know and experience it, demilitarization also contested the way in which police strategies have been transnationalized within circuits that link small US police departments to Israel, which dominates the arena of militarized policing associated with the occupation of Palestine.

I appreciate the more complicated analysis that is embraced by many BLM activists, because it precisely reflects a historical-mindedness that is able to build upon, embrace, and radically critique activisms and antiracist theories of the past. As the BPP attempted—sometimes unsuccessfully—to embrace emergent feminisms and what was then referred to as the gay liberation movement, BLM leader and activists have developed approaches that more productively take up feminist and queer theories and practices. But theories of freedom are always tentative. I have learned from Cedric Robinson that any theory or political strategy that pretends to possess a total theory of freedom, or one that can be categorically understood, has failed to account for the multiplicity of possibilities, which can, perhaps, only be evocatively represented in the realm of culture.

Your most recent scholarship is focused on the question of Palestine, and its connection to the Black freedom movement. When did this connection become obvious to you and what circumstances, or conjunctures, made this insight possible?

Actually my most recent collection of lectures and interviews reflects an increasingly popular understanding of the need for an internationalist framework within which the ongoing work to dismantle structures of racism, heteropatriarchy, and economic injustice inside the United States can become more enduring and more meaningful. In my own political history, Palestine has always occupied a pivotal place, precisely because of the similarities between Israel and the United States—their foundational settler colonialism and their ethnic cleansing processes with respect to indigenous people, their systems of segrega-tion, their use of legal systems to enact systematic repression, and so forth. I often point out that my consciousness of the predicament of Palestine dates back to my undergraduate years at Brandeis University, which was founded in the same year as the State of Israel. Moreover, during my own incarceration, I received support from Palestinian political prisoners as well as from Israeli attorneys defending Palestinians.

In 1973, when I attended the World Festival of Youth and Students in Berlin (in the German Democratic Republic), I had the opportunity to meet Yasir Arafat, who always acknowledged the kinship of the Palestinian struggle and the Black freedom struggle in the United States, and who, like Che, Fidel, Patrice Lumumba, and Amilcar Cabral, was a revered figure within the movement for Black libera-tion. This was a time when communist internationalism—in Africa, the Middle East, Europe, Asia, Australia, South America, and the Caribbean—was a powerful force. If I might speak about my own story, it would have almost certainly led to a different conclusion had not this internationalism played such a pivotal role.

The encounters between Black liberation struggles in the United States and movements against the Israeli occupation of Palestine have a very long history. Alex Lubin's *Geographies of Liberation: The Making of an Afro-Arab Political Imaginary* attempts to chart important aspects of this history. Oftentimes, however, it is not in the explicitly political realm that one discovers moments of contact. As Cedric Robinson emphasized, it is in the cultural realm. Of course Robin Kelley's *Freedom Dreams: The Making of the Black Radical Imagination* accentuates the arena of surrealism as an especially generative contact zone. In the latter twentieth century, it was Black feminist poet June Jordan who pushed the issue of the occupation of Palestine to the fore. Despite the Zionist attacks she suffered, and despite the temporary loss of a very important friendship with Adrienne Rich (who later also became a critic of the occupation), June became a powerful witness for Palestine. In her poetry she felt impelled to embody the juncture of Black and Palestine liberation. "I was born a Black woman / and now / I am become a Palestinian / against the relentless laughter of evil / there is less and less living room / and where are my loved ones / It is time to make our way home."[2] At a time when feminists of color were attempting to fashion strategies of what we now refer to as intersectionality, June, who represents the best of the Black Radical Tradition, taught us about the capacity of political affinities across national, cultural, and supposedly racial boundaries to help us imagine more habitable futures. I miss her deeply and am so sorry that she did not live long enough to experience Black Lives Matter activists across this continent raising banners of resistance to the occupation of Palestine.

As I have remarked on many occasions, when I joined a delegation in 2011 of indigenous and women of color feminist scholar activists to the West Bank

---

2   June Jordan, "Moving Towards Home," in *Living Room*.

and East Jerusalem, I was under the impression that I thoroughly understood the occupation. Although all of us were already linked, to one extent or another, to the solidarity movement, we were all thoroughly shocked by how little we really knew about the quotidian violence of the occupation. At the conclusion of our visit, we collectively decided to devote our energies to participating in BDS and to help elevate the consciousness of our various constituencies with respect to the US role—over $8 million—in sustaining the military occupation. So I remain deeply connected in this project to Chandra Mohanty, Beverly Guy-Sheftall, Barbara Ransby, Gina Dent, and the other members of the delegation.[3]

In the five years following our trip, many other delegations of academics and activists have visited Palestine and have helped to accelerate, broaden, and intensify the Palestine solidarity movement. As the architects of the Boycott, Divestment, and Sanctions movement have modeled their work on the anti-apartheid campaign against South Africa, US activists have attempted to point out that there are profound lessons to be gleaned from earlier boycott politics. Many organizations and movements within the United States have considered how the incorporation of anti-apartheid strategies into their agendas would radically transform their own work. Not only did the anti-apartheid campaign help to strengthen international efforts to take down the apartheid state, it also revived and enriched many domestic movements against racism, misogyny, and economic justice.

In the same way, solidarity with Palestine has the potential to further transform and render more capacious the political consciousness of our contemporary movements. BLM activists and others associated with this very important historical moment of a surging collective consciousness calling for recognition of the persisting structures of racism can play an important role in compelling other areas of social justice activism to take up the cause of Palestine solidarity—specifically the Boycott, Divestment, and Sanctions movement. Alliances on university campuses that bring together Black student organizations, Students for Justice in Palestine, and campus chapters of Jewish Voice for Peace are reminding us of the profound need to unite antiracist efforts with strong challenges to Islamophobia and anti-Semitism, and with the global resistance to the apartheid policies and practices of the State of Israel.

Theoretically and ideologically, Palestine has also helped us to broaden our vision of abolition, which we have characterized in this era as the abolition of imprisonment and policing. The experience of Palestine pushes us to revisit

---

3   The members of the delegation were: Rabab Abdulhadi, San Francisco State University; Ayoka Chenzira, artist and filmmaker, Atlanta, GA; Angela Y. Davis, University of California, Santa Cruz; Gina Dent, University of California, Santa Cruz; G. Melissa Garcia, Dickinson College; Anna Romina Guevarra, author and sociologist, Chicago, IL; Beverly Guy-Sheftall, author, Atlanta, GA; Premilla Nadasen, author, New York, NY; Barbara Ransby, author and historian, Chicago, IL; Chandra Talpade Mohanty, Syracuse University; and Waziyatawin, University of Victoria.

concepts such as "the prison nation" or "the carceral state" in order to seriously understand the quotidian carceralities of the occupation and the ubiquitous policing by not only Israeli forces but also the Palestinian Authority. This, in turn, has stimulated other research directions on the uses of incarceration and its role, for example, in perpetrating notions of a permanent binarism with respect to gender[4] and in naturalizing segregation based on physical, mental, and intellectual ability.[5]

What sort of social movements can, or should, exist at the present conjuncture, given the ascendance of American global hegemony, neoliberal economic relations, militarized counterinsurgency at home, and racial "color blindness"?

At a time when popular discourse is rapidly shifting as a direct response to pressures emanating from sustained protests against state violence, and from representational practices linked to new technologies of communication, I suggest that we need movements that pay as much attention to popular political education as they pay to the mobilizations that have succeeded in placing police violence and mass incarceration on the national political agenda. What this means, I think, is that we try to forge an analysis of the current conjuncture that draws important lessons from the relatively recent campaigns that have pushed our collective consciousness beyond previous limits. In other words, we need movements that are prepared to resist the inevitable seductions of assimilation. The Occupy campaign enabled us to develop an anti-capitalist vocabulary: the 99 percent versus the 1 percent is a concept that has entered into popular parlance. The question is not only how to preserve this vocabulary—as, for example, in the analysis offered by the Bernie Sanders platform leading up to the selection of the 2016 Democratic candidate for president—but rather how to build upon this, or complicate it with the idea of racial capitalism, which cannot be so neatly expressed in quantitative terms that assume the homogeneity that always undergirds racism.

Cedric Robinson never stopped excavating ideas, cultural products, and political movements from the past. He attempted to understand why trajectories of assimilation and of resistance in Black freedom movements in the United States co-existed, and his insights—in *Black Movements in America*, for example—continue to be valuable. Assimilationist strategies that leave intact the circumstances and structures that perpetuate exclusion and marginalization have always been offered as the more reasonable alternative to abolition, which,

---

4   See Eric A. Stanley and Nat Smith, eds., *Captive Genders: Trans Embodiment and the Prison Industrial Complex* (Oakland, CA, and Edinburgh: AK Press, 2015).

5   See Liat Ben-Moshe, Chris Chapman, and Allison C. Carey, *Disability Incarcerated: Imprisonment and Disability in the United States and Canada* (New York: Palgrave Macmillan, 2014).

of course, not only requires resistance and dismantling, but also radical reimag-
inings and radical reconstructions.

Perhaps this is the time to create the groundwork for a new political party,
one that will speak to a far greater number of people than traditional progressive political parties have proved capable of doing. This party would have to be
organically linked to the range of radical movements that have emerged in the
aftermath of the rise of global capitalism. As I reflect on the value of Cedric
Robinson's work in relation to contemporary radical activism, it seems to me
that this party would have to be anchored in the idea of racial capitalism—it
would be antiracist, anti-capitalist, feminist, and abolitionist. But most important of all, it would have to acknowledge the priority of movements on the
ground, movements that acknowledge the intersectionality of current issues—
movements that are sufficiently open to allowing for the future emergence of
issues, ideas, and movements that we cannot even begin to imagine today.

**Do you make a distinction, in your scholarship and activism, between
Marxism and "Black Marxism"?**

I have spent most of my life studying Marxist ideas and have identified with
groups that have not only embraced Marxist-inspired critiques of the dominant
socioeconomic order, but have also struggled to understand the co-constitutive
relationship of racism and capitalism. Having especially followed the theories and
practices of Black communists and anti-imperialists in the United States, Africa,
the Caribbean, and other parts of the world, and having worked inside the
Communist Party for a number of years with a Black formation that took the
names of Che Guevara and Patrice Lumumba, Marxism, from my perspective,
has always been both a method and an object of criticism. Consequently, I don't
necessarily see the terms "Marxism" and "Black Marxism" as oppositional.

I take Cedric Robinson's arguments in *Black Marxism: The Making of the
Black Radical Tradition* very seriously. If we assume the unquestioned centrality
of the West and its economic, philosophical, and cultural development, then the
economic modes, intellectual histories, religions, and cultures associated with
Africa, Asia, and indigenous peoples will not be acknowledged as significant
dimensions of humanity. The very concept of humanity will always conceal an
internal, clandestine racialization, forever foreclosing possibilities of racial
equality. Needless to say, Marxism is firmly anchored in this tradition of the
Enlightenment. Cedric's brilliant analyses revealed new ways of thinking and
acting generated precisely through the encounters between Marxism and Black
intellectuals/activists who helped to constitute the Black Radical Tradition.

The concept associated with *Black Marxism* that I find most productive and
most potentially transformative is the concept of racial capitalism. Even though
Eric Williams's *Capitalism and Slavery* was published in 1944, scholarly efforts
exploring this relationship have remained relatively marginal. Hopefully the

new research on capitalism and slavery will help to further legitimate the notion of racial capitalism. While it is important to acknowledge the pivotal part slavery played in the historical consolidation of capitalism, more recent developments linked to global capitalism cannot be adequately comprehended if the racial dimension of capitalism is ignored.

Part Four

Afterwords

Cedric People

Erica Edwards

I came to Cedric J. Robinson's work through his people, through the jagged network of students, colleagues, and friends that he taught, mentored, laughed with, and argued with over the many years that he was on earth in struggle with us. This thing about Cedric's work—that it travels in the academy and beyond through gestures of affiliation or touch—is significant. If you started graduate school around the time that I did, you would have probably been introduced to Cedric's work by Robin D. G. Kelley or Ruthie Gilmore, or Avery Gordon, or Wahneema Lubiano. And you probably had the University of North Carolina Press reissue of *Black Marxism: The Making of the Black Radical Tradition,* the one with the pristine black matte cover and the simple blue and red geometric letters whose stark clean lines masked what was between the book's cover: more than a history of Black Marxists, the history of the world, the *worlds,* of the Black Radical Tradition which was of course before and more than Marxism. But the other material history of Robinson's work kept on shaping the social world that continued to swell around it, and by "the other material history," I'm referring to the one that Fred Moten describes in the special issue of *African Identities* that H. L. T. Quan and Tiffany Willoughby-Herard edited in 2013:

> For a long time . . . *Black Marxism* circulated underground, as a recurrent seismic event on the edge or over the edge of the university, for those of us who valorized being on or over that edge even if we had been relegated to it. There, at least, we could get together and talk about the bomb that had gone off in our heads. Otherwise we carried around its out, dispersive potenza as contraband, buried under the goods that legitimate parties to exchange can value, until we could get it to the black market, where (the) license has no weight, and *hand it around* out of a suitcase or over a kitchen table or from behind a makeshift counter.[1]

If you had to know someone who had their hands on a copy, there must have been a certain *handedness* that built the discursive and social field around the work—we might even call it a force field in the darkness that now in retrospect, in the tragedy of our time, appears only slightly less obscure. Those were the Reagan–Thatcher years, the post-1968 decades of prison and police buildup and

---

1   Fred Moten, "The Subprime and the Beautiful," *African Identities* 11, no. 2 (2013): 239.

privatization, the invasions of everywhere from Grenada to the Gulf, the neoliberal assault on everything that resists possession.

Now in the wake of the 2016 election I have found myself turning even more urgently to Cedric and his people, our people, Cedric people. I started by returning to Tiffany Willoughby-Herard's *Waste of a White Skin*, a stunning book about the history of white vulnerability and the Carnegie Corporation's *Poor White Study*, where she writes:

> As human being and the realization of human rationality in the aspiration toward and the achievement of the nation and the bureaucracy that organizes it is imagined, the racial politics that rely on black people as the fundamental antagonists of human being and the nation must continually erect new racial regimes and forgeries of memory [of course, that's Robinson's term] to paper over this relation. The study of poor whites, white poverty, and the idea that poor whites were an intractable social problem was one such racial regime. That the racialization of poor whites could occur both as privilege and misery is fundamental to the workings of this relation.[2]

Willoughby-Herard's work, like Robinson's, is the work of Black Studies, as Robinson says, as a critique of Western Civilization, where "critique" signifies, more than criticism, the kind of negation and other world-building that is necessary for the survival of Black thought and Black being. The time for the Robinson intervention is here with us in the work of his people, and it is also here with us in its urgent demands that we stand with and struggle with those of us who are protecting the water, those of us who are abolishing the prisons, those of us who are building the sanctuaries, those of us who are finding other ways to refuse the terms of our present order.

The work Robinson left us is a record of radical thought, of efforts to rethink and remake the world in a historical epoch when such activity has been deemed not only dangerous or subversive (by conservative ideologues and architects of defense) but also naive and idealistic (by those on the decimated Left). And Robinson's metaphysics of the anti-political in books such as *The Terms of Order* and *Anthropology of Marxism* are not only based in Robinson's "deeply historical"[3] work; they are also based in the heresy, the dreamworlds, the ancestral visions, the folktales, the church life, the non-evidentiary stuff that makes up that other authority, that other call to duty, that Robinson theorizes.[4] Against security and order, Robinson gives us—gifted us—a sacred universe of disorder that confounds politics.

---

2   Tiffany Willoughby-Herard, *Waste of a White Skin: The Carnegie Corporation and the Racial Logic of White Vulnerability* (Oakland, CA: University of California Press), 128.

3   Robin D. G. Kelley, "Foreword," in Cedric J. Robinson, *Black Marxism: The Making of the Black Radical Tradition* (Chapel Hill: University of North Carolina Press, 2000), xx.

4   Ibid.

There are two vital strands within Robinson's work that, for me, are central to how we will remember him and his work. One is what his work made recognizable: not only the history of white supremacy but the nature of those worlds exiting alongside and in negation of the culture of capital. The Black Radical Tradition is not simply the dialectical antithesis of capitalism or the blind spot of those movements that have posed a challenge to capitalism (such as Marxism); the Black Radical Tradition is, in Avery Gordon's words, the "living and breathing" entity that "stands in the place blinded from view."[5] And the nature of that tradition is a collective consciousness informed by the history of liberation struggles and spurred by "the shared sense of obligation to preserve the *collective being*, the ontological totality."[6] Let's remember the claim that Robinson makes about African captives who took to the bush or who denied themselves salt to sustain their belief that they could "fly, really fly, home."[7] While captives often attempted to escape to Africa or to the maroon communities, their attempts to flee cannot be understood as simple individualistic reactions to plantation servitude. Rather they must be understood as *complete rejections of their lot*, generative instances of collective world-building in the face of utter devastation and in refusal of the world that still must be refused.

The work asks profound questions over and over again: What are we made of? What is *all* the stuff that we are made of? What is the nature of the "we" that has survived the world?

The other important impulse in Robinson's work that I want to remember is its measured optimism. At the end of *Black Marxism,* Robinson leaves us with a profoundly prescient statement about Black people and the new world order. Diagnosing what he calls the "degenerating mechanism" of Western culture, Robinson writes:

> Physically and ideologically . . . African peoples bridge the decline of one world order and the eruption (we may surmise) of another. It is a frightful and uncertain space of being. If we are to survive, we must take nothing that is dead and choose wisely from among the dying.[8]

This was after Nixon, in the midst of Reagan, and Robinson was writing of the new world erupting into the darkness. Robinson's work across his monographs was to invite us into this "frightful and uncertain place of being," moving in the profound expectation that the Western powers had already been weakened by Third World resistance and were facing their ultimate decline even as he wrote.

---

5 Avery Gordon, "Preface," in Cedric J. Robinson, ed., *An Anthropology of Marxism* (Aldershot, Hampshire, UK: Burlington Ashgate, 2001), xi.

6 Robinson, *Black Marxism*, 171. Emphasis added.

7 Ibid., 169.

8 Ibid., 316.

For so many of us, Robinson's work continues teaching us in excess of itself: teaching us something about the social, collective labor of our work; pushing against the headlong drive toward the professionalization of the knowledge commodity; and calling into being, into actual being, the world he imagines when he writes of that ontological totality, the deceptively simple creed that oppression is only *one* of our realities.

The time for the Robinson intervention is, has to be, now, and we must move in that same expectation that propelled it: that Western culture is degenerating and we are the bridge to the *new* new world order. Let us dance on ocean water, let us take to the interior. Plan and study, as we say, organize, as we can, protect, as we must, and keep responding to the call of this giant who we will all so terribly miss. As we remember.

Winston Whiteside and the Politics of the Possible

Robin D. G. Kelley

On the evening of September 20, 2013, Cedric Robinson addressed the Critical Ethnic Studies Conference in Chicago. As he was part of a huge roundtable titled "What Is to Be Done? The Future of Critical Ethnic Studies," he only talked for about ten minutes, mostly extemporaneously. Choosing his words carefully, he spoke in his customarily slow and deliberate style, occasionally pausing to allow his subtle humor to catch hold of the audience. "Critical Ethnic Studies is not really about the academy," he intoned. It was about the people who believed that our presence in the academy might make a difference in the lives of the most vulnerable. "We are not possible without, in effect, the encouragement, the urgency, and the requirement that we be here by those who are being trampled on." By which he meant the imprisoned, the under-housed, the underemployed, the undocumented, the people who sacrificed for us and whom the state sacrifices for capital. He warned of the moral catastrophe we face if we succeed in the academy while those who insisted we be here continue to suffer premature death, in the streets or behind bars.

Near the end of his remarks he began to speak wistfully about the spiritual and communitarian traditions in which he was raised.

> One of the things I was exposed to was this immense notion of the possible through the construction of the notion of faith. So Christian faith trained me to be able to believe in, to anticipate, something coming into being that was not in being. That's called by the Greek word "utopia," which means the good society. It also means no society, no such place. That gave me a framework for looking at what others, before me, had imagined was possible in their lifetime. And that's why it was so important for me to look at the notion of radicalism from the vantage point of slaves . . . According to some scholars, the slaves . . . [had] no ambitions, except to perhaps live or perhaps to die. They had experienced social death. *Well that's nonsense.* Because they were something more than what was expected of them, they could invent, manufacture, conspire, and organize way beyond the possibilities.[1]

Cedric Robinson always wrote about Black radical futures, but history was his pathway for comprehending what others "imagined was possible in their

---

1   Cedric J. Robinson, remarks at Critical Ethnic Studies Conference (September 20, 2013), audio recording in author's possession.

lifetime." He consistently turned to the past to understand the Black Radical Tradition and its capacity to envision a world beyond the possibilities. The essays gathered here, as well as his entire oeuvre, bear this out. Futures of self-determined, collective democracy find flashes in seventeenth-century marronage, in nineteenth-century camp revivals, in anticolonial millenarian uprisings. W. E. B. Du Bois and C. L. R. James turned to slave rebellions in order to chart a future beyond fascism. Amilcar Cabral, one of Robinson's favorite subjects, understood that a radical future for Africa required that we "return to the source."[2]

Cedric revealed in those brief but profound remarks in 2013 that the source of his own conception of the possible was not some seminal text or archival revelation but his West Oakland upbringing, his Alabama roots, his family and the community that nurtured him. While Cedric was reluctant to dwell in the autobiographical, he never hid the enormous respect and admiration he held for his maternal grandfather, Winston Whiteside, whom he often cited as a formative intellectual influence.[3] Affectionately known as "Cap" or "Daddy" Whiteside, he and his wife Cecilia were largely responsible for raising Cedric. By acknowledging Winston Whiteside, Cedric was telling us something about the nature of the Black Radical Tradition, signaling what he meant by "a revolutionary consciousness that proceeded from the whole historical experience of Black people and not merely from the social formations of capitalist slavery or the relations of production of colonialism."[4] Cedric listened to elders and ancestors, heeded memories, spirits, and "ghostly matters," learned from the extraordinary folks whom professional historians mistook for ordinary, and discovered in the Black Radical Tradition whole communities in motion—full of imperfections and contradictions but holding on to each other because they had to and because their culture demanded it.

But I'm the first to confess that I missed the cues. Only after Cedric joined the ancestors did I recognize the importance of *his* ancestors. Again, Cedric left us a hint, buried in a short paragraph from his book *Black Movements in America*:

> Many did not need the [Chicago] *Defender* or the railroads or the agents [to decide to move North]. Like "Cap" Whiteside, who left Mobile, Alabama, in the late 1920s, they relied on family who had already migrated. A few like Whiteside punctuated their leaving the South with their own unique parting gestures. The white manager at the Battle House, an exclusive hotel in Mobile, had tried to exercise his sexual privileges with a young maid, Cecilia, Whiteside's wife. When Cap was told, he returned to the Battle House that evening, beat the manager up, and hung him in

---

2   Cedric J. Robinson, "Amilcar Cabral and the Dialectic of Portuguese Colonialism," *Radical America* 15, no. 3 (May–June 1981): 39–57.

3   Go to Cedric's Wikipedia page and you will see Mr. Whiteside mentioned, but nothing identifying him or his history.

4   Cedric J. Robinson, *Black Marxism: The Making of the Black Radical Tradition* (Chapel Hill: University of North Carolina Press, 2000), 169.

the hotel's cold storage. In a few days, Whiteside headed for Oakland, California. When he earned their fare, he sent for his family: Cecilia and his daughters, Clara, Lillian, and Wilma. Chastened, the manager gained a reputation as one of the best friends of the Negro in Mobile.[5]

I'd read this extraordinary passage a few times (always with James Brown's "Papa Don't Take No Mess" playing in my head). I'd even assigned *Black Movements in America* in my undergraduate social movements course before Routledge jacked up the price, but had not realized that Whiteside was his grandfather. And yet, as the author of a book about Black radicals in Alabama, familiar with crime reports in the *Mobile Register* about Black men and women hanged, shot, and jailed for lesser violations, I understood that Cap had risked death to protect and avenge his wife. What I did not know was the degree to which Cap's act of defiance— inspired clearly by "an immense notion of the possible"—changed history.

So who is "Cap" Whiteside? And what about his precious Cecilia? What did they teach their grandson? Who and what made them? Who are his people? How did they live and organize beyond the possibilities of the Jim Crow racial regime?

Born in Mobile, Alabama, on June 7, 1893, Winston Wilmer Whiteside was the youngest of seven children belonging to Clara and Benjamin Whiteside Sr. The four oldest children were each two years apart, with Benjamin Jr. born in 1872, followed by Spencer, Addison, and Nellie. Although by 1900 they all resided in the family's rambling house at 615 North Jackson Street in the First Ward, just a few blocks from the Mobile River, the four eldest worked as day laborers while Winston's sisters Clara and Lillian attended school.[6] Separated by seven and three years, respectively, Winston grew up much closer to Clara and Lillian.

Winston's parents had been slaves. Benjamin was born in September 1847, on Richard Whiteside's plantation in Coopers Gap, North Carolina, in the Western part of the state near the South Carolina border. Born in 1808, Richard was the child of William and Elizabeth Whiteside, part of a very distinguished and powerful planter family whose branches extended from Illinois to South Carolina. Of Richard and Sarah Whiteside's nineteen Negroes recorded as property on their 1860 slave schedules, twelve-year-old Benjamin appeared simply as "M" for mulatto, without a name and without acknowledgment of his master's paternity. Incidentally, he was the only "mulatto" in the group. I have not been able to determine his mother's name.[7]

---

5   Cedric J. Robinson, *Black Movements in America* (New York and London: Routledge, 1997), 116. Note that in most of the archival documents Mrs. Whiteside's first name is spelled "Cecelia," but for the purposes of consistency I will use "Cecilia" as it appears in *Black Movements in America*.

6   US Bureau of the Census, *Twelfth Census of the United States, 1900* (Washington, DC: National Archives and Records Administration, 1900), T623.

7   US Census, *1850, Polk, Rutherford, North Carolina*, roll M432_644, page 250A, image 44. US Bureau of the Census, *Eighth Census of the United States, 1860: Slave Schedules* (Washington, DC: National Archives and Records Administration, 1860), M653.

As the Whiteside plantation was situated in Polk County at the edge of the Appalachian Mountains, whites vastly outnumbered Black people. In fact, in 1860 western North Carolina held about 9,000 enslaved people, of which only sixty-two resided in Polk County.[8] The Union Army did not invade that part of the state until 1865, so it is unlikely that Benjamin became "contraband" and traveled the march route with the troops.[9] We do know that he left North Carolina as soon as he could and made his way as far south as he could go, finally settling in the port city of Mobile, Alabama. Around 1870, he met a pretty, young domestic worker named Clara Mercer. She lived with her sixty-five-year-old widowed mother, a former slave from Virginia who also went by Clara.[10] Like Benjamin, they were seeking a new beginning in an era when the South was poised to achieve the impossible dream of a multiracial, popular democracy. They lived through the ratification of the Thirteenth and Fourteenth Amendments, the democratization of state constitutions in 1868 under Republican-ruled "military Reconstruction," and the rise of the Ku Klux Klan and other forms of organized racial terror. They found each other in a whirl-wind of movement, when families broken up under bondage sought to reunite, and marriage, family, and community building were the priorities of freed people. They came together at a moment when the ratification of the Fifteenth Amendment and the question of "Negro suffrage" dominated the press and presumably a good deal of informal street chatter. The *Mobile Register* ran an editorial titled "The Future of the Negro" (March 13, 1870) warning Black people to disavow Northern Republicans and stop biting the hand that fed them—namely the good white people of the South. The editorial declared,

> In these states [Black people's] physical condition has, heretofore, been better than anywhere in the world. In these states they have more sympathy and kindness than has yet been shown to them anywhere in the world by the other races. In these States, by preserving their proper relations to the white people, they stand their only chance for safety and preservation.

When Black leaders and their Republican allies "war on the interests of the property holders who employ the great mass of their race they do injury to themselves."

On May 16, 1870, Benjamin and Clara were married; he was twenty-three and she was nineteen. Clara's mother moved in as well, and on the meager

---

8   Lenwood Davis, *The Black Heritage of Western North Carolina* (Asheville, NC: The Southern Highlands Research Collection, University of North Carolina at Asheville, 1986), 13.

9   There was another Benjamin Whiteside who joined the Sixtieth Regiment US Colored Troops and fought in Arkansas, but he hailed from Missouri where he enlisted in 1863. *Compiled Military Service Records of Volunteer Union Soldiers Who Served the United States Colored Troops: 56th–138th USCT Infantry, 1864–1866,* National Archives, available at https://www.fold3.com/document/302330834.

10   US Census, *1870, Mobile Ward 7, Mobile, Alabama,* roll M593_31, page 224B.

earnings of two domestic workers and a day laborer, they started a family.[11] Within a few years, they bought the house on the corner of Jackson and Adams Streets, which would remain their home for the remainder of their lives, mortgage-free.[12] Benjamin took whatever job he could find to make ends meet. During the early 1880s he worked for the southern Alabama lumber and coal giant A.C. Danner & Co., followed by several years at the Mobile stockyards under the employ of R. L. Maupin & Co. At the stockyards he acquired skills as a drayman—running deliveries in a flatbed horse-drawn cart (an occupation later taken up by his son Spencer). By 1901, Benjamin had parlayed those skills into his own business, renting the house next door and turning it into a wood retail and delivery company.[13] Meanwhile, Clara turned her prodigious cooking skills into yet another family business. Sometime in the late 1890s, they rented the other house next door (616 N. Jackson) and transformed it into Clara's "cook shop," where she prepared home-cooked meals for customers to take away and, perhaps, to eat at the shop as well.[14]

As the baby of the house, Winston received both the benefits and the burdens of his parents and older siblings' tireless work ethic. Unlike his parents, who could neither read nor write, he attended school and most likely received some tutoring from his doting sisters, Lillian and Clara. Being the youngest, he could always rely on their protection, though he matured into an incredibly handsome, well-built, and determined young man with a reputation as a skilled fighter. But, as his parents aged, they could no longer maintain the pace of entrepreneurship supplemented by waged work. By 1910, their respective businesses had come to an end and Clara, most likely beset by health problems, stopped working altogether.[15] Winston had no choice but to seek full-time employment. The situation became even more dire on August 17, 1910, when his beloved sister, Lillian, barely twenty years old, died suddenly.[16] Less than four years later, their mother would die as well at only fifty-nine years old.[17] As

11   US Census, *1870, Mobile Ward 7, Mobile, Alabama*, roll M593_31, page 224B; *Alabama, Select Marriages, 1816–1942*, available at ancestry.com.

12   *Mobile, Alabama, City Directory*, 1876.

13   *Mobile, Alabama, City Directory*, 1883, 1885, 1901, 1909; US Census, *1900*, T623. The first notice I found of Benjamin Whiteside's wood business was in the 1901 city directory, listed at 613 N. Jackson Street, which would have been next door to their house. The 1900 census lists the family residence as 613 N. Jackson, but all city directories and other documents identified their residence as 615. Since other families would come to occupy 613, it can be assumed that Benjamin Whiteside either rented it or purchased it and later rented it out. To settle this matter will require further research. On A. C. Danner & Co. and R. L. Maupin & Co., see John E. Land, *Mobile: Her Trade, Commerce and Industries, 1883–1884* (Mobile: Author, 1884), 55 and 84; Don H. Doyle, *New Men, New Cities, New South: Atlanta, Nashville, Charleston, Mobile, 1860–1910* (Chapel Hill: University of North Carolina Press, 1990), 135.

14   *Mobile, Alabama, City Directory*, 1898 and 1899.

15   US Census, *1910, Mobile Ward 1, Mobile, Alabama*, roll T624_27, page 4B, enumeration district 0078, FHL microfilm 1374040.

16   *Alabama, Deaths and Burials Index, 1881–1974*, film number 1894077, available at ancestry.com.

17   *Alabama, Death Index, 1908–1959*, vol. 28, certificate 335, available at ancestry.com.

his siblings left the Jackson Street home to start their own families, Winston took responsibility for the house and the care of his father. And he started his own family.

Sometime around 1916, Winston married a girl from the neighborhood named Corine Cunningham. Six years his junior, Corine was the daughter of Ella McLean, a fifteen-year-old unwed mother who still lived at home. Corine's grandmother, an independent widower and survivor of slavery named Clara McLean, helped raise her.[18] Corine was about seventeen years old when she moved into the Whiteside house on Jackson. Winston made a living as a porter for the United Cigar Company while Corine kept house, caring for her father-in-law and giving birth to three daughters in succession: Ella May (b. 1917), Wilma May (b. 1918), and Dorothy (b. 1920).[19]

The marriage proved to be short-lived. By 1924, Winston was living at 1011 Caroline Avenue with his new wife, Cecilia. He had left United Cigar Company to take a job with the railway company L&N Shops, and Cecilia, a year older than Winston, found work as a maid. At some point the three girls moved in with them and their father decided to change two of his daughters' names. His eldest, Ella May, was renamed Clara after Winston's mother, grandmother, and sister. Clara Whiteside was Cedric's mother. Dorothy, the baby, was named after her recently deceased aunt Lillian.[20]

Cap's confrontation with the Battle House manager, as Cedric reported it, hastened the Whiteside's family exodus from the deep South. Winston had no interest in the "future" that the city fathers had conceived for the Negro, and no desire to confront the police or a mob anxious to exact punishment for his insolence. So he went West, arriving in Oakland, California, in 1927. He found work as a janitor and lodging at 1448 Jackson Street, not far from Lake Merritt and downtown Oakland. Cecilia and the girls joined him the following year, first renting a house on 34th and West Streets in West Oakland before settling into what would become their permanent home at 3020 Adeline Street.[21]

---

18 US Census, *1900, Mobile Ward 1, Mobile, Alabama*, roll 31, page 4B, enumeration district 0095, FHL microfilm 1240031. According to family lore, Ella was "three-quarters Indian and one-quarter French" and Corine's father was an Irishman named Lorenzo Cunningham. But, according to the Census, Ella was just another Negro like the rest of her family and neighbors, and the two Lorenzo Cunninghams I could find in Mobile at the time were both "colored"—one a barber and the other a public-school teacher. Handwritten letter in Elizabeth Robinson's possession dated 1975; *Mobile, Alabama, City Directory*, 1900 and 1901; US Census, *1900, Mobile Ward 7, Mobile, Alabama*, roll 32, page 15A, enumeration district 0106, FHL microfilm 1240032.

19 US Census, *1920, Mobile Ward 1, Mobile, Alabama*, roll T625_34, page 3B, enumeration district 96, image 860; Winston Wilmer Whiteside, WWI Draft Registration Card, *Mobile, Alabama*, roll 1509409, Draft Board 1; *Mobile, City Directory*, 1918, 1920, 1922.

20 *Mobile, Alabama, City Directory*, 1924 and 1926; Cecelia T. Whiteside, Social Security Death Index; their daughters are identified by their new names in the 1930 Census. US Census, *1930, Oakland, Alameda, California*, roll 102, page 14B, enumeration district 0023, image 28.0, FHL microfilm 2339837.

21 *Oakland City Directory*, 1927, 1928, 1933; US Census, *1930, Oakland, Alameda, California*, roll 102, page 14B, enumeration district 0023, image 28.0, FHL microfilm 2339837.

The kindness, patience, and generosity that Cedric had experienced from his grandfather was not shared by his mother or aunts growing up on Adeline. A strict disciplinarian and patriarch tasked with raising three beautiful girls, "Daddy" imposed suffocating limits on his daughters. I suspect that their conversion from Baptists to Seventh-day Adventists may have exacerbated the situation, as new rules with respect to diet, behavior, and worship were enforced. Elizabeth Robinson heard stories of Daddy Whiteside waiting around the corner for the girls' boyfriends to show up and then beating them mercilessly.[22] The result was predictable: rebellion. When their father's authority prevailed, they left home. Clara, the eldest, found her escape in the fast life of clubs, bars, and dance halls. She fell for a married San Francisco nightclub owner about twenty years her senior named Frederick Hill, known to his friends as "B. Hill." The affair may have been brief, but on November 5, 1940, Clara gave birth to her one and only child, who she named Cedric James Hill. Frederick Hill acknowledged his paternity and opened his home to Cedric on occasion. Shortly after their split, however, Clara briefly married Dwight Robinson and decided to give Cedric, known to his family simply as "Ricky," the last name of his new stepfather.[23]

Clara was not in a position to care for Cedric, so he sometimes stayed with his Aunt Wilma and sometimes with Frederick Hill. He spent the lion's share of his time, however, with his grandparents on Adeline Street. What Cedric saw in Daddy and Mama Whiteside was a quiet dignity, a deep spiritual grounding, and a work ethic that he would go on to emulate. He watched his aging grandfather head to the County Courthouse in downtown Oakland, where he would spend hours cleaning and polishing the floors and banisters with great pride.[24] He watched his grandmother spend all day every Friday preparing the Sabbath meal, which often included a visit from the pastor. Beryl Warren, a family friend from Mobile who stayed with Clara for about a year in 1960–61 and grew quite close to Cedric, remembers the Whitesides as "a very loving couple. Not well educated, just down to earth. They welcomed me like I was their child. They were friendly toward all the neighbors, and well respected in the church. Daddy Whiteside had a big influence on [Cedric's] life."[25]

The nature of his influence may appear simple at first glance. As we've already seen, Cedric himself traced his discovery of the notion of faith to his grandfather's church. For him this was less about the existence of God than the

22   Elizabeth Robinson interview with author, August 12, 2016.

23   Elizabeth Robinson interview with author, June 28, 2016; State of California, *California Birth Index, 1905–1995* (Sacramento, CA: State of California Department of Health Services, Center for Health Statistics).

24   In 1942, Whiteside lists his place of employment as the County Courthouse, 200 Grand Ave., Oakland. Winston Wilmer Whiteside, *Draft Registration Cards for Fourth Registration for California, 04/27/1942–04/27/1942*, NAI number 603155, *Records of the Selective Service System*, record group number 147.

25   Beryl Warren interview with author, July 5, 2016.

recognition of what he later described in *Black Marxism* as "a metaphysical system that had never allowed for property in either the physical, philosophical, temporal, legal, social, or psychic senses." In other words, slavery and racial capitalism were incapable of what Aimé Césaire called "thingification" so long as Black people could preserve this "ontological totality."[26] As Beryl Warren recalls, Cedric continued to attend church services and to derive both enjoyment and intellectual stimulation from them, despite not being "very religious at the time. He called himself an atheist."

But in addition to bringing his grandson into his church, Daddy Whiteside both modeled and engaged in a kind of ontological affirmation of Blackness that consistently beat back the prevailing logic of Black inferiority—a logic accepted by many within Cedric's own family. A three-page handwritten family history dated 1975 reveals an obsession with race and a consistent denial of African heritage. Each family member is identified in terms of racial percentages— mostly Irish, French, Indian, English, and the like. In fact, Winston Whiteside was identified as "Blk, Puerto Rican, and white." But as Elizabeth Robinson explained to me, "For all this stuff about denial about race, that didn't come from Daddy . . . Cedric had fond memories of listening to a Joe Louis fight on the radio with Daddy and other Black men, and how much race pride they had rooting for Louis over some white boxer." And when Cedric was old enough to grasp the implications and consequences of race, he peppered his grandfather with questions about the South—a request that his grandfather was always happy to oblige. Even while Cedric felt that he was treated as the "black sheep" of the family because of his dark complexion, his grandparents loved and embraced him unconditionally.

Perhaps it all boils down to this: love and affirmation; holding on to the notion of the possible; preserving the ontological totality. Cap's stories and lessons—those he lived and those he received—pervade all of Cedric's work, even if they are not readily apparent. And as ancestors, Cap and Cecilia, Benjamin and Clara, the whole Whiteside clan and more served as the scaffolding for his brilliance, continually steering him back to the Black Radical Tradition.

Cecilia Whiteside passed on December 17, 1966, nine months before Cedric and Elizabeth were married. Winston Whiteside returned South, settling down in Georgia. He died on September 21, 1979, just months before the publication of Ricky's first book, *The Terms of Order: Political Science and the Myth of Leadership*. He would have appreciated the dedication: "For Winston (Cap) Whiteside, grandson of slaves / a man of extraordinary courage and profound understanding / . . . my grandfather and my first teacher."

---

26 Robinson, *Black Marxism*, 168. Césaire introduces the concept of "thingification" in *Discourse on Colonialism* (New York: Monthly Review Press, 2000[1950]), 62.

Acknowledgements

This book is the fulfillment of a wish. As the idea for this edited volume came to fruition, it was Cedric Robinson himself, with Elizabeth Robinson's insights, who devised the list of scholars whose offerings would eventually grace these pages in critical engagement with the Black Radical Tradition. Cedric, himself a voracious and meticulous reader, saw something in these scholars' work that he wished to draw out in conversation with his own. He looked forward to reading these essays, and as his eyesight failed, the authors agreed to read them aloud in what would culminate in an audio book meant for his own enjoyment. This is articulated here so that the reader may note that while every scholar invited to do so wrote as a student (or colleague) obligingly answering a teacher's instruction, there is also love and gratitude in the writing. We, the editors, feel abundantly fortunate to have been called to this endeavor.

Our greatest thanks go to Cedric Robinson and Elizabeth Peters Robinson. Cedric's scholarship serves as a home for many of us who have committed ourselves to the invocation and incitement of the Black Radical Tradition, and we intended for him to enjoy and respond to these essays. Though we lost him before the book was finished, every page of the volume bears his imprint. It was Elizabeth, in the end, who completed their contribution, who read our introduction, and encouraged us heartily. For her efforts in particular we are deeply grateful. We also recognize an important source of inspiration for several of the writers included here, a conference organized by Ruth Wilson Gilmore, Christina Heatherton, and Jordan Camp entitled "Confronting Racial Capitalism: The Black Radical Tradition and Cultures of Liberation," which took place in 2014. Though the request for this book came nearly two years later, the spark for some of these essays began in conversation with Cedric Robinson at the Center for Place, Culture and Politics at City University of New York.

Our scholarship means nothing without the people who work in mostly unacknowledged ways to get us all free. While it is Cedric's engagement with the Black Radical Tradition that inspires the work presented here, we presume to argue on behalf of the authors that it is equally the brilliant inventiveness practiced by radical social actors, by freedom seekers and freedom dreamers across the diaspora that serves as the incitement.

Freedom. Unqualified liberation. Abolition. Nothing less.

Contributor Bios

Greg Burris is Assistant Professor of Media Studies at the American University of Beirut. His writings have appeared in *CineAction, Cinema Journal, Electronic Intifada, The Guardian, Jadaliyya, Middle Eastern Studies, Quarterly Review of Film and Video*, and other publications.

Jordan T. Camp is Postdoctoral Fellow in Race and Ethnicity and International and Public Affairs at Brown University. He is the author of *Incarcerating the Crisis: Freedom Struggles and the Rise of the Neoliberal State*, and coeditor (with Christina Heatherton) of *Policing the Planet: Why the Policing Crisis Led to Black Lives Matter*.

Angela Y. Davis is Emeritus Professor in the History of Consciousness program at University of California, Santa Cruz. Her most recent book is *Freedom in a Constant Struggle: Ferguson, Palestine, and the Foundations of a Movement*.

Erica Edwards is Associate Professor of English at Rutgers University. She is the author of *Charisma and the Fictions of Black Leadership* and wrote the foreword to Cedric J. Robinson's reprinted, *Terms of Order: Political Science and the Myth of Leadership* (2016).

Ruth Wilson Gilmore is Director of the Center for Place, Culture, and Politics and Professor of Geography in Earth and Environmental Sciences at The City University of New York. She is the author of *Golden Gulag: Prisons, Surplus, Crisis, and Opposition in Globalizing California*.

Avery F. Gordon is Professor of Sociology at the University of California, Santa Barbara, and Visiting Professor in the School of Law, Birkbeck University of London. Her most recent book is *The Hawthorn Archive: Letters from the Utopian Margins*.

Stefano Harney is coauthor with Fred Moten of *The Undercommons: Fugitive Planning and Black Study*. He teaches in Singapore.

Christina Heatherton is Assistant Professor of American Studies at Trinity College, coeditor of *Policing the Planet: Why the Policing Crisis Led to Black Lives Matter*, and author of *The Color Line and the Class Struggle: The Mexican Revolution, Internationalism, and the American Century*.

Gaye Theresa Johnson is Associate Professor of Black and Chicana/o Studies at UCLA and author of *Spaces of Conflict, Sounds of Solidarity: Music, Race, and Spatial Entitlement in Los Angeles*.

Robin D. G. Kelley teaches History and Black Studies at UCLA. His latest book is *Africa Speaks, America Answers: Modern Jazz in Revolutionary Times*.

George Lipsitz is Professor of Black Studies and Sociology at the University of California, Santa Barbara. His publications include *How Racism Takes Place, The Possessive Investment in Whiteness*, and *A Life in the Struggle*.

Alex Lubin is Professor and Chair of American Studies at the University of New Mexico. He is the author of *Geographies of Liberation: The Making of an Afro-Arab Political Imaginary* and coeditor of *American Studies Encounters the Middle East.*

Fred Moten is coauthor with Stefano Harney of *The Undercommons: Fugitive Planning and Black Study.* He teaches at the University of California, Riverside.

Paul Ortiz is Director of the award-winning Samuel Proctor Oral History Program and Associate Professor of History at the University of Florida. His forthcoming book, *An African American and Latinx History of the United States,* will be published by Beacon Press as part of its ReVisioning American History series.

Steven Osuna is Assistant Professor in the Department of Sociology at California State University, Long Beach. His contribution to this anthology began in Cedric Robinson's "Black Radical Thought" graduate seminar at the University of California, Santa Barbara.

Kwame M. Philips is Assistant Professor in the Department of Communications, John Cabot University, specializing in visual and sensory media production, ethnographic documentary, visual anthropology and audio culture. Phillips's work centers on multidisciplinary engagement and focuses on resilience, race, and social justice.

H. L. T. Quan is a political theorist and a documentary filmmaker. She currently teaches Justice Studies in the School of Social Transformation at Arizona State University.

Shana L. Redmond is Associate Professor of Musicology in the Alpert School of Music and African American Studies at the University of California, Los Angeles. She is the author of *Anthem: Social Movements and the Sound of Solidarity in the African Diaspora,* and coeditor of *Critical Ethnic Studies: A Reader.*

Cedric J. Robinson was a professor for more than forty years and author of several books, including *Forgeries of Memory and Meaning.* **Elizabeth P. Robinson** was a media advocate and local, national, and international activist. Together they produced "Third World News Review" for more than 35 years.

Nikhil Pal Singh is the author of *Black is a Country: Race and the Unfinished Struggle for Democracy.* He teaches in the Department of Social and Cultural Analysis and the Department of History at New York University, where he also directs the NYU Prison Education Program.

Damien M. Sojoyner is Assistant Professor at the University of California, Irvine, in the Department of Anthropology. Sojoyner researches the relationship among the public education system, prisons, and the construction of Black masculinity in Southern California.

Darryl C. Thomas is Associate Professor of African American and Diaspora Studies at Pennsylvania State University. He has published widely on the international politics of the Third World, African and Africana studies, globalization, democratization and global Africa, and resistance to globalization including US hegemony and empire.

Françoise Vergès, Ph.D. from the University of California at Berkeley, is Chair Global South(s) at the Collège d'études mondiales, Fondation maison des sciences de l'homme, Paris. She writes, curates shows, and is a film director and activist.